TROUBLED DAWN
OF THE 21st CENTURY

authorship international

Published by authorship international
Paris, France
authorpol@gmail.com

Cover photo: Jiro Mochizuki
Design: Aaron Levin

ISBN 9780-9887119-8-3

NIDRA POLLER

TROUBLED DAWN
OF THE 21st CENTURY

CHRONICLE

authorship intl

Contents

Prologue

Before the advent of the blog, above and beyond the blog, stands an authentic genre: the writer's notebook. At the end of September 2000 I was mentally constructing my next novel that would expand from the mother-daughter axis of the previous work, *Madonna Madonna*, to the third generation, from mother to daughter to grandchild. The challenge I had set for myself—an extended conversation between a grandmother and a grandchild that do not speak the same language—was abruptly replaced by the existential conflict that has occupied me ever since. The alleged provocation of Ariel Sharon's visit to the Temple Mount, followed two days later by the al Dura blood libel, jolted the course of contemporary history.

I recognized immediately that a real life novel was unfolding before my eyes. And I began to grasp it in terms that only a novelist could perceive and elaborate. Since the late 1970s I had been writing almost exclusively in French. Including the novel referred to above. Neither assimilated nor integrated nor expatriated, I lived harmoniously with my share of France. Like a bird, briefly pausing on a branch. I felt no need for roots. Immigration was my homeland. From Mittleuropa to the United States to Western Europe, why not?

But the tree that supported that branch began to shake violently and sent me flying into emergency mode. I responded, naturally, in French. *Cahier d'une honnête citoyenne* [Notes from a simple citizen] was addressed to the society in which I lived, the media, old and soon to be lost friends, new friends and allies, political leaders, younger generations, my native land, and my newfound Zionist rebirthplace.

Like so many cosmopolitan Jews that did not wear that identity on their lapels or on a fine gold chain, I was thrust into a virtual ghetto, a frenzy of meetings, lectures, broadsides, facts & figures sustained by newly formed groups and revitalized institutions. In that atmosphere of heightened awareness and concrete danger—violent antisemitic acts were counted by the hundreds, adding up to thousands—I would occasionally print out several copes of my *Cahier*-in-progress and offer them to people I met at one or another of these events. My *Notes* were highly appreciated. Gérard Marx (B'nai B'rith hatikvah lodge) tried valiantly but in vain to get me a column in the Jewish newspaper *Actualité Juive*. Journalist Véronique Chemla introduced me to Stéphane Juffa, director of the *Metula News Agency*, leading to the publication of "*Un Sac de billes*" [followed by the English version "A Bag of Marbles"] and launching my journalistic career.

Meanwhile, writers were asking me to translate their texts into English. "Our voices can't be heard here. They have to be projected to the English-speaking world and bounced back to France to have any legitimacy." I translated tens of thousands of words, free of charge, for the cause. This went on for several years before I asked myself why I was writing in French when I could write in English and reach a far wider audience.

It worked. I was published in prestigious outlets: *Commentary*, *The New York Sun*, *Wall Street Journal Europe*, *National Post* (Canada), *City Journal*, *National Review Online*, *Jerusalem Post*, *Makor Rishon*, and many others too numerous to mention. I went on speaking tours, was interviewed on the radio, took part in television debates, and earned an international reputation as a reliable source and eloquent writer.

I courageously adapted to 500 and 1,000-word formats, with an occasional opportunity to publish in-depth magazine articles, but my natural scope has always been book-length. After the publication of "Betrayed by Europe" in *Commentary*, two literary agents offered their services. The first quickly revealed that she wanted me to recompose my fantastically interesting Notebook, to reshape it into a retrospective conventional vision of the period covered, with proper subject categories and all the rest. "But I was writing about these things as they happened. No one knew what would come next. That's the beauty of it," I objected. She sighed: "That's true, but publishers don't like this format."

The other agent stood by me for years, asking me to write and rewrite presentations, treatments, chapter by chapter summaries and other paraphernalia required by publishers that only rarely look at an actual manuscript. His agency rose to heights of success, but there was no place for me in his stable of interchangeable popular hits.

Troubled Dawn of the 21ˢᵗ Century is the chronicle as I wrote it: a mixture of notebook entries [the *Cahier*], published articles, and miscellaneous letters to editors, friends, and colleagues. My working title, *Notes from a Simple Citizen,* was an English translation of the French original but I decided, as editor, that it was too weak. I tried *Torched Synagogues, Scorched Democracy* before deciding on *Troubled Dawn.* Though I have not indicated the original language of material written before 2003, the notebook entries and many of the articles were written in French and later translated (by me, of course) into English. I will soon publish a French version—a collection all the texts written originally in French, including some that I haven't had time to translate into English. Whenever possible I have given credit to outlets for published articles but sometimes I can't find any traces and don't know if or where certain texts appeared.

The art of the novel is the creation —even in non-realistic styles—of scale models of life as it feels when it is being lived. Intricate literary compositions of events, characters, atmosphere, with circumstantial and essential details, incidentals, light and color, the odd and inexplicable, and the thrust of profound forces, may come closer to the truth than conventional non-fictional treatment of current events. I have allowed myself to use these skills while respecting journalistic standards. I treat facts with meticulous care, while making no pretense to objectivity. The chronicle stands here as it was written, in a context that cannot be recreated by explanatory notes. I did not see fit to reprint the articles to which

I react, though they can be found with the references provided. With the exception of one letter published in the *International Herald Tribune* on November 3 2000, all the other letters to the editors are unpublished and some were not even sent. I was so raw to the trade that when I wanted to follow up on the first published letter with an extensive op-ed—the rebuttal to Karen Armstrong's lesson on sharing Jerusalem— I sent it to the *International Herald Tribune* as an attached file. It was undoubtedly trashed on reception.

A few years later I was publishing regularly in the likes of the *Wall Street Journal Europe*; I didn't need the indulgence of lesser pages stingily offered to the unknown. A few of the articles that appeared in 2001-4 are included here. By 2005 they were too numerous to cite. They will all be posted on a dedicated website.

Currents foreshadowed at the dawn of the century are concretely visible today— 27 October 2016: thousands gathered in front of the Quai d'Orsay, seat of the Foreign Affairs Ministry, to protest France's failure to vote against the infamous UNESCO resolution honed to destroy, by legalese, the Jewish connection to Jerusalem, while Daesh was destroying Palmyra with sledgehammers. The difference is, Israel can defend Jerusalem.

That same week, policemen and women, overstepping strict limits on their right to demonstrate in uniform, were in the streets, on foot and in patrol cars, sirens keening to express their utter exasperation with rules of engagement that leave them prey to murderous attacks from freelance jihadis that slit throats (Magnanville) and barbaric urban commandos that engulf them in flames (quai Valmy, Place de la République, Ivry Chatillon). Marching behind banners that proclaim *Police attaquée, citoyens en danger*, law enforcement echoed the *Synagogues brûlées, République en danger* [torched synagogues, scorched République] of 2002. Polls show that close to 90% of the population supported the police protests.

The point being missed is that a new world order is taking shape before our eyes, and we are responsible for the shape it takes. Will it be a world faithful to democratic values in all their imperfection and largely huddled under the umbrella of American military might, or a world delivered up to the logic of blackmail: we can do this to you because you don't know how much we suffer and it's all your fault, and you can't hit back at us because if you do we'll send the whole world down the tubes.

What is happening to Israelis today will happen to every one of us tomorrow. It all comes down to a five year-old girl shot in cold blood as she hid under her bed. And Israeli troops going into Hebron and killing the man who sent the man who killed that child.

Troubled Dawn, April 2002

PASSIONATELY JERUSALEM
July 2000

In the aftermath of the recent Camp David negotiations it might be instructive to look back at Karen Armstrong's essay, "After All These Centuries, No One People Owns Jerusalem" (*International Herald Tribune* 17 July 2000). Drawing on historical precedents, the author of *The Battle for God* and *Jerusalem: One City Three Faiths* argues against undivided Israeli sovereignty on the grounds that attempts at exclusive possession are unjustified and unviable.

Though the broad lines of her argument, stated alternately as principles, assertions, and admonishments, are more or less defendable they function as circular arguments, undermined rather than substantiated by curiously unbalanced specifics. Karen Armstrong's model of level-headed sobriety collapses, leaving us with the naked reality of two small nations locked in conflicting claims to a land so small that the hopes of one disturb the dreams of the other, the tears of one wet the cheeks of the other.

The idea that politicians must cut through the jungle of myths and passions in order to arrive at a viable pragmatic solution is certainly enticing, especially when couched in terms of honest concern for the welfare of all parties. All the more reason to face up to the rather laborious analysis required to identify the structural weaknesses of a slanted discourse. First, we must be careful not to confuse the notion of compromise—which is the very definition of peaceful solution of conflict—

with division—splitting a cake and sharing it between two squabbling children. Some things cannot be divided without losing their viability. The question here is not if but how the parties should compromise.

K. Armstrong is not alone in believing that divided sovereignty is the appropriate compromise for Jerusalem. However, a call for dispassionate rational debate should be judged on the merits of the argument. If, as she claims, attachment to Jerusalem is systematically exacerbated by the threat of dispossession and, consequently, generous sharing is the optimum solution for peace, the burning question remains: who can be entrusted to generously share Jerusalem? On what rational basis should this judgment be made?

It soon becomes apparent that the call for *a rational debate about rights and sovereignty* concerns only one party to the debate. [*All passages in italics, with the exception of book titles, are quoted from Armstrong's 17 July article*]. Both sides contend that Jerusalem is their sacred capital, but their contentions do not have equal force: Though it is not *politically expedient,* the claim to Jerusalem as eternal, indivisible capital of Israel *has acquired the force of a mantra in Israeli politics.* But, she says, the entire Muslim world categorically refuses *total, permanent Israeli sovereignty* in Jerusalem. By simple permutation the same logic would lead to the opposite conclusion: though politically inexpedient, the claim to Jerusalem as eternal capital has become a mantra in Islamic politics; but the entire Jewish world, in Israel as in the Diaspora, categorically refuses Palestinian sovereignty in Jerusalem. Why is Israel's claim nothing more than a mantra and, incidentally, why do Israelis need a mantra to express their attachment to Jerusalem? Isn't the Bible enough?

Logically, this Muslim refusal of Israeli sovereignty would be classified among the unrealistic stances that get in the way of proper negotiations. But Karen Armstrong makes it a categorical imperative: there can be no peace in the Middle East unless the conditions are acceptable to the entire Muslim world. Given that Iraq and Iran, among others, absolutely refuse the existence of Israel, the title of her essay should have been: Jerusalem belongs to everyone but one people.

Following the author into the meanders of Jerusalem's history we find some curious turns and shortcuts. As far as *all these centuries* are concerned, she chooses to log in just after the destruction of the first

Temple, skipping over the period 1000-585 BC as if it didn't exist. The most powerful tyrant on earth can't destroy a temple unless someone first built it; what about that Temple, those centuries, that presence? Nothing notable? We are asked to believe that the most salient fact of those times is a certain policy of exclusion from the Temple practiced by the *new* [post-exile] *cult of Jerusalem* which happens to correspond, according to K. Armstrong's logic, with the Muslim exclusion of other faiths from the city *when Saladin took Jerusalem from the Crusaders*.

And so it goes: every example hides more than it reveals, and all the examples put together give an overriding impression of Israeli bad faith and stubborn intransigence. Jewish attachment to Jerusalem is minimized (it only became *central to Judaism* after the Babylonian exile in 586 BC) and Muslim attachment is firmly established on weaker grounds (Jerusalem has been sacred to Muslims since 610 when Mohammed preached there). Carried forward into recent times this argumentation gives: *After the Holocaust, Jerusalem has become even more sacred to Jewish identity* ...counterbalanced by: *But Palestinians see Jerusalem...as a symbol of their...beleaguered identity and 'rightly or wrongly,' the Muslim world feels humiliated by the West, with the loss of Jerusalem an intolerable symbol.* What logical conclusion can be drawn from these radically disparate experiences? Is the loss of an empire to be measured against the near-extermination of European Jewry?

Karen Armstrong calls on Israel to be reasonable like the early pragmatic Zionists who *accepted anything they were offered, even if it fell lamentably short of what was required....* And clinches the argument with a curious anecdote: *Jerusalem has not always been the 'eternal and indivisible' capital of Israel...* Theodor Herzl thought it might be best to tear the Old City down!

A hop skip and a jump over the Arab-Israeli wars (conveniently avoiding the question of their causes and aims) is given as further proof of Israel's erstwhile willingness to forego total sovereignty in Jerusalem: in 1947 Zionists did not reject the idea of a divided internationalized Jerusalem, Israel just took the western half of the city in the 1948 Arab-Israeli war, only claiming *exclusive control of the whole city* after the 1967 war. Bam! An Armstrong girder comes crashing down on Israeli heads: *Such exclusive policies do not work in Jerusalem.*

It is difficult for someone who has not studied the history of Jerusalem to judge the validity of examples drawn from the distant past. But the period 1947-2000, divided roughly into two decades of Arab sovereignty followed by an equivalent period of Israeli sovereignty, is fully documented. If the status of Jerusalem is to be decided on the basis of rational arguments would it not be levelheaded, sober, dispassionate and absolutely necessary to look into conditions during these two periods? Can anyone deny that the period of Arab sovereignty is marked by abominable desecration of all that is sacred to Jews, and absolute exclusion not only of Jews but of anyone who had dared to set foot in Israel: the very example of *exclusive policies* that do not work! The Muslim world has recently, tentatively, and with notable holdouts downgraded its policy from extermination to dismemberment of Israel. We can logically conclude within the very terms of Karen Armstrong's argument that Israel has shown itself to be the more trustworthy party.

Avoiding these uncomfortable realities, Karen Armstrong flashes back to the Arab reconquest of Jerusalem, with Jewish help, in 634, after a long period of banishment imposed by the Byzantine Christians. Morally tolerant and politically shrewd, the Arabs lived in relative harmony with the Jews, proving once more that *Pragmatic coexistence has worked better in Jerusalem than rigid ideology*. But if it was good for the Jews in 634 why isn't it good for the Palestinians in 2001 to accept pragmatic coexistence over rigid ideology and live in relative harmony under Jewish sovereignty?

In the last analysis, Karen Armstrong wonders if the Vatican might not be *a model for the future Jerusalem*, unwittingly throwing us back into the vicious cycle of alternating Arab & Christian conquest of Jerusalem; this time around the Christians would stand on high as a disinterested disembodied Idea, leaving the Muslims to take care of things on the ground. Rational debate should take us to the here and now. We stand at the dawn of the 21st century. The glorious period of Arab conquest is no more. Neither Romans nor Christians will chase the Jews from the land of Israel. Israel's steadfast defense of its birthright may well be the greatest contribution to peace in the region.

An honest compromise on Jerusalem—Islam's third holiest city and Israel's only capital—could be the turning point of a new era for Palestinians. By deflecting their desires from that one tiny unattainable city, could they not see the way to a new role as a viable state within a vast Muslim world of great wealth and under exploited potential? Palestine, instead of seething in a tangle of explosive frustration, could be an Al Quds, a guiding light for an Islamic world desperately seeking a new dynamics. In the place of a stingy compromise that would satisfy no one, we have the possibility of a brilliant compromise that would finally bring an end to centuries of violence and give Jerusalem its rightful place as a holy city in a holy world that belongs to all people. After all these centuries, wouldn't it be worth a try?

(See Daniel Sibony's brilliant work, *Les Trois Monothéismes,* for a profound understanding of how Jerusalem came to be sacred to Muslims and Christians).

Chapter 1/ Al Aqsa Intifada

NOTEBOOK SEPTEMBER-OCTOBER 2000

If the dead were not dead, if the dead were not dead and gone, never to return, if the dead were not dead but simply outmoded like the discourses that pushed them, accompanied them, buried them and then deflated and disappeared without leaving the words by which they could be brought down to earth and sent back to their authors, if the dead were not really dead but just characters in a play then we could say today that this cheap melodrama, this Al Aqsa Intifada is a flop. And go on to other things.

A flop. Shoddy scenario, sloppy staging, top to bottom has-beens casting, a lousy film that starts off with a bang and a minute later falls on its face, and if it were just a show we'd pack it up and forget the whole thing. But they're playing for real. And the stakes are terrible. The harm is done, more harm will be done. I cannot offer myself the luxury—like that French radio commentator whose hysterical voice is still ringing in my ears—I don't have the luxury of replacing mad cow with enraged Palestinian and too bad for the burned synagogues. No, I can't afford to zap. I have to focus my thinking on these events that have poured clouds of black ink into troubled waters, the better to strangle us in the tentacles of a seemingly incurable political delirium.

Yes, it's true, from a Parisian viewpoint this Al Aqsa Intifada is a flop, a miserable media bust. Despite unfailing logistical support from a good (or rather bad) part of the French press, the extraordinary Palestinian propaganda machine did not produce the desired results. I won't linger over their clumsy strategic errors or the blatant lies called, for a reason that escapes me, counter-truths—but I'm keeping a helluva file for the future—because I think there is such a fervent desire to believe, that no truth could possibly pierce the armor. In fact the décor was changed once a day and that didn't change anything in the hearts of the fans that picked up the slogan du jour and chanted it until the next tune came along. Monday it was "our children are not out there demonstrating," and the song was sung from the early morning news flash to the evening's in-depth coverage and all the way into the letters to the editors. Wednesday it was "we can't keep our children out of the demonstrations, we can't keep them from running up to the front line," and hop! your little local journalist swore it on his mother's head, and the TV news suddenly showed the children right up there in the front lines. Friday we found out that not only were they there, but they wanted to die and furthermore their mothers wanted them to die. As for Yasser Arafat he promised they would die in ever increasing numbers and keep on dying until a little Palestinian boy or maybe even a girl would plant the Palestinian flag on the Palestinian *esplanade des mosquées* [or Noble sanctuary, which is French for Temple Mount]. The strategic zigzags, the unfounded accusations, the gross fabrications did not bother those who wanted to believe in the Long March, Middle-Eastern flavor. Forget about serious investigations that could cast doubt on the martyrological narratives; believers kept on believing.

Nevertheless the believers finally walked out of the theater. Not because the truth rose up and demolished the slipshod structure of doubtful details, but simply because the timing was disastrous. The whole thing had to be brought off at diabolical speed, bringing new shocks bigger and more shocking every day than the day before. Things had to jump, explode, spurt out, the blood had to flow in rivers and not in drops, the hatred burn with incandescent flame and spread over the face of the earth like the lava of hundreds of volcanoes erupting, there had to be the sharp crack of gigantic whiplashes wherever a Jew dared to set foot, sharp blows had to assail them, knife blows and UN blows, and the whole thing had to gallop and the whole surface of the earth tremble under the thundering hooves of millions of Arab thoroughbreds. It had to be done on an endless panoramic screen with earbreaking Dolby sound and the spectators holding their breaths from beginning to end and the end had to come quick as light!

Instead of which and because so many blows missed their mark the dramatic tension dropped, the attention of idle onlookers was distracted and, after two weeks of bumpy progress with no triumphant march into Jerusalem, the Al Aqsa Intifada was exposed for its own miserable self.

Three hours after writing the above I want to redo the whole thing. My argument isn't bad, in fact it's very strong. But it's loaded down with stylistic effects. I wanted to speak simply, and not get caught up in the fight of battling discourses. I do not want to add linguistic confusion to the confusion in the field and in people's minds. I want to see clearly! And I want to speak out now. Not because I'm sure I know better than the others but because I have a duty to risk analyzing in the heat of the action events whose meaning and consequences will be known much later. I've read too much, listened to too much, collected too many press clippings with scholarly care. I know how to organize these clippings and use them to construct arguments, deconstruct *prises de position*, analyze and compare and pounce upon aberrations big and small, bring to light the logical faults, trace out the determinant subtext and prove whatever I decide to prove.

I've already done it in my head and I know how to do it on paper. I know that I'll keep my press files just like I did during the Gulf War, promising myself that one day I'll do my novelist-historian's work, but first I have to set aside the details and dig to the depths of my thought within the few hours left to me to devote to the cause before the year's end.

At times I am so illuminated by the rightness of my thought that I feel like I absolutely must bring it out into the public arena and block the path of this disaster in the making. Then I listen to other people, and I observe that they're floating around inside a bubble of discourse. Facts bump up against the bubble but it holds together with constant patching, and the person can at least remain reassured in his sense of a stable personal identity. It's like a religion, like confessions of faith. Unshakable. So, instead of reassuring myself by making fun of the discourse across from me, I wonder if I too am using one as a shield.

Still, the idea developed above, the image of the Al Aqsa Intifada as a flop, seems to me very strong. And even if in expressing it I let myself go with the typical swishes and furbelows of the French tongue, the image holds up. This Intifada, judged from its explosive beginnings, its pretensions to the absolute and compared to the enthusiasm it initially cooked up in the crowd, has gotten nowhere. Yes, even from my declared enemy I demand a minimum of logical rigor. I do not want to have to be ashamed of my enemy. I don't want him to force me to have contempt for him. And, yes, this flop reminds me of the Thousand-year Reich. Ten years later it was a whole nation on its knees scratching for crumbs in the ruins of pulverized cities. They too went marching to the tune of humiliation arguments. So now I wouldn't touch one of these arguments based on humiliation with a ten-foot pole

But tell me, frankly, where can I put myself in this world? I cannot bear the absence of logic. I detest uninterrupted flows of emotion. When I see the crowd rushing to the fool's market I want to shout: can't you see how they're flummoxing you? So, there was Camp David that was supposed to wrap up the peace negotiations, and there is this Intifada that has come to bury both sides' hopes of living in peace, and today there are talks here and meetings there, a bit of a proposal, a tiny little declaration, in short, on the Palestinian side where just a month ago they were screaming how they'll never again come to our cruddy negotiations because they're going to grab with their bare hands what we don't want to give them by talking, now they're asking for... negotiations. And that's what they call *jusqu'au boutisme*? Should we laugh or cry?

I ask friends what they think. Painful enterprise. It's never the right time, mustn't spoil the party, you never get past the opening arguments. When I try to put them to the test one by one, not to demolish them, not because I think I'm right and everyone else is wrong, but so that someone finally can convince me... no one wants to play with me. Right-thinking Jews, left wing Israelis, peace activists can tell me a long tale of Israel's wrongdoing and I must listen without veiling my ears. Even if it hurts.

And even if I accept all these arguments—the abject poverty of the Palestinians, the mistreatment, spoliation, injustice done to Israeli Arabs, the violence of orthodox Jews and hardheaded reckless *colons* [= colonists, French for settlers], and the terrorist acts of the early Zionists—even if I deny none of that, is it any reason for believing that Israel should commit suicide today? Be ashamed, maybe, compared to our (messianic?) hopes and fully justified expectations, but who are we to take ourselves for G. and chastise Israel?

We live in comfort and security in countries built up without undue scruples over the span of centuries. We accept to live under all kinds of governments without overdue concern about the absolute honesty of those who govern us. Our States protect us against claims—sometimes justified—that might seriously compromise their integrity and this is where, safe inside this home, we express ourselves freely, from the height of our conscience.

Can all the sins of Israel justify its destruction? A very intelligent, perspicacious (Jewish) friend tells me that Jews are mistaken in thinking that anyone wants to destroy the State of Israel. I understand what motivates his cautionary words: it's about our paranoia that becomes self-fulfilling prophecy by turning the whole world against us. How much more elegant is this premise than the litany of grievances of those who are convinced that the opposite is true. Except that the project of extermination of the Jews happens to be a repetitive historical fact. The day the world decides to dismount the mental structures that uphold this project, which has so well served such an amazing diversity of potential exterminators, we'll know it. And it will be marvelous. And not only the Jews but the entire world will be transformed by it. In the right direction.

N.B. 40 people including 16 *lycéens* were massacred in Algeria this weekend.

You won't hear any one in France crying to the high heavens "stop the massacres." What do the butchers want? Who, outside the narrow circle of these rabid throat-cutters will support their action, listen to their discourse, take seriously the slightest project set forth by their leadership? They want to slaughter, they slaughter, the number of slaughtered victims is tallied up, no comment. Remember the Jolo Island kidnappers? The guys who chop off arms in Sierra Leone, the

Rwandan exterminators, the Somali warlords, the barbarians called talibans but students of nothing? Remember Pol Pot? Here we are in the last dregs of history's garbage cans. The pretty revolutions of olden days, slightly shadowed with a few clouds of terror but bearing millenary hopes, have become naked no-future terror. But the discourse hangs on and hangs in. So the Palestinians can jump into their umpteenth suicidal enterprise and these Cartesian French minds weren't bothered in the least by the first act. But when the synagogues started burning it damped down the ardor of the fans, shocked to see, in such a short time, the real path of the stones they themselves had tossed in favor of the cause. Despite an obstinate refusal of any self-doubt the press was too embarrassed by the results of an investigation that smashed the finest icons of the Palestinian struggle. Never honest enough to reexamine the hasty judgments made at the beginning of the crisis, the press drew a curtain over the drama. Which is why I dare to say that from a media viewpoint this Al Aqsa Intifada is a flop. In the early days of the affair the Palestinian Authority was lavishly congratulated for propaganda genius. Now haven't they shown themselves up in all their miserable clumsiness?

Why not say it? Why not say that to this day the Palestinians are still trying to get the Jews to leave Palestine. Of course there is no way to know what the Palestinians taken one by one want because they are not free to express themselves. So I am talking about their leadership. Why say the half-truth about Palestinian objectives instead of going all the way to the bottom of their reasoning and finally holding the key to their behavior for decades or even centuries? Why accept their complaints and desires halfway instead of accepting them fully as they express them in their own words? Why underwrite the image of the Palestinians as victims of a colonial occupation and then turn around and encourage them to be satisfied with crumbs?

Why? In my opinion this confusion of genres is used in order to blame Israel for all the past, present and future suffering of the Palestinians. Whereas the sincere honest acknowledgement of the true PA objectives should open the way to a new peace process.

To persist in bandying about the prettied-up images of Yasser Arafat, his *shebabs*, his *tanzim*, his stones, can only encourage the Palestinians to pursue a desperate struggle in which they have everything to lose, nothing to gain. Israel is not an occupant, the Jews will not be pushed out, the grizzly old man is not going to get back his orchards on Dizengoff Street. What's to be done? Admit and then cure! Admit the true nature of the conflict—the Israelis know that they can't live in peace unless the Palestinians can feel themselves to be fully alive, but the Palestinians think their lives depend on the death of Israel—and help the Palestinians give up and get over their murderous rage. But every time there is an exacerbation of the Middle East crisis international opinion and especially, especially French opinion, does the opposite. It encourages the Palestinians to drape themselves in rags scavenged from the garbage heap of romantic revolutions. It feeds their mental confusion by swallowing stories like "the provocation of Ariel Sharon's visit to *l'esplanade des mosquées*," followed by "the use of excessive force by the Israeli army."

Interview on *France-Info* with Eli Barnavi, the new Israeli ambassador to France. The tone was rather polite but the soft arrogance no less stinging. Barnavi says that the next move is up to Arafat. Journalist: "What can he give you? You have everything, he has nothing. The proposals made at Camp David in July? What you offer the Palestinians is nothing. David Grossman said so. Really monsieur Barnavi, as a historian you should know that by answering stones with bullets and guns with helicopters, Israel has seriously discredited itself." Upon which the ambassador shot back most diplomatically: "If Israel had used its force there would have been many more deaths and the whole business would have been settled in the space of two days. I know you would have liked to see as many Israeli dead as Palestinians…" There, the journalist interrupts, insists it's not true. Not because it's not true, but because it put him on the hot seat and that's not the way it was supposed to be; it's the ambassador who was supposed to suffer.

I say that the Intifada Show is a flop but we can clearly see that the lines drawn at the beginning are still holding: Israel doesn't offer anything worthwhile in those damned negotiations, then over-reacts when the other guys try to grab by force what they'll never get through talks, and now Israel has the nerve to get tangled up in electoral doings while the Palestinians are dying and sinking into destitution.

Well that's what I call the CNRS [*Centre national de recherché scientifique*] party line. With the exception of Jacques Tarnero, who offers sharp clear analyses of the situation, the enlightened CNRS doctors and their fellow travelers all give the same arguments: if the Palestinians are rebelling today it's the fault of Israel for always giving too little too late: We are in a colonial situation. Wisdom would dictate to Israel to fall back to the 1967 line. The Palestinians thus established in a sovereign state would retrieve their full dignity, and peace with justice would spread across the land like honey. The Israeli Arabs? Once again it's all Israel's fault for treating them like second-class citizens. Once they are fully established in their rights, no longer mistreated and underprivileged, they will become loyal citizens who pose no threat to the integrity of the State. In fact, they say, the real problem is neither inside Arabs nor outside Arabs... it's the ultra-orthodox. Violent, extremist, and ferociously power-hungry they are the Jewish version of the fundamentalist phenomenon that began in Iran and spread all over the world.

The difference between history and politics is that the former is written after the fact, when everyone knows what happened. And then again, it's written and rewritten and each time it's a different story that arranges the facts in its own way to the extent that they can be known. It's like my texts on current events, composed from day to day, under the influence of circumstantial developments and conversations, readings and intuitions. My truth is the changing truth of the documentary journal.

The UN has decided not to send observers, that is, protectors for the Palestinians. *Ouf!* More than a month ago, when the battle was raging, I wanted to write about the comical aspects of the Palestinian Authority. We heard that they (seriously) considered creating a Kosovo situation. And no one thought to ask them who would play the role of the Americans in their remake? But don't underestimate them! A little later we found out they thought the European Community would do that job. It's beyond all understanding, the way our intellectuals who are so courageous on the media front, can encourage such nonsensical expectations. First of all, unlike Israeli intellectuals they are not soldiers and, second, they are too intelligent to imagine that someone could stand in front of the snipers who are shooting at Gilo, for example, and protect them from the Israeli riposte. It is totally unheard of. Even the Serbs in the finest days of the siege of Sarajevo never dared to make such a demand. Allow me to say that this is a perfect illustration of the Palestinians' profound cultural confusion: they make a mishmash of elements taken from a very sophisticated international culture but don't have the slightest understanding of the underlying logic. The PA tried to mix up *misérabilisme*, guerilla warfare, *la lutte finale*, martyrology and humanitarian intervention, the whole thing under the umbrella of the Arab League.

I can just see the scene. A kid is throwing stones at soldiers... and shielding a bunch of men in ski masks who are firing with kalashnikovs. The brave UN soldier steps forward, determined to protect the child as his UN mandate obliges when suddenly a tanzim foot soldier pushes him out of the way (if he doesn't shoot him to oblivion) shouting, not that one, he's our martyr *du jour*.

Neither the UN nor the EU and not even the boys from the CNRS will play that game.

So let's get back to the negotiating table. Not the big table at Camp David just a little table here at my place in Paris. Me too, I would like to make peace with the Palestinians. And with the boys from the CNRS while I'm at it. And above all with myself. *Chez moi* also the negotiations will be inspired by a desire for justice. For all parties. I see this as an opportunity to transform the world. For the better. By putting an end to centuries of revolutionary romanticism and starting to imagine new liberation strategies for oppressed peoples. By bringing an end to thousands of years of persecution of the Jews by granting them once and for the first time fully the right to enjoy their rights and the fruits of their devotion. That's my platform.

A full page ad placed in the *International Herald Tribune* by the American-Arab Anti-Discrimination Committee shows a young man naked to the waist, seen from the back, arm upraised, fist clutching a big stone, facing a mean Israeli soldier The ADC shouts: Today's David & Goliath / Stop the aggression against the Palestinian People / End the Israeli Occupation.

Commenting on the injustice not to say the *injustesse* of this image, Daniel Sibony points out that in the story David wins but in reality the Palestinians lose. So, double cruelty: against the Palestinians who are encouraged to pursue wishful fantasy strategies under cover of ill-conceived images, and against the Jews robbed of their own story in an attempt to rob them of their land.

Because if you take the trouble to go back a bit in time you see that the first colonizer in this story is Christianity. And the second, evidently, Islam.

They're constantly talking about holy land and holy places and it's grating on my ears. If there is one jiveass argument among all the false arguments on Jerusalem it's this one: the holy land for the three mono-theist religions, the holy city that should be a place of peace and harmo-ny, torn by the struggle between these three religions, so much blood spilled, it's mine, no it's mine, when it should belong to us.

Who us? Place of peace, why? Perhaps the harsh struggle of the mind seeking the truth is not adapted to this Christian peace or this Muslim holy war. For each his own Jerusalem and we'll try this time in a spirit of justice to juxtapose them, all right. But we'll never do it without first facing up to a few realities.

The three monotheisms were not born out of Jupiter's thigh as simul-taneous triplets, with equal firstborn son's rights. It is Judaism that in-vested Jerusalem with an eternal meaning that neither the peoples who came before nor the peoples who came afterward could ever dislodge. It is obvious! The mufti of Jerusalem can shout from the rooftops that not a single stone in all the extent of Palestine testifies to the slightest Jewish presence (meaning prior to the Zionist occupation) he himself doesn't believe his own screaming. Al Aqsa is the third holiest place in Islam: the journalists take it from the agency releases and pour it into the ears of the public that sucks it in without asking questions and sends it echoing back all the way to the true believers prostrate on the *Esplanade des mosquées*. And yet it's easy to find out why this mosque was set on top of the foundations of Salomon's temple. Just go to Istanbul and see the church that became the Blue Mosque. Anyone who wants to know how Jerusalem became a holy city for the Christians followed by the Moslems just has to lift a finger. The question is not how to find the historical documentation but how to explain to yourself why you don't try to find out, why you absolutely do not want to know.

Strangely enough, recognition of the Jewish priority in Jerusalem, far from preventing the harmonious coexistence that is supposedly the aim of so many talks and proposals and so much pressure, would be a first step toward the resolution of the present crisis. I would like to try to show how this recognition could clarify the situation, and sort out the symbolic by revealing the mechanisms, the chain of events, the aberra-tions that entertain the present violent confusion. Because we have to figure out why these self-declared progressives can slump into this collective obscurantism, denying all their values in the name of... their values! Why does the classic mirror-effect of persecution work so well in the context of the Palestinian conflict when almost everyone can recognize it and combat it in a neo-Nazi context?

They shout "stop the massacres," and no one laughs. It's awful! They call for a halt to the Israeli aggression against the Palestinians and they, the same they, are exploding bombs every day in the path of Israeli school busses. They say: those European meanies tried to exterminate the Jews (but can't resist adding a wink of approval) and then to make up for it they've dumped them on our backs, but we never did anything bad to the Jews. The European side of this argument goes like this: just because the Jews had it hard during the Shoah we're not allowed to criticize them anymore.

Turn the mirror and look yourselves in the eyes. You have not yet drawn the right lesson from the Shoah. You don't understand yet that the Jewish question is your problem. It's no use to say "never again." Because it's not true, as so many recent little demi-semi-genocides amply prove, and still less true since we started seeing a revival of synagogue burning, attacks on Jews, chants of death to the Jews in organized demonstrations, and a Mediterranean radio that spits out hatred all day long and calls for the de-zionization of France, all of this set off by the umpteenth little "Israeli-Arab" crisis as they call it. We believed "never again" and in the space of a few days I don't know if I can still dare to do my shopping on rue des Rosiers, *ça va pas, non*? You don't understand that this is unforgivable?

No, you can't say with a snide giggle, that all because of a little Shoah that doesn't amount to a hill of beans we think we're above suspicion from here to eternity. It's just the opposite. Turn the mirror: because of the Shoah, umpteenth tentative to exterminate the Jews, you must refrain from upholding any and all attempts to unjustly accuse the Jews. You're the ones who have to watch out for your tendency to want to believe once again and simply with a few slight modifications of the scenario that it's the Jews who keep you from living and breathing!

And what did you do? You went for it in spades. The accusation of child murder, traditional prelude to pogroms, went through without the slightest resistance. We are waiting for the rectification but it's not coming and it will never come. And the David and Goliath switch? Still running strong: the Palestinians are standing so small and so alone when it suits their purposes and absolutely backed up the x billion Muslim souls in the world when necessary to put pressure on Israel, the Jews, the whole Western world. These are but a few details and I could pile up hundreds but I am afraid I'll lose sight of the main line of my reasoning. I'll come back to it: the persecution of the Jews is not a closed and settled affair. We Jews have, at least I hope we have, drawn lessons from the Shoah. We can sincerely say "never again." But you haven't understood yet, which makes you one of the targets of this persecution while still being accomplices. You didn't want to find out how this persecution poisons our world and blocks its spiritual development.

I dare to say that is in fully recognizing the rights of Jews in and to Israel that you will finally help the Israelis and the Palestinians find a way to coexist. Instead of pointing the finger at the "colonists" and their "implantations" as the troublemakers ... [unfinished]

LETTER TO THE EDITOR/ *IHT*
"Who Will Protect Palestine's Children?" by Jumana Odeh, dateline Ramallah, West Bank. *International Herald Tribune* 27 October 2000

Under cover of a heartfelt plea for protection for Palestinian children, Dr. Jumana Odeh adds one more stone to the concerted campaign to convince the world that Israelis are child killers. Indeed, who will protect Palestine's children if their own people send them into battle and, as if that weren't enough, kill them a second time by using their deaths as an incitement to murderous hatred!

Mohammed Durra was not killed "in cold blood," he was caught in a cross-fire. And Sarrah "not yet two years old" was not "killed by an Israeli settler," she was shot accidentally in a tragic domestic accident. By her own people.

No, Israelis are not child-killers. Jews do not rejoice in the death of children, even when those children are throwing stones at them, even when those stone-throwing children are fronting for heavily armed men.

It will be a long long time before any plea arising from Ramallah can speak "to all those who still believe in humanity." When the propaganda smoke screen has dissipated the truth will stand, indelible: a heinous crime was committed against two Israeli men in Ramallah and the savagery unleashed there will turn against its perpetrators a hundredfold.

published IHT 3 November 2000

OCTOBER-NOVEMBER 2000

"Three months later, I saw members of the special commandos… playing soccer with a victim's head…. Thirteen corpses would be found, some of them beheaded… His head is displayed on a parabolic antenna. It stayed there for fifteen days…. It's 11:30 PM and the helicopter is still circling overhead…when suddenly the population is awakened by awful conflagrations…. A man shouts: 'They're slaughtering everyone!' There are more than two hundred assailants… They go from house to house… planting bombs, they kill and plunder everything in their path, they force the kids to carry the booty…. the air is filled with the sounds of supplications, children crying, then the piercing screams and groans of people whose throats are slit… women beg to be shot instead of being slaughtered. They are hacked to death with axes or pinned to the ground and their throats slit. This descent into horror lasted six hours."

Who would not be revolted by such barbaric acts? Who could be surprised by the outburst of indignation in the media, the chancelleries, the streets? The United Nations reacts, passes a resolution condemning these crimes against humanity, but the international community, horrified, cannot be satisfied with words alone. Voices call out for action, vociferous demands for the immediate expedition of UN troops to protect the population against this inhumane aggression.

Cut the comedy. The scenes of horror described above did not arouse the conscience of fellow nations, distant cousins, or like-minded buddies. No demonstrations, resolutions, or demands for UN intervention. This savagery, repeated night after night, year after year, has already caused more casualties than the total of American soldiers killed during the Vietnam War. But it happened in Algeria (*Libération*, 25 October 2000, "Le 'J'accuse' de Nesroulah Yous").

And it is still going on.

So how did they manage in the space of a few short days to turn the Jews into child killers? What is this public opinion that can make gentleman's agreements with Algerians who slit the throats of women and children, isn't bothered by the rise to power of a Chechnya-beating Putin, takes its own good time to get Milosevic, Karadzic, Mladic behind bars, accepts a whitewash of crimes in Rwanda but cannot bear the sight of big bad Israel persecuting those poor little Palestinians? Hubert Védrine runs into the arms of the new providential leader Kostunica, who's hiding Milosevic behind his back, but it's Ariel Sharon, "the butcher of Lebanon" (*Radio France Internationale*), who stands for absolute Evil!

How does it happen? How did the press, the state and, consequently, French public opinion gullibly swallow this propaganda treat—so blatant it couldn't fool a 2nd grader—and start spitting out anti-Jewish garbage we thought we'd never hear again? Trashing Jews, burning down synagogues, attacking Jews in the street, shouting "death to the Jews"?

The past few days [end of November 2000] there has been a sort of embarrassed semi-silence. As if the press, practically forced to face the truth, has decided that the less said the better. Which is probably true, but we're not going to leave it at that. The harm is done. Now we have to undo it.

On the cover of *Paris Match*: "THIS WAR THAT KILLS CHILDREN"

Baby Sarah is in our face, plastered all up and down the city on big ads for this week's *Paris Match*. "Killed by a Jewish colonist." Accusation. Machination. And then the truth comes out: the child was accidentally shot by her father, who belongs to the Tanzim. Does *Paris Match* admit the mistake? No. *Paris Match* does its own investigation, which boils down to going back and asking the father if by chance he didn't kill his daughter... accidentally of course. No, no, the father says, there's no doubt, it was a Jewish colonist. And you think Monsieur Genestar is going to trust an official Israeli investigation? You're joking! Shortly afterward a *Paris Match* journalist is wounded. Caught in crossfire? No sir, deliberately targeted by an Israeli soldier. As you can clearly see, this "war" that kills children will not forgive the honest journalists who told it to the world.

Anyway, who exactly is "this war?" It's Israel = the Jews = Jews kill children. Pretext for so many pogroms. The Jews kill Christian children and use their blood to make matzot.

Therefore on this festival the Jews, sufficiently hated for their religion, their wealth, and the debts due to them, were entirely in the hands of their enemies, who could easily bring about their destruction by spreading the report of such a child-murder, perhaps even secretly putting a bloody infant's corpse in the house of a Jew thus accused. Then there would be an attack by night on the Jews at their prayers, where there was murder, plunder, and baptism; and great miracles wrought by the dead child aforesaid, whom the Church eventually canonized.

Heinrich Heine, "The Rabbi of Bacherach"[1]

This war that kills children... The images do not speak for themselves, they say what they are told to say. Though a few of the most blatant errors have been belatedly recognized, no critical reexamination of the Al Aqsa Intifada images within the broader context of Palestinian propaganda has been undertaken. Without this propaganda campaign it would not be possible to accuse Israel (= the Jews) of attacks against civilians, savagery, massacres, crimes.

One single act of savagery was in fact perpetrated, filmed, and broadcast worldwide: the massacre of two Israeli reservists by a Palestinian mob in Ramallah. But these unbearable images of unforgivable barbarity have little weight in a dirty war that doesn't even try to hide its methods. It looks like the formula still holds good: the bigger the lie, the better it works.

How can the truth reply to propaganda? The truth is complex, it speaks with a human voice, it requires intellectual effort from listeners/viewers. Propaganda is intoxicating. It demands blood money. In fact I wonder if what looks like a clumsy failure to hide methods might not be essential to this kind of propaganda. It appeals to the lowest, most ignoble human impulses; so it has to give a wink now and then to show it's ready to stoop to the worst.

Let's go back to the death of Mohamad al Dirah.

According to his uncle Ziad, Jamal [the father] had no problem
passing by Netzarim. A crowd of Palestinian demonstrators,
who couldn't go to Jerusalem, had gathered on the side of the
road in front of the colony to protest against the visit of rightist
Israeli leader Ariel Sharon to l'esplanade des Mosquées the day
before. However, on their way back in the collective taxi the
driver stopped a bit short of Netzarim because the shooting
had started. He [Jamal] wanted to continue on foot across the
area where the agitation was going on, and get to the camp on
the other side. But there was this shooting.

"Mohamad, simple child of Gaza," Gilles Paris,
le Monde, 11 October 2000.

Now the dead child is the Al Aqsa Intifada mascot. First they denied, swore on the heads of the Palestinian children, declared, proclaimed, shouted and screamed that they do not put children on the front lines of their anti-Israeli "demonstrations." These Palestinian denials were relayed by the French press with the appropriate profound conviction and complete disregard for the reality clearly visible in illustrated news magazines and TV reports: Palestinian children are there, in the front lines, when Jewish soldiers and civilians are attacked.

Gradually the discourse changes. Yes, the children are there and proud to be there. They want to die for Jerusalem and nothing and no one could keep them from fighting the glorious fight *jusqu'au bout.* So, first the death of children is used to prove the savagery of the Jews who seek them out on their way to school, in their mother's arms, in their peaceful homes. And then the child martyrs become proof of the determination of the Palestinians to fight for their land.

The images show savage mobs and the text speaks of kind souls asking for bread and freedom. All those Davids armed with slingshots facing up to the Israeli Goliath. How's that for expropriation? They take our very name. David-Judaism-Jerusalem becomes David-Palestinian-Jerusalem and, ultimate nastiness, the Goliath label is torn from the ancient *philistim* and stuck on the Jews. The reality of those crowds is another story. As we saw in Ramallah, the poor little stone-throwers can kill a man with greater savagery than a wild beast.

And yet Israel is accused of using excessive force to suppress "demonstrations" of anger. Anger that is fully justified. And it goes all the way to the United Nations. War crimes, crimes against humanity, worse than the Nazis. The victims are tallied. Ten, twenty, thirty, sixty. Most of them Palestinian. Proof, for those who might have doubted, of the brutal repression practiced by the "fourth ranking army in the world."

Sincerely, every Palestinian casualty is to be deplored. But on the scale of values in this real world and if words still have meaning the Palestinian death toll proves exactly the opposite: Israeli restraint. It's too horrible to play with the figures. But we have to recognize that there is an enormous difference between the figures and the accusations they supposedly prove. Such an enormous difference that it is astounding that the press can give the count day after day without ever asking what the numbers mean in reality. Has Timisoara been so quickly forgotten?

The 24 year-old kid laced with explosives who died yesterday trying to blow up a military post; the children wounded, handicapped for life; the men wounded or dead; this bloodshed, these mutilated bodies, why are they wounded, why are they dead?

To put an end to the Israeli occupation, to create a Palestinian State! To live in *liberté, fraternité, égalité* like you and me? And because they have no alternative to martyrdom. They tried everything. Nothing to be done. *La lutte finale. Aux armes, citoyens.*

Isn't that the subtext at work in French minds today? The reasoning that has etched like acid, wiping out every trace of peace negotiations, Oslo agreements, Camp David meetings. These desperate people who have been offered nothing but crumbs have taken destiny in hand and nothing will stop them.

The Palestinians don't like the peace process. Their Arab brothers don't like it either. Moderate intellectuals, enraged *shebabs*, imams, mothers, schoolchildren, Palestinian negotiators, and a good proportion of the French population—Muslims, Christians and secular unbelievers lumped together—proudly declare that nothing good came of this peace process and anyway it was rigged from the start by American partiality. Whatever was signed, promised, given... it's all worthless. Yasser Arafat was subject to unbearable pressure from an American president motivated by shameful career ambitions who tricked him into signing one agreement after another, all of them unfair and unfavorable to the Palestinians.

The peace they want is an altogether different kind of peace, a peace that's knotted to alliances with Hamas, Djihad, FPLP, Hezbollah and all the rest of the "front of refusal" of Israel's existence, and embroidered with marvelous international commissions and, why not, the United Nations in person.

Anyway, Israel should just comply with United Nations resolutions x and y and that's the end of it.

Really? And that's the end of it?

I can understand that Palestinians or certain Palestinians might cherish the dream of getting back the whole of what they consider to be their land. It should be equally clear that the State of Israel has no intention of committing suicide. But when public opinion, at least in France, lines up behind the Palestinians with no questions asked, I am stunned. How can reasonable people living in a democracy and protected by a strong state that is relatively respectful of human rights swallow a scenario that simply does not hold up under rational analysis?

It's not even worth the trouble to mention the heavy-handed *mise en scène* that supposedly explains the outbreak of the crisis and its ramifications. Any pretext would do. What counts is to imagine the consequences—especially for the Palestinians—of the strategy chosen in place of the disparaged negotiations. Are we to believe that the current violence will have no effect on the future power balance? That the warriors, once the enemy is defeated, will lay down their arms and throw themselves into start-ups? That the refugees holed up in the camps of despair in neighboring countries will rejoice in the victory without claiming their share? That the extremists will become moderate intellectuals, and Djihad terrorists will be bureaucrats in the brand new administrations of the bright new state?

Tear away the veil of 19th century romanticism and this struggle will be revealed as a malediction for the Palestinians themselves. And who can judge the scope of damage for the rest of the world, and especially for the Israelis, who are on the front lines?

Where will the *tifosi* of October 2000 be when the Palestinians are defeated?

Because it can't be denied that they have more than once lost by armed struggle what they could have obtained through negotiation. Instead of awarding the Palestinians unlimited privileges as the supposedly most oppressed of all the oppressed peoples in the world, wouldn't it be more intelligent to imagine—along with them—different solutions to the conflict? Solutions that don't depend on the destruction of the State of Israel or worldwide war against the Jews. Instead of believing, *à la française*, that everything the Americans think or do is bad by definition, wouldn't it be more intelligent to break out of the Franco-French *huis-clos*, abandon the exercises in casuistry, and open your minds to the thought that there is something reasonable about the American analysis of the situation? Instead of counting the number of Jews in America and concluding that they pull the foreign policy strings (not bothering to mention that they make up less than 2% of the population) isn't it time to admit that these Jews, who have been quite well-behaved down through the ages, have good reasons for supporting Israel in such great numbers. That they are not just rooting for their own team? That they are defending noble values, values which, if we are to believe your solemn proclamations, are widely shared in these parts.

It is time to wake up from a nightmare, emerge from a long night's slumber, and ask some fundamental questions about, precisely, the holy places. People who consider themselves reasonable are saying enough of this bloodshed over Jerusalem, holy land of the three great monotheisms, it's about time to stop haggling and share it. What matter if it's the Christians and Muslims who abundantly shed each other's blood and jointly shed the blood of the Jews; our right minded folks don't suspect that the solution to this earth-wrenching conflict requires close study of this rivalry, which is anything but symmetrical.

They haven't caught on: recognition of the priority of the Jews in Jerusalem is the prerequisite for unraveling passions and enlightening minds. From there on, everything becomes possible: freedom of access, harmonious development, respect for differences, fruitful exchanges, sharing what can be shared and clear ownership of that which cannot be.

So that's what's killing Palestinian children: the fact that the Jews have priority in Jerusalem. The more it can't be denied the more the Islamists twist the facts. At the very moment when the Palestinians could have begun to build a state, the extremist current threw them into reverse, into a new cycle of suicidal violence. Days of wrath. Whose flames leap out and ignite our French Maghrebis. Listen to the talk show on *Méditerranée FM*. Hysterical Jew bashing. Boycott the Jews, vilify the

Jews, denounce the Jews as disloyal citizens who support a foreign government... yes, we have the right to shout "death to the Jews" because they deserve it, they have no rights in Palestine.

Look at the full–page ad in the *International Herald Tribune*, sponsored by the American-Arab Anti-Discrimination Committee:

WHO IS THE AGGRESSOR IN PALESTINE?

On the left, THE OCCUPIED: a handsome young man in a tank top about to throw a tiny little harmless stone. On the right, THE OCCUPANT: two Israeli soldiers in combat gear, one of them aiming his gun at the young man with the stone. .

STOP BLAMING THE VICTIMS. END THE OCCUPATION

There has been much talk about a Kosovo-type situation—who's going to play NATO in the remake?—and great hopes built with the paraphernalia of fast-struggles. The masses in the streets, the tyrant overthrown, the victory parade. Can one dare to compare the Arab-Israeli conflict with those situations? First of all, who is the aggressor in Israel? The Palestinians. They say so themselves. They decided to drop a worthless peace process, roll up their sleeves, and blast their state into existence by good old armed struggle. Okay, they think their cause is just; but they can't have it both ways. Either they are fiercely determined no-holds-barred liberators. Or poor innocent victims. In fact they're playing a game of mirrors. They attack Israeli soldiers and Jewish neighborhoods, they stab right into the heart of Israel, and when the inevitable riposte comes, they scream bloody murder. Help! They're being attacked. Same trick for the massacres, the occupation, the murder of children: the Palestinian project is mirror-imaged and switched into accusations against Israel.

Beyond and beneath the deliberate strategy of provoking attacks and then calling on the international community to punish Israel, lie the profound reasons for Islam's murderous hatred of Jews. The Jews were there first. Because of the Jews, Jerusalem is a holy place.

The Palestinians, unable to express the real reasons for their distress, are paying for Islam's angst. What a waste! They're being used as mad dogs to tear the Jews limb from limb and, instead of resisting this instrumentalization and seeking the path to development, they go along with the machination.

And how do you expect the Palestinians to resist when intelligent, cultured, well-fed, comfortably housed French people snap at the first bit of bait and run with the pack? Virtually of course. It's indecent. And they know it, and that's why they justify it by griping: "Because of the Shoah we don't even have the right to criticize Israel." Instead of asking themselves whether, because of the Shoah, they should think twice before griping about the Jews.

These nostalgic Frenchmen with their perverse logic make *Les Misérables* heroes out of Palestinian kids who are more like black shirts of the thirties. It's indecent. As if they didn't know about the millions who have been mutilated, massacred, tortured, hacked up; as if they never heard of Pol Pot, of Rwanda's genociders, of Foday Sankoh's baby monsters. These people get sick pleasure out of cheerleading a movement of blatantly uncontrollable violence. And they do it without a care in the world for the fate of the Palestinians.

The Arabs and Muslims who call in to *Méditerranée FM* say it in their way: *the press in our country is under pressure from the Jews, it's a scandal! TF1 invited Netanyahu, that war criminal. French television showed the lynching of the Jewish soldiers but why don't they show when Palestinian soldiers are lynched...*

Why indeed!

I suppose that mainstream journalists delight in getting slammed with alternate blows of Jewish and Arab indignation. "They shout at us from both sides, that proves we're neutral."

It's a cheap way of getting off the hook! Saul Bellow calls it moral tourism:

> *What Switzerland is to winter holidays and the Dalmatian coast to summer tourists, Israel and the Palestinians are to the West's need for justice - a sort of moral resort area.*
> Saul Bellow, *To Jerusalem and Back*[2]

APRIL- JUNE 2001

23 April 2001

Forty people were killed in Addis Ababa the other day. A student demonstration turned into some kind of a riot and the result is more than 40 dead in one day, giving rise to a brief news item with no further details. A week or two ago forty-seven died at Ellis Park in South Africa, stomped to death because thousands of fans without tickets broke into the stadium, smashing and crushing everything that stood in their way. No one is talking about massacres in Addis Ababa, the affair isn't brought before the UN Security Council. As for declarations of solidarity with the ticketless masses of Ellis Park, perish the thought.

Since the outbreak of this Intifada II at least seventy Israeli Jews are dead and hundreds more injured. Where are the voices that rang out in November 2000? Fifty dead brought outcries of massacre, war crime and crime against humanity, urgent calls for international intervention to protect civilians... meaning Palestinian civilians. Today international public opinion is hardly disturbed by the death of 70 Israelis. Is it because the Palestinian toll has reached 400? Is that the definition of a massacre? Is it a question of proportion? A total of eight thousand dead on each side would make it a just war? A little quarrel between friends?

You still don't get it. News is news, you have to follow it day to day and from all sides if you don't want to look like a pathetic Don Quijote fighting windmills. We are not talking about massacres anymore and the smart aleck who thought she could throw her little update into the opponent's face should stroll over to the open line at *Radio Méditerranée FM*: the talk show host declares, in perfect harmony with a caller shocked by Israeli army operations in Palestine, "It's not a war anymore, it's an extermination... ethnic cleansing..." (*22 April '01, 1:45 PM*).

It would be funny if it weren't deadly serious. Our *Radio des Mille Collines* gaily pursues its weekly hate mongering and the CSA stuffs cotton in its ears so it won't have to take action. An earlier attempt—in fact, a shabby demonstration of symmetrism by which representatives of the Jewish and the Arab stations were sat down and given a joint lesson in good behavior—led to unveiled threats on *Rad Méd* against the Jews if they dared to lift a hand against its broadcast freedom.

Listen to the Jew hatred spewed out on this radio station freely operating in our lovely country and imagine the state of mind of Palestinians in Gaza. How can we get to the bottom of this persecution complex, justification of the most terrible persecutions? Because there can be no doubt about the sincerity of these people. He believes what he says, our perfectly integrated Tunisian intellectual, fully enjoying European political freedom and encouraging his fellow Muslims to do likewise so that one day they will have the real political influence their numbers deserve. He believes it: it's not a war anymore it's an extermination. Those who came before him believed it too: it's the war mongering revolution-making Jews who got us into this mess. It's the Jews who keep us from developing, getting rich, eating, drinking and breathing. It's the Jews who poison the wells, carry the plague, killed Jesus. Anyway they have no business here. Kick them out. Like he says, the talk show host on *Rad Méd*: the Jews don't belong in Palestine. They should go back where they came from.

And there is even worse. There is a child named Shelavet Pas, murdered by a Palestinian sniper. To my knowledge she didn't make it to the cover of *Paris Match*. No *Cette guerre qui tue les enfants / part 2* for a 10 month-old Jewish baby killed by a sharpshooter who knew what he was doing as he aimed for her head and then aimed for the legs of her father as he knelt down to gather in his arms his mortally injured baby. No symmetrism for the Jewish child.

The Betar put Shelavet Pas posters all up and down the rue des Rosiers. And it had to happen: She was killed twice, five times, fifteen times, yes, here in Paris, in the intimate space of our rue des Rosiers, the posters were defaced. Here the child's face is torn to shreds, there it's crossed out with an X, further on she's ridiculed with a red clown's nose, and elsewhere cancelled with the word "false." These are human beings who do such a thing? Instant negationists.

As the *Rad Méd* host said: it's not a war, it's an extermination.

We have to look beyond the suffering of this Israeli family, beyond the suffering of Israelis, beyond this hatred seemingly aimed only at a small minority—a minority smeared with reprobation that justifies by ricochet the evil done to them—and ask ourselves what is the principle that is being insidiously established in our society:

The end justifies the means and the declaration of a state of oppression justifies everything.

If I remember correctly the term previously used was "occupied territories." Then, by one of those slides in meaning that turns history tragic, it becomes "the Occupation." And this word "Occupation" acquires extraordinary powers. It explains everything, justifies everything, replaces the entire historical dimension, silences all political argument, closes the door to any peaceful solution. Don't bother your head. From now on everything is clear. Why do they shoot rockets into Israeli towns? Answer: the Occupation. Why do they shoot at Israeli Jews on the highway, in their apartments, in their fields and kindergartens? The Occupation. Why take the bus in order to blow it up? The Occupation. Why set off remote control bombs under school busses? The Occupation. Why spend three months chatting on the Net to seduce an Israeli teenager and deliver him for death in a carefully prepared trap, why boast about catching this boy in a death trap? It's simple, it's because of the Occupation.

And by the way, why did the Palestinians reject every peace proposal put on the table last year? The Occupation. If you don't understand that, you don't understand anything. The Palestinian Authority could not sign an agreement to end the occupation of the occupied territories because of the Occupation. And it's true. The occupation of Israel by the Jews is the reason for the rejection of a peace agreement. Of any peace agreement already proposed or eventually to be offered. *Sacré dilemme.*

24 April 2001

Ideas churn in my mind. And put themselves in order. I write sitting or standing or walking, I write during lectures, conversations, dinner parties and while reading books, newspapers, reviews. I write, in the streets, entire books and then in the space of the small life-size hours available to develop my arguments, I don't know where to begin.

Public opinion. Geopolitical conflicts are subject these days to the wishes and whims of the ratings. Personally that wouldn't be my choice but it is an unavoidable reality. So let's try to make good of it. Today, the war is being fought on... hey, what am I saying? Wars have always been fought as much on the propaganda front as on the battlefield. But how can we alert public opinion in our democracies? How can we show them that they are digging themselves a monumental tomb by giving in to this massive aggression against their own rational humanistic foundations?

Let's go back to this OCCUPATION, to its simplistic deceiving fabrication. The Palestinians live in misery, their lives are a nightmare, they have no state, no jobs, no freedom of movement, no hope. And as if that weren't enough, they are now "mowed down" by the over-armed soldiers of an over-powerful army. The suffering of the Palestinians, visible to the naked eye, is taken at face value. *Ils souffrent donc ils sont occupés /*

they suffer therefore they are occupied. And who is that OCCUPATION? Well, it's the same as "this war that kills children." It's the Jews.

History is what couldn't be avoided despite good intentions here and there, despite efforts by the well-intentioned to block the projects of the ill-intentioned. The Palestinians and the Israelis are here where history left them. Today, when the consequences of their choices are too hard to bear, the Palestinians want to sweep them under the rug. Since they can't go back in time and change them. There's no way to replay the years and the centuries. It's life, not a video game. But the future is ours, it's up to us to trace it.

And yet anyone who speaks out loud and clear for Israel's right to exist as a Jewish State is considered by definition criminally indifferent to Palestinian suffering. Of course the argument is twisted and turned, embroidered with a thousand details meant to separate the good pro-Israelis from the bad ones, but it's a cloud of phony nuances that vanish without a trace. They say, they are constantly saying: the colonies! The thorn in Palestine's foot. *Les colons*, those horrible colonists who spoil everything. Stunning proof of Israeli bad faith: they negotiate with one hand and build new housing for the *colons* with the other.

You feel like you are dragged into a sinister poker game where the stakes are catastrophic. And every time you put forth a reasonable argument and despite your spirit of peace and conciliation, the adversary is going to pull out his "colonies" card and shut you out forever.

It happens sometimes that a reality condenses into an image that is so dense, so tight, so compact that it operates like the core of a nuclear weapon: Israel throws Jews into the territories and the Palestinians shoot rockets into Israel. That's how they reason: you throw people we throw bombs!

What I want to say today about the issue of the "colonies" is that it's a red herring. And the suffering of the Palestinians, as real as it is, is the direct consequence of the strategy followed by their leadership ever since the creation of the State of Israel (and well before). Trying to explain their seething rage and readiness to do the worst as an inevitable outcome of this suffering is a flagrant denial of historical evidence. I speak for example of Jews murdered in Palestine during the 19th and early 20th centuries, before the creation of the State of Israel... not to mention preceding centuries.

The Jews in those long ago times had no power over the inhabitants of what was then called Palestine and before then, among other biblical names, Israel. Jews who settled in Palestine, in Eretz Yisroel, did not have a powerful army, they did not rule over Jerusalem. There had been no creation of a State, no proposal for partition and nothing like an Oslo Agreement. There were no checkpoints, no curfews, no closures. And yet it can't be denied that for Arabs living in Palestine under Ottoman or British occupation the Jews were already *colons*, it was already the Occupation and, from time to time, for one reason or another, their anger boiled over, they went on the rampage and slaughtered Jews.

You'll say: they were visionaries. They knew what all that would come to. It was preventive therapy. Okay, but it didn't work and here we are today with the result: Palestinian humiliation.

Due to this Palestinian humiliation, Jews are killed in Israel because they are Jews, and that's just for starters. Sticking a *colon* label on the corpses is not going to make the truth disappear, and recent incidents confirm that there is no difference between a good Jew (*chez lui* in Tel Aviv) and a bad one (*chez nous* in Hebron). And shouldn't we ask why Arabs can live in Israel but Jews can't live in Palestine? Don't even bother, the answer is indelibly engraved in minds so closed that the question is never asked or else it's asked in a couplet with a single-choice answer. Israeli Arabs accept to live under Jewish administration but the *colons* wouldn't accept to live under Palestinian authority.

And how about you? Would you accept to live under a corrupt inefficient authority? Would you freely choose to live under a dictatorship without the slightest hope of democracy on the horizon?

But I'm not going to go round in circles on the by-pass roads. I want to get back to my own starting point, the "colonies." The issue is a red herring and there's no way it can hide the real problem, a huge problem: the Palestinian State whose creation will, theoretically, sooner or later, bring an end to the conflict, on condition that it conforms in all respects to the Palestinian wish list and, further, satisfies the entire Arab-Muslim world down to the last billionth true believer, this state cannot exist without the extermination or at the very least the expulsion of the Jews from Israel.

Whereas the miserable piecemeal state, that bundle of Bantustans, the lowdown shackled and handcuffed apartheid state, this contemptible mincemeat state the nasty Jews are trying to pawn off on us, baah! We spit on it and grind into the dust.

Well at the present time it's the best that can be offered. Because history is what couldn't be avoided and current events are what there is and the two together are why we can't trust any able bodied Palestinian authority to respect a security agreement worth the paper it's written on.

It's as simple as that. It's not because I say it, it's because of simple everyday reality, the violence, the violence that some would explain and won't hesitate to justify in the name of the Occupation, it's this violence that proves that a Palestinian State created under the present circumstances will be an Al Aqsa Intifada multiplied by x, and I don't dare give a numerical value to this x.

It's not true because I pieced together a good argument, it's true because of the way the party of the second part is behaving right now at this very moment. It's the logic of reality. Not theoretical logic. I did not reach these conclusions, which might seem shocking, by way of any hatred for Palestinians but on the contrary because I grant them a minimum of respect: I take their words and deeds as an authentic expression of their policies.

Let's say that the PA realizes they made a strategic mistake; the Al Aqsa Intifada should have defeated Israeli determination and imposed a just (in their eyes) solution of the conflict, but it didn't work. So they decide to lower the temperature and go back, as people like to say, "to the negotiating table." And suppose that the PA gives in a bit and reluctantly accepts a few compromises refused at Camp David in the summer of 2000. None of the above is even imaginable today but let's just imagine it in order to imagine what would follow:

The PA signs and is immediately overtaken by its hardliners; lacking the force to resist, it falls, replaced by Hamas and Cie. Or the PA signs, igniting a rebellion that endangers its power; it reneges on its commitments, stays in place, and plunges into ...

One guess? The Al Qods Intifada.

I am neither cynical nor pessimistic. I'm simple. Someone who bonks you every time he disagrees with you will hit you the next time he disagrees. If you're not stupid or masochistic you don't give him the stick to beat you with. Israel will not grant to a Palestinian entity, under the present circumstances, a real state that can arm itself to the teeth and destroy Israel. And the Palestinians won't accept anything less than a sovereign state that can arm itself to the teeth and destroy Israel.

Okay, that's the way it is. I can deal with it. It's not the end of the world.

All I'm trying to say is that you can't swim in two different logics at the same time. Either you accept the explanations given to justify the Al Aqsa Intifada, in which case you have to accept Intifadas Ad Infinitum, or you brush away all these justifications as so many counterproductive fantasies and you start to ask the Palestinians to behave like adults.

How can we find the way out of this nightmare of violence? How can I explain why I reject all arguments based on the principle that Israel must make more and still more concessions? How can I show that this demand for concessions is not based on any notion of justice, it is simply inspired by fear and laziness.

This story of land-for-peace concessions ended in August 2000. Once again the Palestinians find themselves exactly where their ethical and strategic choices left them. Terribly weakened. At a dead end. Because the destruction of the State of Israel does not fall within the range of possibilities. Reality itself can no longer bear such projects! The extermination of the Jews in all or any part of the world is not workable. It's no use thinking you can keep the project secret up to the fateful hour of its implementation. You can't get there on tiptoes, and not by giant steps either.

The only hope for the Palestinians is to accept their position of weakness, take responsibility for it (oh no oh no, I'm not talking about puffed up declarations and oriental rhetoric, I'm talking about politics) and negotiate sincerely from a position of weakness. Abandon their rear guard combat and accept modest pragmatic solutions so they can finally enter into a positive dynamics.

Ah! I'm going to get hollered at! They'll say I don't understand anything about the Palestinian (Arab-Muslim, Middle Eastern and why not fundamentalist Islamist) mentality, that I don't understand anything about realities on the ground, nothing about the determination of an oppressed people.

But I do understand. That's why I keep writing day after day, with no self censorship, without deforming my thought to make it more presentable. I write this way to say the truth of what I think today. I write this way so I can reread what I've written three months from now, one year, ten years later and see if I saw straight on this or that issue.

I don't know how many years it will take for the Palestinians to finally start acting in their own interest. I have great hopes for the future.

Who's crying?

"I had orchards in Tel Aviv. In that place they call Tel Aviv. I had a house and orchards, I had olive groves, orange groves, I had goats and a big family and I contemplated the moon from my rooftop terrace and we were happy and here's the key to my house, I have been carrying it for 53 years."

"Well, I had a temple in Jerusalem."

So let's have a good cry and then rebuild our lives.

25 April 2001

Suddenly the *International Herald Tribune* (24 April '01)—usually pretty fair and honest—sends us a volley of mortar shells. What in the world could have triggered this storm of thundering reproaches? These hysterical accents? They're beamed over the radio (television too I suppose, but the astute reader will have noticed that I don't have TV) in the French print media, and now the *IHT* has joined in. These hysterical accents are a sign that a sensitive nerve has been touched.

What is provoking this hysteria? The Israeli army incursion into zone A of Gaza last week? No. It's not the military operation, it's the official American reaction that explains the outburst. You have to understand: the world's conscience is not shocked by the use of "excessive force" it is excited by the scolding of Israel that mobilizes deeply buried Christian schemas. We are hearing the hysterical voice that cries out, calling the villagers to join in the Jew hunt.

The early Christians quoted the prophets of Israel to curse the Jews for refusing the messiah, for killing Christ. Today, in the same way for the same purpose, our enemies cite *Haaretz* journalists and Meretz MKs.

The villagers are giddy with delight because big bad Colin Powell smacked the Israelis and sent them off with their tails between their legs.

The Israeli public does not yet fully understand the most important consideration of all: that the Palestinians are, in a ter-

rible way, winning. Their suffering is robbing Israel of its moral substance.

... The Palestinians assault civilians, carry out indiscriminate terrorist bombings... But that does not change the fact that they are Israel's victims.

Naturally they would like to see Israel destroyed. But they might accept simply getting back what was taken from them in the 1967 war...

(William Pfaff, "The Outlook is Ominous for Both Israel and the Palestinians" *IHT / LA Times Syndicate* 24 April 2001)

21:20: And when ye shall see Jerusalem compassed with armies, then know that the desolation thereof is nigh.

21:22: For these be the days of vengeance, that all things which are written may be fulfilled.

21:24: And they shall fall by the edge of the sword, and shall be led away captive into all nations: and Jerusalem shall be trodden down of the Gentiles, until the times of the Gentiles be fulfilled.

Luke[3]

And this helps us understand why the Palestinians are always the victims. When they attack they are the victims, when they're hit back they're the victims. When they commit terrorist actions they are the victims, when they "naturally" want to destroy Israel they are victims. Why? Because they are "*Israel's victims*." Just like Jesus once was. And the territories, that red herring, is the miracle of the loaves and fish.

I haven't got the heart to write anymore today. When you're constantly defending yourself against crazy ideas you end up a bit loony yourself. Where does she get that nonsense! The Palestinians as Jesus and what else?

P.S. and why is it called the West Bank, *Cisjordanie* in French, and who owned it in 1967? If the West Bank was taken from the Palestinians in 1967, the young king Hussein shouldn't be surprised if his Palestinian brothers come one day to take back the East Bank too.

I want to write hope. I want to go into the 21st century. I want to show how one can find in the heart of Jewish thought a liberation program that is infinitely more practical, more noble, more humanist than all those revolutions that massacred the 20th century. I want to reflect on the application of the lesson of Pesach to the mistakes of terrorist liberation movements.

(later)

Who said crazy ideas? Ira Berkow (*IHT* 25 April '01) reports on "Charlie Ward, the Knick guard and true believer...[and] his teammate Allan Houston" as quoted in Sunday's *New York Times Magazine*:

> *Jews are stubborn... There are Christians getting persecuted by Jews every day.... But tell me, why did they persecute Jesus unless he knew something they didn't want to accept?... They had his blood on their hands... [Jews] spit in Jesus' face and hit him with their fists.*

Okay, Charlie Ward was not (or not yet?) talking about Israel but he confirms, faster than I would have wished, the urgency of facing up to the problem of the basic anti-Judaism—associated with the birth, development, spread, and dominion of Christianity—that today informs the shifting, changing, malleable anti-Jewish thought underlying a discourse that claims to be secular, political, and above the fray.

26 April 2001

Talk about Palestinian suffering and Israel is automatically accused, no need for explanations. Talk about the misfortunes of Egyptians, Lebanese, Syrians, Libyans, Iraqis, okay, on condition that it can be used to blame Israel or the United States (handmaiden of the Zionists). And if there's no way of avoiding talk about the miseries inflicted on these people by their own governments, it's slipped in between commas, it's yes of course but insignificant, it's okay you're right but that doesn't excuse... the suffering of Palestinians, so let's talk about that.

Where do the Muslim residents of our democratic, high tech, western countries come from? How is it that their numbers have raised Islam to the rank of France's second most practiced religion? These are, if I'm not mistaken, people who left their native lands, who came to live for better or worse *chez nous*? Despite the red tape, flagrant discrimination, and gray skies, despite their nostalgia for native landscapes and traditional dishes, most of these immigrants prefer to remain in their adopted homes in Europe, Canada, the United States.

Whatever their reason for leaving home and settling in another country, it seems like a rather good solution. Immigration often turns out to be a nice surprise. A fresh start, new dynamics, enriching, broadening. You can't always leave, not everyone can leave, but the choice of leaving is not by definition bad or tragic.

Why should it be any different for Palestinians?

Can we say with certainty that this person is an economic immigrant, the other is political, this one was chased and the other left willingly? What explains the presence of over 5 million Muslims in France and the nearly total absence of Jews in the Muslim world? The Jewish communities were chased out of Egypt, Iraq, Iran, Libya, Syria. And what became of the Jews of Poland, Rumania, Lithuania?

If you ask me, the Arab countries should stop fooling themselves and the rest of the world. Instead of boasting about their great relations with the Jews during somber periods of European history, instead of trying to make the statute of dhimmi look like an improved version of 1st class citizenship, instead of pretending they were lily white innocent during the Shoah, they could show a bit of up to date, verifiable, non-mythical generosity. How? By welcoming Israel as a Jewish State in the heart of their region.

Isn't it ridiculous to be obsessed with grabbing up more land when you already have more than anyone could handle and the other guy has hardly enough room to stretch his arms? Isn't it stupid to stir up the good old anti-Israeli boycott when the whole world is organizing for international trade and you've got nothing but oil and sand? Does it make sense to keep plugging up the volcano of popular discontent that feeds into the hands of the Islamists instead of opening new roads to democratic development that would relieve oppression?

The day when it is widely recognized that the Arab-Israeli conflict, violently imposed on Israel, is a rear guard combat bogged down in outdated discourse that brings no good to anyone, hope will be reborn in the Middle East. And let me reassure you: you'll still have the right to criticize Israel. Because it is a country built and inhabited by human beings. It's not a Platonic Idea, not a Christian holy place, not a Muslim paradise, it's a Jewish country churning with contradictions that will continue to provide all the arguments you need to badmouth it. So, even if my dream of peace comes true, no one will be deprived of the pleasure of criticizing Israel.

Israel is a chance for the Arab world, starting with the Palestinians. And the Europeans should finally wake up and exert a good influence on them, to help them escape from the trap of revolutionary discourses—spawned, incidentally, in Europe—that have repeatedly demonstrated their harmful nature. When I see French leftists succumbing once again to these grisly dreams it reminds me of the 1983 invasion of Grenada: disheartened by the Vietnam debacle the Americans found a cute little operation to cheer them up. And French leftists, still suffering from an indigestion of Communism, grab at a Palestinian snack to reassure themselves that their ideology still makes sense.

Try a little harder, boys. The challenge should be marvelously tonic for my French compatriots, world champions in discourse: rethink the Palestinian condition.

To begin with, face the facts: a state can't be thrown together on a whim. Creating one from the bottom up is difficult, almost impossible. But since it's a life or death question, we have to attempt the impossible. A state can't be built out of rhetoric. It's serious work that demands meaningful intellectual effort. So we have to stop encouraging the Palestinians to believe that they are going to brutally tear their state out of the maw of those nasty Jews. How can you expect people in such a state of distress to build a better future if you encourage their dismal confusion by naming "violence" the actions of the army of a democratic state defending its population, and "self defense" the action of a person who wraps himself in explosives and blows himself up at a bus stop for the sole purpose of taking dozens of Jewish school children with him into death?

The grouch who pokes a gun out of his eighth floor window and shoots at the insolent kids who were making a racket downstairs into the wee hours... he too thinks he's acting in self-defense. But you didn't fall for that one, did you?

Anyway, and outside of any moral consideration, the terrorist violence we are talking about will never meet with any response other than military, with its lot of human casualties and property destruction. Precisely because we are not in a "Vietnam war" model, not even a "Lebanese quagmire." We are not dealing with a *maquis* or guerilla warfare, invincible in the long term. And again, for pity's sake, take a look at Colombia. For example! The dregs of guerilla warfare.

Let's forget about this shoddy guerilla warfare and turn our attention to things that can, that could be done. Structures, infrastructures, administrations, accountability. Frenchies, you're champs in administration. C'mon and help the Palestinians get it together. Don't be cowardly. Until now it seems to me they're willing to accept help as long as you shut your mouth and do as you're told, open it to spread their propaganda, dutifully bow to their rule of might makes right.

Strange manners, *n'est-ce pas*? Israel is condemned for the excessive use of force, pilloried for using its superior force against poor under-armed creatures, but the same critics who wag their fingers at Israel unquestioningly accept might makes right in the Palestinian territories. They are terribly, horribly respectful of it. Shhh! Don't say that. You might anger Hamas. I'm told that the Italian cameraman guilty of filming the lynching (that's not even the word, we don't even have words for it) of two Israelis in Ramallah is still getting death threats.

9 May 2001

the day after the *huit mai*, [8th of May] that is, the *oui mais* [yes but]...

I don't want to spend all my days in a state of indignation, I don't want my joie de vivre to be eaten away by indignation, I don't want to cry out every time I look at a newspaper or listen to a newscast, I do not want to defend my version of things just because it's mine, I cannot stand by, helpless, when Israelis are being killed and here in our democratic countries people learn so quickly, oh how quickly, I would say my g-d how quickly to hide the realities under the drapings of millenary ideologies.

What, in reality, was the news this day, the 9th of May, the day after the *huit mai* of the *oui mais*, the *yes but* of the victory over Nazi Germany? Two Israelis, fourteen year-old boys, were savagely murdered, stoned to death (we say stoned to death but that's not it, we don't even have words to say how they were crushed, pulverized with rocks, bludgeoned, beaten to a pulp, and even that is not enough) and their battered corpses slashed and stabbed. This, I repeat, is the news this day. How was this news reported on *France Inter* at 1PM?

Horror follows upon horror in the Middle East (I summarize without deforming): yesterday a 4 month-old Palestinian child was killed, today two *colons* were savagely assassinated. Then the subject is developed at 1:30, following the same plot: blow N° 1, the Palestinian baby killed in a bombing, blow N° 2 (that is, the counterpunch) two young *colons* savagely assassinated. Their age is not mentioned. And if we are too dumb to understand why these *colons* were assassinated, Pierre Weill, reporting from Jerusalem, explains that a Palestinian official, deploring the death of innocents whether Israeli or Palestinian, insists that the only way to stop the violence is to resume negotiations but, our correspondent pursues, Ariel Sharon categorically refuses to negotiate without a total end to violence, but the Palestinian Authority cannot control every-thing and everyone; armed groups are operating in total independence. In short, you get it: Ariel Sharon refuses to negotiate and that's why armed groups with absolutely no connection to the PA run around savagely assassinating creatures who, after all, are neither children nor adolescents, nor Jews, nor Israelis but simply *colons*.

Where is the reality in all of that? Where did that reality begin? And if I were face to face with you, monsieur or madame chief of the news desk, you would have an answer for everything. You would tell me that my objection is invalid, my problem is I want to hear my version of the facts. I'm partisan, I can't handle your objectivity, your supreme impartiality.

Is that so? How do you defend your logic? Your score-keeping method? Because I know you well enough to know that the case will be closed: a 4 month-old baby against 2 *colons*, full stop. If Israel should take some initiative tomorrow you'll start from there, it will be 1 incursion and, if horror follows upon horror, it will just be x *colons* killed or injured in revenge for the incursion and again, case closed, full stop.

And that's not all and it's far from all.

I was riding in a cab on Sunday April 30th. The driver noticed my accent and engaged me in one of those where do you come from conversations between foreigners: he says he's Algerian. Suddenly *France Info* announces that fifty Kabyles were just killed in the course of a peaceful civil rights demonstration. Hubert Védrine solemnly deplores this tragic situation, but says that France has no intention of telling the Algerians what to do. How about that? The cab driver tells me that he is Kabyle and I reply that I'm Jewish and France is too busy telling Israel what to do so there'll be a bit of a wait for Kabylie.

From now on when I hear "deplore" I'll know what's behind it.

But let's get back to logic: Deborah Sontag, writing in the *IHT*, congratulates the Mitchell Report for its objectivity; it doesn't blame the Palestinians or the Israelis for the outburst of violence in the summer of 2000, neither does it exonerate one or the other. This is what goes for objectivity in our times.

Bashar al Assad is not burdened with such scruples. He blames the Israelis today, and the Jews forever. His slurs, upheld and relayed by homegrown religious authorities, were repeatedly thrown in the face of the visiting Pope without provoking the slightest reaction. To each his mission, to each his logic: the Pope's spokesman maintains that his opposition to antisemitism being established beyond the shadow of a doubt there was no need to reiterate it in front of his Syrian hosts who, apparently satisfied by this eloquent silence, explained that the Pope didn't have to articulate approval of this condemnation of the Jews because his presence alone was sufficient proof of assent.

To top it off, as if we needed topping, we get a slap from a Jewish pen, a young man who brings his family squabbles to the "*Letters & Opinions*" page of the *IHT*. His aunt isn't speaking to him anymore. Just because he thinks it's wrong for his Israeli commando cousin to be making incursions in the territories. And told him so. This misunderstanding leads the young man to reflections on the Jewish soul, which is more suited to peace than war, more peaceful and pacific in diaspora than in Israel. He wonders:

"*A Jewish Lament: 'Israel Brings Out the Worst in Us,'*" Radio France Internationale journalist Daniel Brown. IHT 8 May 2001

> *What is it with Israel that brings out the worst in us Jews?*
> *My family, for the most part, has never picked up a weapon.*
> *They somehow escaped taking up arms in the vicious wars of*
> *humanity's bloodiest century, the 20th. Not by fleeing them,*
> *how could they? But maybe by trying to resist tyranny with*
> *the Jewish traditions of dialogue and humanism.*

Oh my g-d! The young man has made the biggest revisionist blunder in history. In the name of the "very Jewish humanism we have been so proudly advocating for thousands of years," and on the strength of citations from the Talmud and Buber, he dumped into oblivion not 6 million but 6 times 6 million Jews proud of their humanism who, seeking for how many thousands of years to pursue the dialogue, have met with violent death for lack of someone to dialogue with!

As if we—people like me—were indifferent to Palestinian suffering. As if we were not aware of the dangers, for the Jewish soul in general and the Israeli soul in particular, of life in a state of war, of this violence that forcibly calls for a military response. How could we ignore those dangers when we ourselves, comfortably settled here in France, can't even follow the news without being pushed into a state of self-defense?

As for me, I'm tired of having to react day in day out to endless insults (to my intelligence). I have something to say... a lot to say to humanists who'd like to pursue the dialogue with us: I beg them to begin by dialoguing with the Palestinians.

P.S.

Discovered only the other day, in the February 2001 issue of l'*Arche*, two illustrations from *Intifada,* a little Palestinian newspaper. *Palestine*, a frail young woman nailed to the cross, is bleeding to death while hook-nosed Jews in *talit* stand at her feet spitting insults and shooting arrows at her.

11 May 2001

A tempest rains down on us this week, as one more dike gives way under the pressure of hatred that has been stewing for 2,000 years. You can't hit back at every outrage without becoming an outrageous pillar of indignation yourself. No, they're not going to give me a hundred verbal lashes a day just for the fun of hearing my screams. No, I will not scream in pain, not in indignation. From now on I will be imperturbable. Talk your talk, mesdames messieurs, spin your fantasies, I'm here, I'm listening.

Jim Hoagland, who sincerely wishes to be objective, who has no intention of blaming Israel without also blaming the Palestinians for everything that has happened since the beginning of the Intifada, who sincerely hopes to convince both parties to bury the hatchet and smoke the peace pipe, writes an editorial that belies, by its vocabulary, the apparent effort to respect human values. Here are adjectives attached to Israel in the space of 16 short paragraphs:

- *harsh military and political tactics*
- *a new campaign of conquest and vengeance*
- *inflexible*
- *...urged Americans to combat Palestinian "terrorism"... as a one-size-fits-all threat that requires no thought or discrimination*
- *not simple opportunism*
- *war and peace are not total opposites for besieged Israelis*
- *Particularly revealing is the [Mitchell] report's focus on Israeli settlements*
- *pure idealism to greed for land*
- *religious fervor and mysticism that defies rational political discourse*
- *stealthy and invasive expansion of settlements*

I repeat, all of these expressions defend an argument constructed with an obvious intention to be fair. Hoagland holds the Palestinians largely responsible for the conflict. But can't seem to find the harsh words to uphold the analysis:

- *ugly overreaction to Mr. Sharon's walk around the Al Aqsa mosque compound...*
- *stop the violence they inaugurated*
- *deal with the underlying causes of conflict.*
- *reversing the slide into religious hatred*
- *unvarnished, odious bigotry*

         (*"Israel's Upper Hand is a Mixed Blessing," IHT,* 10 May 2001)

If you please, Mister Hoagland, <u>not</u> having the upper hand would be a <u>total</u> disaster for Israel, so leave us with the mixed blessing, we're used to it.

How can we explain the feelings that underlie such a choice of words? How can we expect the Palestinians to deprive themselves of *unvarnished, odious bigotry* when a Hoagland harbinger of peace indulges in those good old stereotypes? How can we understand such lack of literary sensitivity from a lettered man?

And how can we calmly go on with our lives when the front page of today's paper announces *Life on the West Bank: An Eye for an Eye* (the murder of the two adolescents in Tekoa).

26 May 2001

Where are they trying to lead us? How low can they sink? Tell me, please, where is French public radio coming from?

Continental breakfast this morning on *France Inter* and *Radio France Internationale:* a little jaunt into the blazing core of Hamas demonstrations in Gaza to go with our morning coffee. Gilles Perez puts our ears right up against the loudspeakers and if that doesn't chill your blood then you're already on ice. These town crier loudspeakers march through Gaza announcing in a nasal voice the explosion of the day's first martyr (the panel-truck stuffed with explosives) and, shortly after, the second lucky number (in Hadera)... a special brand of fireworks to celebrate the anniversary of Israel's pull out from Southern Lebanon. And you want Israel to pull out of the territories before nightfall? So tell me how Hamas will celebrate the anniversary of that momentous event?

The *RFI r*eporter with the feathery voice is no less at ease in Hamas-land; tears well up in her eyes as she invites us to coo over the determination of these young men who are willing to die "to have a country."

So much for local color. We mustn't neglect the strategic aspect, as we are often reminded. We must be objective, we need a wide screen view of the overall situation in the Middle East. Well, how about this?

Dominique Roque, reporting from Jerusalem, announces the 2 suicide-attacks claimed by Hamas (see above "demonstration") and the death of a Fatah militant in the explosion of his car. The PA says he was assassinated. Israel claims it was a work accident but Ms. Roque reminds us that the Israelis have often used "this method" to eliminate Palestinians. As for the cease-fire proclaimed by the Israeli government, the Palestinians say it's not worth a dime.

Conclusion? Precisely, what is one to conclude from this gobbledygook?

The same menu is served again at 1 PM. Gaza, Hamas, loudspeakers, sizzling voice, strident cries, overheated atmosphere and, on the other station, the young woman in ecstasy over budding martyrs. Where we learn that Hamas is going to pursue the Intifada "as long as the *colons* are here." Can anyone in this day and age pretend to not know that Hamas considers all the Jews as *colons* on the land of Palestine from the Jordan to the sea? Must we point out that this demonstration is taking place in zone A under Palestinian Authority control. Therefore, with PA approval. Mitchell Report, getting back to the negotiating table, Sharmel-Sheik & Cie. notwithstanding.

So I suppose it's logical to begin the newscast (*France Inter* 1-2 PM) with: "despite the cease-fire there were two attacks in Israel yesterday." Funny kind of logic, isn't it? Funny kind of despite. In fact it's despite the attacks that the cease-fire was maintained. Despite being attacked Israel respected its unilaterally declared ceasefire. But that little shift of a "despite" gives the distracted listener a chance to heave a sigh of exasperation. Those big bad Israelis can't even respect a cease-fire. It's subtle but I'm sure it works.

Then *France Inter* gives some details provided by the Palestinian Authority: in fact the Fatah activist was killed accidentally while "manipulating explosives" that blew up his car. Another "despite" to stick on Tsahal. Despite the fact that the Israelis did not assassinate the guy there's no reason to ask what he was doing with explosives in his car. But a half hour later on *RFI* the car was still blasted by an Israeli strike. Why not? A few more hours of Israeli guilt tallied up at no extra cost. Tomorrow there will be new violence to report, they'll forget to rectify yesterday's incident, the idea is to keep things moving... on the right track.

Now, with a bit of distance from the crackling loudspeakers and the feathery voice shimmering to the tune of young Hamas desperados, I cut and shuffle the reports and observe that:

Despite the unambiguous urgent demands from ex-senator Mitchell himself, asking the Palestinian Authority to make a total effort to stop the violence, the PA heartland welcomes Hamas celebrations of suicide attacks.

Despite the hand on the heart good faith declarations of the President of the Authority, no later than the 24th of May in a buddy-buddy act with President Chirac, his own Fatah boys drive around in bomb mobiles. And that's not all. They travel in distinguished company.

The man killed apparently was an activist in the Fatah movement.... Two of the wounded were identified as Fatah gunmen

*and the third as a follower of the radical Popular Front for the
Liberation of Palestine.*

(IHT / Associated Press / 26-27 May 200)

But it's clear as day. Hamas gets a thrill out of blowing up Jews, I could spend my whole day blowing up French media coverage, misguided citizens shrieking with glee run full speed into the wall, okay, but where's the pleasure in all that? Where is the hope?

The cavalry is coming. Dum de tee tum. Colin Powell and his boys. Sock it to 'em brother! Lightskin & streetwise, good grades & no fool, Brother Colin knows a passel about this kind of violence, these shoot from the hipsters running riot in the 'hood. Better don't invite Colin Powell to no Hamas bashes let me tell you. Today—birds are singing, flowers are prancing in window boxes, the sun is shining on our roofs as it shines in our hearts and it's good, it's so good to be alive—I'll place a twig of hope on Colin Powell. Amen.

9 June 2001

Cease-fire? Me too. For some time now I have been observing a cease-fire: I read the press but I don't clip any articles. I shout, but I shout in the privacy of my home. I cry but I don't cry in public I cry in the depths of my heart. And I speak to you [*vous*], I speak to you [*tu*], I speak to you to myself:

Listen, neighbor, listen and take heed. You couldn't take it, wouldn't want it... the unspeakable world in which this kind of Intifada carries the day. Look, neighbor, can't you see the vocations you are spawning? Think it over, neighbor, before it's too late, give a thought to some of the gripes and claims stewing in the hot spicy sauce that spikes your appetite today, at a distance, by proxy. Think of it, neighbor, the cauldron they're boiling up for you, a *colon* in spite of yourself, unknowingly treading on someone's hypersensitive turf.

Friday evening June 1st, I'm doing some ironing. This activity always inspires—please excuse the pretension—philosophical thoughts. I say to J., my friend for life and love: I think all human beings can tell the difference between good and evil. We are born with the ability to distinguish good and evil and no one can turn off this inner light. People can be indoctrinated, fanaticized, brainwashed, pressured, mistreated, oppressed... there remains a point in the body-mind, an articulation no less

61

vital than the heart, the brain, the carotid artery, a place where knowledge of good and evil is intact, protected against all aggression, consubstantial with life itself. No, I didn't say all that while I was ironing his shirts; I laid down the basics. The ramifications developed naturally after the fact, here at the keyboard.

I said: I think those young men who do the "suicide" attacks know that they are doing evil. Yes, they are fanaticized, manipulated, artificially enraged. But I think they know that what they do is evil.

Upon which, for some strange reason at that late hour, I turn on the radio. And the news explodes. Suicide attack in Tel Aviv. Young people who wanted to go dancing, seaside discothèque, a hot summer's night...

In Tel Aviv, my neighbor, in Tel Aviv.

You're surprised? I'm not. And you shouldn't be. Didn't you party with Hamas just last week?

The world waits for the reprisal. But the awaited reprisal doesn't come. The silence is deafening. And so, terrified by this silence, the other one doesn't triumphantly hold up his bloodied hands, no, this time he mumbles in a barely audible voice, okay, me too, cease-fire.

And suddenly the level of this spontaneous, popular, diversified and downright multinational violence whose author in spite of being the authority was, as you saw it, neighbor, powerless to control, as if by magic radically decreased.

Where are the *tifosi* of November 2000? I didn't expect them to do any soul-searching and I wasn't disappointed. Yes, they were shocked, they deplored, they almost told the old man straight out that this time he went a bit too far. All of that is perfectly normal. But could this lead them to review and question their guidelines? Don't even dream of it.

Over at *Rad Méd* they are shocked too. Scandalized. And downright furious! Hosts and callers in one voice and beside themselves deplore the indecent media attention slathered on the Tel Aviv suicide attack. As if Palestinians weren't being killed every day in their own land! Who would dare to deny them the right to resist? By all means at their disposal! Who would presume to deny them a right granted by the Qur'an itself--and a few surahs are read then and there in a mellifluent voice to prove it—to defend themselves against those who robbed them of their land? As for poor Farhid who called in to say what everyone knows—that killing innocent children is evil, is against Islam—he is torn to shreds for hours that day and every day for the rest of the week. You don't play around with *Rad Méd's* open mike! Farhid what? Farhid who? And they kick and punch Farhid, and they can't be fooled: behind the shameful remarks of this so-called Farhid crouches a poorly disguised Moshe, an Isaac, or a David.

No cease-fire on *Rad Méd*, no, they won't put up with this media hype about the Tel Aviv incident. This undue attention has fanned the flames of an already raging hatred. No fear of reprisals either. Here in France, land of liberty, there are no taboos when it comes to apologetics for suicide attacks. Hour after hour the calls pour in. And don't think they're coming from dumb brutes. No, these are well-informed educated Frenchified Muslims, who read everything including the Jewish press, who cleverly develop apparently rational arguments forged in the flames of virulent hatred. Hatred, jealousy, covetousness, murderous impulses; passions that twist and tangle a burgeoning will to overturn and conquer, to rule as masters, alone and unchallenged. Energy that spins in a void because it is void of meaning, void of project, and void of identity.

I grit my teeth and listen to *Rad Med*, telling myself I have to know what the other guy thinks and feels. And what he's planning to do about it. I tell myself I'm strong, I can listen without losing my cool. I listen and I ask myself if you, neighbor, ever thought of listening. Then a mouth opens and blasts out from a seething furnace of bitterness words that rip us to shreds. The Jews... the Zionists... they're fascists... they're little Nazis... they're Nazis, that's what they are, Nazis.

The imperturbable hostess, the very one who had read the Qur'anic verses, confirms the accusation in eloquent silence. I listened, and made solemn vows: I hold you responsible for your words, I hold responsible those who give you freedom to broadcast them on an authorized radio station. And what shall I do? What can I do, what can I say, what can I write, where shall I write so that these words will never be transformed into acts... before these words are transformed into acts.

Do you know, neighbor, the vocations that you are spawning?

"Rabbi Slain In Zurich" / *The Associated Press*
ZURICH—A 70-year-old Israeli rabbi has been shot and killed on a street in Switzerland's financial capital.../The police, who declined to identify the victim beyond saying that he was the

head of a Talmud college in Israel, said their investigation had
yet to determine a motive for the slaying.../ The Hebrew Con-
gregation of Zurich issued a statement saying it was "shaken
by the new attack on a recognizable Jewish person."/ The vic-
tim, dressed in black, "was clearly recognizable as an orthodox
Jew," said Werner Benz, a police spokesman, but he added that
he did not want to speculate on whether the attack had anti-
Semitic overtones./ Mr. Benz said a single gunman had fired
several shots at the victim and fled.

(IHT 9-10 June 2001)

26 June 2001

Bashar al Assad is at one and the same time a figure of continuity, pursuing his father's efforts to achieve a just and lasting peace in the Middle East, and a president in rupture with the legacy, initiating tremendous changes in Syria: freedom of speech and association, an open economic system ...

We mustn't forget that for twenty years Syria disputed Lebanon with Israel before finally expelling the Israelis from Lebanese territory, a major victory for Syria. Now we must understand that Syria had never accepted being separated from Lebanon, which it considers to be an integral part of its territory. This is why there is no Syrian ambassador to Lebanon.

The visit of Bashar al Assad is an opportunity for France to expand its role in the resolution of the Mideast conflict. Syria hopes to see France, with the European Union, act as a counterweight to the crushing pro-Israel influence of the United States that, it should be said, has done nothing to solve the conflict.

It's true that President Bashar al Assad has made some awkward statements. But we know that those who contest his visit are motivated by the intention to embarrass the President of the République, in fact, to embarrass France. Those awkward statements were meant for domestic consumption. Day after day Syria sees Palestinians killed, bombarded, humiliated, occupied. The Golan Heights are occupied. I do not think he will repeat those statements during his visit in France.

I know what you think, after reading the above. You think I stopped by the Syrian embassy (we are not yet a province of Syria) to pick up some literature on my way to the demonstration (intended to undermine the foundations of the République française). No, I simply tuned in to *Radio France Internationale* at about 9:30 PM. A specialist on Syria and an ambassador—no doubt former—got the red carpet mike treatment from one of those journalists who invites you to say what's on your mind and would never have the effrontery to contradict or even question you.

It's crystal clear and unambiguous. State-owned and operated, tax-payer- financed *RFI* is not at all bothered by the "awkward statements" of Bashar al Assad nor by his War Minister's call to murder. When the glory of France is at stake and an opportunity is offered to hoist itself to the level of the big bad superpower, the folks targeted by those little awkward statements can just move over and clear the way.

And what are we supposed to do? What should we say? It's not a reprimand, not a rhetorical question. We say and do so very much and why is it that the message just doesn't get through?

France is sinking, France is excluding itself from the best conflict of the decade, France lowers itself, shrinks, makes a fool of itself and our boys at *RFI* think they're so clever to throw mud at us, Jews of France, with a shilling-for-Syria broadcast. Bashar al Assad dines at the Élysée and our public radio rolls out the red carpet for two airheads and all these punks are so proud to be doing an advert for the Syrial killers. They still think it's going to stop with the Jews!

TO JOHNS HOPKINS ALUMNI MAGAZINE

"Q & A / Hopkins Assistant Professor of Sociology, James Ron" *Johns Hopkins Alumni Magazine,* June 2001

I will not be reading James Ron's soon to be published *Frontier and Ghetto: State Violence in Serbia and Israel.* Serbia and Israel? What a curious binary choice! I readily admit that my reaction is based exclusively on the short Q & A interview published in the June issue of the *Johns Hopkins Alumni Magazine.* But it is more than enough. Whatever the time frame for the writing of this curious work, the interview was certainly conducted in the light of current events, giving the Serbia-Israel juxtaposition an additional sting.

We are told that the author observed an inside/outside-the-borders correlation for the level of Serbian violence against Bosnian Muslims. But no explanation is given for the quantum leap to Israel. For the lay reader, un-steeped in the latest sociological methodology but quite alert to international affairs, it would seem that the Serbian example opens on to a large field of possible comparisons.

Why Serbia and Israel? Without deliberately seeking any hidden agenda behind this choice, the reader cannot help but notice the radical difference of levels of state violence as conveyed by the language of the loaded Questions & Answers. Serbia: Muslims in Serbia were harassed and their property was stolen, Muslims in Bosnia were subject to so-called ethnic cleansing, softened by quotation marks. Israel: "Some Palestinians living in the West Bank or Gaza have been viewed as enemies of Zionism in Israel but only Palestinians in Lebanon were killed in large numbers...." And "Israel's police-style repression has moved to more despotic measures."

If sociology has even the vaguest connection with real life and if the wording of the J. Ron interview has any connection with reality, one would advise Palestinians to run over and settle in Serbia to save their skins.

No, I won't be reading about ghettoes and frontiers in Serbia and Israel. I don't need it. We get this kind of comparison ad nauseam in the French press: Israel is accused of child-killing, colonization, apartheid, state terrorism, torture, war crimes, violation of human rights, land-grabbing, water diversion, carpet bombing, and worse. On a fast trip to "Palestine" the people's favorite agitator, José Bové, declared that Israel

is practicing ethnic cleansing (without quotation marks). The star political commentator of a local Islamic hate radio, *Radio Méditerranée*, tells
us that Israel is exterminating the Palestinians.

But of course all of that is politics, and Assistant Professor Ron is apparently dealing in unadulterated sociology. He has scientifically pin-
pointed the inside-outside factor for state violence against a group, and
nothing else would seem to matter. If the cohort "states" includes only
two possible subjects—Serbia and Israel—and no observable differences
other than the inside-outsideness of the "group" can be considered significant; if no political, historical, strategic or other factor could weigh on
the situation; if the borders of the said states were equally established
and recognized, and if history began somewhere around 1989...all of
which is most unlikely if not simply untrue, then might the comparison
be, even sociologically, justified?

State Violence in Serbia and Israel? Why? Why not, just for fun, Serbia and Sudan?

"...although 2 million people have died [in Sudan's 18-year civil war]
it was also among the most obscure." "The Islamist military regime in
Khartoum is waging a brutal counter-insurgency campaign against black
African southerners..."During the past year government forces have
carried on a ruthless bombing campaign to depopulate areas around oil
fields..."(*New York Times / International Herald Tribune, 24 July
2001*)

What about women in Afghanistan? Are they a group subject to state
violence? Police repression? Despotic measures? Are they inside or outside Afghanistan? Is Afghanistan a state? Or must the group be half inside and half outside the borders to qualify for entry into James Ron's
study? Now how about the bodies of murdered Kosovar civilians brought
back to Serbia and dumped in the lakes? That's an interesting outside
turned inside variation that certainly deserves further study. And East
Timor? But Indonesia is a string of islands, so full of insides and outsides
that even a hefty young sociologist might be excused for preferring other
fields of study. Cambodia, perhaps? Cambodia doesn't qualify? Not
enough despotic measures, not enough millions killed, not the right vic-
tim-group? Iraq? Kurds in and out of the borders? Chad? Nigeria?

With such a wealth of exquisite variations on the theme of despotic
measures on this poor earth does it really help to play silly sociological

games behind a mask of political innocence? Forgive me if I choose to steer clear of the numerous articles on the subject of state violence published by James Ron. Until of course one of them is pushed in my face by way of *Le Monde* or, even more likely, Belgium's *Le Matin*.

Nidra Poller
MLA, Writing Seminars, 1969

Chapter 2/   9/11

Somewhere near Washington DC, USA 15 September 2001

X., you are surprised that I haven't written more about what we are living through in these momentous, portentous days. And this is the same kind of silence, the same kind of absence we see all day in the area where the World Trade Center once stood. The masses of wounded and injured have not emerged from the wreckage. This is a wreckage such as we have never seen. And yet I have often imagined such a blow. And the dismay. The repercussions. So I am living in a series of unreal realities. Seeing things that aren't believable. A hundred times, the towers, the airplane, the fireball, black smoke, and then the whole thing crashing down. I saw it. And no matter how many times I tell myself that some creatures with the form of human beings but having nothing human about them flew airplanes into buildings and killed at least five thousand people in one blow, I can't make it fit anywhere.

There is a burnout of information. The television... I can watch it all day long. Sometimes it is just filler, and then suddenly there you are in Lebanon in the home of one of the suicide bombers (yes, I use the same name for them in Israel as in New York), you see his whole family, a nice house, reasonable looking people, and they are saying that this is a tragic event, that they are against it, and their son (brother, etc.) is not a hijacker, he was a victim, an innocent traveler on the plane.

While we are watching the television, J. is on the Net, bringing us dispatches from the *Jerusalem Post*, fresh as hot morning bagels. People call, and tell us about eyewitness stories, bereaved widows. The morning paper is there, but when can we find time to read it?

The stories unfold like that incredible thick smoke rising up like a mushroom cloud as the building and all those who were still trapped inside crashed to the ground in utter despair. The stories of people searching desperately for their loved ones. Wedding pictures taken last year, and now the beloved is gone. A woman who just gave birth, and her husband died in the mass murder. The stories of bereavement, the stories of miraculous misses, lives saved by a sudden change in plans or a slight shift of position.

And another plume of filthy choking blinding smoke of stories spirals out. The hijackers. No one can find Chandra Levy, no one knows who murdered a little girl somewhere in Texas, no one can really prove that OJ Simpson was guilty, but we know how the terrorists spent their evenings in Hamburg, went through a highway toll booth without paying, shaved their beards and dressed in Western clothes, how much money was in their pockets, what kind of cars they rented, when they sent their families home, how many engineering degrees they earned....

There are discussion programs, round tables with national and international journalists, messages from you my dearly loved ... and other family. I can't process any of this yet. These are just notes jotted down at ground zero.

Ground zero, and here we are in this unreal suburb, spanking clean houses, bright clean sidewalks with no dog shit, quiet streets, well kept lawns and well kept children. The sky is blue, the sun is African strong. Gaggles of geese fly overhead. We shop for food, gather in the kitchen to prepare meals, talk and laugh about other times and long ago memories, endlessly admire R. But the days are not days, time is not time, it is one endless stretch of stunned silence underlying all we do. I always feel a bit disconnected when I am in the U. S., because of the American way of life, but this time it is increased a hundredfold. Since I left Paris on the 5th of

September the world is totally transformed. I am not going back to where I came from, that place no longer exists.

We are stranded here, but I can't feel the reality of being stranded, because the two points, departure and return, have been wiped out. I know, rationally, that the only way S. and I can get back to Paris is by taking the plane, so all we want is to get on the plane and come home. How can I dissociate that plane we want to get on with those planes that were weapons of mass destruction? I will. But this is nothing like going home after being stranded by a snowstorm, a hurricane, not even an unexpected family tragedy. This is about going home to nothing settled, nothing resolved. There will be no *ouf*!

But of course there will be an *ouf*!

And for me another agony, added to the anguish of concern for family here in the US, for family here in France. There will be the agony of watching the French do their thing. I don't know how much you have heard about what the French ambassador to Israel said about terrorism. It's like the wicked king who gives a nice banquet to his three ugly daughters and then turns to Cinderella and gives her a kick in the ass. What? You thought you were going to eat too? Out you little urchin!

I find it profoundly distressing that they did not do the three minutes' of silence in C.'s school. So the French are going to do their appeasement bit. And they're going to claim that they know better how to deal with the Arabs than Americans do, so just let them do their thing. Don't ask for details, don't ask for proof, don't ask for results. Just trust the French, they have savoir faire.

In fact the Americans do have some enormous gaps in their under-standing of all those guys out there. But I don't think it's nearly as big a handicap as symmetrism. X., I loved your reportage on that one. Yes, the Americans are a bit corny. A flag on every house, people wearing red white & blue, and so many outpouring hearts of simple people. But there is something very decent and honest about it, and I will feel safer in a world where their resolve materializes in concrete action than in our European world where so many will look down their noses at the honest anger of legitimate suffering, and an honest determination to FIGHT BACK.

I just want to come home now and be with all of you again. But I know I am riding into a storm. Several storms. Yes, somewhere in my muscles I want this to be the war to end all wars. And I know too much about history to believe in that. Okay, that isn't possible. But neither is it possible for the world to stumble like a gigantic bloodthirsty madman from one horror to another. I am not buying any apocalypse stock. I want a brighter future. For everyone.

You see the WTC site on TV. How many thousands are working at that hopeless task. You would think that humanity *toute entière* would lift its arms to the heavens and cry out "How do you expect me to clean up this mess for G-d's sake!" No. They go about their business. Knowing that crushed and murdered under that rubble and twisted steel lie, among others, the bodies of other rescue workers who came before them. All those modest heroes, and a population, not any population, a population of tough New Yorkers stand on the sidewalk and cheer them as they go by.

Lee Hockstader, the Washington Post bureau chief in Jerusalem, recently sent J. a nasty reply to a letter taking issue with his analyses of the situation there. Hockstader said that any journalist worth his salt on that beat knows that there are no good guys in the Middle East (meaning in the Israeli-Palestine conflict). I wonder if he thinks there are no good guys in lower Manhattan.

I cannot bereave myself of my unbounded optimism. And so I imagine the wonderful changes that are going to take place. Americans will rediscover their founding principles. The entire free world will regain its mettle. Lucidity will grow from that upside down mushroom cloud. The ashes of the dead that are drifting down on the heads of the living will awaken them from this thick torpor that has besmirched our world. I am for luxury, comfort, modern appliances, communication & transportation, clean bathrooms and tasty food, love and peace, and I think we can have it without torpor, without air rage, without suffocating inanity.

If thousands of people can remove thousands of tons of debris, if thousands of people can find the courage to live after seeing the fireball that consumed their loved ones, and still hearing the sounds of a voice calling to say "I am going to die. I love you," then tens of thousands will find the courage to be soldiers and hundreds of thousands will find the intellectual resources to track down these mass murderers and put them out of commission, and millions of people can awaken from a nightmare of cruel fanaticism, and how many hundreds of millions can act to make this world better.

I can't wait for the outcome of this war as if it were a fatality. I have to fight it single handed. As every one of us must do.

If we get on the flight on Monday, J. will e-mail to tell you.

Washington DC 16.9.01

GOOD NEWS!

Osama bin Laden has joined the anti-terrorism coalition! Surprising as it may seem, this unusual development has opened the way to a peaceful resolution of the terrible conflict between warmongers and peaceniks, equally shocked by the flaming wreckage of passenger planes accidentally plowing into noted American landmarks, namely the Pentagon, the World Trade Center, and the Somerset PA cornfield. Bin Laden, seen in a secret video shot by a secret cameraman in a secret hiding place, put his hand over his heart and swore on the bible that he has absolutely nothing to do with any of these shocking accidents. In fact, he ordered one hour of silence for all shepherds in the area where he is actually located but which we are not free to disclose. It is to be noted that this hour of silence is a full 57 minutes more than the maximum 3 minutes of silence observed in decadent Western nations on the same occasion. Further, bin Laden, excuse me, Mister bin Laden, has imposed eternal silence on all people within his reach who have dared to connect him to this really regrettable and heart rending incident, of seeing innocent decadent money grubbing imperialist minded fornicating pig-eating kosher-keeping simple men and women going about their business in various infamous places such as the aforementioned WTC, Pentagon, and cornfield (Jose Bové, world renowned liberator of humanity has suggested in an off the record interview that the corn in the field was... genetically modified!!!! But denies any involvement in the planning and execution of the accident.)

Mister bin Laden, who turns out to be a reasonable leader inspired by a peace loving religion, has explained that he is against our terrorism and we are against his terrorism, which proves that we are united against terrorism, and that should settle all outstanding grievances. He is perfectly willing to surrender to the Pakistan posse which informed sources inform us is to leave Islamabad tomorrow, laden with gifts and precious stones, and committed to bringing him back in glory to be protected somewhere out of harm's reach of any ill-conceived evil intentioned bombing campaign which might strike the poor beleaguered nation of Afghanistan. However, given his commitment to the anti-terrorism coalition, Mister bin Laden thinks it would be better for him to stay right where he is, just in case some meanie might take advantage of his sudden flight to move in on his camps and set up a real terrorist operation which, as you can easily understand, the coalition would never be able to uproot.

Yasser Arafat, president of the Palestinian Authority, who is known to be somewhat slippery when it comes to negotiations, made a brief attempt to take credit for bringing Mister bin Laden into the coalition. Mister Arafat maintains that he was the first to suggest that all Arab countries join in the anti-terrorism coalition, giving as evidence on-line reports from the *Jerusalem Post*. The dispatch he refers to does in fact exist, and can easily be consulted. In his heartwarming call for volunteers, Mister Arafat took care to point out that terrorism will be defined as all military or other aggressive actions, speeches, theories, and thoughts perpetrated by the Zionist entity against the innocent beleaguered Palestinian people.

Mister bin Laden dismissed Chairman Arafat's claims, and tossed the said Chairman into the dustbins of history, claiming he was a handmaiden of the decadent west. Certainly not content to redefine the key word, TERRORISM, Mister bin Laden set down the rules for membership in the coalition and the guidelines for its eventual operation. The following countries are expressly excluded from membership; Guatemala, Costa Rica, Great Britain, Nicaragua, Italy, Canada with the exception of Québec, Greece, Denmark, Spain with the exception of the Basque autonomous region, Turkey, Russia, Senegal, Brazil, Norway and Sweden, Luxembourg, Andorra, Monaco, Japan, South Korea, the infidel half of the Philippines, same for Nigeria, ex-Yugoslavia and so on and so forth.... Israel is not excluded from the coalition. Israel is excluded from the world. The United States cannot be excluded from the coalition, for obvious reasons, but the American government and military will operate under Taliban command.

We trust this announcement will be met with a big sigh of relief. And if not, just remember, those who ain't with us are against us, and they know what's coming to them! Just remember that fireball and come on and coalition with us now. Before it's too late.

WHAT SHALL I WEAR TO THE WAR?

The above is just a tepid reaction to the news that the U. S. is thinking seriously of keeping Israel out of the anti-terrorist coalition so that Pakistan will join. Now let me get back to my running account...

It may seem strange to you that I didn't mention the Pentagon in my first letter. In truth we are equally removed from firsthand contact with both targets. The WTC provides more metaphors, more varied human interest stories. I'm not playing any numbers games, though anyone would be transfixed by the more than 5 000 dead in one blow. And that's nothing yet, that's just the first step. Many more are planned and underway. (This is my intuition, not something coming from informed sources). We haven't gone to look at the Pentagon. A combination of reasons... Leaving the routes open for people who really have to come and go. Not wanting to torture ourselves with the horrible sight and smells. Being dependent on J. for transportation, and he has other things to do. We get daily firsthand reports from L. who spends her whole day out in the streets of NY, and has so much to tell us.

We are living in a summer mode. S. and I spend hours on the deck sunbathing, reading, talking about the situation. It is so hot, so sunny, so suburban. The other day, by the way, I was talking to one of J.'s neighbors about what's going down, and suddenly I saw a small deer standing on the lawn. It turned to look at me, like a deer in a nature documentary. Then it walked slowly across the emerald green lawn in dappled sunlight, crossed the road, and went nibbling in the undergrowth on the edge of the woods, perfectly unflappable. We sit in the sun, come in for delicious meals or hot news, look at TV, try to catch the latest developments or tune in on a good discussion program (there are quite a few), check out J.'s Net printouts, then shower and dress for a long leisurely walk before dinner.

So I dreamed last night that I was in a restaurant with my new fiancé; S. and her fiancé were with me. And I was very happy but I just couldn't decide what I wanted to order. I had a great suntan in the dream, as I do in reality. And finally I leaned over to the waiter and apologized for all this fumbling, explaining that I'd been on vacation and it had worn me out!

It's now almost ten-thirty. We spent the evening dining, laughing, and enjoying each other's company. It's not all la de da, we are seriously debating the dangers that lie ahead. Looking beyond all the red white and blue reactions, we are starting to get edgy. Are the Americans going to winch out? Is this nothing more than a high school pep rally that will fade away at graduation? The gaps in security are chasms, and that's just talking about airports and intelligence. Illegal aliens, felons, illiterate slouches, and Islamic fundamentalists are running the security checks at the airports. All of that has to be transformed by a magic wand. As for intelligence, our chiefs in troublemaking spots don't even speak the local tongue. And now they are hoping to be able to recruit spies. Real bad guys who can infiltrate dirty organizations and wiggle through narrow dusty mountain paths. In fact, I suggested to R. that we open a recruiting agency: Help Wanted / Unsavory characters with experience in terror-ism. So who's going to size up the agents and figure out which ones are unsavory but trustworthy?

And meanwhile no one is bombing Afghanistan. Is this an indication of what's to come? A clever strategic move? A sign of faint hearted back-ing down? An erroneous stalling operation while waiting for the coalition boys to sign on? Fears of mass destruction of harmless civilian popula-tions are exaggerated. No one is looking for that kind of backward behav-ior and futile waste of energy.

And please don't think I am faint-hearted if I break off here. I hope my next message will come to you from Paris. By the way if we do get on that Monday flight, shana tova...

A rabbi, asked in a TV interview "what shall we say to the children," replied: we should hug them and hold them and, yes, tell them we are doing everything we can to protect them, but also tell them that we too are afraid. I think it is important. Because it is inhuman to not be afraid, seeing what we have seen, knowing what we know. And if we don't tell them the truth, the children will feel even less protected.

Paris 10 October 2001

Dear S & G,

Let me begin with good news: the bougainvillea finally decided to bloom. There are still small miracles to soothe our hearts. Next, I want to apologize for any mistakes I might make [in French]; I've lost my taste for the French language. *Rien à faire*. Yes, I know, you're thinking that the pendulum will swing in a year or ten, and I'll be loving our country again.

My call this morning was meant to be brief. I was looking for an all-clear after the deluge, the latest minor catastrophe. I wanted to be sure you were all on terra firma and your apartment wasn't flooded from above or below. But one word led to another, we started talking about "the situation," we disagreed, and here I am again reading, reflecting, analyzing discourses, and wondering how to express my thoughts, how to make myself understood, at least by my loved ones. It's not because of what I say or how I say it, no, that's not the problem. It's the crushing weight of the ambient discourse. I'm not being contrary for the fun of it. Why do I desperately reject those arguments against American politics, the American way of life, fast food, air conditioning and tutti quanti? Because we are in a life or death situation. If we want to survive we have to define the danger at our door. And what keeps us from defining the danger, recognizing the enemy? Our Western values! We have been taught to keep an open mind, reject stereotypes, live in peace with people who are different from us.

Because we cannot clearly say where the evil comes from today, people turn against themselves. Instead of mobilizing to defend ourselves, we go into a depression. The holier-than-thou, firmly convinced that we must not wage the war against Islam fervently desired by bin Laden and his henchmen, reach out in endless salamalekems, fall all over themselves in promises of benevolence, become overnight specialists on Islam in the sole aim of persuading the world that Islam is a religion of peace... And I know one who wants us to wear hijab in solidarity with Muslim women!

But bin Laden is not trying to drag us into a war against Islam, he is making war against us. And he thinks he'll win, because we are degenerate. I am not playing with words. If we fall into the trap—the trap of believing that we must at all costs avoid giving the impression that we are at war with Islam—we will lose sight of the vital necessity of winning that war. Muslims the world over are trying to figure out what foot to stand on. As you rightly said, X., it is in our interest to leave the door wide open to moderate Muslims willing to take sides with us in this multifaceted war. And that's why we have to stop believing their lies. So that they will have to take position honestly on the side of the law and against brute force. From what I have read in the press, it seems that the so-called moderates are especially and with rare exceptions preoccupied today with defending Islam against all criticism, whether general or specific. That's wrong. What they have to do is defend our shared values. Otherwise, they stand with Islam and against us, while pretending to be on our side.

Do you really think that I am not in favor of a better world, better for everyone in the world? That I don't want greater justice, more generosity, more bounty everywhere and always? Do you think I ignore the evil committed in the pursuit of profit at all costs? Yes, I want, I wanted a better world. I am not disillusioned, but experience has taught me to be wary of purifiers. In fact, their supposed disinterest is just as dangerous as the decried free play of competition. We have to ask why there is—concretely—more generosity from the rich than from the illuminati, those self-appointed benefactors of humanity...in spite of itself.

Room for improvement, yes, that's the slogan of all epochs. We have to strive to improve. But the time has come to interrupt the soul-searching if we don't want our principles to disappear under the ruins of our civilization. I want the debate to continue, the world to evolve. I want good ideas and good deeds to gain ground. I want the new century to be the one in which we learn how to handle conflicts without violence. And that is why I am going to fight now with all my might and on all levels against the primitive, savage, barbarous and terribly modern violence that befalls us. So let me tell you why I find inadmissible all arguments that "explain without excusing" the 9/11 terrorist attacks (and others to come, for sure...).

We are told that the Arab-Muslim world is angered by the suffering of Palestinians at the hands of Israelis. Indeed. But it's a terribly thin explanation and I don't care if it is repeated *ad nauseum*, I'm not convinced. If Palestinian suffering provokes anger, then someone has to explain why the suffering of Afghans at the hands of the Taliban doesn't have the same effect. Yes, their suffering today under American bombs has suddenly become as unbearable as the miseries of Palestinians. But the suffering of Algerians doesn't seem to provoke anything in the heart of the champions of Islam. No, it's the Israel-Palestine conflict, an open wound in the Middle East, that poisons the world and explains a good 90% of the famous Arab anger. The argument goes like this: Israel does have a right to exist in security, but is making a big mistake by refusing to give the Palestinians the authentic state they deserve. In fact, it's just the opposite: the same terrorist movements that don't want Jews in the Middle East don't want infidels in Muslim lands, and they haven't finished and never will finish defining the limits of their lands. We have to set the limits!

You have to look at how the terrorists, first, and then the bleeding hearts reverse the order of truths. It is the terrorists who prevent the creation of a Palestinian State but the blame is placed on Israel. Then the United States is blamed for defending Israel (which is its right as a sovereign country and cannot justify a military attack against the US), and confusion blurs reality, and obscures the connection between terrorism against Israel and terrorism against the West. I could give you a hundred examples gathered here and there in the past month.

If there were no Palestinian suffering, no Israeli bad faith, no American self-interest, and no injustice inherent in the history of the peoples involved, such reasoning could not be developed. It takes a dose of truth to concoct a good lie.

And the same goes for the argument "it's all the fault of *ultralibéralisme*." It's a cascade of sleights of hand. They cast a harsh light on the inequalities of the American system and black out the great opportunities it offers. They scream about "capital punishment, fast food, pollution" and draw a veil over our remarkable progress in science and technology. [*16 October-I'm picking up where I left off*]. They point a finger at the shameful exploitation of poor Third World peasants, and forget to remember that the United States is still a haven for the tired, hungry and poor, the wretched masses yearning to be free... (Is that how it goes?) And, first last and worst they omit to mention that the poverty and misery that supposedly nourishes terrorism is primarily the fault of governments that make their own people miserable.

They claim, without fear of contradiction, that misery is fertile soil for terrorism. Bravo! Aren't the wretched masses good soil for every sort of enlistment imaginable? Hitlers, Napoléons, and warlords who send out their ragged troops to lop off arms, to rape and eviscerate, don't they all draw from the ranks of the poor? So does the Church. If you want a multitude of disciples, it's better to recruit among the poor than try to attract the rich. Leaders, however, usually come from the bourgeoisie, or even the aristocracy. Terrorism is certainly not a monopoly of the wretched of the earth. Whatever... it's not misery that paves the way for bin Laden's brand of terrorism. There's no dearth of misery all over the world, but that terrorism, the one we are dealing with right now, develops only in Arab-Muslim milieux. So that is where we have to look for the causes and reasons.

The danger is immediate, mortal, growing. This isn't a good old days war with front lines and all the landmarks, but that doesn't mean we can't localize the enemy. But, precisely because this enemy is disseminated, it is all the more urgent to localize it in our minds. Bin Laden, like Hitler, unambiguously announces his project, his objectives, his motivations, his plan of action. He clearly defines his enemy. He expresses his gripes and says they go back 80 years... that is, to the fall of the Ottoman Empire. And who is trying to convince me that if we gave "Palestine" back to the "Palestinians" and pulled the American troops out of Saudi Arabia he would fold up his tents and slip away? Fat chance!

I don't understand why people refuse to grant a minimum of respect to the bin Ladens, the leaders of Hamas and Hizbullah, the Pol Pots & Cie, and just believe what they say. Their combat is not ours. Ok, I'm told, that's obvious, everyone knows it but it doesn't change the fact that... And then I get an earful of everything the Americans do wrong. Well, bin Laden doesn't have any scruples! He uses anything that will further his goals: ultra liberalism, misery, high tech, obscurantism... Maids in Saudi Arabia are raped, it leaves him cold. Little girls in Afghanistan are raped, it doesn't disturb his sleep. People can play the stock market instead of feeding drought ridden peasants, what does he care? He rakes in the profits. No shame.

Giuliani was more royal than the Saudi prince who thought a check for 10 million dollars would buy him the right to *noyer le poisson* (what's the English expression for "drowning the fish?") Why did Giuliani refuse the check? Isn't it the same as my rejection of the argument that 9/11 is all the fault of the Americans for increasing the gap between the rich and the poor?

There are and there always will be contradictions and grievances. It's the ongoing history of our world. Our founded or unfounded criticism of American culture will be no more nor less valid tomorrow than yesterday, and fixing up the world will always be nearly impossible. Today we have to make war to protect our right to live, to criticize, to nourish our social conscience. It is a real war and it has already begun. It is modern, it is globalized. The enemy is everywhere, but so is civilization. The values we defend exist everywhere, sometimes in a state of unfulfilled wishes, and we must rely on that force. We have to pull the veil away from the enemy's contradictions, not our own. As I write those words I hear you thinking "*Elle est folle* ..." She wants to keep us from curing the causes of evil. She defends the Americans as stubbornly as she once demolished them. She's playing at war without a care for the dead and wounded. She defends the way the American government is handling this military campaign when everyone in his right mind knows it is already a disaster. And to top it all off, she sabotages her bright and often perspicacious insights by insisting against all evidence on points where she is wrong.

I can't defend myself against such criticism. I am not authorized to speak on geopolitical questions. I don't know where it comes from... this word that has chosen me as loudspeaker. Is it madness or the highest reason? I don't take myself for Jeanne d'Arc, you know! And if, in fact, I see (on certain questions) the future, I am no fortuneteller. When I argue with you—my loved ones, my well-informed friends—I really think I'm wrong and you are right. And yet, as soon as I sit down to write, I find myself taking strong and indefensible positions and there's nothing I can do to oppose myself. I have to forge ahead while constantly trying to understand where these perceptions are coming from. I can't just push them aside to make myself presentable.

So here's the meaning of this missive: what can we do so we won't fall victim to the violence aimed at us? Among the numerous troops of a totally bad man like bin Laden, very few would be acting out without his charismatic leadership. Among the vast Arab-Muslim populations in this world, there are in fact very few who would spend their lives trying to die while taking the maximum of Jews, Americans, Christians with them, if they weren't encouraged 24 hours a day to act that way. In Muslim communities in France and other European countries, few would channel all their energy into exercises of murderous hatred if they weren't deformed by imams and other extremist *maîtres à penser*.

We don't try to exterminate the enemy, we don't even want to exterminate him. But it is neither honorable nor healthy to continue to submit to his violence. I am seeking means of defense on my own level, side by side with whatever police, military, or political operations are underway. I think we must stand against the twisted discourse that underlies and nourishes this violence. It is the only way to put pressure on the perpetrators of violence, make them back up, reflect, reform, and finally channel their energies toward projects that are positive for them as for us. They have to feel that they are up against a wall!!!!

Well, every time we accept, in good faith of course, to dialogue with their supposed grievances it makes a breech in the wall. Tens of thousands of *Beurs* booed the Marseillaise during the France-Algeria game? And how do people react? Oh yes, they booed, isn't it a shame. But after all, it was a mistake to package the match as the championship of Arab-French reconciliation; besides, the security was inadequate, another mistake; of course the Beurs have a gripe against France, we're playing a two-faced game in Algeria and our government doesn't lift a finger to stop the massacres; well, what do you expect, we flunked out on the integration of these youths into our society... In short, one more "you reap what you sow" discourse. A huge breech in the wall.

You don't boo the national anthem. You don't use commercial airplanes to destroy skyscrapers and all the people working inside them. You don't strike civilians, policemen, countries without exposing yourself to outsize retaliation. That is reality. When you attack, you are not master of the response. You're not the boss. You're not the one who decides if you should be hit hard, harder, or totally destroyed... because you place yourself in the hands of your victims. When you put yourself outside the law you are not protected by the law. Crime doesn't pay!

Putting up a wall to block the falsified grievances of terrorists doesn't mean shirking our civic responsibilities elsewhere. It means separating our responsibilities from their fake grievances. However, it is impossible to make a sharp separation between a people, its government, and the bandidos who have taken up residence in their country. You can't strike the guilty without the risk of hurting the innocent but if we do not strike the guilty the innocent will definitely continue to suffer. Afghans are suffering right now because of the bombing, even though modern warfare is cleaner than old warfare. Wouldn't they have suffered if there had been no 9/11 and the retaliation it provoked? The family man who was killed accidentally when an explosives warehouse was bombed might have been killed by a Taliban guardian of virtue if we didn't intervene. People love to say that the terrorists have nothing to lose. And what about the people of Kabul? Did they have much to lose? After this military intervention they will at least have a fair chance to live in peace in a country undergoing reconstruction. Their future will depend on what the different Afghan factions do, not on the good will of the big bad Americans.

But let me go back to the wall. By erecting a wall against the massively lopsided discourse circulating in the Arab-Muslim world we will manage some day, by virtue of great effort, to push back the wave of hatred that threatens to engulf us. And there it's no longer a question of discourse, but of life and death reality. As long as so-called moderate Muslims persist in hoodwinking us with their lopsided arguments, they will not be forced to question themselves, and the hatred will keep billowing and boiling and coming at us like ten million dragons.

I am not racist. I don't think that ideas circulate in the blood. They are built in the mind, and can be modified. I'm not the one who is making war against Islam, it's Islam that is making war against me. And I am going to say it, and repeat it, and prove it by infallible arguments. Until they decide to stop. And make peace with themselves and, finally, with me too. I believe that the Arab-Muslim world can change, and it will be as much to their benefit as for ours; that's why I reject all arguments that claim to explain without justifying. Because I do not think you can explain without justifying.

After all, what world do we want to live in? A world with no rules for living in society, no rules for international relations, no rules of warfare? A world where words have no meaning because they are applied to everything and its opposite (state terrorism, violence of exclusion...)? A world doomed to die because reality counts for nothing compared to discourse? Of course not. But that's exactly the world that is built by this claim to explain without justifying.

First, let's sweep in front of the door of this world dirtied by poverty, inequalities, social injustice, misery, hunger. Who, since the beginning of time, has been able to purify the world of these scourges? Who, between capitalism with all its defects and all those utopias convinced of their rights, has succeeded in bringing material goods to the common people? We are at leisure to criticize capitalism in its so-called ultra-liberal form because we are well fed, well housed, well educated and in good health. Pakistanis in their Qur'anic schools can't enjoy the benefits of the most primitive capitalism and aren't free to criticize the ultra-Islamism that is stuffed into them. We have the strength to fight against "ultra-liberal" capitalism because we live in democracies where we can speak and act freely. So be careful not to aim at the wrong enemy; we don't have the leisure to fight both the forces determined to destroy us and the economic forces that act freely in search of high profits. There are a thousand ways of defending ourselves against the latter. And only one way to counter those who want to destroy us.

What do they want to destroy, what must we defend? The law. Man cannot live in society without law. The attack against the WTC is an attack against the laws of peace and, what's more, against the laws of war. Whatever the grievance, no one has the right to perpetrate such attacks. The well-intentioned think they can reduce the 9/11 attacks to their essence—violence against innocent civilians—and condemn both the terrorist attacks and the military retaliation they provoked. But a military response to an unprovoked attack is within the rights of international law. Is it an arbitrary occidental privilege, blind to cultural differences, insensitive to social, military, and strategic inequalities? No. In our judgment the suicider strapped up with explosives who kills people eating pizza is an outlaw, whereas military action against a training camp for suicide bombers falls under the heading of self defense. Is that arbitrary? The Arab League thinks so; they've just redefined terrorism to exclude actions conducted for the purpose of national liberation... theirs, of course.

Every attempt to explain without justifying, to deny the difference between terrorism and armed defense, is doomed to failure for the simple reason that the sponsors of terrorism win only in the short term. The law is stronger, those who respect it are stronger and always win in the end. And life continues to flourish on this earth despite countless imperfections.

A kid who steals a car risks getting killed in a crash or shot by a policeman. I'm not advocating the death penalty for car thieves. It's just an example of the long-term consequences of this kind of revolt that does no good for anyone. Putting himself outside the law the car thief puts himself in a position of weakness: the law is stronger, and it's the law not the thief that decides how much force to apply. Depending on the circumstances he will get a scolding, a punishment, or death. And he has no control over the circumstances.

The law draws its legitimacy from the community and from the patrimony of humanity. The car thief has no legitimacy. He takes a shot at might-makes-right, double or nothing. Despite the imperfections of the law as established in our democratic countries, it is far superior to the might-makes-right systems preferred by some people, countries, cultures, movements or beliefs. OK, let them opt for brute force. But they have to take the consequences.

As a matter of fact the terrorists and those who understand them want nothing to do with consequences. They are trying to impose a logic in which each one strikes according to his means and is struck according to his desires. The victims of 9/11 are deplored but the United States is denied the right to use its power against the perpetrators of the attacks and the countries that give them refuge. In the same way Israel is accused of disproportionate response. "Palestine" is defined as a poor defenseless entity, and Israel as a bully and outlaw. The Intifada is kids throwing stones. And the big bad Israelis who shoot at them are terrorists!

The kids throw stones and the soldiers should respond by throwing stones? So then what would be the appropriate punishment for someone who rapes a child? To be raped by someone bigger than him? Or how about this? The terrorists killed thousands of employees of the WTC, the Americans should find jobs for thousands of poor Muslims.

They say: we must not add violence to violence, we must not kill innocent civilians. Then the moderate Arab-Muslims add a detail: we must not attack a Muslim country, we must not kill innocent Muslims. They want to make us think that their tribal customs are superior to the law and deserve our respectful obedience.

So let's have it tribal! They killed 6,000 Americans? We'll massacre 60,000 of theirs... designated at random as ours were. And so on, tit for tat, they kill 600,000 and we do in 6,000,000 (oops! I didn't see where those figures were leading me), and may the best man win. We too want to be understood without being justified. Our leaders follow the street, like all self-respecting leaders.

Bin Laden is super rich, he uses his money to kill thousands of human beings. A CEO is super rich, he uses his money to make computers and sell them to hundreds of thousands of consumers. Bin Laden's executives died at the controls of "their" planes. The CEO's executives got stock options. Bin Laden's employees now risk being killed by American soldiers. The CEO's employees feel like they are being exploited and, way down at the bottom of the ladder, peasants from Burkina Fasso feel like they are being impoverished by an economic system far too favorable to CEOs and terribly unfavorable to African peasants. Bin Laden 's employees will have the choice of dying for him or slipping across the frontier and pretending they don't know him. So, everyone is in his place and the peasants—whether African, South American, Egyptian or others—will be just as underprivileged under the bin Laden/Taliban system as under the capitalist system. With just one small difference: sooner or later the CEO will have to take those grievances into account. Bin Laden, never.

Setting aside the rhetoric, what is the difference between bin Laden and ultra-liberalism, from the viewpoint of the starving peasant? And even if the African peasant and the Palestinian student, convinced that bin Laden is working for them, are ready to kill for him, it just proves their dismal moral and intellectual poverty. And doesn't add an iota to sustain the arguments that draw a straight line from poverty to terrorism. As for the effectiveness of strategies based on such an analysis, it's zero. Discourse permits logical leaps by pasting words over huge gaps in reasoning. Reality is far more rigorous. How does poverty make people want to kill? How can murder help anyone get out of poverty? (I know, we've already argued about this. I stand by what I said. It's not the poverty that creates the violence, it's the violent nature that explains, at least partially, the poverty. An immigrant who reacts with hatred against the frustrations endured won't find the avenues that are in fact open to him. As for the Palestinians, they destroy themselves with their hatred of Jews. Is it Israel's fault? Israel shouldn't have fallen into the trap? Why is it always up to us not to generalize, not to fall into the trap?)

These garbled explanations for the unmitigated horror that has befallen us sound to me like dumb people in an uproar because an airplane crashed. And they're clucking, what a disgrace. People never should have made airplanes. Can't they see? A big heavy thing like that can't fly. Shit, they didn't learn anything since Icarus? Greek tragedy, hubris, occidental values trampled in the name of what arrogance, crazy projects, unbridled will! An airplane, filled with people. Every person dies at the appointed hour. So you put all those people in an airplane, of course it's the appointed hour for at least one of them. And all the others go down with him! Disgraceful. Look at the Indians, they didn't build airplanes. And they were here long before us. By the way, we weren't very kind to them... one more good reason why that airplane fell from the sky. Never heard of Humpty Dumpty? It's Nostradamus, if I'm not mistaken. He warned you but no, you high techies just had to tempt the devil, well, he gave you your comeuppance!

According to that logic, instead of accepting the imperfection of all technologies, even the highest, you create an imaginary world where no one ever makes a mistake; you trash everyone involved in airplane travel, knowing full well that they will keep on flying. You give yourself a fleeting moment of private, cowardly relief. Is it true that more than 100,000 people in Rome demonstrated against the American bombardments in Afghanistan?

I have already gone beyond the limits of this letter and probably beyond the limits of your patience. I'm using the letter as a sketchpad for a text that has been going through my mind since 9/11. I have to sign off but, you know, being an immigrant here in France... and American... my heart is heavy today. Why are they so haughty? I don't have the means to do a systematic study... I read, I listen, I debate... I don't think I'm far off in judging the general attitude: it's a sort of shamed indifference. People know perfectly well that we are all concerned. The subject gets broad media coverage. But it seems that this whole society is positioned at a safe distance from reality; they talk about a war as if it were a hypothesis to defend or demolish but definitely not as a series of concrete actions that are decisive for our future. They criticize everything the Americans do, or don't do, did or will do but don't feel called upon to do anything whatsoever along with us. They delight in highlighting everything the Americans don't know how to do. Do they offer to do anything in our stead?

Then there's that *Paris Match* journalist still in the hands of the Talibans. You don't hear anything more about him. Why? Is it because the government is wheely dealing? Shamefully and maybe ineffectively? Is it normal to not mention it anymore? [*17 October: it's back in the news,* Paris Match *is making a big deal about it, they're talking to him in prison, hoping and striving. Give me a zero on that one.*] At the same time we are suddenly getting all this praise for Al Jazeera, "the Arab CNN." I've been hearing about Al Jazeera for years. They have unspeakable programs where so-called scholars lecture on Judaism (a religion that explicitly grants the right to rape non-Jewish women), the "purported" Jewish presence in Jerusalem (there never was a Temple, never any Jewish presence until recent times... I can't remember if they said 1940 or 1920...). And suddenly al Jazeera is the Arab CNN, a model of pluralism. Well if Al Jazeera is the Arab CNN, the burka is the Afghan miniskirt. Robert Ménard of Reporters without Borders complained to Colin Powell in person. Ménard accuses the US of imposing the same censorship as Middle Eastern dictators. What did we do wrong now? The administration doesn't want Western media to relay the propaganda operations of bin Laden and his network. That's censorship? Asking our allies to refrain from spreading his call to murder Jews, Christians, and Americans! It's okay for the Quai d'Orsay to have a grip on the *AFP* that supplies most of the news broadcast in France. Did you know that Jewish journalists who work for the French media are not free to express themselves, personally, outside the job, on the Arab-Israel conflict? But we mustn't censor Al Jazeera, and we must help pour bin Laden's sermons into the ears of our housing projects. In the meantime *Radio Méditerranée*, unhindered, distills its murderous hatred.

[19 *October 2001: we learn in the IHT and through the Net that the ruling clique in Afghanistan is rapidly falling apart; the moderate Taliban are breaking away from the extremists and both of them from the mudjahidin who are partially cut off from bin Laden and his garde rapprochée, while mullah Omar is isolated and so on. And here's the cover of* l'Express: *a close up of bin Laden in battledress, taken from the first Al Jazeera video, with the headline "*BIN LADEN *can strike again." Maybe it was "where is he going to strike next?" Anyway, the idea was to show that he's so strong we should give up without a fight. They had the same attitude when Saddam Hussein invaded Kuwait.*]

Did you hear? They're saying the AZF explosion in Toulouse was definitely not a terror attack? No further investigation needed in that direction. Ok with me. But I don't understand how this monsieur Jandoubi could be hired to work on such a sensitive site. The *IHT,* quoting French sources, says he "was connected to a group of four or five men in the area belonging to the Takfir movement... that preaches a radical form of Islam. Two of those men are believed to have spent time in Afghanistan." The CIA is dumb, the FBI is stupid, but (*IHT 6.10.01*) "The Interior Ministry confirmed that French intelligence had made inquiries into Mr. Jandoubi, but found nothing troubling. 'A lot has been exaggerated,' a spokesman said." And yet, the day before, it was reported in the same *IHT*: "So far, investigators have not linked him to the Osama bin Laden groups, a connection that would send a shock wave through France. An investigator in Toulouse complained that a search of Mr. Jandoubi's apartment for clues was 'spoiled' because magistrates took five days to issue a search warrant. The apartment had been completely cleaned out—'no clothes, no photos, nothing'—by the time the police got in..." Not really reassuring, *n'est-ce pas*?

(P.S. *France Info* starts the morning newscast with wounded Afghans in a Peshawar hospital, in the style of their reports on hospitalized Palestinians during the Intifada. But Palestinians are being wounded by their own police these days so no one is holding a mike out to capture their agonizing screams. We are reminded hourly that George Bush, Tony Blair, everyone and his brother has promised the Palestinians a state but no one mentions the revolt against Arafat that is enflaming Gaza and the territories. *18 October: that's old news. An Israeli minister is assassinated and suddenly there is unanimous understanding that Arafat has to stop fooling around. I predicted last week, after the Gaza riots, that Arafat is finished. We'll see.)*

It all (*we're back to the French attitude*) seems terribly petty. And old hat. When I get the courage to open my Gulf War notebooks I'm sure I'll find the same behavior, the same arguments, the same attitudes. How can the French thinking-classes discourse day after day and page after page on American faux pas and clumsy boots, CIA mistakes, FBI bungling, errors of past U. S. administrations, and never give a thought to local problems? The French still haven't found the guys who murdered Préfet Erignac, they can't snuff out violence in Corsica, they allow the ETA to act freely on both sides of the frontier, and haven't lifted a finger to help the Algerians.

To sum it up, I am shocked on all sides. Like you. Like others. The discourse shocks me, the news shocks me, the lack of news shocks me, conversations leave me exhausted and dismayed, analyses seem futile and unfounded, I have nightmares, not the normal kind of frightening nightmares, immense, dense, bottomless nightmares without images without representation, as if I were in the heart of something nameless. It is awful. Nightmares that are not frightening. That do not invoke pain that can be felt. Without flesh without body. Nightmares of the end of the world.

This, too, is why I have to write. To place myself in a line of heroic résistance. To tell myself over and over: it's war. We can't say that we don't know. The view from my window looks perfectly normal. It is deceiving.

I think not enough has been said, almost nothing has been said about the plane that crashed in a Pennsylvania cornfield. By virtue of modern technology the passengers knew, almost in real time, what was going to happen to them, how they would be used. They revolted. They won. And it's marvelous. They are heroes. Is the revolt less noble because the heroes are dead?

Bin Laden is cringing deep inside his cavern. What could be more inglorious than this arch-terrorist trying to save his skin, letting innocent Afghan civilians die instead of coming out of his rat hole and facing the adversary man to man. Can't we get through to the Arab-Muslim world, without the help of Al Jazeera, and tell them a thing or two? Osama bin Laden is afraid of us. The Taliban are afraid of us. The masters of Qur'anic schools-of-hatred are afraid of us. All those men are lying low, hiding behind women, children, and old people. They are afraid of us because they are outlaws and their game of might-makes-right has back-fired. Today they reap what they sowed. We should not only break up their networks, freeze their bank accounts, tear away their charitable organization masks, destroy their bases and their artillery batteries, we must also dismantle the arguments that give them legitimacy in the eyes of the wretched of the earth.

That's why I'm writing this endless letter. To say that you have to pull out the rug from under their feet, not lay out a red carpet in front of them. We have to set a trap for them, not fall into their trap. A few people are really evil, you have to fight them with all your might. Others are just bad, and go along with the evil ones. You have to fight them too. And then there is a multitude of disingenuous people who want to play the game without suffering the losses. They write letters-to-the-editor like this:

> I write to you as an Arab Muslim who was deeply shocked and horrified by the tragedy that took place on Sept. 11 in America. It is my belief that such acts of terrorism against innocent civilians violate the principles of democratic life, freedom and above all the most fundamental of all human rights, the right to life.
>
> .... All countries should join to combat terrorism, regardless of race or religion....
>
> We in the Arab world have also suffered for decades from the evils of terrorism from various extremist groups, which have, unfortunately and on various occasions, been granted asylum by some European countries as well as the United States. We have... called for the convening of an international conference to define terrorism and distinguish between terrorism and people's rights to struggle for independence and freedom.
>
> The Palestinians, in that sense, are equally the victims of contemporary "state terrorism." They have been for almost half a century denied their right to existence. The targeting of innocent victims on Sept. 11, as well as the targeting of innocent Palestinian civilians in the occupied territories, is both illegal and morally unacceptable.

...the United States...has to...embark on a fair and balanced "dialogue"...with the intention of eliminating cultural and political misconceptions, stereotypes and all other forms of prejudices.

(IHT 17 October '01) Maha K. Altorki, Cairo

I am an Arab-American, a Muslim woman and a New Yorker.
....The Middle East is home to great injustices: the continued oppression of the Palestinian people; the starvation of the Iraqi people; the massacres of Sabra and Shatilla....
When bin Laden's agents attacked the World Trade Center, they hijacked the legitimate despair that is so much a part of the reality of the non-Western world....
We Americans can no longer turn our backs on the helplessness and desperation that is rampant in so many regions of the world. We must take human anguish out of the hands of bin Laden and his cohorts by righting the wrongs committed against humanity.....
I do not want to live in a world determined by bin Laden, where my pen and my camera are taken from me.... Let us meet in the uncharted territory between East and West and begin a dialogue to build a world beyond despair.

(IHT 10 October '01) Anissa Mariam Bouziane

And that's how the terrible tragedy of Sept. 11 turns into a lesson in cultural tolerance for the United States, and a heartfelt cry for justice that includes some rather suspicious specifics (Sabra and Shatilla, yeah, we know that one!) All based on the supposition that America can right all wrongs, combined with the underlying threat that if they don't, bin Laden and his boys will have a nice long field day.

In conclusion here are some excerpts from an interview with Soheib Bencheikh, Grand Mufti of Marseille (*Libération* 17 September 2001):

My first reaction [to 9/11] is indignation and spontaneous sympathy for the American people, who are totally innocent and apolitical. No cause...can make itself heard by way of that barbaric act. I am in favor of a reprisal called justice. The perpetrators of the murders should be punished. But we must stop the escalade.

If the American reprisal is to have "wisdom," it must, first, avoid confusing that crime with Islam. Second, it must make the perpetrators, not the people, pay for their crime. If the Palestinians are made to pay, if the Afghans are made to pay, it will radicalize Muslims and accomplish the aim of the terrorists. Third, the Americans must look for the cause, namely, poor policy.

American policy has often been based on total ignorance of the causes of peoples, namely Palestinians, which has led the United States to cover and protect certain dangerous archaic regimes. We see how the Americans defend their ally, Israel, and close their eyes to daily exactions by that state.

Many nations have had a taste of criminal Islamism and are absolutely disgusted with it: Algerians, Egyptians, Afghans…The Americans weren't the least bit troubled to see Islamism flourishing everywhere.

Before looking for Islamism in Kabul or Nablus, one should look first in London and Berlin, where the Islamists enjoy the right of asylum. You have to see the hate literature published in London. The logistics of Islamism are centered primarily in European capitals, with the exception of Paris, because Interior Ministers Pasqua and Chevènement did not allow the networks to develop.

On other occasions Bencheikh has spoken harshly about "that crazy Ben Laden." The Mufti criticizes the French government for inviting virulent extremists to a recent consultation of representatives of French Islam. But it doesn't keep him from following the Muslim party line.

And it all comes down to: it's the fault of the Jews.

I hear every day all day that it's the fault of Israel. Now it's also the fault of the Americans. And, again, it's the fault of the Americans who stand by and defend Israel and it's the fault of Israel for not making a magical agreement with the Palestinians because, again, this situation excites the Muslims just when we want to calm them down. No one is afraid of exciting the Jews, no one says hush! You are going to provoke the anger of Nidra Poller. And I'm so kind, I feel I have to ask you to forgive me for the passion, the length, the disproportion of this letter. (sigh) There are days when the only thing that agrees with me is reality.

Email to a friend

dear A.,

I didn't respond to your forwarded messages, because I disagree so profoundly with them and that deserves a full response, which I was not able to formulate at the time... not because it wasn't formulated in my heart and mind, but because I had so many things to catch up on after my unexpectedly prolonged visit to the US.

I did write a 12-page beginning of an essay on the subject... it's in French. Shall I send it to you? And D. has had interesting exchanges with friends here who sent him some of the same messages, and others in the same vein.

I feel called upon to respond to these messages of peace, because I am a peaceful, tolerant, generous person and I believe that this is a time for war. In fact, I respond with such passion, whenever the subject is discussed among friends and family, that I might sometimes give the impression that I think there should be no dissenting voices.

Of course there is room for dissent. And room for me to dissent with that particular dissent which is coming from people more or less like myself.

Did I already tell you this: Over the past few years I have been receiving those SOS help the Afghan women petitions that were circulating on the Net. And each time I delete the message, and shake my head, and exclaim to myself that the only way to help the Afghan women is to make war against the taliban, and the day we decide to do it, the same people are going to send me pacifist petitions.

Well, I was right on that one. And that's the kernel of my dissent with the peace loving dissenters. You can't be against terrorism and against the war against terrorism. Yes, I know, you can build a case for every other possible treatment of the problem... it's what we call in French *t'as qu'à*, you just have te'...

The best cases are the retroactive ones. You never should've backed bin Laden when you wanted to beat the Russians out of Afghanistan, you shouldn't let people go hungry and poor, you should've watched out for airport security so the terrorists wouldn't have been able to do their dirty deed... We can eliminate all these arguments on the simple grounds that history moves forward, and has never been known to back up and allow all our stupid democratic governments to do what they should've done so that the wicked ones who feed on oppression would have nothing to feed on.

And then there are the arguments that claim that with infinite finesse and brilliant strategy it is not too late to do what you should've done, and take out these terrorists as delicately as a woman plucking her eyebrows.

And then there is reality. Reality has never offered anyone a pure field in which to operate. In reality wickedness knows how to sidle up to despair, and there is no way to fight back against wickedness without harming a hair on the head of despair.

As for wearing hijab in solidarity with Muslim women, isn't that precisely the kind of turning otherness into same that feeds the oppression of Muslim women and non-Muslims living in Muslim lands? If a Muslim woman freely wants to wear hijab or even tchadri, that is certainly her right, but to me it is oppression, so I am not going to use my precious freedom to defend her right to be oppressed. No more would I dress in a miniskirt up to my belly button as a sign of solidarity with prostitutes.

I reject this "we are all..." kind of movement. We are not all besieged Berliners, exterminated Jews, attacked Americans, AIDS victims, oppressed peasants, and so on. It is because we are all different that I defend the rights of human beings to affirm their ideas and be judged on something other than their appearance or membership in a group.

I am furious against all Muslims who explain (without justifying...) the WTC bombings as a reaction against the sufferings of the Palestinians and the deaths of countless Iraqi children. I am furious against Muslims who spread the most virulent antisemitism seen or heard since the 30s. I hate them. They are my enemy and I will defeat them. And I don't care if they declare themselves moderates, and say they are against the terrorist attacks and tell us in soft voices that Islam is a religion of peace.

But when I am face to face with an individual Muslim, I don't have any feelings of hatred or rejection. And if we come down to discussing ideas, I react to the ideas, not to the hijab! Solidarity with all Muslim women is no less reprehensible than hatred of all Muslim women.

Personally I would like to help enlightened Muslims to learn to speak out strongly and clearly against the bad ideas that are spreading like wildfire among their people. And believe me, it is no easy task for them.

That is why they so often express themselves in ambiguous terms, if not in sheer hypocrisy, while claiming that they are reaching out for common understanding. If they really condemned this tide of wickedness that is swelling, they would get so much flak from their own people. And they are afraid of that. Because it is violent flak.

I don't want to hate anyone, and certainly not two billion of anyone!!! So how can we start to turn back this tide of destruction? How can we engage in real dialogue with these Muslims who live in our democratic countries?

Well, A., that's a sort of prelude to what I might have to say on the subject. Argue back with me, friend. I am looking for strong arguments to tear down whatever is faulty in my own reasoning. I want to fight, friend. A fair fight.

Chapter 3/ Arab-Israel Conflict, Antisemitism

Marina Niforos, Esther Dijkman, Lars Rosdahl
French Chapter – JHU Alumni Association
e-mail 21 December 2001

Dear fellow alumni,

As promised in my telephone conversation with Marina Niforos, I am writing to take issue with the one-sided presentation made by the tandem Remy Leveau/Christophe Ayad on November 28th at Marina's home, and to ask you to invite other, equally competent speakers, who can defend a different point of view on the vital question of "the impact of the latest political events following the attacks of Sept. 11 in the United States."

In fact, the invited speakers did not lead a discussion, and were not open to discussion: Professor Leveau presented a well-worn vision of the Arab-Israeli conflict as if it were the gospel truth, and Christophe Ayad filled in with an evasive profile of the situation as seen from Egypt and Saudi Arabia.

I would have expected a greater sophistication on international affairs from an SAIS alumni organization, and a higher degree of sensitivity to the controversial nature of the issue chosen for discussion. After my conversation with Marina, I wonder what you really heard.

I would like to remind you that Prof. Leveau clearly established a parallel between the Arab-Israeli conflict and the French-Algerian war, and concluded by saying that unless the Americans can put pressure on both parties and force them to negotiate he feared that the situation in Israel would more likely end "*à l'algérienne*." What does this mean?

This means the end of the State of Israel. Prof. Leveau was not talking about a situation "*à l'algérienne*" in the occupied territories. He was not talking about an Israeli withdrawal from the territories. Such a withdrawal, within the easily recognizable framework of his discourse, would not be feared but desired. Along with many other concessions, of course.

Working back through the multiple accusations made in the course of professor Leveau's talk one might easily conclude that the *défaite programmée d'Israël est bien méritée*. And why not? Many people—politicians, journalists, intellectuals, activists, and ordinary citizens or subjects—share this point of view. It is defendable, and it is arguable. But it is not objective. Nor moderate.

If none of you are aware of the strong arguments developed against that point of view, it would be most appropriate to schedule another meeting, with other speakers, and thus open an authentic discussion on the subject.

Though I cannot guarantee the availability of any given person, I am sure that you could find at least two people on this list that could enlighten us all:

Alexandre Del Valle: Etudes stratégiques
Frédéric Encel : Professor of International Relations / l'Institut de Sciences politiques de Rennes
Michel Gurfinkiel: Director, *Valeurs Actuelles*
Marc Knobel: researcher-Centre Simon Wiesenthal
Pierre-André Taguieff: Researcher, author
Jacques Tarnero: Researcher in sociology and philosophy - CNRS
Shmuel Trigano: University professor, director of the Collège des études juives
Meïr Waintruter: Editorial director- *l'Arche*

Clément Weill-Raynal: journalist at France 3
And of course I would be ready and willing to help you in any way to organize such a meeting.

I hope that you will receive this message in the spirit in which it is transmitted and with the respect for an honestly critical approach to human affairs which is the pride of Johns Hopkins University.

With my best wishes for the holiday season,

Nidra Poller, JHU Writing Seminars 1969

TO THE *WASHINGTON POST* OMBUDSMAN
Paris, 19 March 2002

Dear Michael Getler,

Is there any illusion more obstructive to the search for truth than the illusion of objectivity in the face of life and death conflicts over essential human values? What does objectivity mean for a journalist covering events in Israel and the Palestinian territories today? Can a journalist who betrays the ethical imperative be trustworthy?

These questions churned in my mind during a recent 3-week visit with family in the Washington area (15 Feb. - 7 March) where I had the opportunity to read the *Washington Post* every day. I am an American writer and translator living in Paris. Since the start of the "intifada" in September 2000, the *International Herald Tribune* has been one of my prime sources of information and a healthy antidote to the biased French press. Again, with the September 11th terrorist attacks and the American riposte, I would not have known what was happening in Afghanistan without the *IHT*. So, I was looking forward to a rest from dubious French reporting and concomitant antisemitism.

I was rather disappointed. I must admit that I had already observed a curious shift in attitude following the interception of the Karine A; as if this illegal arms shipment from Iran to the Palestinian Authority had capsized the theoretical constructs for reporting on the conflict, leaving journalists adrift and paddling to stay afloat.

We who defend Israel's right to exist are subjected to daily affronts. We are wracked with pain to the depths of our souls for every victim of suicide bombers and vicious armed killers who open fire on civilians. We are distraught by the deaths of Palestinians caught in the crossfire, and horrified by the senseless martyrdom of murderous young Palestinians. As if this were not enough, we are exposed to the slings and arrows of outrageous disapproval. . . of Israel. Our voices are hoarse, our minds are hoarse, our hearts are hoarse from vainly trying to be heard.

What are we asking for? Do we expect journalists to solve the conflict? Do we think they should defend "our side"? No. That's not what we are asking... it's what we ourselves do... we study this conflict in depth, write books and articles, give lectures. We take a stand, take sides, defend our positions, make ethical judgments, and stand by our word.

All we ask of journalists who have been covering this conflict for 18 months is to question their initial hypotheses in the light of subsequent developments. We ask you to seriously question the scenario: the intifada was caused by Ariel Sharon's visit to the Temple Mount, motivated by Palestinian determination to recover occupied territories and create a state, whipped by reciprocal hatred into an infernal "cycle of violence" that no one could extinguish until Prince Abdullah of Saudi Arabia came forth with a peace plan... Will that stand up to re-examination even one year from now?

Imagine stepping into the Second World War just when Hitler marched into Czechoslovakia, and covering the conflict without ever backtracking to question Hitler's aims and motives. Imagine reporting the war day by day, giving equal credence to statements by the Germans and the Czechs (Poles, Belgians, Dutch, Jews, gypsies, etc.) It would be absurd!

None of us can be certain how history will judge the events we are living, but we can be certain that they will be judged. We have to make an effort to judge fairly even though we are partisan; your readers are partisan. . . and so are your journalists! If the real nature of the Mideast conflict were recognized, everyone would be partisan. But that is the crux of the problem: this conflict, which concerns everyone, is the most poorly defined in the mind of the general public and, tragically, this is one of the reasons for the persistent violence.

A journalist can't simply tell what he sees and report what he hears. He needs an ongoing story that gives coherence to day to day events. Whatever the reason for initially accepting the Palestinian version of this "intifada," how can serious journalists keep sticking to the same story, filling in details and awkwardly keeping score? I saw *Washington Post* graphs that compared the number of casualties in each camp with stick figures, and maps with explosive bursts—red for one side, black for the other—counting the week's attacks. What do the figures prove? X + Y Palestinian deaths = Israeli brutality? X + Y Israeli deaths = Palestinian victory? The figures prove nothing but themselves.

I do not doubt the honesty and devotion of reporters who risk their lives to cover events. I am sincerely grateful to you. And I sincerely believe that you could question your suppositions and refocus your perspective on the Mideast conflict. The elements are right there in your columns.

The Palestinians are engaged in a Resistance movement. This supposition is usually accepted without question. Is it upheld by realities on the ground? An honest observer would have to admit that the facts do not exactly bear out this noble image. And a rarely posed question—why haven't the Palestinians tried non-violent resistance—(occasionally raised in a naïve letter to the editor) gives us an important clue: the Palestinians are not fighting for national liberation. They are engaged in a hopeless war of conquest. To my knowledge there is no such thing as a non-violent movement of conquest.

Palestinians and Israelis are equally to blame for this infernal cycle of violence. If an armed gang attacks a Manhattan bank the police are expected to try to foil the attack, free the hostages, kill or arrest the armed robbers, recover the money. So what if five armed gangs attack five banks? And the police do their job. That makes a lot more police action, a lot more shooting, a lot more risk of collateral damage. So make it twenty attacks. And twenty successful police operations, and a lot of dead or wounded bank robbers. Can this be described as an infernal cycle of violence, with the implication that if the police had just allowed the first gang to peacefully rob the first bank none of the other attacks would have occurred? No. The law says you can't rob banks at gunpoint and the number of attacks doesn't change the law. Well, the laws of war prohibit deliberately blowing civilians to bits by the dozens. And it is pernicious to count every military action aimed at foiling these attacks as one more notch in the ladder of violence, to be condemned on the same score as the terrorist attacks themselves.

The intifada was provoked by Ariel Sharon's visit to the Temple Mount. Eighteen months of war, more than a thousand deaths, thousands of injuries, billions of dollars' worth of property destruction, incalculable economic damage, uncontrollable international repercussions. . . all of this is attributed to the fact that one political figure walked on a piece of ground that matters deeply (and on the surface) to two different peoples. Isn't it time to backtrack and check that out? If that were really the cause, what would prevent similar causes from arising once "peace" is established? The Palestinians dropped this "Sharon's visit" version more than a year ago, but it keeps cropping up in the in-depth analyses you publish. So it's false, and at the same time it is a threat of future little wars based on similar false pretexts.

The Palestinians are fighting desperately to retrieve the occupied territories, create a state, and live peacefully side by side with Israel. What in fact do the Palestinians want? Do they want a state or do they want to destroy Israel? Your analysts assume that they want a state, they want the territories, they want an end to the occupation (of what?). This supposedly explains the barbaric counter-productive method of suicide bombing as a measure of intensity of the Palestinian desire for a state. If they didn't want it so badly they would never blow themselves to bits in order to kill dozens of Israeli teenagers. People like you and I don't do such things, which proves that we are not in a state of such terrible want as the Palestinians. But the fact is that a large proportion of the Palestinian population, an even larger proportion of the PA, and the totality of terrorist organizations such as Hamas, FPLP, Islamic Jihad, Al Aqsa Brigade, Hizbollah, etc. are against the existence of the State of Israel on any terms. Doesn't <u>that</u> explain the suicide bombers?

If Israel would just hand over the territories and give the Palestinians their State, the conflict would end. Why should Israel drop its defenses and run back to the negotiating table? Who should Israel make peace with? It is freely admitted (and often but not always blamed on Israel) that Arafat can't control the terrorist organizations, including his own Al Fatah movement. But Arafat himself recently called for a million martyrs for Jerusalem. And when it's not Arafat, it's some other component of the PLO. After Israel makes concessions and signs a peace agreement with the Palestinian Authority, how will Arafat control the terrorists? Will they snuggle under his wing and forget about repatriating the refugees down to the fifth generation and ending the occupation (of the rest of what they call Palestine)? If Arafat can't control the terrorists today when the whole world has promised him a state if he can stop the violence, how will he control them tomorrow after shamefully writing off a big chunk of occupied Palestine (i.e. Tel Aviv and the rest) and the rights of millions of refugees to return to their homes... in Israel? There is nothing clear cut about Palestinian demands, nothing inevitable about their methods, nothing reassuring about the future. . . and no citizen of a democratic country would accept to live with the level of violence that Israelis have endured for 18 months.

The Saudi peace plan is a breakthrough. From 1993 to 2000 Israel was engaged in long-term negotiations with the Palestinians with the aim of reaching a peaceful resolution of the conflict. Months, weeks, and years have been devoted to exhausting discussions; heads of state have wracked their brains, risked their careers, lost their lives without reaching this sincerely desired peace. And along comes the dazzling Saudi peace plan. Why is it better than the Barak-Clinton Camp David proposals? How does it differ? The answer is that no one knows, because no one has the faintest idea of the details, or even if there are any details. What's more, within the space of a few days it became clear (simply from reading your reports) that the plan is a take it or leave it no-discussion deal. Is that what well-meaning international opinion makers call a breakthrough? Forget about the details, just make peace and get this over with!

The Mideast conflict is some kind of an eye-for-an-eye biblical throwback. What about Jihad? What about Arafat haranguing his Palestinian audience with guttural cries of Jihad, Jihad, Jihad? What about the Jihad sermons given in mosques in Gaza (or London or Paris or New York?) Palestinian children have been taught <u>for decades</u> to hate and kill Jews. Have you seen images of this indoctrination in Pierre Rehov's film *Contrechamps* (copy available on request)? The region is soaked in Jihad blood and yet Lee Hockstader writes (*IHT* May 10, 2001)

> *"A pair of fresh-faced Israeli 14-year-olds skipped school Tuesday and went strolling near their homes in a Jewish settlement on the West Bank..../ Early Wednesday the boys' battered bodies were found in a rocky cave.... They had been bludgeoned to death with bowling-ball-sized boulders...so badly mutilated that one could be identified only by his fingerprints."*

Hockstader takes a quote from *Ha'aretz*—"*brutal acts recalling grisly Old Testament killings*"— and gives it a clever twist:

> *"Horrific as the latest murders were, they were welcomed by some Palestinians as the eye-for-an-eye consequence of the killing of a 4-month-old Palestinian girl in a Gaza refugee camp earlier this week."*

The article was published in the *International Herald Tribune* under the headline: "Life on the West Bank: An Eye for an Eye." With a legend above the photo: "Old Testament Killings."

But this was a typical <u>Jihad</u> killing! Picking up on the *Ha'aretz* image, Hockstader got Jewish permission to make the unspeakably brutal Jihad murder of two Israeli youngsters into. . . a Jewish thing. The "grisly Old Testament killing" of two Israeli Jews becomes one episode in the grisly eye-for-an-eye behavior of those vengeful Old Testament Jews. Lee Hockstader might object that he was just reporting what *Ha'aretz* said, and what "some Palestinians" said, while keeping his own thoughts to himself. If this is really an eye-for-an-eye story, why didn't Yasser Arafat walk around Joseph's Tomb as a riposte against Ariel Sharon's visit to the Temple Mount? And I wonder if Lee Hockstader doesn't give himself away in this recent dispatch from Gaza:

(*IHT* 14 March 2002) *"Few places in the Middle East are as poor, overcrowded, desperate and radicalized as Jabaliya, a teeming camp of 100,000 that is fertile ground for Hamas, which has carried out suicide bombings and other attacks on Israelis."* This time he doesn't quote *Ha'aretz* but authentic Jabaliya graffiti: '*Hey, Jews, you cowards! We swear we'll answer your aggression. Just wait.*' / *Jabilaya has a long, bitter history of fighting the Jews* [sic: this is Hockstader speaking in his own voice... 'fighting the Jews.'] *Fifteen years ago, it was where the first Palestinian uprising against Israeli occupation erupted.*" Anyone who thinks the graffitists of Jabilaya will be satisfied with a little state, some territories, and an end to the occupation (of what?) doesn't know how to read the writing on the wall.

And so in the squalid "refugee camp" of Jabilaya that the Israelis evacuated in 1994 (and the PA left in squalor) we come face to face with the real Mideast conflict. Who are these refugees, why are they still refugees, what do they want, what will they accept? Do they want a Saudi

Peace Plan? Or do they want Jihad? Do they want Hamas or Arafat, or Hamas and Arafat? Do they want a State or martyrdom? Why do they think Jews are cowards? Because Israel sends an army into the camp instead of a suicide bomber? Because Jews want to live and the boys from Jabilaya want to die?

How can journalists from a democratic nation like the United States—itself a victim of Jihad and the target of further Jihad operations—fall into the trap of the objective fallacy? The Palestinians cultivate martyrdom, journalists record their screams, measure the dripping blood, and point the finger at Israel. Unwittingly this intensifies international pressure for a peace sellout of Israel, whereas hopes for peace in the world depend on the survival of the State of Israel. Misguided tit for tat reporting obscures the terrible fact of suicide bombings, an absolutely unjustifiable atrocity that should not be committed against any human being on this earth. Fallacious objectivity leads to ethical blindness. Refusing to judge right and wrong on all sides, it fabricates wrongs to count against Israel and balance out the wrongs committed against Israelis. So we get scorekeeping: one terrorist attack, bad; one incursion to root out terrorists, bad... Ethical blindness leads into a bottomless pit.

The Palestinians are trapped. Hostage to a Jihad mentality, hijacked by terrorist gangs, they have no outlet for the expression and pursuit of legitimate aspirations. International opinion captivated by their distress and blind to its causes (or delighted in blaming it all on Israel) reinforces this tragic situation. If we truly respect the Palestinians we must treat them like responsible human beings: call them to account for their atrocities, confront them with their lies, expect them to choose once and for all between a state (= compromise) and jihad (= endless martyrdom).

No other conflict in our times is more sensitive to public opinion, and rightfully so. We are all, if you will, at stake. We need well-informed reporting based on an awareness of the universal impact of events playing out in the Middle East today. We deserve something better than exasperated begging for a settlement that doesn't know right from wrong. Am I wrong, then, to ask more of you? And more of myself by engaging this dialogue with you?

With sincere best wishes,

(Ms.) Nidra Poller

LETTER TO THE EDITOR/ *IHT*
April 2002

IHT's extensive coverage of the Israeli-Palestinian conflict is certainly appreciated. By giving voice to a wide range of opinions and perspectives you give readers a chance to be informed without being indoctrinated. And I think that your editorial staff makes a sincere effort to keep the debate open, fair, and lively. So I trust that you will be receptive to my request for an even more lively, fair and open debate that will fill in some missing details and draw conclusions instead of stopping midway where no one is responsible for anything. Over and above our warring opinions, we share a responsibility to our common humanity.

And humanity is in danger when the collective mind is so disconnected from reality that verifiable facts can be blown away like a cloud of dust and fantasies can outweigh tanks and buildings. The collective mind is disconnected from reality when the lessons of recent history, of 7 months ago history, count for nothing and speculations based on wishful thinking or simple fear are dished out in all you can eat abundance. Six months after the WTC attacks followed by the brilliant intervention in Afghanistan, we are told that there can be no military solution to Palestinian terrorism. The Arab street is going to blow up in our faces, thousands of innocent Palestinian civilians are being massacred, a new generation of terrorists is being spawned every day, every hour, every minute... and so on. I still have the forwarded e-mails sent by well-meaning friends in the aftermath of 9/11. Nothing happened the way they said it would, none of the dire consequences occurred, a high proportion of the immediate objectives were accomplished, the tens of thousands of casualties they invented lie in limbo, waiting for Arundhati Roy and Jim Garrison and all the others to admit the imagined deaths didn't happen. And all the better for humanity.

To come back to the Israeli-Palestinian conflict... there was no dearth of civilian deaths to count in Israel over the Passover weekend. The summary execution by Palestinians of alleged collaborators is also well-documented. Israeli military authorities report Palestinian deaths during this phase of the military operation... almost all of them are armed men killed in combat. There is no massacre of innocent civilians. What then led Dan Williams to shame himself by publishing a concocted story of summary execution of five Palestinian policemen by Israeli soldiers? His story should be taught in journalism schools as a model of the eyewitness account by a person who saw nothing and knows all.

We are hearing for 18 months from keen analysts that Yasser Arafat can't stop the terrorist attacks because: he can't possibly have control over all the different factions operation in the territories, and besides no one would listen to him if he did order a halt because he has no political perspectives to offer them and no compensation for the 30 (and then 40, 80, 100, etc.) dead since the beginning of the intifada and, more recently, he can't stop the terrorists because Israel is undermining his authority, destroying his infrastructure, arresting his policemen and now, ultimate humiliation, imprisoning him in a two-room suite in Ramallah. All of this sophisticated reasoning has the advantage of placing the blame squarely on Israel. But the facts exist. Arafat has never ordered his people to stop terrorism against Israel, he has constantly and unequivocally justified the murder of Israeli civilians. The very journalists who write these articles, these editorials, have seen the evidence. They know. The CIA knows. Admiral Zinni knows. The Arab League knows, Prince Abdullah knows, Shimon Peres knows... And now tons of new evidence is being gathered by the Israeli army and presented to the appropriate reliable authorities. So will the real Yasser Arafat please stand up? Is he the Christ figure adored by a gaggle of mainly European "pacifists"? Is he the enigmatic political genius invented by subtle minds, the nation-builder whose little nation lies in ruins while he floats on dreams of glory?

While the well- intentioned continue to invent fake Yasser Arafats to puzzle over, the very Arab League conference in Beirut called to approve the Saudi Peace Plan acknowledged that Yasser Arafat is the leader of a Palestinian strategy of "intifada" (= suicide bombings, drive-by shootings, etc.) and the assembled Arab leaders approved this strategy, agreed to continue to fund it, and declared that it will continue until the Palestinians achieve their goals.

And even Mahathir bin Mohamad, prime minister of Malaysia, who actually condemns "armed attacks against civilians" including the "human bomb attacks by Palestinians," even this prince of peace writing under the heading "Killing innocent people is not Islamic," even Mahathir bin Mohamad acknowledges without actually naming Arafat that the Palestinians pursue a strategy of human bomb attacks against civilians. And what's more, we should understand that these acts, this terrorism, will continue. Even though it may be misguided, counterproductive, harmful to their cause. Terrorism will continue because Muslims are bitter, angry, and frustrated. And the world must remove the causes of their anger, the world must bring an end to the oppression of Palestinians in particular and Muslims in general. In the meantime, the world must force the Israelis to de-escalate. The Israelis must be forced to stop fighting terror. "But," concludes M b M, "Muslims everywhere must condemn terrorism once it is clearly defined."

That's the noble position. Now here's the reality:

It would come to light if you would no longer exclude—or downplay almost to oblivion—what we might call simply the djihad factor. Muslim spokesmen, leaders, specialists and apologists have ample space to lecture us on Islam, the religion of peace, and then go on to condemn Israeli attempts to bring an end to such attacks, qualifying this as "terrorizing the terrorists" However exhilarating it may be to describe scenes of war and echo the hue and cry of "stop this violence," readers and journalists alike in this dawning twenty-first century cannot ignore the far-reaching consequences of current events.

Is this "stop the violence" a cry for justice or the bleating of lambs eager to run to slaughter?

And it's high time the world caught on. Today we stand, transfixed, on the line of battle. The world's attention is focused on this conflict. And rightfully so. But how many of us know what is at stake? When will the hysterical condemnation of Israel die down and let the voices of human decency be heard? The battle line is clearly drawn. We are asked to choose between ethics that encompasses the whole of humanity and a village logic that sees no further than the end of the street. Humanism stands on the Law. Village logic ends at the last house on the street and bows to the biggest tough on the block. . .

LETTER TO THE EDITOR/ *IHT*

3 April 2002

"Killing Innocent People is Not Islamic," *IHT* 2 April 2002

Malaysian PM Mahathir bin Mohamad offers a faint glimmer of hope; he actually condemns "human bomb attacks by Palestinians."

However, if we follow the reasoning of this prince of peace—who acknowledges without actually naming Arafat that the Palestinians pursue a strategy of human bomb attacks against civilians—we reach a dead end: these reprehensible acts, this terrorism, cannot be stopped. Even though the terrorists may be misguided, counter-productive, harmful to their cause, terrorism will continue because Muslims are bitter, angry, and frustrated. And the world must remove the causes of their anger, the world must bring an end to the oppression of Palestinians in particular and Muslims in general. In the meantime, the Israelis must "de-escalate." They cannot defeat terror with military force. "But," concludes Mahathir bin Mohamad, "Muslims everywhere must condemn terrorism once it is clearly defined."

In fact the Islamic Conference at Kuala Lampur justified human bomb attacks, but let us nourish the glimmer of hope and examine by its faint light the moral precepts we are invited to share. We—the world—must take our human bomb attacks stoically until we can remove, totally and absolutely, the causes of anger and frustration that misguide the terrorists. In the prime minister's own words, "The insistence that everyone must accept the same ideology and set of values must be relaxed."

So there you have it, world. Saudi Sunday pilots barreling into the WTC and exploding more than 3,000 lives, frustrated Palestinians disguised as Elijah crashing the Natanya seder and blowing 25 Jews to bits, maiming a hundred others... these are not horrendous, unacceptable acts of war that call for appropriate military action. Then what are they? A knife held to the world's throat. Some people are going to define their grievances according to their own system of values, and the world just has to take it on the chin until and unless it can satisfy their demands.

Doesn't this cast a bright light on the current Israeli military campaign? Israel is saying no to this deal. No, you cannot blow civilians to bits. No you cannot get away with it. No this strategy is not an indomitable juggernaut. Yes, terrorist cells can be dismantled, arms can be captured, and terrorist leaders can be neutralized.

Think it over, world. Is the current uproar, outrage, outcry against Israeli military operations really inspired by enlightened humanism? Or is it a hysterical headlong plunge into disaster?

Let us rather join with Mahathir bin Mohamad in bringing a glimmer of hope to light. Surrender to blackmail is just as bad for Muslims as for the world. The Law is for everyone, suicide bombers are against everyone. And Israel's refusal of blackmail is a glimmer of hope for the Arab world.

"Riyadh misses the point" Washington Post. IHT 29 April 2002

Prince Abdullah does indeed "miss the point" that the United States cannot act to solve the Israeli-Palestinian conflict unless Arab governments are willing to accept and shoulder their own responsibility. Missing the point is precisely his strategy and woe unto us if it works. But why does the *Washington Post* editorialist miss the point? Putting Ariel Sharon's refusal of a call for an immediate military withdrawal on the same level as Arab leaders' ignoring the call to denounce suicide bombings is a logical insanity. Why did the troops go into the territories in the first place? Can any honest person, whatever his sympathies or antipathies, deny that the troops went in to dismantle terrorist networks? Am I the only person who remembers how the Palestinian Authority responded to repeated demands from, yes, the American administration and its emissaries, asking them to dismantle terrorist networks and stop terrorist attacks? The answer was NO. No, we will not do Israel's dirty work.

So now Israel is doing the PA's dirty work, and the *Washington Post* heaps adjectives on Ariel Sharon, the *stubborn Israeli leader* who *ruthlessly exploit[s]*, *defies*, commits *reckless excesses...*

Glorifying suicide bombers, nurturing, fostering and supporting terrorism, and floating a peace plan that bears no discussion... these are not reckless excesses. Nothing ruthless about fostering terrorism? Nothing defiant about ignoring pleas to denounce suicide bombers... notice, nobody is asking them to stop fomenting and funding suicide bombers, just a few words of faint denunciation, maybe a tiny little hypocritical declaration.

If logical insanity were not contagious, this kind of reasoning could be dismissed as laughable. But it is contagious. And deadly.

The point being missed is that a new world order is taking shape before our eyes, and we are responsible for the shape it takes. Will it be a world faithful to democratic values in all their imperfection and largely huddled under the umbrella of American military might, or a world delivered up to the logic of blackmail: we can do this to you because you don't know how much we suffer and it's all your fault, and you can't hit back at us because if you do we'll send the whole world down the tubes.

What is happening to Israelis today will happen to every one of us tomorrow. It all comes down to a five year-old girl shot in cold blood as she hid under her bed. And Israeli troops going into Hebron and killing the man who sent the man who killed that child.

Will the real ruthless defiant recklessly excessive killer please stand up?

FRANCE IS NOT AN ANTISEMITIC COUNTRY
"A slander on France" François Bujon d'Estaing. *Washington Post* 22.6.02
IHT 24.6.02

Nous voilà rassurés. France is not an antisemitic country. The proof? Policemen are posted in front of schools and synagogues. To protect them. And rain is not wet! The proof? We use umbrellas.

The honorable French ambassador to the United States admits that the violence against Jews in France is terribly distressing... but clearly shows he can take it in his stride. His rage and fury is reserved for the outrageous comparisons elicited by this regrettable but after all understandable antisemitism. The assaults are "inexcusable" but those who dare to describe them in dramatic terms backed up by historical precedents are "blatantly malicious." The "unforgiveable acts... must be seen for what they are: a spillover from the Israeli-Palestinian conflict."

Since these acts are condemned by the highest authorities and the perpetrators are severely punished (that's news to us!) what can explain the slanderous accusations against *la belle France*? A hidden agenda! Some people who are opposed to the eminently reasonable French solution to the Mideast conflict "are distorting the truth in a despicable way."

Did anyone mention *le complot juif*? Certainly not the diplomatic ambassador. He is just giving the facts. And what are the facts that prove that France is not an antisemitic country? *Pitié!* Captain Dreyfus was defended and cleared of the false charges levelled against him, and three quarters of French Jews were saved from the death camps. *Nous voilà donc rassurés*. France is not an antisemitic country, just as it wasn't when Dreyfus was dishonored, just as it wasn't in 1936 when Léon Blum was in office, and just as it wasn't when one quarter of French Jews perished in the camps.

And who is guilty of "an insult to victims of the Holocaust?"

Israel Hasbara Committee

A BAG OF MARBLES

« Israël-Palestine: le cancer » Edgar Morin, Sami Naïr and Danièle Sallenave. *Le Monde,* 3 June 2002

> *"The Israeli-Palestine cancer was formed on a territorial pathology: the formation of two nations in the same land, a source of two political pathologies of which one is an outgrowth of domination and the other of privation. It developed by feeding on the historical anxiety of a people that had been persecuted in the past and their geographical insecurity, and on the misfortune of a people persecuted in the present and deprived of political rights."*

What in The World has come over Edgar, Sami, and Danièle? Did they want to squawk back at a conflict they can't understand or influence? Did they honestly think they'd convince someone of something? Or maybe, knowing they'd provoke a flood of indignation, they were looking for a chance to say you see you can't criticize them without being accused of... Did they just want a slap in the face? For the fun of it? What else could explain this shameful display of dismal intellectual poverty? The Gang of Three dumped out their bag of marbles....and broke their own necks! Dragging us—as if we had nothing better to do—into this catch-22: let them holler who cares but still in all you don't accept that kind of insult; or dig in and waste precious time underlining, making marginal notes, tallying up errors, getting exasperated. *Pitié.*

Their text is sheer hooliganism, and calling it a text is a compliment. They pulled the rabbi's beard, tripped him up, and when he fell in the mud they shouted dirty Jew and ran.

Naughty kids! Watch out your own selves. A whole lot of clear-minded clear-hearted people might get so fed up with the way this society is going that they'll scoot out and leave France to her darlings of *dé-*

raison. And in that shoddy new world you're begging for... there won't be any place for Ed, or Sam, or Dan.

In the meantime, let's see what's true and what's false in this bag of marbles.

"*The Israeli-Palestine cancer was formed on a territorial pathology: the formation of two nations in the same land...*" How about that? Not a territorial conflict, not a religious war... a pathology. Idiots all over the world have been wasting time thinking, negotiating, peaceplanning and summitmeeting when what we needed was a doctor. A sort of Supreme Doctor-in-Chief about half as big as God who graduated from universities that don't even exist yet, because territorial pathology is even more avant-garde than AIDS and scarier than mad cow disease.

Forget about the scientific angle. It takes a bigger brain than me to analyze that one. I prefer to begin with the crime of crimes: it seems that the Jews have endured such terrible persecutions that they ended up changing places and turning into the worst kind of persecutioners you could imagine. It sounds simple (backed up by a quote from V. Hugo) but in fact it's complicated. As you tread through this minefield of marbles, slipping, sliding and breaking your neck, you can't tell if the Jews really suffered a whole lot or just a little. Because they're so perfidious they went and named their suffering (not all of it, just the last little incident) with a word in their own language: *Shoah.* And this deprives other victims—"*those of the gulag*" for example—of getting their fair share of suffering. So they really went too far. The Jews of course, not the "*Noirs esclavagisés.*" (Slaverized blacks! Wouldn't a nice Bantu word do more for their cause than this barbarized term?) The slaverized Blacks didn't go settling in Palestine and causing grief to Palestinians did they? Even though they're always singing *Go down Moses.* The Gypsies didn't barge in on them. Ditto for the American Indians. Only those shoahized Jews. And then they have the nerve to see "*The right of return of Palestinian refugees... not as symmetrical to the right of return of Jews who never lived in Palestine, but as... a demand for Israel's demographic suicide.*"

It's not always easy to piece things together when three different writers, each with his or her own temperament, go off and write each in his or her own corner and then get together, who knows, by e-mail or more likely at dinners where wine flows like water... but I'm writing here all by myself and I'd like to know if, according to this trio, the Jews were in fact persecuted and if so how much. "*Israel presents itself as spokes-man for the Jews, victims of a multisecular persecution up to the Nazi's attempted extermination.*" Let's forget about this pretentious Israel taking itself for spokesman and concentrate on things that can be weighed and measured. So the Jews, who are now oppressors, did in fact suffer a lot and for a long time. But that's not all. The birth of that same Israel "*attacked by its Arab neighbors came near to being its death.*" So this suffering is rather recent. But, not to worry! It's all over now. It's a "*passé aboli,*" over and done with, leaving just a tiny trace of anxiety unfortunately awakened by a really tiny little teeny new Intifada. Don't forget: "*The word Shoah…singularizes the Jewish victimary destiny and makes all the others ordinary…*"

But… another marble underfoot: "*It is hard to imagine that a nation of fugitives, born of a people who suffered the most extended persecu-tions in the history of humanity, who suffered the worst humiliations and the worst contempt could in the space of two generations turn itself into 'un people dominateur et sûr de lui'…*" (Hugo and now de Gaulle, *décidément* we deserve the best in famous quotations! The nerve! Hardly two steps out of the camps and already overbearing & over-confident…*)* Okay, they were the most and the most but it's no reason to singularize themselves. Weren't the other victims the most and the most of the most?

Maybe so. What I understand is that the Jews don't understand that now it's the Palestinians turn to suffer the worst humiliations and the worst contempt. Even victim isn't a sinecure. Too bad. Because "*rights and justice are on the side of the oppressed.*" Instead of which those Jews, who could easily have stayed on the right path, decided to become strong, get themselves a "*reconquistador*" Prime Minister, perpetuate massacres, demolish houses, in short dilapidate in just 2 generations a victimary credit good for 3 centuries and renewable on request.

Even their almighty God couldn't get them out of this quagmire. *Peuple élu,* chosen people, okay, but incumbents have been known to lose elections, it's quite commonplace. "*The French case is significant*" as our authors so wisely observed. So no providential bailout, but, but their luck has not run out! They're so good at playing the oppressors that now they've got the whole world on their case. Yeah! Daring to respond to human bomb attacks by dressing up as soldiers and using harsh military tactics, targeting so-called terrorists and destroying homes, swaggering around, their arrogance visible to the naked eye, their tanks and their missiles, in short, with their "*state terrorism*" they've ended up awakening "a *new wave of antijudaism.*"

They have such high hopes of becoming victims once again that if History doesn't pay close attention it might not even notice the brief transition between the *passé aboli* and this New-Wave antisemitism. Will History at least realize that by the fault of the "*merciless repression led by Sharon, mental antijudaism*" has assumed concrete and even incendiary forms?

Our trio will see to it . Valliant wrong-righters, mathematical whizzes, agile acrobats they spin and squash disequilibriated interpretations with astonishing dexterity! For example: saying it's Arafat's fault that the Camp David festivities exploded in human bombs... that kind of fibbery is *unilateralism*. Talking about an Israelo-Palestinian war, the way they do in western media, is indulging in false symmetrism (and if you're like me and never heard tell of any such war, then you're not just disequilibrated you're also deaf).

Never fear. Thanks to an oh so well-known, richly awarded, recognizable method that we might call but without or at least I hope without the least suspicion of stooping to anti-seniorism (he who knows me knows my age) with, then, what we might call the rocking-chair slowdance version of the marbles method, all of this can be set straight. Here's an example of this brilliant what am I saying dazzling blinding thought:

> "*Unilateralism masks the infernal repression-attack dialectic, itself fed by extremist forces in both camps. It masks the fact that Sharon's visit to the esplanade des Mosquées [French for Temple Mount] could only reinforce the infernal vicious circle that favors the worst in each of the two camps.*"

Which by the way reminds us that you can recognize the distinctive touch of each distinct pair within this composition for six hands. And we have to give the authors a hand for going beyond the (bitter) statement of the facts and suggesting positive steps. A really great idea: the Checkpoints Reality Show or, if you want it in French, le Loft Story. Because "*The media can't really show the incessant multiple demonstrations of contempt, incessant multiple humiliations suffered at checkpoints, in the homes, in the street,"* what we need (I'm extrapolating) is to show them in real time and, as in the Loft, the camera will be covered with a modest veil only when *"those young men and young ladies who have become human bombs"* go by.

And this brings us to the hands of the delicate seamstress that embroider a petit-point portrait of the young people inspired with their *"strong motivation of vendetta"* who, in *"a superbly Mediterranean gesture…. have the feeling that they restore a lost honor and finally find in a murderous death [their] own dignity, [their] own freedom."* Nothing about the 70 virgins. We're feminist *jusqu'au bout, n'est-ce pas*?

Might it be that the hand that claims to think that *"it is terrible to kill civilians… this way, by suicide attacks"* doesn't know how tenderly the other hand is patting the killers on the head? Take it easy! Don't go looking for *La Complexité* all over the place! The above condemnation was just a way of condemning the condemned—I sniff essence of Sabra & Shatila —and according to our authors it's always Israel that started the fight. What's more, Zionism from its very *"beginning… obscured the right of the Palestinians to their nation."* C'mon, don't stop halfway, say it: they started out by killing God and when (already) they were kicked out of their little sh…. country, not content to sit down and cry by the waters of Babylon they started plotting a comeback that denied the rights of another people yet to be born. And that's serious! You should always look out for future generations.

You might wonder where I get the nerve to snap back in the face of such a solemn statement from three such French and distinguished intellectuals? I'll tell you why. They're talking to me. That's it, to me. And don't think, just because of a certain style *dans le texte,* that we're dealing with inoffensive *beaux parleurs*. The fact is these guys have written a genuine call to action! Yessir! It's subtle, not so say hidden… almost shamefully slipped in not far from the pyrotechnical conclusion where the cancer conjugated with the confrontation of confrontations in the *"seismic zone"* of the Middle East where, not having had the good sense to appreciate *"the 100-volt shock"* of the Saudi peace plan, we're now in danger of croaking en masse from metastases spurting to the four corners of the world, hidden as I said but to my eyes highly visible, this appeal to the *"United States, that bears a crushing responsibility."* So this 5-page argument that I only quoted in snippets here, is addressed to me, *l'Américaine*. I can handle it. Okay for the crushing responsibility and okay for the obligation to reply. The United States, "*disposant du moyen de pression décisif en menaçant de suspendre leur aide, et du moyen de garantie décisif en signant une alliance de protection avec Israël*," disposing, as they put it, "*of a decisive means of pressure in threatening to suspend their aid and a decisive means of reassurance in signing a protective alliance with Israel. . .*" First of all I wonder why this sentence is turned so tricky. Do they think they can talk to me in crooked *Français* just because I'm *américaine*? You don't have to be bilingual to see what I mean. "...the United States disposing...in threatening..." What happened to the coulds and woulds of intelligent discourse? Okay, I'm not saying who concocted that one.

Let's get down to the nitty gritty. Invited to intervene along the lines of the ideas bandied about thereabove, I reply (*en anglais dans le texte*): No way! You naughty kids, go on home and tell your ol' man he better keep ye outta trouble. And pick up those damn marbles before someone breaks his neck. Make it snappy!

Hopeless intellectual poverty. These guys are human bombs. These three lost souls, equipped with identical opaque hearts, wrap themselves in belts of explosive conceit loaded with adulterated words and, in a superbly Mediterranean gesture, blow themselves up in a crowd of discourse and go down the tubes on a field of shattered truths. Shameful.

And they think *l'Américaine* is going to rush to the rescue? *En anglais dans le texte*: Yeeeah, riiiiight, gotche! I'm going to cut out my buddy, Israel, and put my money on some cool cat like Syria. Come to think of it, the Bashar kid is an ophthalmologist. Maybe he can refer me to a good International Strategic Oncologist... No, forget it. *Je n'ai plus le cœur à ça*. You want help in badmouthing the Jews? No problem. *Embarrass de choix*. But not the Americans. Leave us out of this. We may not be as smart as you guys, but at least we know the time of day. This is the 21st century, boys and girls. Time is on the fast track. Your little funny games there might be the height of fashion in Paris today but who knows, tomorrow this kind of shtick might be so old hat that not even *Le Monde* will publish it.

Metula News Agency[4]

ALL OUR MISERIES ARE NOT IN FRENCH
26 August 2002

Yes, we're tough and brave and we won't give up...but we need a break once in a while. *Des vacances*, a change of climate, a piece of good news or *faute de mieux* a change of language.

Summertime and the living is easy... until you catch Alain Krivine (*Ligue Communiste Révolutionaire*) on the radio one fine day (*France Inter*, 1 August '02, 08:52) with his nice deep voice telling how Picasso's *Guernica* speaks for all massacres—Oradour sur Glane, Sabra & Shatila, Jenine—and all people who resist. So how about a little hate-bath on *Radio Méditerrannée*? An interview with Thierry Meyssan, author of that groundbreaking muckraking investigation (already selling in the hundreds of thousands in French and an English version now on the Net). Only Thierry and his fans know that no airplane crashed into the Pentagon on September 11th. The whole thing was a montage, virtual images, easy as pie, a setup job to make the Muslims look bad.

Don't despair, there are heroes galore. José Bové's coming out party at Villeneuve lès Maguelonne announced in detail, in earnest voices, in heightened awareness. He lost weight, he's going to lead an intifada for all the prisoners in this unjust country, *lotta continua* and all the rest, my eye. Does the excited lady on *France Info* happen to know that this José Bové fellow deprived me of a lovely bucket of huckleberries at the Marché Bio des Arceaux at Montpellier? Yes, I was about to buy real huckleberries, the kind we used to get in the Poconos when I was a girl, not those mushy modern blueberries. The genuine bio producer was just slipping them into a paper bag when my eyes fell upon a leaflet sitting next to his green beans: *Libérez José Bové*. Sign here. I just blurted out, *non, finalement je ne les prends pas*. Well, I hope he made the connection: my eyes>the leaflet>the no huckleberries. I should have said, *gardez-les pour José Bové*.

But if I start telling French stories you'll never hear the end of it. The point I wanted to make is that outrageous statements can be found in other languages. English, for example. Not that it can console us here in the *pays des droits de l'homme, des lumières*, and *des* silly French intellectuals. We still take the cake. But it is terribly instructive to have a look at other versions of the same insidious campaign. Campaign to...or against...or for? Let's see.

Take the *International Herald Tribune*. It has often been my refuge and solace. I turned to the *IHT* during the Gulf War when I realized that no truth could be forthcoming from my favorite French newspapers. And over the years I had endless occasions to quote articles, nod in agreement with editorials, delight in the crisp clean lettuce of factual reporting.

No longer so. What happened? I have the distinct impression that the *IHT* is bending over backwards to please European and Arab readers. Gradually the choice of *NY Times* and *Washington Post* articles and opinion pieces has narrowed down and slanted in one direction. While US readers of these papers were bombarding ombudsmen and canceling subscriptions, the *IHT* smoothly pursued its new route. Lee Hockstader (*c'est toute une histoire*) has disappeared from the pages of the *Washington Post*. Is he still bureau chief in Jerusalem? Does he still think that "any journalist worth his salt knows there are no good guys or bad guys in the Middle East," is he still touched to the heartstrings by Hamas leaders mowed down as they tended their pigeons in a sundrenched orchard? Wherever he is at the moment—hunkering down waiting for better or for worse days—he's not on the pages of the *Washington Post* and not even in the *IHT*.

But brilliant no-nonsense Pulitzer-prize winner Charles Krauthammer is regularly published in the *Washington Post*... and in the *IHT*? Nevermore. And Thomas Friedman, rarely. Granted, since he invented the Saudi Peace Plan he's lost a bit of credibility, but even with one wing bandaged he flies a lot higher than the likes of Marwan Bishara and Henry Siegman.

Siegman, "*senior fellow on the Middle East at the Council on Foreign Relations in New York,*" informs us in an exclusive commentary (*IHT* 14.8.02) "*Hardening Palestinian views suggest worse to come.*" The article is illustrated by a cartoon showing Arafat and Sharon face to face like two faces of the same Bad Guy, haggling like drinking buddies who fight and make up from binge to binge.

Siegman comments on an opinion poll showing that the majority of Palestinians will vote for Arafat in the coming elections (nya nya nya on Dubya) and, while 42% are in favor of a democratic political system, a corresponding 42% are in favor of an Islamic system. Those are the figures, and here's Siegman's explanation: "*To the extent that the policies of Prime Minister Ariel Sharon's government toward Palestinians can be said to have rational content, it is to provoke ever greater Palestinian extremism, which in turn provides justification for ever more severe Israeli measures intended to destroy what is left of civilized Palestinian existence.... The escalation of Palestinian extremism plays directly into such a strategy, one that Israel's rightist government hopes will lead to Palestinian surrender to its terms."*

Wagging a stiff finger, Siegman announces that, despite it all, 50% of Palestinians are optimistic about the future. Explanation? *"The Palestinians' alternative to capitulation is to embrace the Islamic agenda and the 'blessings' it offers."* Given that *"For Israelis...there is not available a comparable political or religious ideology that offers optimism in the face of their suffering,"* Siegman concludes ,*"Israelis are likely to fold before Palestinians do."*

In a Greek chorus of Letters to the Editor Bush is scolded for prejudice against Palestinians because he reacted with fury against the Mt. Scopus bombing but hardly condemned the Gaza bombing, Arafat is given credit for refusing the Barak-Clinton plan because it offered the Palestinians nothing but polluted dry landfills. A letter reminding that current Palestinian hardships are a direct result of their intifada strategy is sandwiched in between all of the above and a harrowing account by the general secretary of the Tulkarm Blood Bank Society of his voyage to a conference in Toledo, via endless obstacles, checkpoints, closures and assorted injustices.

But the worst is yet to come.

The Guardian's sweetheart, Suzanne Goldenberg, *"reports from Dura... on a reviled collaborator whose treachery cost him his life"* (10 August '02). A full-page article illustrated with a huge photo of *"one of the collaborators... ignominiously strung up for the mob to vent its rage,"* hanging by one foot from a pylon and I spare you the details. The article deserves a 10-page analysis but I will have to limit myself here to a rapid review. *"Musa Rajub died a traitor's death.... He must have known he had it coming to him."* When local Al Aqsa Brigades commander Marwin Zaloom was eliminated by an Israel helicopter gunship, *"Rajub's fate was sealed."*

Musa and two other accused collaborators were dragged out of prison, *"beaten for nearly 24 hours,"* 20 bullets pumped into each one and the half-naked carcasses strung up, stoned, spat upon and *"cigarettes stubbed out on the cold and graying flesh."* Are these vivid not to say sickening details presented as a shocking image of Palestinian brutality?

Don't forget, Musa knew he had it coming.

Drawing on a broad spectrum of remarks by friends and neighbors, Suzanne tells us what a bad guy Musa was, a gun-toting showoff bullying wheeler-dealer. And what a good guy he was, how he used his influence with the Israelis to help people, how he was forced to sell secrets so he could feed his seven children. In the interests of common sense she mentions that Musa had been in jail for 18 months; one would be hard put to say what he had to do with the elimination of Zaloom. His wife had been paying monthly protection money and trying, for 18 months, to sell a piece of land to pay the bribe that would liberate him. Just when she was about to clinch the deal... well, you understand, it was too late.

So what can be wrong with this well-balanced mixture of lurid details, statistics from Palestinian Human rights Monitoring Group (71 suspected collaborators killed since September 2000) and touching words from Rajub's widow? It is all so reasonable. Mrs. Rajub is shocked, Palestinian security officials deny there was any prison-releasing deal on or under the table, and the Al Aqsa Brigades boys had to take revenge on someone. And what are we to think, we rational, intelligent, humane, concerned readers of this article? Khalid Amayreh, a Palestinian journalist from Dura, is given the last word:

"What happened is the epitome of the entire Palestinian tragedy: Palestinians killing Palestinians. Musa Rajub and the likes of him are not immaculate people. But they themselves are victims of the Israeli occupation."

Occupation. Collaborator. Remind you of anything? And the missing partner: resistance fighter. Check it out. Israel is the enemy (we're talking about the Oslo years). People like Musa are collaborators, selling *"snippets of information about militant Palestinian groups..."* and benefiting from modest Israeli largesse. And the resistance fighters? Evident my dear Watson: the Al Aqsa Brigades. The ones who send human bombs to Jerusalem and Tel Aviv. A brigade commander gets knocked off by the Occupying troops, a collaborator gets strung up, and it all makes sense. Unless you happen to think that Israel has a right to exist, that the Al Aqsa Brigades are terrorists, and the Palestinian Authority was supposed to prevent terrorist attacks. Wouldn't that make Musa more like a peacenick? Even a profiteering peacenick, if we must absolutely make him a bad guy. But a collaborator?

It's so insidious. The inset quote to the right of the photo— *"Collaborators are the worst and most diabolical product of the Israeli occupation"*—somehow cancels out the horror of this creature strung up by one leg, a huge bloodstain on his tee shirt where his head once had been. Collaborator, occupation... and the Nazis are not far behind. Okay, it's a bit rough, but this is the Middle East. Nobody loves a collaborator.

What compassionate title crowned this article? Terrorists lynch father of seven. Gun slinging Al Aqsa Brigade members make the law in Dura. Targeted killing blind revenge / prisoners killed like dogs. Or simply *"They stomped out their cigarettes in the cold and graying flesh."* Other words, different reality. So what do these words mean? *"He pointed the finger and pulled the strings, but the protection ran out."*

It means that a Palestinian who informs an Israeli official of a plan to send a human bomb or maybe a car bomb into Israel or yes go ahead if you must into the settlements or into Israel proper, and kill dozens of civilians and maim hundreds for life, or even better kill hundreds and maim thousands, just because they are Jews living in Israel or happen to be standing or sitting next to Jews living in Israel, a Palestinian who gives information that might help the Israeli government prevent this attack from taking place is morally equivalent to a Frenchman, not a bigshot like Maurice Papon but just a sort of local guy operating on a modest scale in the period 1940-45, also known as the Occupation, who pointed the finger and helped the Vichy government round up Jews and send them to the death camps. *Faut le faire!*

And when your name is Goldenberg, pointing the finger at Israel is a goldmine.

It is no accident, then, that the day's Letters to *The Guardian* come down hard on... the Jews! *"As a British citizen who happens to be Jewish [x] ... believe[s] he has the right to... [Israeli] citizenship because of his religion.... this democracy necessitated the ethnic cleansing of thousands of Palestinians.... The current Palestinian terrorism, appalling as it is, differs from Jewish terrorism of the 1940s in only one respect: it is committed by people trying to reclaim their own land, not by foreigners trying to conquer another people's land."*

Another reader declares that *"The basic racism of the state of Israel has been going on since 1948..."* and comments on a recent article about rabbis converting Peruvian Indians *"... cynical battening on to poverty-stricken peasants, rendering them 'kosher' in two weeks and shipping them over to the settlements, providing they'll agree to say that Palestinians have no rights. If I had a laugh left, I'd be knocking myself out at the irony."*

The letters just happen to draw the appropriate conclusions from the article published the same day: Jewish presence in Israel is unjustified if not outright evil and anything done to bring an end to it is justified even if evil. How did we get from the article to the conclusions? For on the face of it, the article makes no sense. Can a *Guardian* byliner stoop so low as to do a zapping on this high profile subject? Lynch the collaborator and get your kicks, cry with his widow, cluck cluck with a neighbor who badmouths him, sigh with another who speaks kindly, string him up and spit on him with the street boys, shrug your shoulders with the PA police, bow your head and shed a tear with a Palestinian reporter who gives him absolution: after all, he was a victim. No, this seemingly nonsensical article is fraught with meaning. It's a benchmark of the progressive dismantling of the State of Israel. The fact that Israel is a sovereign state guaranteed by international law counts for nothing in the minds of its heartless critics.

What does count? The laissez passer. Permission to vent vicious hatred, justify abject brutality, not know right from wrong, wallow in sin and boast about it. Stick out your chest and receive the distinguished medal for cowardice. Congratulations! Your name is Seigman, you're a senior fellow, and you feed the Yasser Arafat party line to the sophisticated readership of the *IHT*: the Israelis are soft, they only know from startups and cocacola, Palestinians love to die, we can hold out longer, so give them Intifada, and don't worry, I'll cover for you. *Félicitations*, all of you, and when the day of reckoning comes, you'll say, "I didn't know, honestly, I didn't know. I know they went out, the boys from Al Aqsa Brigade, but I didn't know where they were going. We couldn't hear the explosions from here. What concerned us was the Occupation. You understand..."

Make no mistake about it. The avalanche of press coverage of the "Middle East situation" is not innocent. The media don't waste words. We are literally submerged by a massive campaign for... against... to?

To let Islamism take up where Nazism left off.

This is a terrible thing to say. And even more terrible to prove. Because the undeniable absolutely conclusive proof would be after the fact. And we are determined to make that impossible. As Europe gathers its forces—one might say its weaknesses—to stand up to Big Bad Little Bush and keep him from attacking Saddam, Saddam is loading up his diabolical arsenal and aiming it at... Washington DC? Paris? London? No. Israel. For all the corrupt and outright stupid historical comparisons dragged in by the hair in the form of a totally unjustified ideological vocabulary (Occupation, collaborator, etc.) there is a remarkable absence of awareness of the authentic historical comparison playing out before our eyes. The planned destruction of Israel (in the first place) the Jews (in the second place) and Western civilization (for the grand finale).

Last week an *RFI* journalist announced that several Palestinian activist organizations had decided to curtail suicide bombing but Hamas intends to continue attacking Israeli civilians "until Israel ends its Occupation of the Autonomous Territories." Clever, isn't it? Just add a few words and turn the truth upside down. *NY Times* correspondent John Kifner got it straight: *"Hamas, whose ideological goal is the establishment of an Islamic State in all of what was once Britain's post-World War 1 Palestine mandate."* His article, picked up in the *IHT*, is illustrated by a picture of the rubble of a Palestinian home destroyed by the Israeli army. These rubble photos, inevitably © Agence France Presse, now illustrate most *IHT* articles on the conflict.

Has it occurred to these Israel bashers that the rubble might illustrate their own bankrupt humanity? The demolition of their own civilized decency?

No human being should die blown to bits by a human-bomb. No human being should live maimed for life by a human-bomb. No human being anywhere on this earth for any reason whatsoever should die or be maimed by explosives wrapped around the body of another human being and loaded with sharp objects and venomous substances.

A human heart is infinitely elastic. It can sorrow for countless incidents of human suffering, with no temporal or spatial limits. A human mind can be reconciled to death by accident, disease, natural disasters, poverty, bad luck, domestic passions and gangster shootouts. A human being <u>cannot</u> accept these deaths by explosion of hapless civilians in public places. I have not digested a single one of these deaths, a single case of mutilating injury, I will never digest them, I will never forget.

This is the salient fact of the war against Israel. An inhuman, cowardly, basely abject method of torture and assassination—suicide-bomb-murder—systematized, industrialized, and grafted onto the Palestinian body politic, has gained acceptance in the very hearts of otherwise civilized people in the Western world. This abomination has awakened deep-seated primitive passions, a bestial bloodlust. This despicably cowardly military tactic—suicide-bomb-murder—that they dare to call the poor people's weapon, insulting the billions of humane, civilized poor people on this imperfect earth, this most cowardly strategy of blowing civilians to bits has awakened cowardice in the souls of so many otherwise decent people.

And we stand there naked before them, with our facts. But they are impervious to facts. Bloodlust and cowardice blind the mind to reason. We show them the facts in black and white and they spit out a factitious vocabulary of apartheids and ethnic cleansing, bantustans and colonization. And in fact, the more the facts are "on our side" the more vicious the accusations against Israel and the Jews. At the beginning of this misnamed Intifada, outraged readers and editorialists accused Israel of killing children, using excessive force, making unrealistic demands on Yasser Arafat, expanding colonies. Today it is the very notion of a Jewish State that is being blown to bits. (Yes, and what's to be said of the countless Arab / Muslim immigrants living in Europe and the Americas who write letters to editors, indignantly asking why Jews who were not born in "Palestine" should have the right to live there?).

This is not 1942. The trains are not sneaking through occupied towns whose inhabitants huddle behind closed shutters. This is Global Village, and grandmothers are being blown to bits down the street. All other questions aside... I repeat... all other questions aside, all other sufferings, injustices, deaths in battle and terrible mishaps aside... this abomination—suicide-bomb-murder—should not exist. And it would cease to exist if international opinion so decided. Yes, it would cease to exist. The problems would still be there, the conflict, the who struck John and I was here first, all of this would persist, and even war would persist, but this abomination would be reduced to a straggling minimum.

And where is world opinion? In the pits! Seized with bloodlust, cringing in cowardice, and simply too wimpy to take a stand. Impervious to reason. Go ahead, say it, just once—suicide-bomb-murder is absolutely unacceptable—and you'll see, all the rest, the conflict you can't live without, it will still be there. End this abomination and we'll be able to fight in peace!!!

Believe me, I have tried every way possible to understand the attitudes of these people who do not agree with me. I have tried every way to reason with them and myself. I have tried to understand why charming French friends I've known for decades can look me in the eye and give me, as if it were the depths of their own hard earned thought, arguments developed by Hamas and passed through several filters to reach them in beautiful French words upheld by serious French media.

I have patiently listened to intermediaries willing to explain to me European attitudes, French-Arab relations, Leftist traditions, non-Jewish indifference, and these explanations can't touch more than a tenth of what is going down. None of them can explain the sheer volume of vicious hatred, the crushing tons of unfair criticism, the hue and cry, the blinding incongruities, the suffocating sophism, the shell game of mirror reversal of every last shred of truth and the world itself turned upside down and stomping with all its force on Israel, on the Jews.

They intend to watch it happen, do nothing about it, go along with the crowd and, faced with absolute barbarity, they'll say with *The Guardian's* Suzanne Goldenberg: *"[they] must have known [they] had it coming."* And that will efface the image of the Palestinian man beaten to a pulp and strung up from a pylon? And that will hide the image of the Israeli baby blown to smithereens?

Give the barbarians a field day and, preparing for the worst, heap vindictive slander on their victims. Let it happen and pretend you don't know. That's the mechanism I see in operation. That's the only lens setting that gives a clear focus. That is the formula that accounts for the motion, speed, direction, acceleration, impact, and damage. It fits historically, it fits psychologically, it fits politically. It makes sense out of the hundreds of senseless lies and distortions heaped on us daily.

And the big front page story in today's (19 August '02) *International Herald Tribune*? *Washington Post* reporters Molly Moore and John Ward have a scoop: *Suicide bombers give an edge to Palestinians. Tactics shift military balance in conflict*. Well, friends, it seems that "*one of the world's best trained and equipped armies*" has met its match: the suicide bomb. In a well-balanced report supported by statistics from the Israeli government and quotes from Hamas chief Rantisi, statistics from human rights organization and quotes from Tsahal's Olivier Rafowicz, the journalists explain how the Palestinians have found their weapon of choice and stymied the Israeli army. Do you remember how the high ratio of Palestinian to Israeli casualties in the early months of the conflict proved Israel's use of excessive force? Well, the ratio has changed, the difference has narrowed. So, logically, the increase in Israeli casualties would indicate excessive use of force by the Palestinians? Not at all! It indicates the weakness of the Israeli army, the strength of the Palestinian strategy and, I might add, the triumph of even-handed reporting.

As for the inevitable © AFP photo, I guess they are out of rubble for the moment. It shows "*Red Crescent workers distributing food and household items Sunday in Rafah to people whose homes were destroyed by Israel.*"

Metula News Agency[5]

JEAN DANIEL, THE FRENCH AMBASSADOR'S AMBASSADOR

23 August 2002

Antisemitic? France? Perish the thought!

And perish the thinkers. Since it is no longer possible to deny the distressing proliferation of anti-Semitic violence in France, apologetics has turned to obscuring both the roots and the implications of the phenomenon. And the best way to begin is by asking if France is antisemitic. Very clever! Once the question is put that way, anyone can argue yes... or no... and win. But we're not in a sophomoric debating society. Events have forced us to ask how the contemporary form of antisemitism is taking shape and taking root in France today. And what can be done about it.

Accusations of antisemitism provoked outrage from France's ambassador to the US, François Bujon de l'Estang *(Washington Post* 22 June '02). When Jean Daniel, director of the elegant Left-ish weekly *Le Nouvel Observateur,* uses the same twisted logic as the ambassador, demonstrating the opposite of what he purports to prove, we realize the extent of the damage!

In a 4th of July [sic] editorial *"Lettre à un ami américain"* Jean Daniel asks, *"Antisémites les Français?"* The answer is a resounding NON. His arguments are more extensive than Bujon de l'Estang's brief diplomatic slap in the face, but no less shocking. As he tells it, the French people loved Israel as long as it was fragile and endangered; when the Israeli army became strong, the French, *"taking a lesson from the Algerian war,"* shifted their concern to the colonized Palestinians. The French loved Israelis when they were making peace with Arafat; in those days French Jews and French Muslims also lived in peaceful harmony. The first Intifada cast a long shadow, presaging the second, when *"Islamic terrorism and Sharon's Machiavellianism"* would destroy hopes for peace, shattered in a *"cycle of violence"* of suicide attacks and Israel's *"exclusively military riposte."* Jewish communities, led astray by this tense situation, over-react to the slightest criticism (legitimate, by definition) of Sharon. And start thinking that everyone wants to destroy Israel and exterminate the Jews.

Further, this unjustified Jewish reaction has tripped off the seething anger of French people of Arab origin, directly provoking the (regrettable) antisemitic incidents that have indeed occurred. Deeply convinced that only a minority of the French Muslim community is truly motivated by hatred of Jews, J. Daniel is equally convinced that the French react to *"Islamist barbarity...[with] deep compassion for the victims..."* but (rightfully) *"condemn Sharon no less than...Hamas or Islamic Jihad."*

I am not Jean Daniel's *ami américain* but, like his American friend I have lived in France for decades. And I am not reassured by this kind of argument. On the contrary! I do not see the slightest place for any notion of human dignity, moral rectitude, forthright honesty or even lucid common sense in this kind of thinking. It is an excellent example of the vicious mushiness currently in fashion here. Loving Israel because it is weak, putting Ariel Sharon on the same level as Hamas because he is strong, suggesting that Jews should keep mum and not stir up the Muslim hornet's nest and, more generally, accusing Jews of being the cause of everything that is done against them... aren't these the classical ingredients of antisemitism?

Jean Daniel admits that there have been antisemitic incidents in France... then downgrades them because they were done by "*young Muslim immigrants.*" A bit tricky! The French media have been particularly stingy with information about the authors of these crimes; in the rare cases where they were actually apprehended and identified, the culprits were French... whatever the origins of their parents or grandparents. *Beurs* are French when they win Olympic medals but turn into native born foreigners when they attack Jews and burn synagogues. In fact they are one face of today's France and cannot be written off so conveniently.

Drawing himself up to full height, J. Daniel solemnly declares: "*Il est faux et grave, très faux et très grave to say that France is an antisemitic country.*" [Meaning it is terrible and false... but it's so much more imprecatory in French.] This is a golden age for Jews in France, *n'est-ce pas*? They can join in the boycott of Israeli scholars and heap scorn on Israel in the pages of *Le Monde*, blithely tripping from Sharon to Israelis to Zionists to Jews. Nothing antisemitic about that, is there? Though Daniel agrees that we shouldn't underestimate Islamists and Lepenists he says—on the 4th of July, 10 days before the attempted assassination of President Chirac—that these extreme right fascist movements are down on Arabs, not Jews.

Unfortunately they manage to be down on both and on occasion can get together with the Arabs to attack Jews. Maxime Brunerie, the accused assailant, belonged to *Unité radicale* an extreme right radical fringe. As reported in *Le Monde* (3 August '02), UR's website justified antisemitic attacks as self-defense in "Occupied" (by the Jews of course) Europe, and the firebombing of the Djerba synagogue as an act of "résistance." *Unité radicale's* lawyer wonders what all the fuss is about when fervent anti-Zionism runs the gamut from Rony Brauman to José Bové. In other words, falls within the range of acceptable opinions.

How are we to react when Jean Daniel, echoing the ambassador, heaps scathing scorn on the very idea of an antisemitic France: infamous, slander, paroxysm, psychosis, a deliberate campaign to get French Jews to flee and American Jews to shun! Well, the second half of this long letter literally follows Bujon de l'Estang step by step and detail by detail. The arguments are richer, broader, and deeper as befits the doyen of a high class intellectual weekly, but the anchorage is the same.

The Dreyfus Affair becomes a proof of France's devotion to her Jews! By persecuting Dreyfus, France gave Theodore Herzl the idea of creating a Jewish state. And by rehabilitating Dreyfus the French so impressed Emmanuel Levinas' father that he encouraged his son to go there. Not even the Vichy government can darken this bright image: *"two out of three Jews were protected by the French people."*

France is a model of tolerance compared to the US. Racial and religious discrimination was banished in 1791 (followed by "all men are created equal" in 1776?); unlike Yale, Princeton, and Harvard, French universities never excluded Jews and Blacks! True, my uncles had to find clever ways around the numerus clausus and get their degrees at dumpy places like MIT before jumping into uniform and going to war against Hitler, while lucky French Jews were excluded from all professions and sent into hiding and/or off to the death camps.

Jean Daniel pulls the same names—Léon Blum and Pierre Mendès France—out of the same hat as Bujon de l'Estang, to prove that Jews can be elected to high office in France. Then, giving full expression to attitudes that the distinguished ambassador could only hint at, he aims and fires at his usual suspect, arch- villain Ariel Sharon. Sharon has nothing good to offer the Palestinians and never did; he has no respect for Yasser Arafat; he has wound George Bush around his finger and, with the help of the Jewish lobby and the Christian coalition, made Bush turn his back on the democratically elected Arafat. Leaving Sharon free to pursue his wicked designs: he wants all of Palestine for Israel, can't tell the difference between Arafat and Hamas, and will never be forgiven by history for sinfully rebuffing the Saudi peace plan.

So whose fault is it if France, which is not antisemitic, is antisemitic? Follow this logic:

As long as the conflict continues, nothing can stop the explosion of anti-Israeli passions and their *"terrible antisemitic"* throw offs.

Instead of accusing France of deep-seated antisemitism you (the American friend) had better take stock of America's responsibility for this mess.

The Americans have a nerve blaming the French for the effects (anti-semitic incidents) when they, the Americans, are the real <u>cause</u> of the problem: *"History will say... that we have all suffered the consequences of American failures in the Middle East. Because the Israeli problem is an element of American domestic politics."*

And that's a highly respected French intellectual thinking! *C'est très faux et très grave* to accuse France of antisemitism because this dishonors the memory of the real victims of the real antisemitism known as the Shoah. But there's nothing grave about some French people—of Arab origin—expressing their seething anger against Israel by attacking Jews in France while the rest of the population looks on and says it's all Sharon's fault and Sharon is all America's fault, and we never mistreated Jews the way Americans mistreated Blacks so shut your mouth.

Is that any way to treat an American friend?

Israel Hasbara Committee

FRENCH RADIO CELEBRATES 9/11 WITH M...F...ING GLEE

9 September 2002

Too polite to dance in the streets and hand out sweets for the first anniversary of the big tower crash, too Cartesian to admit they half way subscribe to evangelical Meyssanism, but so eaten up with spite that they can't hide their emotions, our *compères de la radio française* are indulging in orgies of geostrategic folly. And this is just for starters.

The future is full of promise. Here are a few of the gems displayed today. Mister Arafat himself wouldn't hear of it—I'm talking about the twin towers / occupied territories link—but French public opinion has gobbled it. From the editorialist admiringly quoted in a press review (advising the Americans to leave poor Saddam alone and put their weight on the Israelis, kick them out of Gaza, and make them give the Palestinians their State) to the simple citizen calling in and lining himself up with the Arab street (to say no to any intervention against Iraq as long as the Israelis get to do whatever they want) the WTC / Israel-Palestine connection is solid. And our superfine analysts drill it in. The murder of Israeli civilians is manna from heaven for Sharon, delivering a free permit to pursue a merciless war against the Palestinians. The unfortunate incident in Lower Manhattan is a godsend for the diabolical couple Bush – Sharon, united in their fight against so-called terrorism. And the collapsible towers were made to order for two-gun Georgie, smashing in the wake of their spectacular crash the last obstacle blocking him from lashing out for no reason at that poor li'l Saddam Hussein. Not exactly the USA-Israel conspiracy, but maybe its twin.

True, for a few days back there in September 2001 our neutral observers were choked with simply human simple emotions that I prefer to leave to your imagination given that their speedy-as-light flipflop leaves me in all my united states of indignation and riposte. But they had no problem switching right back into rational mode. And how do they rationalize in their elegant European minds circulating among the stone façades of centuries of exemplary civilization? Well they reason just like the Arab street! It's so cute. The kids from the CNRS [Centre national de recherché scientifique in case you don't know] with their slingshots, side by side with public radio journalists in raggedy t-shirts, brave boys standing up to those over-armed warmongering Americans, unilateralist and haughtily indifferent to the international institutions which alone have the right to act and then only in an emergency and within the rules and with the agreement of all parties to the conflict.

Ici Saudi Arabia, the downtrodden masses *vous parlent*. Yes but Americans don't know how to pick up a phone and say *allô j'écoute*. Walled up in their arrogance, driven by hegemonic ambitions, drunk on cocacola, enriched by the poverty of others, bloated with greenhouse emissions, and endowed with the brains of a second grader here they come terrorizing us yes <u>terrorizing</u> us with their goose-stepping march over the living bodies of this wonderful multicolor world, *la gloire de nos pères*. Here in Europe we know how to live together with our differences, here we reach out body-and-soul to the 4 corners of the earth. We know how to treat problems and people with respect *m'sieu*. And we will not allow, let this be clear, we will not allow any hasty operations. And the simple folk hooked up to the program call in to say forcefully and with the help of English words that burn their tongues: *halte au cowboy, le monde n'est pas un saloon*.

The Yanks don't have a clue. We understand everything, including the Americans. They've been traumatized. Poor things. Thinking they were invulnerable (dummies) they went doodiddling down the highway while we were trudging along bent under the weight of History and bearing monuments to the war dead in the hearts of our villages. We've seen it all, had it all, and we don't want anymore. Just give us our *vendanges*, our peasants, our church towers and feisty labor unions... and a rocking chair on the front porch.

9/11 in case you didn't get it was a tragedy. A tragedy (as in Greek tragedy, y'see? so there's no way of escaping from European culture even when you're a dumb American—and most likely Chinese to boot—thinking you're so smart to be slaving away in a stockbroker's office on the 99th floor of a skyscraper so skyscraping it's literally begging to be brought down.) What do they mean, a tragedy? The tragic loss of every single person assassinated in cold blood that day, yes, a tragedy for the grieving families. But these multiple, immeasurable, incomparable tragedies are the consequences of an act of war.

And that's what they want to cover up with the seemingly innocent tragedy label. When tragedy strikes you shed a tear, heave a sigh, shrug your shoulders and go on to the horse race results. An act of war demands a response. And the French today don't want to know about it. Iraq? Terra incognita. Vast country shot through with underground tunnels stuffed with fatal illnesses ready for delivery, terra dolorosa where the screams of the tortured get no hearing from the associated bleeding hearts, a people oppressed by the millions but holding no interest for our ideologically drunk NGOs... An imminent danger. Reduced, in the French mind, to a stub. They know nothing about Iraq and they definitely do not want to know anything more. Imminent danger? Prove it! Imminent danger? Not enough. We want an obvious danger. We, the champions of abstraction, we want a palpable danger. Okay, if Saddam keeps his word, like if he reduces Israel to a pile of ashes, then we might believe what you're claiming but until then you're nothing but warmongers.

Why try to prove that an imminent intervention is justified when you can have such a good time fooling around with 3 thousand innocent victims? A *France Inter* journalist (8-9 AM newscast, 8 Sept.) tossed them into a mass grave: one layer of WTC dead, one layer of Afghan civilians "killed by American bombs," one layer of Middle East victims, "2 000 dead, of which ¾ are Palestinian," and a layer of quicklime— "victims (Afghan, Palestinian) whose death is not commemorated, victims that don't get the benefits of media coverage." A Senegalese journalist (*Radio France Internationale* this weekend) explains that there was real empathy in his country for the 9/11 victims at first, but when everyone started talking about Islamism that was too much, if it was going to be a war against Islam, no, not for them. Because there's a detail that may be missed by those who don't know how to listen to the people, the street, the oppressed and *tutti quanti*: in Islamism there's Islam, so don't be surprised to hear that Arab-Muslims do not accept the hooking on of this ism... and they won't accept its slicing off. *C'est clair, non?*

Anyway the cause of the 11 September tragedy is the worldwide *fracture sociale*. There are no culprits, no enemy, no anti-Western political agenda, no hostile project aimed at democratic nations, and nothing to worry you and me as long as we are broad minded Europeans, gentlemen and gentlewomen you can talk to because you know we will listen, with whom you play by the rules because you know we won't ever make the slightest misstep. We are simple workers and peasants on strike, the salt of the earth, we like sports and hunting and visiting historical monuments. And we understand your despair. Do whatever you want to those arrogant, reckless Americans, handmaidens of Israel. Take note: we do not go along with their crazy shenanigans. We're not silly little Blairie follow-the-leaders! Look, we're not crying over their ultraliberal casualties perched up in the tops of the towers of arrogant capitalism, we absolutely do not condone or collaborate in their thoughtless action against a Muslim country, victim of an unjust embargo that is killing thousands of children every day—and we said it a long time ago already, Iraq, arms inspections, the embargo, we're tired of it, wrap it up and throw it in the garbage and let's get on with business—and that's why we are saying today if Iraq bothers you, call the UN, send in the inspectors, of course they have to accept the inspectors as we've always said, and keep their hands off weapons of mass destruction if they happen to have any but it's hardly likely.

This is linguistic mass murder. The words aren't connected to each other and have no connection with reality. Words are piled up as ramparts against reality. And the more meaningless the words the more there's talk of talking. Again today we get the 9/11 lesson (*France Inter*, 1-2 PM newscast, interview with 3 of the 11 filmmakers who took part in that collective film we can't miss): we have to learn to respect each other in spite of our differences, we have to talk to each other. Who started this fashion of marshmallow-coated bombs? And then they wonder why I insist on putting quotes in English in the middle of my French texts?

"The United States government has made a decision that it will not permit either mass terror by Baghdad or random terror by the many Palestinian militias to set the norms of how others, in the region and beyond, live or die. This is the critical principle underlying our Iraqi policy and our Palestinian policy. It is, at root, a statement about how we define civilization and how we defend it from its unconventionally armed discontents."

Martin Peretz, "The New Bush Doctrine / Son Shine." *The New Republic*, 9 September '02

I read that, I remember who I am, where I come from, what has to be done. Courage.

Then when the dust has settled, when I've finished hollering back at all those pious voices telling Americans to wake up before it's too late and learn their lesson from this "tragedy," I realize that in all this river of thought there wasn't the slightest mention of the European welcome mat held out to the authors of this forfeit, complete with room & board & laundering. And one absence leading to another I notice that this winter's top tune –"The whereabouts of Osama bin Laden remains a mystery"—has fallen off the French media hit parade. No surprise. His Al Qaeda colleagues can't even pull him out of hiding for a glitzy book signing party, a chic UNESCO cocktail party. So if you follow the logic built up and hammered into your head on French public radio and you figure that if only these terribly reasonable people were allowed to run the world instead of Americans so arrogant that they deserve to die in the most horrible suffering, the whereabouts of Osama bin Laden and Mullah Omar would be no mystery. Because they would still be riding high in Afghanistan, aided and abetted by taliban super-ruffians, and regularly invited to sumptuous international peace conferences... preferably held in Paris.

SPME Faculty Forum[6]

LETTER TO THE EDITOR / *IHT*

"For the world's Muslims, a special night, a magical night"
IHT 9 Dec. 2002 / from *The Daily Star,* Beirut

Is this supposed to be cute? Or maybe it's part of the worldwide reconciliation movement wherein distinguished newspapers and magazines in democratic countries make demure little curtsies to the dark forces gathering on the horizon?

Jesy Chahine invites us into the Oriental mysteries of *Lailat al-Qadr.* In a deep, dark, mounting crescendo of Orientalism we are lead step by step into the mysteries of this awesome Muslim holiday, a night-long ecstasy of fervent prayer, a night when the fervor of true believers is rewarded with celestial cleansing of sin.

And finally we reach the summits. "Although every *Lailat al-Qadr* is sacred, some are more memorable than others." Bilal, a student at the American University in Beirut, recounts the February 4, 1997 Night of Destiny when two Israeli helicopters entering Lebanese airspace crashed, killing 73 Israeli soldiers. The true believers shouted "God is great!" and left the mosque at dawn, "cleansed of their sins and reborn."

Isn't that just one beautiful spiritual lesson of peace and goodwill brought to you unblemished from Syrian occupied Beirut?

And how about the mysterious magical cleansing night of fervent prayer and forgiveness of sins in the last ten days of Ramadan 2002? Was its fervor intensified by the deaths of Africans and Israelis in a hotel in Mombassa? Would it have been even more holy if two missiles hadn't missed their target? Or did *Lailat al-Qadr* fall—uneventfully—this year.

I know of a religion that teaches that we must not rejoice in the deaths of our enemies. Apparently the *IHT* doesn't. So you don't understand why I find this article inappropriate, distasteful, and dishonest.

FRANCE CAN BE PROUD OF HER MEDIEVAL UNIVERSITIES

23 December 2002

France can be proud of her medieval universities... if they remain back in the past where history left them... When they bring medieval methods into the 21st century, it is shameful.

The *Conseil d'Adminstration* (governing body) of Paris VI-l'université Pierre et Marie Curie made a quantum leap into obscurantism this week by launching a backhanded boycott of Israeli academics in the form of a motion requesting that the European Union refuse to renew the EU-Israel cooperation agreement that expires in 2003. The Paris VI board is spearheading a university-wide boycott campaign by taking the issue to the Conference of Presidents of French Universities. News sources report that Paris VII will sign on in the first week of January.

To fully understand the extent of this disgrace, take a look at what Paris VI encompasses: l'École nationale supérieure de chimie de Paris, parts of the Jussieu and Orsay Faculties, and a handful of teaching hospitals (Pitié-Salpétrière, Broussais-Hôtel-Dieu, Saint-Antoine.) Scientists!

The motion passed by the Paris VI administration blames the Israeli occupation for preventing Palestinian colleagues in Gaza and the West Bank from teaching and doing research. Further, it claims that renewal of the EU-Israel cooperation agreement would amount to tacit support of current Israeli policy, in violation of the very terms of the agreement which explicitly states that relations between the parties are based on respect for human rights and democratic principles. The motion enjoins Israeli colleagues to take a clear stand on the treatment of Palestinian faculty and students, and authorizes Paris VI president Gilbert Béréziat to make contacts with Israeli and Palestinian university authorities, and spur efforts for peace. Yes, they manage to drag in the password: peace. Anything goes as long as it claims to aim for peace.

That's how it stands as France drags its way through the last days of the year 2002: burning synagogues is (temporarily) out, beating up Jews here and there is stable, and persecuting Israel, Israeli-sympathizers, and anyone who refuses to persecute Israel is definitely IN. Publishing companies compete to bring out the most ferociously perversely anti-Zionist books, intellectuals stand in line to spit on anything remotely connected to Jews and/or Israel and, when the community stands up for itself, the invectives start flying—paranoia, extremism, repression of free speech, Islamophobia, and all the rest.

But this call for boycott from Paris VI is causing an uproar that will not be stifled, and it is certainly not limited to the Jewish community. Paris VI has gone too far. The motion is so spiteful, hateful, and blatantly political, a mockery of university democracy, a betrayal of the principles of academic freedom, and a disgrace to the values of scientific research. Voices that count are speaking out and full-scale action is being organized despite the Christmas break.

Speaking on *Radio Shalom* this evening Gideon Kurtz (the accredited French-Israeli journalist thrown out of the *Sommet de la francophonie* in Beirut last month) broadened the scope of the debate by reminding that boycotters can be boycotted. Especially when they are scientists working on international projects. Colleagues from certain enlightened countries may start cutting ties when they get word about the abstruse discriminatory nonsense oozing out of this Pierre and Marie Curie University. *N'est-ce pas?*

Reliable sources insist that the French government is firmly opposed to this boycott. I believe them. But we won't sit on our hands and wait to see how they will counter it. The poison is spreading fast.

SPME Daily Digest

DEMONSTRATION SHEMONSTRATION
6 January 2003

The demonstration was a success! *A los cincos de la tarde...* thousands of people gathered at the feet of the shamefully ugly Jussieu campus, a complex of shabby asbestos-ridden buildings where parts of Paris VI and Paris VII are miserably installed. Braving freezing temperatures and a sharp wind we came to listen to a rich array of intelligent, sometimes brilliant speakers, and to join them in saying no to the ignominious boycott of Israeli scholars and scientists. Squads of CRS in full riot dress stood between the vast crowd of peaceable academic type people and a small group of hostile hissers pushed up against the bars of a campus gate, hissing "Bush Sharon assassins, assassins, Bush Sharon assassins assassins." Our heads are still reeling from the ghastly news of the murder-bomber attack in Tel Aviv last night, our ears are tuned to strong words from courageous people on the podium, and this bunch of hate mongers huddled behind the gate like self-imprisoned beasts never stop hissing and howling. They have no words, no ideas, no arguments, no flags, no allegiance, only self-righteous buzz.

I don't have official figures yet but there must have been at least three thousand people demonstrating against the boycott and for Israel, against narrow-minded nasty antisemitism and for scientific integrity, courage, hope and yes, someday, peace. I stood on the fringes of the filled-to-overflowing Jussieu Square, and took my place in an assembly of eminently civilized people that could have been instantly transposed to any international congress of learned men and women.

I arrived late—a previous engagement that could not be rescheduled—and missed fine speeches by the likes of Alain Finkielkraut and Pierre Lellouche, but just in time to hear Alexandre Adler call out loud and clear in his booming operatic voice: we are not afraid of antisemites. And boycotts don't work. They didn't even work in Nazi Germany. They had to arrest the Jews, torture them, force them to sign over their property, they had to deport the Jews, they had to steal Jewish property. Other speakers—Bernard-Henri Levy, D. Assouline representing the mayor of Paris, Roger Cukierman president of the CRIF—spoke words that the Paris VI *Conseil d'Administration* should have been ashamed to hear. There were messages from Jack Lang, Claude Lanzman, distinguished professors, world-renowned scientists, and there was a feeling of quiet pride. I looked around me. Many of the people were my age, they had lived through the Shoah, and even the youngest among us had seen films and photos of Jews like us, well dressed ladies and gentlemen who had been leading thoughtful well-constructed lives. And suddenly... no, very gradually, almost imperceptibly to many, the ground was chipped away under their feet and then, yes, suddenly they found themselves gathered together in tragic haste, standing together, dismayed, right here in Paris, in a square like this, this Place de Jussieu. With their suitcases. Then bussed away, interned, deported, gassed or tortured and killed slowly.

Adler said "we are not afraid of antisemites." The hissers could be heard in the background. A half-dozen flags—French, Israeli, and Jewish Defense League—were brandished in the Square, a few discreet signs poked up in the crowd, our sweet security service boychicks dressed in black with red armbands were a reassuring presence and the CRS were there to protect us just in case the Jussieu rowdies tried any thuggery... but we were in the thousands and they prefer to gang up against lone disarmed victims. We braved the icy cold, craned our necks to get a view of the podium, basked in the warm familiar voice of the moderator, Shlomo Malka, author of a biography of Emmanuel Levinas and president of *Radio Communauté Juive*. Further out on the edges of the demonstration a thin lightskin black guy wearing a campesino cap doggedly tried to peddle his shoddy ideological merchandise to a group of women who, you can be sure, have read a hundred books and a thousand Net postings on the subject. Voices rang out from the podium, unanimously decrying the shameful boycott, tearing away the pseudo-humanitarian mask of its perpetrators. Bernard Henri-Levy reminded us that to this day the French universities have still not expressed repentance for the exclusion of Jews under the Vichy government. The police, the church, the bus and railroad companies have come forth to admit their crimes and ask forgiveness. Not the universities. Campesino didn't hear a word of this. All but one of the women gave up on him and blended back into the crowd. Old friends and colleagues met and formed little circles of conversation. People who had never seen each other before exchanged quiet comments, agreed and disagreed with the fine points of one or another speaker, applauded discreetly or wholeheartedly. There was a feeling of relief. This ignoble deed was not triumphant, it was shameful. And the shame was brought out into the open, into the public square.

This demonstration, the flow of letters and articles, and more than 22,000 signatures to the anti-boycott petition added up to a moment of hope, a fleeting moment of believing we might actually turn the tide here in France, bring this country to its senses. We are brought up short by the announcement that someone had set fire to the car of Gabriel Fahri, the rabbi who was stabbed in his synagogue Friday afternoon. Where will we find the battalions to oppose this relentless hatred? The hissers have not stopped. But no one can deprive us of this feeling of quiet pride. We were standing up for Israel by standing up for ourselves and it was the same thing. We came in large numbers to the public square, the organizers (UEJF, CRIF, Filles et Fils des déportés, MNEF) had set up a professional podium and invited intelligent speakers who came with carefully constructed arguments to defend clear and noble values with a supplement of oratorical talent straight from the heart. This is our way: no compact masses marching behind blaring sound trucks, no huge garish gas balloons, no idiotic slogans blasted out for kilometers.

The CRS surround us, politely ask us to move into the Square or disperse. We leave reluctantly, frozen to the bone, feeling a bit guilty about not staying to the very end. We walk all the way around the back of the Jussieu campus. Desolation. It looks like a communist era factory. The waters of the Seine are icy black, the wind whips at us, trains rumble along the quai heading for Gare d'Austerlitz, everything takes on a sinister cast. Finally we are on the other side of the river, moving up into the genteel streets of Saint Paul, past the elegant Place des Vosges that has taken on the sheen of an ice skating rink, and home again to our warm interior, our well ordered lives. Our uneasy stability.

And where was the Conseil d'administration of Paris VI all this time? Where was the president? Lurking half-hidden on the fringes of a sixth story window, looking down on the demonstration and thinking vile thoughts? Skulking behind closed shutters in a bourgeois apartment and mumbling curses against us? Standing bare-breasted on the ice cold banks of the Seine, crying I have erred, forgive me? Or perhaps feasting on dates in lush chambers at the nearby *Institut du Monde Arabe*?

No my friends, Paris VI was on its website lying through its teeth. A message from the *Etoile-liante* was waiting in my inbox when I got home, chilled to the bone. I clicked on the link and found myself virtually on the front lawn of Université Pierre et Marie Curie/ *Actualités/ Communiqué de la Présidence/ au jour d'aujourd'hui*. Where we discover that the whole thing was a bad dream. What boycott? (And, follow my logic, what demonstration?) The communiqué has spread fast; sardonic comments from a host of friends and correspondents are pouring into my inbox and clinking as I write this.

Who do they think they're fooling?

The president of Paris VI claims with a straight face that on the 16th of December 2002, at the request of some of its members, the Paris VI board took a look at the academic situation in Palestine [sic]. And needless to say but making sure to say it in the very next sentence of the communiqué, the board rejects out of hand the idea of any such thing as a boycott or even a moratorium on their relations with Israeli universities. They simply asked the president to go and visit colleagues in Israeli and Palestinian universities and see what they could do about making some peace.

Then comes a statement of principle. *La Présidence* draws itself up straight and tall, sniffs contemptuously through slightly flared nostrils, and wishes to remind you that it (he? they?) is firmly opposed to any and all infringement on academic freedom and all acts of terrorism from all sides. In other words the all too familiar underhanded evenhandedness which is chillingly similar to Arafat's ritual condemnation of suicide bombings.

The communiqué concludes by claiming that the University hopes the European Union framework accord can be extended to the Palestinian entity, and is already busy developing detailed programs for academic collaboration with Israeli and Palestinian universities.

Can you believe it? Bald faced lies. Can you believe it? Tens of thousands of signatures on the petition, hundreds of letters, a mathematician from Princeton cancels his visiting professorship to Paris VI, emeritus professors write heartfelt letters, Nobel prize winning scientists make scathing scorning scolding declarations, scientists threaten to pack up their laboratories, with test tubes, budding researchers, and million dollar funding, and hightail it out of Paris VI and all of this based on nothing. Worse than nothing. A vile rumor spread by...well, if it must be said, by Jews.

Isn't that the subtext of the Paris VI communiqué? Motion, what motion? Boycott? No such thing! *La Présidence* of Paris VI is all peace and love and his (her?) heart goes out in equal parts to Israeli and Palestinian colleagues and all is for the best in...

The boycott motion was an outrage. Pretending it never existed is suicidal. Yes, *la Présidence* of a French university has invented a new form of intellectual suicide attack. Anything, even shamefaced silence, would have been better than this silk and ruffles hypocritical LIE. The Seine is rising and threatens to spill over its banks, and Paris VI has sunk to the depths of ignominy. Where is the strong hand of integrity that can wipe out this shame?

Israel Hasbara Committee

Chapter 4/ Intifada, Antisemitism, Anti-war

WAR & PEACE & THE JEWS
19 January 2003

They fell into my inbox on the same day—the bigboss virus and an antiwar petition—but it was simply a coincidence. My in-house super engineer gave bigboss a kick in the pants and sent him flying back into cyberspace, leaving my precious treasures unharmed. As for the antiwar petition, I had to handle that myself. It was forwarded by a Jewish friend. Jewish and what's more Polish and after that Israeli and even a bit American and now living here in my neighborhood. We have known each other for decades. We don't share the same opinions. Friendships can endure in spite of explosive contradictions. But perhaps not forever.

I was not surprised that she had signed the petition fielded by Swedes and zipped around the world by e-mail, but I was astonished that she would send it to me. I trashed it so fast I hardly can remember the details. It was not dangerous like bigboss but I don't want useless messages piling up in an inbox that already requires heroic filing efforts. It said that the Americans were going to attack Iraq and set off the third world war. I think the petitioners were asking the UN to prevent this catastrophe from occurring.

Okay, for the sake of accuracy let me check this out in my trashcan.

It's a bit more garbled than I remembered. The petition claims the US wants to declare war. And the world is so unstable that this might set off the 3rd World War. The UN suggests that opponents to this dastardly war should sign and send this petition (where? not to Baghdad for sure). And even if you don't want to sign it, please pass it on to your friends. My friend's signature stands proudly at the end of a list of hundreds and just after a dozen Israeli names.

Something like 80% of the French people questioned in a recent poll are opposed to the war against Iraq. How could it be otherwise when the press feeds them nothing but tasteless porridge, ideological sermons disguised as news, and pep rally hurrahs for the brave French president who dares to stand up to Bush. You want them to be for this military operation when they haven't got a clue to what is going on in Iraq and couldn't care less? While the inspectors are snooping around in Iraq the French press is preening itself in the mirror mirror on the wall: *tell me that Iraq doesn't have any WMDs at all*. And the mirror replies: *you are the fairest of them all, peace-loving rational leaders of the civilized world*. When the inspectors stumble upon a little stock of chemical warheads how could this perturb a public opinion convinced that the danger comes not from warheads but from warmongers. The danger *chers compatriotes* lies not in evil but in the mouth of the upstart who dared speak of the axis of evil.

Even our Jewish radio, our darling Jewish radio that we are hooked up to six days a week and yearning for on the Sabbath, is talking about *bruits de bottes en Iraq* (echoes of German troops marching roughshod through Europe). That, and calling ticking bomb terrorists *kamikazes*, are two of the most irritating French copouts at the moment. How can you describe the forthcoming American operation in Iraq as *bruit de bottes*. Where are the goose-stepping battalions *s'il vous plaît*?

Officially the French position is: we don't do anything unless the UN tells us to. And the citizens, deeply relieved, go about their business, worry about small nuisances, shed a few tears for the homeless and the unemployed, plan winter and summer vacations and who would blame them. Isn't life to be lived, and all the more so in this beautiful country blessed by man and nature? It used to be you had to ask the *curé*, now you ask the UN. And don't ask yourself who exactly is the UN and where is the slightest proof of its probity. Satisfied with the comforting feeling that somewhere up there, not all the way to heaven because we don't believe in things like that anymore, but up there somewhere is the UN, a higher authority that stands head and shoulders above the bevy of squabbling nations and, like the Church, accumulates power and wealth while claiming to be angelically free of material interests.

The unscrupulous Americans want to get their hands on Iraqi oil? The holy UN wants oil to be distributed like the fish and the loaves, miraculously. And the petitioners claim that the UN in person suggested they proclaim their opposition to this American declaration of war. Where exactly are they proclaiming it? To the high heavens, perhaps. Or to some Saudi backed propaganda operation, more likely. Anyway, let them proclaim. It's nothing but gesticulation.

Gently rocked in the arms of a reassuring government cuddled by a subservient press, the public is not hearing the tiny sirens that go off from time to time in the very heart of the lullaby. The military operation against Iraq is inevitable and the French government has to stop siding with Iraq very soon if they don't want to be caught on the losing side. Their participation will be no less theoretical than their opposition. So be it. What puzzles me is how a Jewish friend could send me a petition claiming that the Americans are going to declare war.

I am shaking my head in dismay. Totalitarian savagery is breathing down our necks and the dragon slayers want to disable the knight in shining armor. We are being attacked on all sides, and the petitioners and the peace mongers want to pet the fiery dragon and say nice doggie. And if that doesn't calm him, then throw him a bone. Israel, for example. Why not? Isn't that better than starting the 3rd World War? Does anyone want to know what our enemies are planning? Help yourself. He has no secrets. Not only can you find out who they want to kill and how and why, you can even get their recipes. Right on the Net. Do you want to see how they kill people? This time around the scenes of horrendous torture and murder are not hidden behind the high walls of death camps, they are out in the open. You can see them on TV. You did see them on TV.

It's the same old story. The ravaging barbarian hordes sweeping through towns and villages. Rape, plunder, massacres. Terror. Untold suffering. Rivers of blood. Atrocities. One thousand years later you can still cry your heart out when you read tales of these inhuman calamities. There can be no distance between me and a human being slaughtered at the hands of these monsters. It is monotonously the same old story. There are a limited number of ways of torturing, killing, defiling. But the number of victims is staggering. Hundreds of thousands, millions of human beings viciously murdered at each onslaught of this same scourge.

And today the peace-loving people who have always been victims of the barbarian hordes can fight back. We are not unarmed and defenseless. We have learned from history. We have assumed our contradictions. Overcome our inhibitions. Yes, I can love peace and develop ultra sophisticated weapons. Yes I can be a peaceful, rational, thoughtful human being and maintain a fully equipped high tech military. And appreciate that army, be grateful for that army. So now you know why there will never be heaven on earth: people wouldn't want it. They wouldn't recognize it. There would be a surplus of ideologists to convince them not to enjoy it. Give us paradise with all the trimmings and the paradise trashers would step up and convince people that this life is no good, the better life is after you're dead, when you can have illness, disease, robberies, tornadoes, automobile accidents, stock market crashes.

The same merciless barbarians who have been plaguing humanity since the earliest days are out to murder us again and well-intentioned people are preaching pacifism. They want the beautifully armed democracies to drop their guns and surrender. French people often attempt to mitigate the shame of the collaboration by explaining that Hitler's tanks rolled right over the border and into Paris, there was no way the French army could defend the country. And today, when all they have to do is whisper a word of faint encouragement to the GIs and stop talking as if George W. Bush were the greatest threat to world peace, they rise up proudly and say no war.

When this don't-hurt-a-fly logic is applied to a question like health it gives the no transfusions, no antibiotics, no surgery, no harsh treatments of any sort policy that leads to glorious decrepitude and precocious death. I interrupted this essay to visit my dentist. It was not particularly amusing and I spare you the details. When you calculate the wasted time, the pain and discomfort, and the extravagant cost, how can you not sign a petition against dentists interfering with peaceful decaying teeth? I can see the screen clearly today because my ophthalmologist removed a cataract two years ago. Another hefty bill, throwing away money that could have been spent on beautiful clothes and accessories, travel, gifts for my loved ones, instead of which I paid someone to cut into my eye. What is the difference between Jack the Ripper and a surgeon who cuts open your abdomen to remove an inflamed appendix? What's the difference between an Algerian Islamic terrorist who rips open the belly of a pregnant peasant, and an obstetrician who does a cesarean? These sound like stupid questions but I feel that I am surrounded by people who can't answer them. They don't know the difference between a murderer and a legitimate soldier. Because both kill, they think they are the same.

And as a result they call for their own defenseless destruction. And think they are saving the world.

In our day, when every image of the Shoah has been shamefully boomeranged against us, at a time when demonstrators can march down French boulevards carrying signs on which the *magen david* is equated with the swastika, we are not only deprived of decent respect for the victims of that extermination, we are also deprived of our own valid arguments drawn from that experience. But no matter how our enemies twist and turn those lessons into knives to slit our throats today, we are not mouthing hypocritical slogans when we say: never again.

Then what do we mean by this never again? We mean not only words but action. Obviously my antiwar friends believe that this never again can be assured with 100% pure actions. I wish they were right. All of reality, all of history proves them to be wrong. Would fiction help? A sort of collage that I see in 3-dimensions with stunning reality.

A Polish shtetl in 1942. Why not Przemysl, where my father was born. The Einsatzgruppen and their Polish henchmen have finished off the neighboring town and, on their way to Lvov, they plan to stop in Przemysl. And kill men, women, and children. In the most atrocious fashion. And deport the "survivors" to nearby Oswiecem. Routine. It's become as natural as a harvest. Good-natured, hard drinking, husky peasants and brave Nazi soldiers doing what has to be done. So sure of themselves, of their rightful domination, of their indomitable power, that it wouldn't even occur to them to be on the alert as they pass from their last killing ground and make way at daybreak for Przemysl.

Surprise! US Marines swoop down upon the advancing column and wipe it out. Forgive me, there is something childish about this dream, this just short of divine intervention. But my father, *olav ha shalom*, was a Marine and I was a child past the age of reason. They wouldn't send him to the front, because of his age and his four children, but he wanted to fight the Nazis and in this dream I give him his chance. He is in the platoon that attacks the Jew-killers who were on their way to Przemysl. His cousins are not herded like beasts into the forest, stripped, shot point blank on the edge of the mass grave, covered with quicklime, with earth, their lives stifled, their voices still choking in our throats. They are not murdered, they live, and I am not an orphan in Europe.

And the American troops, instead of winning the war slowly and at great cost in human lives, win it quickly, almost in a flash, with fantastic weapons and overwhelming military superiority. And the American government makes the rescue of Europe's Jews a priority instead of a hush hush while we're at it task. And my Jewish friends in Europe would not be remnants, they would be loaded down with more family than you could handle, running off to bar mitzvahs in Budapest and weddings in Warsaw.

How could you not wish it had turned out that way? Well of course you do, my friend who sent me the petition, because that was in the past and you know how it turned out and you suffered unbearable loss in your own life because it didn't turn out that way. The Americans didn't get there soon enough.

Today they are ready and willing to get there ahead of time. So the antiwarriors won't hear of it. The World Trade Center attack? Oh, that was a year ago. What has he done to us lately? Besides, Saddam Hussein didn't sign that one. So how can you prove what he was going to do if you have the good fortune of stopping him before he could do it? The antiwarriors want proof. Just as they would have asked for proof, as the Einsatzgruppen trundled along from one shtetl to the next, that they really intended to massacre all the Jews there as well.

And even when they get the proof they pretended to want, they turn it down. Last fall the official French position was: no to Bushy unilateralism. Take the question to the UN. To their great surprise, Bush brought the question to the UN, where the French did their best to undermine his efforts to put real teeth into the resolution. Nevertheless the antiwarrior camp swore by inspections. They got inspections and for the past month you would think there was a journalist under every inspector's collar. The rallying cry was: they haven't found anything... which proves there is nothing to find. And every holier than thou antiwarrior had personally read the 12,000 page report and concluded that, there again, no news is good news. Now the inspectors are saying that something is fishy. The other day they found some very rich material on enriching uranium stashed away in the home of a respectable Iraqi scientist but that won't faze the antiwarriors because nothing proves that the gentleman actually intended to enrich uranium. And by the way, where is Oussama bin Laden? And what do you intend to do about North Korea?

The wriggling-out tunnel is endless. The operation against Iraq will be over and let us hope well-done, and the tunnelers will still be underground.

I just opened a book to check on the spelling of Einsatzgruppen, and came upon a murky photo of Jews beaten to death in a public square by Ukrainians in 1941. The image superimposed in my mind with the unbearable aftermath of a terrorist attack in Israel, torn bodies in a lake of blood. And bystanders—then the local folks, today the TV audience—looking on with blind eyes.

Israel Hasbara Committee

A NATION OF PRIESTS
20 February 2003

One short phrase sums up in my mind the current stance of France and her cronies on the troubled world stage: *une nation de prêtres*. Once again a notion is borrowed from our Jewish heritage—"And you will be *a nation of priests...*"— only to be denatured and turned against us.

France has been taking itself for the world's conscience; it is the ringleader of its *inconscience*. So proud to lead the peace battalions, gloating and self-congratulating, full speed ahead with its Gaullian nose stuck up to the heavens, France is heading straight for the wall. I don't hesitate to predict that when the military operation begins in earnest (all kinds of brilliant commentators here are still talking as if they could stop it) the French will have to relent and go along, dragging their feet, twisting their tongues in confused explanations, getting wrapped up in a volley of turncoat flipflops... and the fun will be over. The government will get the flack it deserves from a misled population, and when the social, economic, and political consequences of this monumental error hit home, the same demonstrators who were marching against the war will be in the streets crying poor, defending retirement pensions and medical care, wailing about unemployment and lost buying power...

All of this is particularly painful to me because I am American. Not the 9/11 kind of American convert overflowing with compassion as the twin towers exploded and collapsed—oh the poor things now they know what it is to suffer—and not American by marriage with Hollywood, Nikes, and fast food. American because my grandparents ran away from Europe (before the First World War), found refuge and opportunity in the United States, and saved a branch of the family from perishing in the Shoah. Thanks to them and the American Way of Life I had the luxury of... well, of coming (back) to Europe.

We who have been trying to defend Israel against a relentless campaign of delegitimization have been trying to tell our compatriots that the semantic sabotage associated with this smear campaign would not stop there. I see the consequences today in the mental confusion of European pacifism: a bundle of ideas that are as full of holes as a ragged sweater. And these European commentators and politicians who take themselves so seriously remind me of rabble-rousing soapbox orators. The kind you see at Speaker's Corner in Hyde Park. They know better than everyone, they can solve all the world's problems, their theories are 100% perfect... as long as they fit onto the upended surface of a soapbox. If you push their logic a few centimeters further it goes over the edge and disappears.

Can diplomacy be practiced that way... on a soapbox?

The latest bright idea (but by the time you read this there will be others) of the immobilist camp is to admit that military pressure—American of course—is in fact an essential element of the inspections system. BUT that's no reason to rush into action. Haste makes waste you know. We should give the inspectors all the time they want and need and then some. They'll find something sooner or later and in that case, yes, we'll have to go to war... under a UN mandate of course...and that too will take a good chunk of time... In the meantime, what are some 200,000 battle ready American troops supposed to do? Polish the silverware?

America with all its hegemony and state of the art weapons is going to take orders from... France? France and her buddies, countries with no military means, no strategy, and no determination are going to give orders to the American army? Tell them when to move and when to stay still? A few European countries, cheered on by their street—yes, now we have the European street running parallel to or maybe intersecting the famous Arab street—are the Masters, and the Americans will be their obedient servants and nobody on this side of the Atlantic realizes that this is utterly unthinkable. What is this supposed to be? Post-modern realpolitik? Who changed the realities of balance of power?

But reality has no place in this discourse: the most unbelievable ideas are turned into fervent beliefs, time and space shrink to nearly nothing, the citizens are disoriented, and the more they're flattered into thinking they're the salt of the earth, the more rude will be the awakening.

Men may be born equal but they don't die equal.

War is terrible, moan the hand-wringers. You don't rush into war that way without giving it a thought. There will be civilian victims. Enter the victims: massive urban bombardments, whole neighborhoods reduced to rubble, gaunt orphans roaming deserted streets. We know what war is, they say, and we don't want any more war.

So what became of the starving Iraqi children, victims of a merciless ridiculous embargo? *Stop the inspections, there's nothing left to inspect. Let bygones be bygones.* Where are the hospitals with no medical supplies, the professors selling their scholarly books on street corners to buy a crust of bread?

Vanished. Because today we must have inspections to disarm Saddam Hussein by peaceful means. *Chase away that disgraceful dictator but please we beg of you, no war.* They don't give a damn for the real suffering imposed on Iraqis by their despot; what makes the *nation des prêtres* cry are the imagined victims of American bombs. Unless the poor souls die under a UN mandate. Unable to come up with a greater European foreign policy these Europeans swear by the UN. Unwilling to defend our democratic values, Europe raises to the rank of *Grand Prêtre* a UN largely discredited by its own words and deeds.

The UN, they say, because we must respect international law (a pure invention but never mind). And the Axis of Good lines up proud and tall. Belgium, rich in congolesque adventures, grants itself a <u>universal</u> right to judge... and applies it to <u>one single country</u>: Israel. But these unilateral final-judgers breathe fire over the shameful unilateralism of Uncle Sam. Russia, struggling to change the course of a long history of tyrannies, still fresh with memories of the glorious Soviet era with its pileup of gulags, mass murder, conquest and oppression, takes sides with the peace camp but for how long? Germany, all-categories champion in 20th century barbarity, seems to be embarrassed to death by something that forcibly recalls the war against democracy so recently undertaken by one of their own. China, model of respect for international and domestic order, recently awakened form its cultural revolution and assorted mao-mao exploits, poses for the group photo with an enigmatic smile. And our sweet lovely France, with her dom-toms, and scattered ex- colonies, sets the tone. Our president solemnly declares that Saddam Hussein must be disarmed but nothing can justify forced regime change. *Ça ne se fait pas.* That's not done

Except perhaps in Côte d'Ivoire where France chose to sidestep explicit defense agreements with an elected government (casting doubt on the legitimacy of Gbagbo's election while turning a blind eye to flagrant cheating in other African countries) and came up with chic little peaceful means to impose regime change by inviting the president to Paris for peace talks and serving him up to an armed rebellion backed by foreign agitators. A Marcoussis-Kléber for Saddam Hussein? An international conference in Paris to solve the Middle East conflict? You give the defense and interior ministries to the rebels, step back, and let the sparks fly. That's the finesse of French diplomacy?

They tell me I should try to understand. Me, the American, I should understand that an ally is not a yes man. A good ally freely expresses disagreement with his partners. Yes, I understand. When it comes to meat laced with hormones Europe says no and I agree. And I would be delighted to see a US ban on those hormones that are remodeling the morphology of my countrymen along the lines of double breasted chickens and heavy uddered milk cows. But today we are talking about allies on the eve of a military conflict. What is an "ally" who digs in his heels and refuses to move when you are facing mortal danger? At the worst that's an enemy, at best a neutral.

An ally is not a yes man. Except if it happens to be a former Eastern bloc country standing at the door to the European Union, begging to be let in. How could they dare to step out of line and take sides with war-mongering America! President Chirac himself wagged his finger, scold-ed, humiliated, and gave them a good kick in the ass, warning them in no uncertain terms that they better shape up and do what they're told, fol-low orders with no questions asked. If not, the European street will fin-ish the job!

One of the dastardly motives attributed to Americans is the intention of smashing up the European Union because it stands in the way of their hunger for world domination. The war against Iraq is really a war against Europe, a tricky empire-building maneuver. Clever, isn't it? The French and the Germans (abetted by hang-on Belgium) struggling to hang on to their hegemony within the EU, undermine the Union and blame it on the good ol' USA. Now the damage is done. Former Eastern bloc countries recently liberated from the yoke of a dismal series of tyrannies might decide to pass on this not so great Greater Europe. Other configurations could be appealing. Why not two zones of influence, one Atlantic and the other Seine-ic?

The Americans, I am told, as if I'd never seen one as they really are, that is, the way the French imagine them, the Americans haven't experi-enced war in their own country. Okay, that's understandable, Europeans have a perfect right to throw in my face their majestic history that spar-kles with an uninterrupted (until just recently) parade of dazzling wars of stunning duration, record-breaking casualties, epic battle scenes, and all the rest. I should be ashamed of the miserable record of my native land. One civil war, count them, one! The Americans, they say, are trau-matized by that World Trade Center attack (they've decided to forget about the Pentagon, why?). Attacked on their own soil *pardi*! With the destruction of the Towers, their feeling of being safe at home collapsed.

So when is the last time they took a look at a crowd of Americans? Anywhere? In the street, on the campus, on TV, at the shopping mall: a nation of survivors. Refugees of all the world's wars. America, yes, if she is someone, stretched from coast to coast, from Canada to the Gulf of Mexico, her mountains and prairies, yes, she is more or less unharmed. But Americans? Haven't experienced war in flesh and blood on their own doorstep? Don't make me laugh.

But I should understand: Boush [French for Bush] and his team ha-ven't been able to convincingly state their case. Maybe so. But why is it that the same people marching against war are carrying posters for justice in "Palestine"? The guy who wants to try to get rid of Saddam Hussein's regime must be 100% pure. When it comes to this question, Europeans act like professors screening candidates for the *agrégation*. Nitpicking guardians of the citadel of knowledge, they close ranks and block all exits: only the finest will pass. They don't like Boush's speeches, they don't like Boush, and even when he's right they can't stomach him. There are no words too harsh for Rumsfeld and Ashcroft... puritanical, tyrannical, extreme right religious power freaks... don't be surprised if you hear them labeled *haredim*. Condoleeza Rice is a problem: being female and black she should appeal to the broad-spectrum Left but she's classified hawk. Rejected. That leaves Colin Powell, erstwhile young hopeful turned into a big disappointment. A total bore the other day at the UN listing all the peccadilloes of Poor L'il Saddam. Those Americans are so naïve it's a pity. Of course he's trying to fool the inspectors, what did they expect? That he'd throw open his closets and say here's my skeletons? You don't make war against a dictator just because he's dishonest!

Nothing the Americans say or do or are can find favor over here. Everything about them is simply repulsive: their arrogance, their hegemony, their economy, their over armed army that wants to kill others without getting killed themselves, their unilateralism, their attempts to drag the UN into this questionable adventure, their impatience... These severe judgments are coming from the same camp that balks at the idea of investigating use or possible misuse of EU funds donated to the Palestinian Authority and, again, the same who want to give the Palestinians a state without bothering their heads to know if it will be a budding democracy or a hideout for terrorists, without being the least bit perturbed by the means used by the Palestinians to get that state. Intifada? What do you expect! The deal offered at Camp David did not meet their expectations, they take up arms, it's perfectly normal, *la résistance*, okay we're not that crazy about "*kamikazes*" [French for human homicide bombers] but the solution is obvious: give them their state, empty the *colonies* [French for settlements], draw back to the '67 line and if things go well just keep on drawing back.

BUT it is forbidden to remodel the Middle East by violent warlike techniques. Everything must be done within the limits of international law. Europe desires from the bottom of its heart peaceful solutions to these conflicts that so worry us.

Don't we have the right to ask how that Middle East, cradle of humanity and of so much inhumanity was modeled in the first place? Syria, Lebanon, Jordan, Iraq, Iran, Egypt: who drew their frontiers and set up their governments if it wasn't European powers in the waning days of their hallmark empire colonialism?

And now we're touching the sensitive spot: imperial colonizing Europe. What splendor, what power, thunder of marching troops, clash of glinting sabers, ornately decorated haute couture uniforms, Republican Guards, chancelleries, battleships, military marches, brilliant strategists and specialists in the art of war. Today the three musketeers—France / Germany / Belgium—are tired. This Europe doesn't even want to hear about balance of power. Weary of realpolitik and temporarily comfortable in their little everyday lives, this Europe has dropped out. These peacefully disarmed countries are recycled. They've turned into NGOs! Isn't that the limit!

But their dreams of power are still afloat. So they take potshots at the *arriviste*, the former colony that grew up to be a great power: the USA. All the other conflicts on the face of the earth can stew, rot, be settled any slapdash way; all the strategies of all the countries in the world can be lopsided, slipshod, sinister, so what? Only one country has to toe the line: the USA. No, two countries: the USA and Israel. Do the Americans really exist for these Grand Inquisitors? They are so obsessed with Boush. What in the world is he up to? He's dumb (we are intelligent), simple-minded (and we are fluttering with subtlety), clumsy (and we're so suave), violent (we're sweet and tender) and to crown it all he claims that there's such a thing as Good and Evil (ho! ho! ho! we nearly died laughing).

And yet and still the Europeans agree that Saddam Hussein has to be disarmed and if he could be dislodged without hurting anyone it would be a gift for his tormented population. Yes, it's true, he's a bastard.

But the American still doesn't understand. We can't make war against Iraq because the terrorists will come bearing down on us with all their might. It will be terrrrrrrible. There will be terrorist attacks with no end. They already hate us, if Boush attacks, they'll tear us limb from limb. That's what we're trying to tell you, what you have to explain to your

Boush of a president: we are for peace because our enemies are for war. Is that so hard to understand?

The coupling peace on Iraq / intifada on Israel bothers the seasonal pacifists. They try to hide it under their napkin like a chicken bone they spit out and don't know how to get rid of. Some friends tell me that the demonstration in Paris on February 15th was "confused." In what way confused? "Well what does Palestine have to do with it?" Pertinent observation, immediately brushed aside by explanations no less confused than the demonstration. "It's folklore, every march you go to there's always a handful of Kurds, a bunch of Turks, a woman's collective and some crazies advocating free sale of hard drugs." I insist: it's not anecdotic, it is the very articulation of the movement. *Non, non*, I can't be right. It would be too grave.

The European Union is not stingy with pronunciamientos these days. Yesterday they did one of those circus tricks that make our heads turn and our hearts sink: no pressure on Iraq without equivalent pressure on you know who to resolve the Israeli-Palestinian conflict. You absolutely want to disarm Iraq? Okay, on condition that you give a good whack to Israel. A vicious idea clothed in measured language. Tune in to the voice of the common people and you'll get the real message. *Radio France Internationale,* 18 February, first caller on the daily Juan Gomez show (Mecca Cola lite): Nasser asks if the real aim of this imminent war in Iraq is not to increase Israel's inordinate overwhelming power in the region. The international editorialist of the international radio station unreservedly confirms this analysis and backs it up with a bevy of details! Isn't that just lovely? A change from the sempiternal "they're doing it so they can get their hands on the oil!"

Beyond the abject nastiness of these variations on the theme of the Jewish conspiracy stands a musty geopolitics aimed at preserving at all costs a disastrous status quo that is generating the worst ills: poverty, resentment, under-development, fanaticism, virulent anti-Semitism, smuggling, financing of terrorism, terrorism, intifada...the list is open-ended. The immobilist's brilliant idea is to leave the region in this state of utter breakdown, let the filth run into open sewers, and put the blame on Israel for the stinking consequences...why? Because all the other parties to the problem are so deathly frightening. And, when the great pragmatic Americans offer to take the first steps in a vast cleanup and renewal project, their so-called European allies spit on them. *Have they thought of the consequences of their acts?* And you? Are you aware of the dangers of your inaction? History will be the final judge but we will have to pay as we go.

I don't underestimate the legitimate concerns of any human being on the eve of a planetary conflict, the fear of unpredictable overwhelming consequences, the difficulty of letting oneself believe that military action is necessary. But one may rightfully wonder about the quality of the halo 'round the head of the French president, leader of the front of refusal. Where are his troops really heading? Massed behind the banner "Yes to disarmament, yes—on condition—to getting rid of the despot, no to war" they're simply asking for results without action. Immaculate Conception! A posture particularly suited to a certain tendency of the French mind, victim of its own power of abstraction, dazzled by the theoretical and frightened by concrete application of thought. Intelligence strangled like a fetus wrapped in the umbilical cord. Discourse that turns on itself in a *huis clos* with no hope of an exit .

Crisis is an opportunity for healthy reexamination. The Europe three-some, turning down the occasion, finds itself locking in to some good old contradictions. Take pugnacious little Belgium. Up front she's trotting behind the Franco-German duo as fast as her little legs can carry her, taking her place in the rampart against American unilateralism. Behind the scenes she's set herself up as the Supremest Court in all the lands. Preemptive war against Iraq? Prohibited! It will establish a dangerous precedent. As far as dangerous precedents go, what's to keep Saudi Arabia from following the Belgian model and declaring Shari'a above and beyond all the world's jurisdictions, competent to judge crimes everywhere and forever with no statute of limitations?

There is something troubling about the way our president has built his popularity on successive waves of questionable mass demonstrations. Elected with an African potentate's score to block the unlikely passage of an outmoded fascist candidate, Chirac rode into office on the euphoric tide of *le peuple* mobilized to save *la République* in a series of joyful demonstrations seriously compromised by the presence of Hamas style keffiehs and flags—and the burning of Israeli and American flags— incendiary antiZionist and antiAmerican slogans...

Racism was vigorously denounced, but nothing said about antisemitism. The *Magen David* cropped up here and there, not to remind *le peuple* of the terrible yellow star, but joined by an equal sign with the Nazi swastika. All of this in the Spring of 2002 when synagogues were burning and Jews were getting beat up. Today, again, our president has taken the lead of a confused movement in which do-gooders go arm in arm with the worst elements, agitated in depth by antidemocratic and anti-occidental currents. This thundering wave, which actually stimulates the virulent hatred that threatens us, will soon slosh to shore without exerting the slightest positive effect in the direction of peace. But, as it rolls back, it may well carry away the debris of shattered institutions: the UN, NATO, and the EU.

Today, Chirac's unconditional fans, drunk with the liquors of certain victory, will not tolerate any criticism of their leader and their nation. For over two years Israel has been called every kind of dirty name, the Zionists are accused of all the ills of the world, any Jew who defends Israel's right to exist is branded an extremist... and suddenly the French are outraged by the Francophobia pouring over our berets! What? A boycott of our products! Scandalous! What? We are accused of ingratitude, the white crosses of Omaha Beach are thrown in our faces! Boundless cruelty.

French radio stations activate their network of contacts, open the mikes to pro-French American expatriates in Paris, anti-war French expatriates in the US, and every possible trans-Atlantic combination as long as it can reassure and console them with soothingly reasonable comments. "We saw signs <u>in French</u> carried in the antiwar demonstrations here in the US: *'merci à la France, non à la guerre.'*" "I've been living in France for twelve years and I too am opposed to this war."

Can't we criticize the policies of Chirac's government without being accused of antiFrenchism? It looks like we can't.

Les jeux sont faits. The intervention is imminent. Let us pray that it goes quickly and well. Let us pray and let us finally extend well-deserved recognition to those who have gone to the pains of taking action. Victory will not fall at the feet of the persnickety ones contemptuously watching the battle from a sidewalk café. As a realistic optimist I dare to believe that at the end of the game honor will fall to the true democrats who accept the heavy responsibility of defending their—imperfect—values with—imperfect—means of action instead of parading under the banner of virtue draped from head to toe in the accoutrements of chaste priests.

We have good reason to not let ourselves be fooled by images of the good guys and the bad guys based on costuming. We know about the big bad fully equipped Tzahal soldier versus the nice little kid in a sleeveless t-shirt armed with a slingshot. The same holds true for all those nice people who demonstrated on February 15th in such great numbers that are counted and recounted like the bounty of the holdup of the century. They are not the ones who will defend our democracies. Our fate depends on the hundreds of thousands of soldiers equipped with the most sophisticated arms, trained, motivated, and led by world class strategists. The emblem of justice is not the kid throwing a molotov cocktail and it's not the crowds massed in the streets of all the cities you want on a pre-war Saturday. Mobilizing the masses behind sophistic slogans is not democracy! It's demagogy.

I think that Europe and our cherished France deserve better than this lukewarm dish of ersatz served on a bed of dishonor.

Spme Faculty Forum[7]

REACTION TO PETER BEAUMONT

March 3, 2003

"The New Antisemitism" The Observer, 17 February

This article deserves a fully documented reply that would expose the weakness of the author's arguments and his total ignorance of a situation he purports not only to explain but to set right. Peter Beaumont obviously doesn't have a clue to the extent and range of the new antisemitism in Europe. This doesn't prevent him from accusing the victims, as usual, of bringing the wrath of antisemites down on their heads. According to his somewhat garbled analysis, Israel is manipulating the whole world and deflecting justified criticism by unjustified name-calling. Jews are overreacting to something that is not—yet—totally unbearable and life-threatening. As for the antisemitism which does, admittedly, exist in Europe, it is not really European because the dirty work is being done by Muslims.

I am sorry I do not have the time to take apart every one of the false arguments lined up in this article, but I can at least expose the ridiculous reasoning that structures it: the new version of antisemitism is, essentially, a reaction to Israel's "heavy-handed" response to the 2nd intifada. Now let's look closely at this: a Muslim living in Belgium beats up a Belgian rabbi, kicks him in the face, insults him, calls him a dirty Jew, threatens to kill him... and this is a reaction to Israel's "heavy-handedness?" Who ever heard of such logic? What does a rabbi in Belgium have to do with Sharon's politics in Israel? What does beating up a rabbi, kicking him in the face, threatening to kill him have to do with criticizing the "heavy-handedness" of Sharon's government? How could any human being claim to be responding to "heavy-handedness" by kicking a man in the face?

This is precisely the antisemitism that Peter Beaumont cannot recognize... because he practices it himself!

First element: Israel is guilty of reacting to something, but that something is guilty of nothing. The Intifada is not heavy handed, it is... what? It is the unquestioned base line from which the objective journalist, a self-appointed judge, will decide who is right and who is wrong. Guilt enters the picture when Israel—Ariel Sharon, the national union government, or the Jews—reacts.

Second element: the honorable journalist is the voice of conscience, reason, and righteousness. He never drove a tank into a Gaza slum, never fired back at a Palestinian who was trying to kill him, and doesn't even get into brawls in pubs. Naturally he is shocked by all of this (Israeli) violence. Israel should know better, should behave with civilized good manners.

And the final soup: the honorable journalist's civilized manners are thrown like a magical veil over the antisemitic hoodlum who kicks a rabbi in the face. By this magic, the connection between the antisemitic hoodlum who kicks the rabbi in the face and the antizionist hoodlum who kills a few dozen Israelis in a restaurant disappears. The murderous hoodlum is endowed with the polite manners of the journalist, and together they tut tut over Sharon and why can't we criticize him and take him to court in Belgium for crimes committed by Lebanese Christians against Lebanese Palestinians?

Choose any period of European history, choose any episode of persecution of the Jews, you will find the same kind of twisted reasoning, the same self-indulgence, the same dismal mental confusion.... and the same murderous hoodlums applying it in the street.

SPME Faculty Forum

PEACE MARCH VERGING ON POGROM
22 March 2003

The so-called peace movement hit the streets of Paris today, following the well-worn route from La République to La Bastille and beyond to La Nation. Isn't it a shame they didn't demonstrate around the Elysées Palace so that president Chirac could admire the crowds he has so skillfully spurred to action? Apparently forewarned of certain unpleasant sidelines to the movement, he made a high-on-his horses call for *dignité* before this latest extravaganza. And the call was heard!!! It literally flew at high altitude over the heads of the actual manifestation that concretely took place, but came through loud and clear in the dutiful French media, for the sake of the president and the innocent masses who had not actually seen the demonstration with their eyes, heard it with their ears, or believed what they were told by people who had seen it. The official version went from president to public and, I fear, back to the president. While the incident I describe below was in full swing, one radio newsman reported that the demonstration was *digne* and silent.

Silent? Oh... perhaps a bit of youthful enthusiasm... but nothing to write home about.

Well I am precisely writing home to tell you some things that actually transpired on Saturday March 22, 2003 in the city of Paris. Most likely you have been told that some 80,000 pacifists demonstrated against the war. And if you imagined sweet faced students with peace doves in their hearts and on their heads, brave American not-in-my-namers proud to defend their country's honor against its better judgment, couples with babies in strollers, and gray-haired hippies, just let me tell you that there might have been 5,000 of those feathered birds in the crowd, but not enough to make a decent fig leaf for the tens of thousands of enraged, bloodthirsty, ranting, raving armies of hatred. *Les nouveaux jihadistes.*

What is the difference between a pro-Saddam rally in Gaza and the latest fashion in Parisian antiwar demonstrations? Read to the end of this article to find the answer.

Here is how it looked to me. I missed the first wave: the legitimate front group and assorted doveniks passed quickly and, I must assume, never looked back. The new wave begins with a booming *Libérez Očalan* sound truck. Two young warriors with legs widespread perched on the roof of the truck carry huge flags bearing portraits of Očalan. Actually he looks like a younger Saddam. Maybe it's the mustache. A compact mass—families with children in the front lines—marches behind the heroic standard bearers. From there on the tone never changes, contingents pass one after another, shouting, screaming, accusing, threatening. Keffiehs all over the place. Some enterprising person had the bright idea of making baseball caps out of Hamas scarves. Little paper Palestinian flags demand an end to the massacres in Palestine. Huge Palestinian flags snap in the breeze, proclaiming allegiance, pride, determination and, make no mistake about it, intifada, jihad, and all the rest. The Oumma is there... Algerian, Moroccan, Hizbollah, Iraqi flags join in the hymn. American flags too, made to order, with a swastika in place of the star-spangled field of blue.

France is not with Saddam. France is only demanding scrupulous respect for international law. France has total confidence in the UN inspectors. France was only asking for the inspections to continue as long as necessary—the current figure batted around in circumlocutory retrospective reasoning is 2 years—until and unless... etc.

This peace-chanting France is not the same crowd that marched down the boulevard Beaumarchais on Saturday, spotted the enemy, closed ranks to savage a 17 year-old Jewish boy, then veered off to terrorize the Hashomer Hazair kids at the Cercle Bernard Lazare and attack one of the older boys with iron bars. Or is it?

What exactly happened?

According to an initial report by three Digipresse journalists that filmed the incident, a group of *Beurs* carrying sticks, their faces covered with keffieh, ran up from the rear of a cortège, shouting "there's Jews over there." [8] The reporters followed them. A 14 year-old Jewish boy who had come with two friends to have a look at the peace march was thrown to the ground, beaten, pummeled and finally rescued. At the next corner the gang turned into rue Saint-Claude and headed for the CBL (Cercle Bernard Lazare where the Hashomer Hazair youngsters meet on Saturday afternoons).

Their numbers swelling, the assailants massed in front of the door of the CBL, shouting insults, injuring two more Jewish boys. Two young women participating in the demonstration tried in vain to stop the violence, a middle-aged woman who tried to help was knocked over, another pacifist who tried to intervene was beaten off.

A demonstrator wearing a Palestinian flag as a cape stood on the roof of a car and delivered a tirade through his megaphone: "We Muslims, we Arabs can walk with our heads high. They [pointing to the Jews] have to hide. The Koran says 'what was inflicted upon you, you may inflict...'"

The incident, according to Digipresse, occurred during the passage of the CAPJPO contingent. Some older members, who managed to hold back the crowd until the CRS arrived, unashamedly explained to the journalists that the boys had been "provoked by members of Betar who attacked two girls..."

Hashomer Hazair counselors deny that there was any provocation from the Betar and explain that it all started when three of their members were insulted and attacked.

The Digipresse journalists were shocked by the violence against the Jewish kids and equally shocked that the demonstrators threatened them with violence if they continued filming. Their courage, at the time of their first Internet report, had found no takers: France2 and France3 news directors turned down their reportage: they "didn't have time to treat the subject."

When I reached the scene the riot police had pushed the mob away from the doors of the CBL, but the sight was hardly reassuring. The demonstration had spilled like scalding lava from the boulevard and down the rue St. Claude to the corner of the rue des Arquebusiers, a churning mass of anger trying to push past a handful of organizers, trample the 10 little riot policeman, and storm the Center. The "imam" with his batman cape and megaphone suddenly reappeared from the other end of rue St. Claude, surrounded by his *aides de camp*, and marched defiantly past the CBL and through the police line to rejoin the demonstration. After a long standoff the "pacifists" let themselves be sucked back into the compact mass on the boulevard. According to reports from reliable sources, the festivities ended at the Place de la Nation with flag-burnings, *allah ou akbars*, prostrate veiled women praying... for peace of course. Meanwhile a few men in blue took depositions or stood guard in front of the CBL until the children safely left the premises.

Patrick Sebag witnessed the incident from his men's clothing showroom next door to the CBL.. He called the police as soon the demonstrators started streaming from the boulevard and into the street, he didn't close the iron shutter like other shopkeepers on the street but he couldn't protect the Jewish boy who was beaten right in front of his plate glass window. He is horrified. The police did come in time to avert a far greater disaster, because the assailants were trying to break down the door of the Center, but Sebag cannot reconcile himself to the situation. The savagery of the mob, the irresponsibility of a government that allows this rage to develop and flourish. He told me how the neighborhood merchants organized their defense 20 years ago. But things seemed to quiet down, it was easy to slip into a comfortable prosperous life. "And now," he says, "we don't defend ourselves." He feels that the government has counted heads and decided to side with the vast and growing Arab population. Each increment of violence confirms his apprehension. "I cannot live this way," he says, "I cannot live in a country where a 17 year-old boy is savagely beaten because he is Jewish. I can't stand by, helpless. The crowd pushed against the window, there is a mezuzah on the door, they would have broken the window... people in the building across the street from the CBL shouted at the mob to stop, but some young people on this side of the street waved Palestinian flags and defended the Jew beaters. The gang that attacked can come back another day, there's no protection, there was no protection on the day of the march. A few more minutes and it would have been..."

Members of Hashomer Hazair interviewed on Jewish radio corroborate the above versions of the incident. They have a video of the attack, the assailants can be identified, they've filed an official complaint with the organizers of the demonstration, calling on them to exclude, in the future, these elements of violent hateful people marching for an altogether different cause, and reminding them that Hashomer Hazair is in the forefront of the movement for peaceful coexistence between Israelis and Palestinians.

One would be tempted to add: big deal. Jews for peace and Jews for defense and Jews for fighting back and even Jewish rabble-rousers are all the same for the iron-bar wielding barbarians who attacked on Saturday. If the up front media squelch the incident and the government doesn't take a stand, it will be our word against theirs. And here's theirs:

For the Digipresse journalists who, let us not forget, filmed the incident it was a clear case of Jews being targeted for attack in the streets of Paris. Interesting to note: the CAPJPO (*Coordination d'appels pour une paix juste au Proche-Orient*) does not deny involvement in the incident.[9]

They simply turn everything upside down, call it "Another Sharonian aggression and provocation Saturday in Paris," and put themselves in the role of the victims. Sound familiar? According to the CAPJPO communiqué, their cortège was peacefully marching behind a portrait of "Rachel Corrie, deliberately crushed by an Israeli bulldozer," and signs protesting the "American-British aggression in Iraq." A group of 4 or 5 boys "violently" jostled two young ladies in keffiehs and shouted racial insults at them. They called for help, dozens and dozens of young people came and the assailants ran away. The defenders chased after them, followed them down a side street, where the "aggressors" met up with about twenty of their friends who were shouting "Israel Israel," carrying baseball bats and iron bars, the "usual equipment of Jewish extremists such as Betar, Jewish Defense League."

A fight ensued, during which one of the good (CAPJPO) guys "apparently grabbed at least one" iron bar from a bad guy.

The incident was reported in several media: France3 described it as a "fight between Jewish extremists from the Betar and pro-Palestinian demonstrators" but, warns the CAPJPO, false and defamatory reports of aggression are circulating on the Internet and on a Jewish radio… "They'll get what they deserve."

The CAPJPO communiqué concludes with a snide snarling analysis of Zionist support for the war and the duplicity of the organized Jewish community that secretly backs Jewish extremists and the war, but adopts a low profile because of the overwhelming antiwar sentiment in France.

How will the organizers of the demonstration reply to Hashomer Hazair's request to hereby refrain from hitching up with these hate mongers? Will they try to wriggle out by reducing the incident to a regrettable scuffle between boys will be boys that must not be allowed to infringe on the hallowed tradition of street protests, basically a healthy democratic freedom and regrettably like all freedom not 100% safe and sure.

But today's Frenchman being a world class specialist in digging out hidden motivations, at least where the US is concerned, shouldn't they take a closer look at their own dubious figures? Five or ten thousand antiwar demonstrators in Paris on 22 March would hardly be a triumph for peaceloving veto-wielding Europe-dominating France. It would be a fiasco.

Add 50 or 60,000 bloodthirsty jihadists and you get a lot of clout. Don't take my word for it, juggle the proportions as you wish, 20,000 purehearts and 70,000 enraged anti-American antisemites... go ahead, make it 50/50. You'll still have a hard time explaining the difference between a pro-Saddam demonstration in Gaza and a peace march in Paris.

Americans and Brits are fighting and dying in Iraq, facing resistance from the army of a despot—who by some accounts was supposed to be toothless and out of commission—facing untold danger from the biological and chemical weapons he supposedly doesn't have. Many soldiers are dead, others are POWS with no hope of being treated humanely, and here in Paris mobs carrying scurrilous banners rumble down the boulevards, co-opting hard won freedoms to give rein to expressions of unmitigated virulent hatred. And these soldiers of shame have the nerve to smear anti-American graffiti all up and down the boulevard, shitting on Americans...

...and calling them cowards.

Spme Faculty Forum[10]

AFTER THE JIHADISTS, THE STATE COMES TO RUE ST. CLAUDE
7 PM, 4 April 2003

The Yanks are in Baghdad, the French are on strike, and the Minister of the Interior is coming to visit the Hashomer Hazairniks at the Cercle Bernard Lazare on rue St. Claude. Policemen came a few hours ago to clear away cars parked in the vicinity. Now CBL officials, Hashomer Hazairniks, secret service men, policemen in uniform, undercover agents, and assorted civilians mill around in front of the Cercle, walk in and out, clacking the heavy *porte cochère*, communicate by cell phone, and wait in an icy blustering wind. Every ten minutes someone opens the garbage cans that stand by the door alongside the welcoming committee, peeks in, drops the lid with a soft bang. All safe.

People coming home from work bear briefcases and groceries; kids go by on scooters, skateboards, roller blades; police cars pull up, linger, drive off, circle around the block. A delivery boy comes down from the supermarket on the boulevard, struggling to control an overloaded cart on the slope, his red coat flashing in the setting sun. Two slightly grungy teenagers scoot by on skateboards, swing around, meet up with some girls, hang around... A secret service agent walks over, flashes an orange fluo Security card, checks their handbags and backpacks. A few neighbors watch the scene from their windows, braving the arctic wind. The sun sets. Night falls. The garbage truck turns in from the rue de Turenne and chugs slowly down the street like a giant green mechanical elephant. People duck back into the Cercle, others come out, wait, send and receive important messages... suddenly all the policemen leave at a brisk trot and disappear on the boulevard. Walkie-talkies squawk. Nothing happens.

An Interior Minister certainly has a busy schedule. But he promised to come and the reception party waits patiently. No doubt chilled to the bone. At least the Minister isn't inconvenienced by the transportation strike. Today's demonstration went from Place de la République to the Grands Boulevards... trade unions, civil servants, with retirement benefits on their minds marching in Paris as coalition tanks roll down a boulevard in Baghdad—tell me who's bogged down now—and I wonder if the jihadists hooked on for the ride, since they can't vent their hateful anger in peace marches these days.

Where's Jihadman with his megaphone and Palestinian cape? Too scared even to come and have a look from the sidelines? The State itself is coming to visit the modest locale he besieged just 13 days ago. He wouldn't dare jump on the roof of a car tonight, but how about standing up against the wall of the supermarket where he'd ignited the mob with his *Allah ou Akbar*? "We Arabs can walk with our heads high, they [the Jews] have to hide..."

The Interior Minister and his delegation finally arrive at 19:45. No screeching sirens. A subdued precision ballet. Sleek silver cars pull up on silent tires, men and women in black appear instantly, doors open, dignitaries step out, doors close with a whisper, cameras turn without a whirr. 3rd arrondissement Mayor Pierre Aidenbaum arrives in the last car, the last of the welcoming party follows him into the building, a handful of policemen stand guard outside.

The Marines are in Baghdad. The French are striking for better retirement pensions. And there are no more peace demonstrations in the streets of Paris. Thirteen days ago this same street was filled with a bloodthirsty mob. Yoni was on the boulevard, a 17 year-old kid, victim of a savage horde out of their minds with hatred, beating Yoni because he is Jewish. He could have been killed. In these times when truth is systematically assassinated by false parallels I try to avoid slimly justified comparisons but, believe me, the mob that attacked these Jewish kids on March 22 was of the same stripe as the one that beat two Israeli reservists to a pulp in Ramallah in October 2000.

What are the words for these things? Pogrom? Lynch? Massacre? They don't apply. This is a new kind of atrocity.

Since that peace march incident other Jews have been insulted, beaten, threatened, harassed. A man was attacked yesterday in the Parc de Bercy, he's in the hospital. We heard that a woman was seriously injured by stone throwers on her way to a synagogue in Garges lès Gonesse. A mysterious report slipped in and out of the news the other day: did a bomb squad blow up a parked car in front of a synagogue in the 16th arrondissement at 5 AM and tow away the debris before worshippers arrived for morning service? A kosher restaurant was definitely set on fire yesterday in Epinay! Relatively minor damage and no injuries. Someone tried to burn down a synagogue in Massy. And how many schoolchildren were hounded, mistreated, chased out of their school, their park, their neighborhood? A grandmother from Lyon tells how some Arab kids pulled her hair as she came out of the metro. She stood up to them, asked if they would treat their own grandmothers that way. They answered back: We're on top now, you're at the bottom. "We Arabs can walk with our heads high, they [the Jews] have to hide."

Solitude of the persecuted and heavy police protection for the Interior Minister; ugly acts in the streets, beautiful words from on high. What shall we believe?

First, give the kids credit. They accomplished miracles. Since the autumn of the year 2000, since the first pro-Palestinian demonstration that incorporated Jew-hating jihadists, since the first cries of Death to the Jews in la Place de la République, how many millions of words have been written to call attention to the danger of stoking this murderous hatred and letting it run wild in the streets. The Socialist government fell, the new Chirac government rode in on a dictator's score as France, running from the far right bogeyman Le Pen, threw itself into the arms of the soon to be Prince of Peace. And nothing we could do or say could stop the jihad marchers. We scolded, analyzed, reasoned, appealed, begged, pleaded, and even demonstrated. Nothing we could say or publish or declare or tally up could stem the tide.

March 22, 2003, three young Hashomer Hazair counselors walked up to the corner of rue St. Claude and boulevard Beaumarchais to have a look at the antiwar demonstration. A half hour earlier, I was standing at about the same spot, and the week before, too... I remember seeing three guys with Hamas scarves tied like do-rags running into the supermarket. I didn't have an American flag in my hand or a *Magen David* around my neck. Yoni was wearing a kippa. Look at his beat up face in the Digipresse film. These guys go for the head. What did they do, kick him in the eye, bang up his face with baseball bats, iron bars? Will he keep his eye? His sight?

Y., retired lycée professor was in the Hashomer locale teaching Yiddish dances to 8 year old kids. Hearing a racket in the hallway she came out to quiet down the rowdy older boys, never imagining... N. L. was there shouting, "they're killing my buddy." He was on his way out to rescue Yoni. Y. still didn't understand what was going on, she tried to hold him back. He wouldn't listen to reason so she went out with him and found herself facing the mob. And realized that this was no boyish scuffle. Things happened fast. Yoni had escaped from the wild men on the boulevard and somehow managed to slip into the Center and close the door against the mob that stood there shouting "Betar you're fucked." Y., slim, springy, courageous and over 60 was knocked down, pushed, shoved, bruised. The mob was kicking at the door, trying to break it down, a ringleader with a megaphone shouting *Allah ou Akbar* was swelling his troops and sparking them to battle...

Finally the riot police drove in from the other end of the street and pushed the crowd back toward the boulevard. Alerted, a 24 year-old former Hashomer counselor came rushing up on his motorcycle. A few minutes later, as he described the incident in front of a camera, someone rushed at him, slammed him on the head with an iron bar, knocking him to the ground, beating him while he was down. In front of the camera.

Words lead to acts. You shout *Death to the Jews* at Place de la République, the powers that be don't take you by the scruff of the neck and send you flying back to your lair... no, they understand. They explain without condoning. Your tender heart is pained by the suffering of your Palestinian brethren. Israel must stop shooting bullets at stone-throwing babies, and la République will recover its stately charm. You shout *Death to the Jews*, you paint swastikas wherever your little heart desires, you burn synagogues, beat up orthodox men in black, promote boycotts of Israeli academics, spurt hellfire hatred on the Mecca Cola airwaves, and the powers that be point the finger at Tzahal. You shout *Death to the Jews* in the year 2000 and beat up a Jewish man in front of the camera in 2003.

Al Qaeda committed a fatal error in attacking the US at home. We can safely assume that if they had attacked Paris they would have been able to go on and do it to Berlin, Rome, and other picturesque capitals without arousing the troops. And it would seem that the jihadists made a deadly mistake in attacking boys from Hashomer Hazair. Their candor has accomplished something that none of us were able to do. They put a stop—at least for now—to Jew-hating demonstrations. Given the scope and speed of the military campaign in Iraq—which normally would have provoked a corresponding increase in antiwar protest—this is a breathtaking feat.

The Hashomer offices are tucked in under a low ceiling on a sort of mezzanine over the meeting hall of the CBL. Jew and Arab stand side by side in idealistic posters, there's a portrait of Rabin (z"l), a Shalom Achshav banner, making no mistake about what these young people stand for. Their reaction to the unthinkable violent hatred that befell them is true to the Zionist spirit they stand for: manly, upright, strong and without a tinge of hatred. Press releases, e-mails, phone calls in all directions... they took matters in their own hands, acted in their own defense, reached out and up for support and explanations and, from the beginning, made clear and concrete demands:

1. Legitimate demonstration organizers should no longer allow anti-semitic slogans and banners, violent hate-filled contingents, Hamas and Hizbullah flags, American and Israeli flags defaced with swastikas.

2. A mixed group of about thirty moderators should be formed to patrol the demonstration and demand the exclusion of objectionable elements.

3. President Chirac himself should appear at the next scheduled demonstration, check it out from head to tail, and see with his own eyes if the above rules are respected.

To this date as far as I know no French TV station has aired the Digipresse film of the aggression. A few seconds, the least horrifying moments, passed in a flash on one newscast. But all the big TV channels sent cameramen and journalists to the press conference organized by Hashomer Hazair on March 26th. Distinguished guests, full house, and good coverage the next day in major newspapers, the same papers that had been consistently underplaying the hateful rage of pro-Palestinian and antiwar demonstrations.

Candor of youth, childlike innocence of Left wing parties and human rights organizations shocked to discover that the hatred they had been stirring up and using as fuel for their rickety wagons could actually run amok. The moment-of-truth atmosphere of the press conference was conducive to certain almost religious confessions, highlighted by a long emotional statement from Aurélie Filipetti, a spokeswoman for the Paris branch of the Green party. Her heartfelt declaration apparently left the Greens cold; she may still be a spokeswoman but they've let it be known that when it comes to Zionism she only speaks for herself!

There was an atmosphere of moral probity at the press conference. All the speakers were lucid, frank, and determined to stand up and be heard. Yoni Smadja, articulate Hashomer Hazaïr spokesman, affirmed his personal opposition to the war but called on President Chirac to make peace in France before trying to make peace in Iraq. Alain Finkielkraut declared that there is no place for Jews in the peace movement in France. Cameras rolled, journalists rushed for exclusive interviews with the distinguished participants after the conference.

And so? So how did it go on Saturday the 29th? Did the jihadists stay home? Or did they drape themselves in pale blue peace dove flags borrowed from their love-not-war buddies? Or did they just decide to beat up Jews on their own turf instead of messing with the "white cap" moderators? As I predicted—no credit for clairvoyance, an idiot could have foreseen it—the turnout was mediocre on what should have been a day of crescendo, and the jihadists were not in the least intimidated. They marched, bearing the same hatespitting banners, shouting the same bloodthirsty slogans, and any whitecap who politely requested removal of swastika banners and other foulmouthed accusations got shoved, pushed, or bonked with a flagpole... and called a dirty Jew, even if he happened to be *Beur*. Not because the rough guy didn't know the difference. There are many ways of being an assimilated Jew. One way is by blending into the woodwork and another is by arousing the ire of an antisemite.

The March 29th antiwar demonstration started in the vicinity of the American embassy, place de la Concorde, but no one spotted President Chirac on the sidelines or looking down from a wrought iron balcony. It would seem that Saddam Hussein pre-recorded a series of lifelike scenes to be rebroadcast during the war while he either hunkered down, flew the coop, or went to his last eternal bunker. President Chirac just disappeared, leaving his lieutenants to backpedal, stutter and stammer, reinvent recent history and, as the Yanks encircle Baghdad and the only true bogging down is in the front lines of the French government, lob a few last grenades of snide criticism before crumpling in a whimper at the feet of the Allies, wagging their tails, licking boots and biting ankles, and generally proving that there is no way to say spin doctor in French.

The figures, let's have the figures. The antiwar marchers numbered 60,000 according to the organizers, 15,000 according to the police. And you want them to kick out the jihadists? The latest and perhaps the last of the great Paris peace marches was rich in incidents. An anti-Saddam Iraqi poet in exile, Salah al Hamdani, was giving an interview before the cameras on bld. St. Germain when a bunch of Saddamites led by Charker Saadi ran up, insulted him, and beat him up. Isn't this Saadi, capo of the *Association des Irakiens en France,* the guy who's invited at least 5 times a week to growl and snap at the Americans on *Radio France Internationale*? Another way of beating people up in front of the cameras.

J., one of the HH boys roughed up the week before, stood dauntless on the sidelines and observed. A journalist was at his side, and a hidden tape recorder was capturing the soundtrack of the, let us not forget, antiwar demonstration. He played the tape back on Jewish radio. A jihadist comes up to him, Jonathan's not wearing a kippa, doesn't have *payes* or *tsitsis* or a royal blue Hashomer Hazair jacket, nothing but his face. And the jihadist tells him, "You're Betar." How does he know? The same way he, or one of his cohorts, knew last week. And now we all know what it means when a CAPJPO communiqué claims that guys from Betar attacked their whiter than snow ladies. Betar means Jew.

The same hateful slogans, the same violent accusations, the same calls to jihad, the same swastika defaced flags, the same insults (a Jew for peace and for Palestine was hooted and threatened); and some of the same men who attacked the HH boys the week before were present and accounted for.

And all the king's horses and all the king's men and all the smartass international law-abiding,UN inspections-respecting, peaceful disarmament-advocating French officials, politicians, and human rights activists couldn't disarm a few tens of thousands of jihad fascists in the streets of Paris. They should have hired Hans Blix to head up the white caps!

A strange silence falls on the boulevards of protest. Will the swastikas never again fly in our breezes? The April 1st march was cancelled. Ditto for April 5th. Other statistics have come forward to smother the impact of the swelling peace movement that was supposed to stop the Apaches in their tracks and send the smart bombs back to their bays. Terrible figures, confirming the shameful increase in antisemitic incidents, and shocking figures, confirming pro-Saddam sentiment in French public opinion. The Chirac government is cringing. This twisted international delusion strategy has brought forth not one but hundreds of thousands of Golem. Heavy monster footsteps shake the Haussmanian glory of Paris to its foundations. A war memorial to the Brits who died to liberate France from those old fashioned Nazis that almost everyone knows to hate... today... is defaced in blood red graffiti and familiar jihad terms. Coalition troops, deaf to the commentaries of French specialists, thrust forward to Baghdad at lightning pace when they were supposed to be bogged down, strung out, underfed, and misguided, dumped in Iraq by hooknosed Washington hawks, left without a trustworthy map or a halfway reliable battle plan, dumbstruck in the face of ferocious Iraqi *résistance. La résistance, quelle magnifique résistance*, ah those stupid Americans underestimated the strength of Iraqi patriotism. They should have asked a French newscaster before rushing into this fearful endeavor my goodness.

SPME Faculty Forum[11]

8 April 2003

It's not exactly mopping-up time but, yes, the military phase of the Iraqi liberation movement is just about *mission accomplie*. But the war is going strong in France. The war against the Americans heats the airwaves to boiling point. Hatred multiplies with each victory. Saddam's faithful are out of action, the local population turns against the remnants of his wonderful domestic terror machine, the crowds welcome British and American troops, the bloody house to house hand to hand combat did not occur, and peace-loving citizens all over the world can begin to breathe a sigh of relief and plan for the future. Not here in gay Paree. Red hot anger pours through tight-clenched lips. The how holy we are syndrome is stoked up to cosmic levels. Draped in the glorious veils of the United Nations, France steps up again on its self-made pinnacle and crows: only the UN can rebuild Iraq, only France can judge the victors and share the spoils, only Europe can stand up to the United States, only France can keep Europe afloat. *Délusions de grandeur, grandeur nature*, a whole nation off its rocker, sunk to the depths of ignominy. And blind! And deaf!

No voice of reason can be heard. It would have to be a whisper to drown out this macabre crowing. Don't you see, *chers amis*, the warriors are decent. Going to war against a tyrant brings out the honor of honorable men. Skulking in a corner, mumbling curses and refusing to stand up when history comes calling turns a people rancid.

The young people of Hashomer Hazair are mobilized. They awakened something decent in a small sector of the antiwar movement. They provoked sincere promises from an Interior Minister who means business. On several occasions recently, Sarkozy has forcefully proclaimed that no Jewish person should ever have to ask himself if he can continue to live in France.

Unfortunately, the question won't go away. It keeps coming back, re-charged with anxiety from the day's account of antisemitic incidents. Jewish youths beat up by adult Arabs in Montreuil, Jewish tombs dese-crated, Jews insulted in the press, in the courts, in news analysis, in the attitude to the war in Iraq... Jews associated with Americans associated with Israel, boiled together in the same cauldron, all hawks and extrem-ists and unconditional backers of Bush and Sharon.

Yes, the coalition troops are in Baghdad, Chemical Ali is dead, the noose around the Iraqi population is loosening, Saddam's golden faucets and chemical warheads are exposed to the world's conscience, while France is floating in an Oriental paradise, wing in wing with the angels...

And there's a big peace bash scheduled at the Fontaine des Innocents on the 11th of April.

They wouldn't dare try to do that in Baghdad!

LET'S BE FRIENDS

14 July 2003

A *JTA* article posted in the June 18-19 SPME Online Digest caught my eye. The article praised—in advance—an event organized by the UEJF (Jewish Student's Union of France) under the slogan "Zionist and pro-Palestinian." I hesitated. Should I throw cold water on well-meaning peace-loving young people? And do I have to take it on myself to set the record straight for anything and everything that goes on in France? An-yway, why do I always react negatively to this type of initiative? Don't I want to be friends with... my enemies?

Something like a very tall fence rises up in my mind every time I hear gushing praise—because it's always gushing—for these Jewish - Arab or Israeli - Palestinian joint ventures. I didn't like the film *Promises*. I don't want to listen to the hyphenated orchestra, see the hyphenated film, follow the hyphenated theater troupe on its triumphant world tour just because they are hyphenated. Why? Am I deliberately closing myself up in a ghetto of prideful rejection of the Other? On the contrary. My whole life is a story of reaching out to Others, trusting them, rendering tribute to their superb exotic cultures and making them my own, becoming Oth-er to myself and indigenous to what had been exotic. I have tasted to the full the joys and sorrows of a real life without frontiers and with no hidden geopolitical agenda.

This may explain my emotional reaction to what seems like contrived relationships as compared to my own authentic life of passion and adventure, but it is not enough to justify any reasoned argument against the undesirable side effects of this kind of wishful thinking. What's wrong with pretending to be friends when you really aren't? Or reaching out to friendly elements within a hostile group? I would say that my objection is based on the conviction that conflicting interests and hostile actions should be squarely faced and if necessary fought over, not sugar coated with sweet intentions. But I don't know if I am convinced by my own argument. Don't people get together to debate and argue, peacefully, while their respective collectivities are at each other's throats? But in fact isn't there always an element of compensated guilt in these groupings? The party of the first part, assumed to be somehow unjustly powerful, reaches out to the party of the second part, assumed to be aggrieved... Would striking workers attend a gala organized by the Employer's Association smack in the middle of a period of acute labor strife?

Whatever my reasons, my immediate reaction to this Pro-Palestinian Zionism was totally negative. And, at least in this case, the facts bear me out. When "anti-war" pro-Palestinians beat up kids from Hashomer Hazair in Paris in March 2003, hardly any of the legitimate organizers of the marches could bring themselves to condemn the attack without condemning Israel, Sharon, the territories, the incursions, Bush, and all the rest. To my knowledge no one has been arrested for this attack, though the incident was filmed and many of the assailants are clearly identifiable. I mention this to give a sense of the context in which the UEJF decides to come out for pro-Palestinian Zionism. Instead of asking those from the other camp to stand up and defend shared civilized values, you give them a pat on the back and say let's be friends. Not the jihadists, of course. No one would expect them to show up for the party. But the pro-Palestinians who would identify themselves as Zionists... where do they stand exactly?

All kinds of distinguished guests—from the Zionist side—were announced. I wouldn't have dreamed of going. But I was not alone: Alain Finkielkraut declared with no ambiguity (on "*Qui vive*" his weekly program on *Radio Communauté Juive*) "as for being pro-Palestinian, no, I am not pro-Palestinian." His partner Ilana Cicurel was shocked. Dropping the usual formulations of a radio pro, she simply blurted out, "Why?" Finkielkraut answered in a voice that came directly from the heart as if a heart could speak without passing through normal channels of vocal chords, tongue, and lips. "No," he said, "I cannot be pro-Palestinian, because *ce peuple n'a rien donné.*" Did he say *rien donné* or *rien montré*? I heard *rien donné.* A simple expression that could be translated as "has nothing to show for itself." Which brings us back to *montré.* A people is judged, explained Finkielkraut, by its leaders, its institutions, its way of conducting the struggle for independence. And he went on to spell out the shameful record of the Palestinian movement judged by these criteria.

I was surprised to learn, the following week, that Alain Finkielkraut had spoken at the event. But his honest appraisal confirmed my misgivings: the great majority of the people in the audience were Jewish, there were very few Muslims. And all the so-called moderate Muslim speakers spoke out for the Palestinian right of return... to Israel of course. Finkielkraut concluded, with a sigh, that there's a long way to go before we can reach any real understanding. And his voice seemed to say that the road was so long as to offer no horizon let alone hope.

Now, Patrick Klugman has left the UEJF and moved up to the Jewish community's umbrella organization, the CRIF (*Conseil représentatif des institutions juives de France*), apparently bringing along his pro-Palestinian Zionism. Or maybe it is just a coincidence? The CRIF website sends readers directly and with no commentary to a long article by Christophe Ayad (*Libération* 3 July 2003) on Al-Rowwad, a Palestinian children's theater troupe currently on tour in France. Ayad reports, among other *misérabilismes*, the real life stories of these children of the camps. Wou'oud: Israeli soldiers stormed into her house, set up an explosive charge to break through the wall into the adjoining house; her mother was injured, the soldiers would not let them call for help, her mother died. Khaled is Palestine's best dancer of *dabké*, "a rural dance where they tap their feet on their beloved soil." Mohamed: loves to play soccer and fight with the soldiers. And Ayad adds for good measure the conclusions of a study by a Gaza psychiatrist: "most Palestinian children idealize the model of the kamikaze [French misnomer for *shahid*] the only one capable, in their eyes, of avenging the flouted dignity of their fathers, condemned to unemployment, humiliated at checkpoints, help-less to protect their families from attack." Abdel Fattah Abou Sourour, founder of Al-Rowwad, describes the desperate conditions in the camp that lies at the feet of the "colony of Gilo." Using culture as an arm of resistance, Abou Sourour is determined to save the children, for they are the future of Palestine. The children worked for three years on their play, presented as a series of tableaux that tell the history of their parents and grandparents. And Ayad appreciates: "The passage where they lampoon the absurd litany of aborted peace plans is hilarious. The one where four of them 'play' at being Israeli soldiers at a checkpoint with sadistic real-ism is chilling." And what strikes the children of the camps about France? Wou'oud notices the changeable weather and, "Oh yes, there aren't any Jews here." Abdel corrects the impression, "There aren't any soldiers. It's not the same thing."

Why in the world would the CRIF post this article? And not even mention the excellent *Metula News Agency* article[12] by Gérard Huber, author of *Contre-expertise d'une mise en scène*, the investigation into the simulated murder of Mohamed Al Dura. Huber does not ride rough-shod over the frail Palestinian "refugee" children as they bask in the spotlight of Ayad's partisan praise. But he does, precisely and intelligent-ly, expose the instrumentalization of the Mohamed Al Dura myth, in connection with their French tour. If the purpose of such cultural activity is to save the children from a dead end *shahid* future, it should not be presented under the patronage of the poster boy whose simulated mur-der was the starting gun for this never ending massacre of innocents. By displacing the responsibility for their culture of murderous martyrdom onto the Jewish victims, the Palestinians lock themselves into the impos-sibility of honest self-critical examination and healing transformation. And the introduction to the children's passion play clearly establishes a connection between their suffering at the hands of the Israeli "occupa-tion," and the sufferings of French Jews during the German occupation.

Without getting into the narrow streets of French Jewish community politics, and without accusing anyone of dastardly motives, I must say that the failure to post Huber's article, at the very least side by side with the *Libération* rave review, was not an oversight. What exactly is the deal? Isn't it let's be friends, we the Jews of France, and you the powers that be will exchange visits, handshakes, moving speeches and you'll post policemen in front of the synagogues—sometimes—and in exchange we won't make waves or call you to account on any of the preceding.

Another indication that something is fishy in this let's be friends approach: the French Jewish community snuggled up to la République just when relations between France and my native land were at their worst. I was home for a visit in late April as the military phase of the Iraq operation was winding up. Any honest observer would have to admit that the whole thing had gone smoothly. The revelation of Saddam's grisly atrocities, the smiles of liberated Iraqis, the discovery of millions of dollars stashed away and other millions paid out to butter up journalists in the most unlikely places was making a mockery of France's hypocritical anti-war stance. I saw Liberty fries on the menu at a DC delicatessen; the waiter was not unhappy to tell us that the nearby Sofitel had taken down its French flag. Everywhere I looked—in the press, on rear windshields, on TV and among friends—there were clever jokes about the French and a wealth of downright serious discussion with sharp insight into their motives and acts. I reveled at the constant flow of news, the full range of opinions expressed and defended. I was delighted by the abundance of concrete details and rational arguments, a sharply outlined sense of reality, everything but the thick ideological pea soup that prevails in French media.

And in the middle of all of this I get e-mail messages telling me the CRIF is planning a *Vive la République* demonstration. Uh-oh, let's be friends. The United States stands up for Israel, stands up to Saddam, stands behind a genuine vision of change for the better in the Middle East and the Jews of France or at least the Jewish institutions want to crow *Vive la République*. When *la République* is pushing all kinds of retrograde pro-Palestinian (in the person of Arafat and Hamas charities) pro-Arab (in the defense of the highly unstable profoundly antisemitic status quo) policies, and allowing home grown jihadists to blithely gnaw at *la République*, the CRIF is going to do a *Vive la République* march? Other messages come to me from the outer space that is my adopted home, explaining that the French-US rift will soon be a thing of the past, and the French dirty dealings a matter for future study by dispassionate historians. Are you guys kidding? This is an <u>international</u> affair. Our Frenchies are not going to wriggle out of it with the local pirouette method: you do a low down dirty trick, it doesn't work to your advantage as you had hoped, you paste a grin on your face and pretend that the whole thing was but a ripple on an ocean of good relations.

French foreign policy had huffed and puffed to shoot down American power wherever it took a stand, and the only power that was really undermined was the smidgeon still left to this small European country with its big ego. But the party line during and after this monumental foreign policy disaster was, "just an honest disagreement between friends." What a sick joke! You side with the enemy and that's a simple difference of opinion with your ally?

The spin is still spinning. But I don't even have the heart to make fun of it. A French hotel website opens with a sugar sweet explanation of the not-really-a-rift, actually daring to give a nicey nice version of that little difference of opinion between allies, and assuring American visitors that they are welcome and loved in France. Reliable reports of French-American handshakes at this and that international powwow are slathered over the truth, while all the time the slimy betrayal goes on as usual: looting and burning in Iraq, the implacable Shi'ite power grab, the Wolfowicz conspiracy, the WMD hype, the GIs sniped... Meanwhile, go into Parisian shops and check out what's missing. American customers. Didn't they get the message? Let's be friends.

What's wrong with being a pro-Palestinian Zionist? Well, first of all it assumes that being just a Zionist is not enough to qualify for caring about the welfare of Palestinians. But that's not the half of it. This kind of reaching out to shake hands with yourself is a way of looking at the world through nearly opaque glasses. Making friends with individuals on the basis of their labels is nothing to brag about. Making friends with nations and groups, even when they are engaged in outright war against you and yours, by way of individuals doesn't add up to anything.

As it turns out the CRIF decided to bring the *Vive la République* demonstration out of the streets and into the hallowed walls of the Paris City hall with its gilded chairs and flowery fruity naked angel frescoes. An uncomfortable pall hung over the assembly every time a speaker (inevitably American or at least not French) spoke out boldly against European and particularly French antisemitism or in favor of the American intervention in Iraq. Something even worse than silence, shocking disrespect, greeted the talk by Adam Rayski, a great hero of the French résistance. Yes, heroes who survive grow old. Rayski spoke hesitatingly, with great difficulty, the people in the audience stood up, turned their backs, and walked out in a steady flow of indifference, leaving the hall emptied by one third.

And then there was the 12-hour bash for French-Israeli friendship in June. Fifty thousand friends of Israel braved the torrid heat of a barely ventilated Parisian convention hall to meet Tzahal officers and Zaka volunteers, taste Israeli foie gras, guzzle Maccabee beer, buy Ahava beauty products, meet the media, buy books and CDs, and listen to heartwarming speeches by friends of Israel, including superstar Nicolas Sarkozy.

What exactly was the French half of this France-Israel friendship? Do you want to guess or should I tell you? For the greater French public the event, and its underlying friendship, didn't exist because it wasn't reported. Anyway, for most of them the very idea would be repulsive. Friends with Israel *et quoi encore*? First let them stop persecuting Palestinians, end the occupation, stop practicing apartheid, tear down the wall, give them food and water, start employing them, stop exploiting them, stop making claims based on a Bible that's old as Methuselah, stop imposing colonial domination by the force of arms, give up all WMDs, in short give in, give them a state, and make peace. Then maybe we can talk about being friends.

In a way, I agree. In my way, that's what I am saying about the pro-Palestinian Zionist movement. True friendship is not so easily won. If we are friends with everyone, we are friends with no one.

And then, mistaking our friends might lead to mistaking our enemies.

Libération 8 July 2003: "Interrogations about an 'anti-Jewish' attack." As reported in a short, vague, non-committal article, two individuals broke into a Beth Lubavitch school in the 19th arrondissement of Paris and hit some students with sticks. Does this mean that the attack was antisemitic? *Et voilà* for the hallowed French tradition of philosophical inquiry. The police arrested the individuals and then released them, but that doesn't mean they won't be judged. Sammy Ghozlan, president of the Office for vigilance against antisemitism, published a communiqué denouncing "another anti-Jewish attack," but Ariel Goldmann of the CRIF's Jewish Community Protection Service declared that there was not yet enough evidence to justify classifying the incident as antisemitic; perhaps these people broke into the school with the intention of stealing.

Meanwhile where are our faint-hearted friends? Out to lunch? On vacation? Applauding the adorable Palestinian (4th generation) refugee child actors or scrambling for new justifications, adjusted excuses. I can just hear them: this kind of incident is on the wane... Besides, it's no kristalnacht... And you have to understand, the Lubavitch in the 19th arrondissement, well, you have your extremists too, they're out to conquer a territory, it's no wonder that they incite this kind of rejection.

And as if that weren't enough, we also have to be on guard against those who want to be friends with our dead. Precisely the case with a distinguished personality widely cited as—just what you were looking for—a Palestinian pro-Zionist: Father Shoufani, the "*curé* of Nazareth." Not really pro-Zionist but certainly pro-Jewish. His peace loving book, *Comme un veilleur attend la paix,* was warmly received, generously admired, rather uncritically accepted. His association, *Mémoire pour la Paix,* is praised to the heavens by Paul Thibaud, president of *l'Amitié Judéo-chrétienne de France*. His ecumenical compassion visit to Auschwitz with a group of Jews, Muslims, Christians, Israelis, Palestinians (no neo-Nazis) would seem to be the very model of what should be expected from peace loving Palestinians.

Why cast doubt on Father Shoufani's motives? Certainly not out of mean-spirited refusal of the warm embrace of friendship. No. The terrible lucidity that reveals the down side of this compassion comes from an understanding of the lurking dangers of replacement theology (see Shmuel Trigano "*Retour sur l'appel du curé de Nazareth*.")[13] When the compassionate gestures are placed in their context, the thrust of the argument is definitely not to our advantage. Put simply it is compassion for the suffering of innocent Jewish victims of the European Shoah, innocence of Arab-Muslim societies in the persecution of Jews, persecution of innocent Palestinians at the hands of a State of Israel haunted by memories and fears of extermination to the point of perpetrating the very evils that were committed against the Jews. By showing compassion, the friends of peace will soothe this anguish and grant, out of the goodness of their hearts, the right of Israel to exist... thereby depriving the state of its international legal foundations and placing it at the mercy of a fickle compassion.

But how could I forget the real flesh and blood friends? My old friends, the friends I haven't seen for the past three years and suddenly we cross paths, share news of our families, our travels and professional lives, the people we used to know. And these old friends who knew me as a model of integration suddenly discover that I am no longer at home in France. Antisemitism. Oh really? They didn't know, but when I tell them they don't seem to be surprised. They ask absurd questions. "Are you directly affected?" As if that would change anything! And when I speak of Jewish children persecuted in schools right here in Paris, a friend asks, "How many?" Another day another friend snaps at me, "Yes, but how about what they do to Arabs in Israel?" It turns out she was referring to the attempted elimination of El Rantissi. I say, "Jews are being attacked!" She replies, "Crime is on the rise everywhere." I object, "No one has been arrested." She snaps back, "Sarkozy's oppressive policy is a disaster... did you hear about the forced repatriation of illegal immigrants?"

The conversations are polite but afterward, remembering what was said, I am filled with seething anger. These friends, who are concerned about poverty, exclusion, deportation of undesirable immigrants, don't seem to care that their country is setting out to impoverish itself of me. They don't really hear what I am telling them. Everything I say is filtered through the thick fog of what they are reading in *Le Monde*, seeing on television, saying to each other. They have already been conditioned to think of antisemitism, even violent antisemitism, as part of the landscape.

Individuals and small groups can make friends, people can fall in love across battle lines. You can always find admirable qualities in the opposite camp, and people in your own camp whom you love to avoid. But there is a battle going on and real friends should come forth with sharp understanding or at least a willingness to find out what is at stake.

Okay, let's be friends, but make no mistake about it...we aren't cuddly toys to hug as you fall off to sleep.

GO FLY A KITE
2 August 2003

Listen, *haverim*, you've got to try harder. All this time you've been getting more than your fair share—more terrorists, more humanocide bombings, more international pressure, more credible threats—it's only normal to ask you to give us something a bit more schmaltzy, you know what I mean? Give us a bit if not a whole lot more Jewish humor. Over here in France where the summer is steaming like never before, we're bombarded with all kinds of jokes and it seems to work because if you notice, *la France* remains the most fabulous country on earth and anyone who thinks otherwise has to say it on one of those little extremist Net sites for unconditional supporters of you know who or you know what. Certainly not in the pages of *Le Monde* or *Libération*!

Granted, French forests are flaming, unemployment is rising, Corsican villas are exploding, our dear little president was hissed and booed by the Canaques, and American tourists don't have the guts to come here and get insulted to their faces but does that keep the French from having a good time? I ask you. They didn't have the heart to keep José Bové in jail. He's too young to bask in restored honor and honorable retirement like good old Maurice Papon, so when our José national gets out of his revolving door prison he's going to grab a hoe and work the land along with a noble peasant on the *plateau du Larzac* and you don't think that's funny? (As for me, if I should commit some big José-burger political-trade union crime, don't be surprised if I'm sentenced to spend 10 months in the South of France. Revolutionaries have to take their punishment!).

Americans are getting popped off in Iraq, how about that? Didn't they say their (nasty) war was over? They got the sons but they haven't found the father, they're up against a relentless *résistance*, they don't know how to talk to the natives, they've been there for months and still haven't managed to set up a democracy and France abstains when the UN Security Council votes to send an international force to the rescue of Liberia, then turns around and tells the Americans they better scuttle over to that war zone and start shooting or else they're going to be guilty of *non-assistance à pays en danger*, and that doesn't make you laugh ?

Excuse me, *haverim*, were you in such a hurry to wash off the smell of fried shtetl onions and remake yourselves into healthy, strong, suntanned, uninhibited new men that you lost your Jewish humor in the process? That incredible Jewish humor that helped us avoid so many catastrophes... though I must admit the exploit is somewhat hidden behind all those countless catastrophes that did occur. Never mind. The day when historians sit down and write the history of everything that didn't happen, these narrow escapes will shine forth in all their glory.

Meanwhile, go fly a kite. Let me explain. For a long three years now we, your friends and relatives living in France, are up to our necks in an acid bath, they're telling us the humanocide bomb attacks (that they call kamikaze) are because of Tsahal's incursions into the Good Guys' camp, and the Camp David fiasco is because of Barak who didn't know how to stimulate Arafat's political G-point, and the dead and mutilated Israelis are because Sharon doesn't want peace, and the torched synagogues and the Jewish kids beat up in France it's because of the unconditional supporters of Sharon, and the war against the Iraq of peaceful Saddam it's because of the Americans who support the unconditional supporters of Sharon, and the source of all that *tsurus* is the colonies and to begin with the colonization of Tel Aviv by the survivors of those European reeducation camps set up in reaction to the aggressions committed by the future unconditional supporters of Sharon whose *shtetlkh* were an insult to the dignity of honest peasants attached to their land as is only natural (I beg you to forgive these long trailing sentences but History is by definition a prolongation of the original anecdote) so for all these years we're getting the fallout from your overarmed policies so we have a right to ask you to use your imagination. Let me explain... That's all I've been doing for the past 3 years but never mind.

And now, when we dared to hope for a bit of a breather, the time of a *hudna*, the space of a road map, no such thing. Our media have you in their headlights and the image they send us is not good. To put it simply: it's execrable. Did you know that there's something worse than the death of innocent bystanders collaterally damaged on the occasion of the liquidation of a political leader of the Palestinian *résistance*? Worse than the destruction of the homes of *shahidin* in the heart of a refugee camp candidate for the Nobel massacre prize? Did you know that the checkpoint in all its horror, sizzling under a merciless sun, and manned by equally merciless Cerberus, the checkpoint with its daily lot of women giving birth in the dust as arrogant Israeli soldiers and soldieresses look on in cold indifference, the checkpoint is nothing compared to a wall.

A wall! Don't you know that the other nations on this earth don't like walls? They don't want any walls of lamentation, ghetto walls, Berlin walls... and even the Great Wall of China is not strictly kosher as they see it.

Don't think you're going to curry favor with them by nitpicking about little failures to respect the road map. Everyone's got his own road map and it's never exactly the same and even if the Palestinians signed you're not going to make a big deal out of a few rockets named Qassam (that's racist!) and hundreds of new recruits in the ranks of Hamas. No. What's keeping the road map from going forward today is THE WALL. The wall of apartheid, the wall of shame, the wall of refusal to see Others, the wall of arrogance, the wall of the unconditional supporters of Sharon.

Because finally our journalists have got the picture. The obstacle to that lovely peace desired by the whole world and to begin with by the Palestinians, exemplary victims, was not the colonization, not the incursions, not the use of excessive force, not the flip flop where the Jews, former exemplary victims, became oppressors. It's the fortress mentality of the Israelis. It's THE WALL. That's what the press says so that's what the people say. A hue and cry rises up from the hamlets and byways of the genuine French homeland: Down with the wall.

Think of us. And go fly a kite. What we need is a huge flight of kites. I know someone who can get them for you wholesale, direct from Japan, no middlemen. Every single Israeli should send at least 5 kites soaring over the other side of that big high wall. Peace doves of course, but why not goldfish, butterflies, pink lace bows, simili falafel sandwiches in hand painted silk, inflated PVC cell phones...put your imagination in the driver's seat and kites in the skies, as numerous as the generations of Abraham, a splendorous display of breathtaking beauty. And even if, for a few short hours, this beauty masks the sky and all it holds, not to worry, the lovely outburst will have imposed its logic, and skies will clear in a sweep of the eye.

Three days later, ready, get set, go again! This time with balloons. In myriad shapes and colors. Then kites again, then balloons...a dozen operations in all.

What's the use?

You're asking me what's the use? Can't you see? It's to squash, smash & demolish the peace process!

What do you mean squash, smash, demolish? With balloons and kites, and they're there with their apprentice humanocide bombers, their snuggling smuggling tunnels, their map where we don't even have a scrap of land, and we're going to squash, smash & demolish the road map with a few picturesque kites from the land of the rising sun? Are you kidding?

Yes.

Guysen Israel News[14]

JEWISH ACTIVIST AT RUTGERS SUPPORTS PALESTINIANS

Article by Sarah Greenblatt, *Home News Tribune* August 17, 2003

As (bad) luck would have it, I read Sarah Greenblatt's article about Abe Greenhouse at midpoint between two breaking news shocks: the bombing of UN headquarters in Baghdad and the bombing of a N° 2 bus in Jerusalem. Forty-two dead, over 250 maimed or injured, who could ask for a more perfect illustration of the Palestinian Solidarity fallacy? And where, under the tons of rubble and the slicing horror of torn bodies and twisted steel, where under the tons of sadness and lacerating pain, shall I find the serenity to explain what is going awry in the minds and hearts of so many well-meaning people.

No one should die in a bus bombing. Not because they are Israelis, not because they are Jews, not because they were coming from the Kotel and going to this or that Jerusalem neighborhood, not because some people have a state and other people claim to want a state, but because no human being should die that way. This is what is meant by a crime against humanity.

No one should kill that way.

And it is a terrible affront to decent Palestinians to perpetrate the lie that humanocide bombings are acts of resistance against occupation.

One would expect that the very minimum degree of academic rigor would preclude hosting such a conference—organized by apologists for crimes against humanity backed up by uncritical advocates of an ill-conceived national movement and the rank and file of vaguely committed, naïve, uninformed students and fellow travelers—and then obstinately defending such unenlightened judgment in the name of freedom of speech.

The ranters and ravers and the sweet talking spokespersons who will mouth, some cynically, some innocently, the full range of jihad rhetoric could never stand up to an honest debate on any one of the questions that will be raised—and immediately shot down—during the so-called Solidarity "conference." The invective position papers of these groups could not pass Freshman composition. The doubtful underpinnings and suspicious financing of these solidarity movements is fully documented. In short, everything a university stands for should stand against the hosting of this conference.

So why does Rutgers insist? Isn't it a case of juvenile emotions and fond memories of the Sixties? Student activism and all that nostalgia? But the times, dear Rutgers, are a changin' and the stakes are too high to allow for latter day Woodstock saints.

No, there is no excuse for hosting this conference. It is action unbefitting a university. Can't they see the difference? A university can host a conference where Communist ideologists explain how capitalism exploits workers. A university cannot host a conference organized in solidarity with bands of terrorists who kidnap rich people, chop them to pieces, and burn their bodies to punish them for exploiting workers. It's that simple.

And how simple Abe Greenhouse, our value added Jew. Change the Abe to Bob, cut off the house and leave the Green, don't mention his grandfather, and suddenly his value for the Palestinian solidarity movement goes down a few big notches. The young man goes for a frolic in Judea and Samaria (yes, that is the real name of this region), he's ~~wined~~ and dined (Israeli forces are still looking for the American yeshiva student who disappeared two weeks ago) and flattered (a young woman from Tiberias is missing; a soldier was kidnapped, tortured and murdered under similar circumstances) and our brave young Greenhouse stands up to the ferocious Israelis who would dare to place a barrier between themselves and those who are waiting for a chance to hop on the next big luscious bus and blow it to smithereens. And this is supposed to be taking a look at both sides of the question? No, my boy. You have to be braver than that! You have to be a human shield on an Israeli bus. Not just any bus, but yesterday's bus that left the Kotel at around 9 PM.

And now, excuse me, no offense meant to our Christian cousins, but the value added Jew, according to this article which rings too true to be inaccurate, stands straight and tall, points the finger at Israel (hospital personnel are treating a one-month old baby injured in the blast, they don't know what became of the parents) and says, more or less, okay, Israel, exist if you must, but get your act together and give us those good Jewish values: compassion and altruism. He must have read too fast. It's not easy to catch up on Judaism, we can all attest to that, even the most learned are called to endless study and exceptional vigilance. But young people today, especially when they are activists for Causes, are in a hurry. So perhaps young Greenhouse skipped right over the Torah and found himself in the Gospels without even realizing he'd crossed into a new territory. Whatever, and however, he missed an important line:

You will choose life.

BEHOLD THE GHOSTS
OF HOLY FRENCH POLITICS
1 September 2003

The official count of victims of this summer's heat wave in France is 11,435 and still climbing. How is it possible in this day and age? Who are these people? How did they die? What could have been done, what can be done in the future, why didn't we know and why does this figure, endlessly repeated, never take on the weight of reality?

They don't exist. They are ghosts come to haunt the land of the Declaration of the Rights of Man. Martyrs sacrificed on the altar of histrionic humanitarianism in a society that worships imaginary human beings and leaves its own to die. In any healthy democratic society this death toll would overturn the chessboard: the public would be up in arms, the press would be digging up stories, experts would explain... Nothing of the sort here. One fall guy fell. No one seems to really care.

The right wing government blames the Socialist's 35-hour work week and the general population for neglecting the old folks, the Socialists blame the government's hard hearted social welfare cutbacks, the Green party blames everyone, doctors and health care workers react with varying degrees of honesty, the press reports it in flat, stale, repetitive, unconvincing prose, and the living savor their last days of vacation and head for September as usual. There is no soul-searching.

Holier than thou France, so holy that only the UN can deserve its blessings, shovels up the dead, stacks them in refrigerated trucks, and rushes to bury them before the promised strikes and demonstrations of *la rentrée*. But these dead civilians give the lie to a torrent of vociferous protestations from a society that makes a profession of defending the wretched of the earth. They said no to military action against Saddam Hussein because heaven forbid it might harm innocent civilians; they wring their hands over Palestinians melting in the blazing sun at Israeli checkpoints; they understand why local Muslims, exacerbated by the deaths of Palestinian civilians, would set fire to synagogues and beat up Jews. As for the excruciating civilian suffering caused by 9/11, the French pursed their lips and advised Americans to question the whys and wherefores of this eloquent expression of legitimate grievances by the Oppressed...instead of lashing out with bombs that might fall on innocent Afghan civilians.

Does life and death really matter to these finger wagers? The hundreds of thousands of Iraqi civilians tortured to death under the reign of Saddam Hussein registered zero on the French humanitarian scale; the only deaths that counted were the victims of American [sic] sanctions, the starving children, the agonizing patients put to the scalpel without anesthesia; brave doctors lifted their scrub masks to decry the American [sic] sanctions (and then went back to slicing off ears and other body parts from suspected opponents of the supreme Saddam?)

But today the torture chambers are visible for all to see, mutilated corpses are dug up, simple Iraqi civilians cry their hearts out over the loss of their loved ones, and French foreign policy doesn't bat an eyelid. Saddam was a bit rough but the enemy is elsewhere. Israel pursues its policy of targeted killings of "activists," destroying all hopes for peace. Americans get picked off in Iraq, destroying their dreams of conquest. Israeli civilians are massacred in a Jerusalem bus because their government insists on hunting down "activists." Iraq is shaken to the timbers by terrorist attacks? Bingo! French media make a beeline for the most strident, nasal, fanatical condemnation of the "Occupation." What's this mess? Where's our security? Funeral processions are a hit in the French media, as long as they are big budget casts of thousands wailing breast-beating revenge- threatening Muslim funerals.

As for the 11,435 civilian casualties they are being dumped quietly into graves as fast as they can be dug, it's so low key, all the way to the buck-passing. Who were these people and why did they die? How can such overwhelming figures lie below the level of public attention in a post-industrial information age nation? On <u>August 13th</u> *Le Monde*, the newspaper of <u>record</u>, reported that the health minister was subject to some criticism for his management of the ongoing crisis which had led to <u>hundreds</u> of deaths.

Where was the press when all this dying was going on? Dancing with José Bové and his *altermondialiste* elves on the *plateau de Larzac*. People were dying because they didn't have fans let alone air conditioners and Arafat's buddy José Bové, *l'homme providentiel* who tears down McDonald's and tears up genetically modified corn, was crucifying capitalism, shitting on globalization, trashing technology, breathing fire at Americans, and ushering in a new world order.

French editorialists gleefully declare that the Americans should admit their dismal failure, go down on their knees and beg the UN to come in and handle the mess they've made in Iraq. Jacques Chirac calls for an international conference to impose a peaceful settlement on recalcitrant Israel. Former Secretary of Foreign Affairs, Hubert Védrine announces that the United States is in a "classical colonial situation" in Iraq. And France still thinks Hamas has a political wing, and wants to keep it flying.

Words no longer have meaning in this society. Information is blocked at the source. Jealousy, envy, and covetousness have hardened the arteries where thought should flow freely. Spiteful pronunciamentos are delivered helter skelter, breaking up the chains of logic that would help people understand complex situations. Disgraceful covenants are concluded out of the public eye by political leaders who drape themselves in pure white togas to preach pacifism in the international agora. A pitiful farce played out on the world stage in the months leading up to the military campaign in Iraq has leeched out the vital intellectual juices that might have helped French citizens assume their responsibilities in these times of mortal danger.

Now the farce is over and reality strikes from an unsuspected angle. Death comes calling on those who took the name of human rights in vain. All those phony causes defended from a distance, all that prancing and preening in NGO mirrors, all that cuddling with evil forces in the name of adulterated justice swings back with a wallop. European record-holder for antisemitic incidents, last ditch defenders of despots and terrorists, France self-destroys, giddy with delusions of grandeur and incapable of respecting the basic rules of civilization. A staggering third-world death toll from a simple unexpected change in the weather!

You would think this might induce a smidgeon of humility? *Tu parles*!

Gérard Araud, newly appointed French ambassador to Israel, was caught spouting the usual anti-Israel blather within earshot of *Yedioth Aharonoth* reporter Boaz Bismuth. Araud branded Ariel Sharon a "rogue" and diagnosed Israel as a "paranoid State."

Incorrigible.

National Review Online

Reply to criticism of the above after it was posted on MoveOn.org

"America, love it or leave it!" Sound familiar? It was a big hit in the late sixties and early seventies. Only it didn't come from the left, it came from the hard hats and other benighted elements. How did it fall into the hands of MoveOn.org readers? And why do you reply with nasty ad hominem arguments instead of addressing the facts? You don't know anything about our family, you don't know how much I loved my adopted country, you are two weeks behind on the official death toll figures, and you react like wounded animals when I shed—eloquent, yes eloquent—light on the terrible irony of professional humanitarians who allow more than 11,000 people to die in the space of 2 weeks. If I am not mistaken, MoveOn.org is home to tens of thousands who severely criticize the American government, society, politics, economy, action, etc. MoveOn faithfuls love Israelis who trash their own government, society, etc. And I am supposed to smile and say (French) cheese?

Why do you squirm when I bring to life those 11,435 people who died in the shadows of human rights cant? Something like half the French population has interpreted this death toll as a sign of serious trouble in our society. And many thousands interpret this serious trouble in the same terms as those presented in my article. And by the way, if you don't believe in ghosts (I don't) the very title would indicate that I was not taking a measured journalistic approach to the subject, with hemming and hawing and this might be and that appears to indicate, and an anonymous official declared.

As for those who would give me lessons in history, what would you say if this were 1938? Do you think the American expats who left France were happy to go home? Do you know what would have happened to them if they had stayed. And the Jews who fled Europe? You think they didn't love their countries? And those who stayed? What price did they pay for loving their countries? This is not 1938, and I stand with people who will not let that history repeat itself.

When a luxury goods label hides shoddy merchandise, you have a choice: believe the label or trust yourself to judge the real value of the merchandise. Instead of accusing me of *lese-majesté*, you should take another look at what is happening in Europe, and particularly in France. France is your enemy. And as long as you keep on thumb sucking those human rights- UN legitimacy-third world excuses, you will misread contemporary history and condemn us (us = *nous* = we who live in France) to rapid decline and heart-breaking destruction of the values of la République.

MoveOn d'accord, c'est très bien, mais il faut aussi wake up. And don't throw the alarm clock at the wall to punish it for ringing.

...OF THE PEOPLE, BY THE PEOPLE, FOR THE PEOPLE
11 September 2003

The French are indignant. Their patience has run out. This Iraqi thing, how much longer is it going to drag on? Though there's no denying the satisfaction derived from the daily tally. Quagmire in Iraq, another American soldier killed today. Chaos in Baghdad, two American soldiers killed the day before yesterday (when there are no fresh bodies, they dig up recent casualties). Bad news for Bush, American soldiers are dying by the dozens. While ordinary French civilians were passing away by the thousands during an August heat wave, these daily specials from Iraq were generously served with a nasty grin. Military deaths in war were proof of American incompetence, civilian deaths at home were an unavoidable side effect of unruly meteorology. And besides, didn't Booush declare on May 1ˢᵗ that the war was over? Hmmmph! They never should have gone in there in the first place. It was against international law. And they better get out before it turns into another Vietnam. You notice they don't say "another Dienbienphu." Yes, if you ask your ordinary French journalist or his equally ordinary reader, the diagnosis is clear and the treatment beyond a doubt: hightail out of there like a woman running away from a mouse, put the UN in for a short stint, and then hand the whole thing over to the Iraqis for heaven's sake. Proof that they know what they are talking about? The Health Minister recently declared that our health services functioned properly and did what had to be done under the circumstances (meaning the extraordinary occurrence of a real sizzling summer). So how could they be wrong about Iraq?

Yes, French patience has run out. This whole Iraq business has been going on since last spring and those stupid Americans still haven't brought democracy to the country they dared to invade and now occupy, in spite of hefty *résistance.* So if the boys turned Iraq into a spic 'n span democracy before the end of October would the French find it in their hearts to forgive us for barging in there with our muddy boots and no UN laissez passer? Don't bet on it.

The fervor for democracy has no bounds. And the defense of democracy is a full time job. When it's not the Americans depriving Iraq of the stability it enjoyed under the regime of what's his name, it's the Israelis plotting openly to banish *le président élu de l'Autorité Palestinienne* Yasser Arafat. How dare they? He is the duly elected legitimate leader of the Palestinian people and the French will never under any circumstances betray the indestructible bonds that bind us to a fellow democratically elected democrat, namely Yasser Arafat.

And if you don't believe he is a democrat, just try creating all those prime ministers, cabinets, over-ministers, under-ministers, supervisory services, parallel services, joint chiefs, united commands, and I won't go on you get the idea, only a real democrat would go to the trouble of all these parliamentary niceties before pulling out his gun and snarling "I'm the boss!"

The European Union does not bandy about its power with a heavy hand. Hamas? Terrorists? Now let's see what could be terroristic about helping widows and orphans. Okay, first they manufacture the widowhood, the orphanhood and even better they get the mothers to be orphaned of their children and the children widowed of their adult futures but handing out goodies is not called terrorism in the Old Country's book. So they hand out goodies when Israelis are blown to bits? By their Hamas buddies? All right, we'll look into that. A careful reading of the mainstream French press yields no information that might corroborate these exaggerated Americano-Israeli claims. There are activists, militants, members... oh yes, and extremists, well that's not too lovely but look at all these spiritual leaders, political leaders, theorists, analysts, engineers, students, camp counselors. Isn't this just the sort of democracy that Americans do not know how to establish in Iraq?

Granted. For the sake of argument. But then what is the use of Road Maps and Quartets? The people chose their leader, their leader chose *la lotta continua,* the result is a fiasco so why can't Israel fight to win and give the world the Middle East peace it has been longing for like an eternal virgin waiting for her prince charming? Ah! Israel can't fight to win, because it might hurt people. Palestinian people, innocent bystanders who seem to always be standing around every time a terrorist, excuse me an activist goes by. But aren't they the voters who democratically elected President Arafat? So why shouldn't they democratically share in the fruits of the wonderful program he has put into action. For once a politician honors his campaign promises and no one seems to appreciate it. He said jihad, jihad, jihad. And he does jihad, jihad, jihad. Rome wasn't destroyed in a day. His electorate is patient. And to while away the time before the Ultimate Victory, they can always opt for the fast track: shahidom

Expel Yasser Arafat? Our American buddies put their feet down! No, no, we mustn't do that. And where would we be without our America? And where would they be without us? Up to their necks in dhimmitude, like the European Union! Did the Americans expel Ousama bin Laden? No. They just hunted him down until he turned into a has-been. His old films turn up every few months on Al Jazeera but I don't know if they get laughs anymore. Did the Americans banish Saddam Hussein? No. They just chased him down until he went underground and if you ask me they're hoping he'll squiggle out of one of those Rafah tunnels some fine day when a Tsahal sharpshooter is waiting for deliveries.

You have to give the French credit. Try to follow their logic. Not only is it naughty to lay your hands on a democratically elected president, especially when he is the founder of a movement whose goal is to expel you from your towns and cities and *kibbutzim* and *yishuvim* and green-houses and universities, it is also counter-productive. Because let's say you refuse to listen to reason or buckle under threats, and you kick him out. Do you think he's going to be replaced by a nice guy in a 3-piece suit? Of course not. Arafat ousted, Hamas will instantly fill the void. And for all their laudable charitable functions, Hamas is not democratically elected.

On the other hand, whatever prime minister might be chosen and confirmed by due process and, further, should manage to present his government and get it running, he better not lift a hand against Hamas. The people won't stand for it. As we saw only last week, if the choice is between Hamas and a PM in a 3-piece or even a casual suit, the people's choice is Hamas. Public opinion polls confirm: if elections were held today, Hamas would win.

Oh? Not Arafat?

Does that explain why the European Union reluctantly, belatedly, but finally decided to give Hamas its coveted AOC terrorist label? I keep wondering if there's not some cute trick lurking behind that—admit it— sudden turnabout. The French were promising to vote *nyet*, and then they didn't. My ear constantly tuned to the nuances of our Pravda radio network has been noticing the repetition of a curious detail. Between the decision and the decree, between the intention and the implementation, falls the shadow. And in the shadows, were the bank accounts already frozen or will they be frozen next week, when the stately European Commission draws up the elegant official decree that will freeze the... already emptied accounts? Maybe the money was transferred to one of Arafat's highly personal richly endowed portfolios.

This might seem far-fetched or downright nasty if you don't know about the recent triumph of French diplomacy. A compromise has been reached, France withdrew its threat of another *nyet* and simply ab-stained when the UN Security Council voted to end sanctions against Libya, another eminently democratic country reintegrated into the con-cert of nations, having promised to pay damages for past errors without, lucky for them, having to make any promises about the future. The bone of contention had nothing to do with bringing terrorists, excuse me, activists, to justice. It was, rather, a question of closing the gap between the generous indemnities offered to victims of the American plane that unfortunately crashed under the unpleasant side effects of a Libyan-planted bomb, and the stingy package offered to victims of a French plane, accidented by the same method.

The gap was not closed, but effectively narrowed. The resolution passed. Another triumph of democracy. And everything should have been more or less satisfactory, as satisfactory as things can be under these horrific circumstances where your loved ones are blown up and scattered to the heavens, except that young Khadafi, president (elected?) of the foundation of the same name which out of the goodness of its heart had promised to fork over what was needed to bring the settlement up to par, immediately announced that the funds would be drawn exclusively and entirely from French firms doing business in Libya. A *jizya*, so to speak.

This should help us understand why Europeans in general and the French in particular are so vehemently opposed to American military intervention in the Middle East. These cultivated people know how to solve problems through negotiation and dialogue. And this should explain why these same cultivated people rush to the rescue of President Arafat whenever his sublime authority is endangered. Because President Arafat, model democrat, believes in solving problems by dialogue and negotiation.

Wrong again. So why can't these arguments ever make ends meet?

The people want Arafat, Arafat wants jihad, but the jihadists must be shielded from excess force, they must be spared the humiliation of checkpoints and the running insult of a security fence. The people want a state, their democratically elected leader wants a state, the international community must give them the state they want, and the state they want goes from the Mediterranean to the Jordan. What they want is what they have to get, and the accumulated frustration of not getting what they want has led to an explosive situation on Israeli street corners, busses, cafés, university cafeterias...

No democratic country can accept the atrocious random murder of its citizens by tens and twenties any day of the week for years on end. Democracy is <u>for</u> the people. Democratic leaders cannot expose their populations to slaughter by a foreign enemy without raising armies, going to battle, and defeating the enemy.

There is a difference between war and a shooting gallery. Democratic citizens accept the sacrifices of war. They do not go clickety click around a ring on the firing range waiting for their turn to be popped off.

Conclusion: someone is lying.

Either Arafat is a pox on his people and someone has to disarm him totally, absolutely, effectively and permanently, or he is the legitimate leader of his people, and his people is engaged in jihad against a sovereign nation, in which case not only Arafat but all of his voters will have to be banished together

How dare I even suggest such a cruel choice? How dare I be so simplistic in writing about such a terribly complex situation?

I dare, because I truly believe in democracy. And I know that President Arafat's constituency extends far beyond the borders of Gaza, Judea, and Samaria to encompass millions of voters prepared at any moment to vote with their kalashnikovs, rockets, missiles and eventually WMDs. These are the famous Palestinian refugees. It may be difficult for your average primitive American congressman who spends his career juggling subsidies, jobs, industrial complexes and the like to appreciate the postmodern democracy of a president Arafat who must repeatedly sign international agreements and agree to international peace plans that provide for all kinds of settlements—and particularly for Israeli withdrawal from same—knowing full well that none of these agreements will be accepted by his voters without the hidden clause: right of return.

These are his people, languishing in sordid refugee camps waiting for the signal to bundle up their belongings, shine up the golden key, and come home. To Tel Aviv and all the rest of Israel to which they hold a supralegitimate claim that no international law can counter.

We hold these truths to be self-evident but they hold us and our truths to be easy targets. They who?

That's the point. Either the people truly vote in real democratic elections and their will has been expressed, in which case they assume the consequences. Or the elections are a sham and Yasser Arafat is no more the legitimately elected president of the Palestinian Authority than a Hamas humanocide bomber is a member of a resistance movement fighting for the creation of a Palestinian State living peacefully side by side with Israel.

Time is running out ...

We, the people, will no longer stand by dumbly as the world loses its reason and the democracies their precious rights.

SEEING IS BELIEVING

18 December 2003:

Seeing is believing... and I'm afraid if you didn't see the December 18, 2003 episode of *Envoyé Spécial* on *France2* you won't believe what follows. I saw it, and I'm not sure I believe it myself. The program was announced during prime time news as the full story of the arrest of Saddam Hussein. Aha! Let's see how they are going to tell it, or spin it, or doctor it.

It was doctored all right. I don't know when they intended to air this film on the hunt for Saddam Hussein, produced by the Capa Agency. Sometime in the near future I suppose. The in-depth investigation of tricky dealings in counterfeit caviar announced in this week's TV guides was bumped. You can understand why. On the 18th of December 2003 this special on the difficulties, what am I saying the impossibility of finding Saddam had a shelf life of minus four days. Too good to be scrapped, with atmosphere shots of the Tigris at sunset, an American colonel with an Arab falcon on his wrist standing in beautifully angled sunlight on a terrace of the fabulous palace that is now his headquarters as he unflaggingly searches for Saddam. And of course he'll never find him. Oh no, all those GIs in top-secret operations rooms staring into computer screens are no match for Saddam. Those callow GIs won't make any headway against implacable traditions, steadfast tribal customs, endless stretches of ancestry, finely calligraphied tribal registers (women and children are not counted) and the anger of ordinary Iraqi citizens who hate them with a vengeance.

Hey, wait a minute. Saddam's been captured. He was shown, hirsute and groggy, in the opening seconds of the film. And we are reminded from time to time that unbeknownst to the GI hunters, and unsuspected by the proud tribal leaders, Saddam will in fact be arrested a few days from now. Now when? He has already been arrested. The film began with a replay of the familiar scenes, the entry to the rat hole, a long view of the farm. So what's going on here?

Believe it or not—I have no proof so it's simply a matter of logic and intuition—the film was intended to show, hee hee, that the Americans can't find Saddam. Then, due to unforeseen circumstances, it was quickly touched up and served as the real story of how they found him. A weary spectator might not have noticed the ploy but it stared me in the face. And then again, what more proof is needed than the film itself? It wasn't planned, produced, and edited in 3 days. Obviously it was made some time ago, and clearly it was made in the *Ousama bin Laden toujours introuvable* spirit.

They can't find bin Laden, they can't find Saddam, their soldiers are getting picked off like ducks in a shooting gallery, nobody wants them in the 'hood. Scenes of GIs armed to the teeth searching vainly for the intrepid leader are interspersed with seething groupings of loyal tribesmen who swear by their mustaches that no one will betray Saddam. I think I recognized some of the very hotheads who turned up in newsreels this week. They're shouting and screaming Saddam forever and we'll slit the American's throats, when suddenly an Iraqi policeman comes up, grabs a guy by the arm and drags him to the hoosegow.

That's now. That's just plain old simple reality. But when this French film was shot the Saddamites got the best lighting, the best billing, the most attention, the fullest respect. This was the people speaking. They're dressed for the part, they fit into the landscape, they're defending their homeland against the Occupation.

At one point a GI is briefing a small patrol that will head into town with him. We hear him say in English, "We're going to try to make friends." In the French translation this becomes, "We're going to look for informers." No easy matter. Nataf, the guy who snitched on Uday and Qusay, was disowned by his family. We get an on-site eye witness account of that dastardly deed from the baker across the street who unwittingly provided bread to Saddam's sons in their hideout. It was as you can imagine terrible. All that firepower, all that destruction. And if it weren't enough to kill the poor boys, they razed the house. Look, here's where it stood. A blind wall. A cute little toddler standing against it. The picture of innocence. Later, the assembled tribal leaders show us the letter in Arabic where the family swears that they had nothing to do with the betrayal and will have nothing more to do with the traitor. A man with a hawk nose and a red and white keffieh turban on his head says that you couldn't get an Iraqi to betray Saddam at any price, not even 2 million dollars.

But, the voice over comments: a few days later Saddam would be found.

How phony can you get?

If I had any doubts about the intentions of the first film they were re-solved by the second film. A full screen Old Glory flapping in the wind introduces a major exposé of the lies that justified the war. WMDs? What WMDs? There are none there were none and everyone knew it.

The American flag pops up at regular intervals throughout this super dramatic political sleuth show. It isn't graffitied with swastikas like it was in the jihadist antiwar demonstrations last year in Paris, but it is defi-nitely sullied. And the bad guys don't need black hats. They are clearly marked by clever camera work that flattens their faces, drains the color, giving them a scary look like macabre Halloween balloons. And they are always shown in power situations: at the UN Security Council, in the hallway of the CIA building, lying to the Senate. Their entries are filmed in slow motion—as if they could be frozen into admitting the truth—and accompanied by horror film music to make your heart beat faster. The point is that this war was justified by deliberately false accusations about Iraq's WMDs. Do you get it? That was the only justification, the whole argument, nothing but the argument, and it was a lie.

The villains are photographed at their worst in dehumanizing close-ups. The finger-pointers walk through tree shaded gardens, enter their homes through beautiful glass doors, sit intelligently in front of double barreled bookshelves and tell us how Bush lied because Cheney lied be-cause Tenet lied and told Powell to lie and dragged America into this senseless war, with soldiers dying every day, and even if all those dirty liars did bring down Saddam, which no one would deny is a good thing, their lies have sullied the very fibers of our democracy. Each in turn and filmed with hushed respect, John Judis of the Carnegie Foundation, Joseph Cirincione, Hans Blix, Greg Thielman, Jacques Baute, Joe Wil-son, and Mitch Mc Connell tell the truth about the liars. These homey or officey scenes with the truth-tellers are interspersed with crescendo passages of lies and liars. And, as in the hunting-for-Saddam film that preceded it, the WMD-lies investigation has been updated with a few words about the insignificant fact that Saddam Hussein has been arrested. The splicing is so obvious you can almost see the masking tape!

An antiwar demonstration on the Washington mall gets big billing, with special focus on families of soldiers, two count them two, who say bring our boys back home and what are we doing there. Scenes of barrels of uranium in Niger with a supporting cast of clever Google-searching prove that the purported Iraqi purchasing contract was a fake. The stars and stripes come in for a quick flap and the whole affair is wound up in the heart of the American Enterprise Institute.

Now these guys—and girls—are thinkers of another stripe. Nothing to do with the relaxed college professor types whose unquestioned veracity serves as base line for the serious allegations that motivate the France2 investigation. These folks are neoconservatives! They were defending the war even before the liars started lying in order to drag the hapless American public into the quagmire. Now they are on the defensive. Because of the WMDs. Oh yes, the by the way, Saddam was found and arrested but what does that have to do with anything. And what could be the value of Danièle Pletka's testimony? Just back from Iraq, telling what she saw? Who cares? Nothing said in the halls of the AEI can be taken seriously. So, tricky cameraman, use your camera like a machine gun, and get that lady! Ratatatatat...

The "investigation" closes on the Iwo Jima monument. Explains that significant battles are engraved on the base. And what of the war in Iraq? Will it be a source of pride, will the results wipe out the dishonor of the lies that led to it? Or, if GIs continue to die, will it be chalked up as a terrible disgrace?

Old Glory. Over and out.

Now we are in the studios and two well-groomed rapacious anchorwomen are eliciting the last word from a young man named Philippe. Unfortunately I didn't get his last name. Maybe he's the producer of the show, or of the films. Whatever. He's so smart he doesn't need a last name. Philippe explains to the birdy ladies that it is impossible to undertake any honest investigation on the subject in the United States today. The whole thing is taboo, the whole field is fenced in, the doors are locked tight. But you can be sure that this affair will be exploited in the current election campaign. And watch out! Howard Dean, who has been unstinting in his opposition to the war, made a phenomenal rise to favor and prominence in the Democratic camp.

Did you get that? Tremble in your boots, George W. Bush. You might not be aware but a good portion of the French public, unhampered by your muzzled press, does know that Howard Dean is packing a punch you'll be hard put to parry. The truth will out! And maybe, says Philippe, if American soldiers keep getting killed over there... Well, you understand, Bush, your goose will be cooked.

Cut.

So, if you want to know how the French swallowed the capture of Saddam Hussein, *Envoyé Spécial* is a good indication: like a bitter pill. It wasn't supposed to pan out that way, and we're not going to let this minor incident spoil our fun.

Film N° 1 was obviously meant to show that the war is going badly. All Bush's forces and all of his men cannot find the great Saddam. And *la résistance* is waiting behind every tree! The 2nd film, a marvel of impressionism, is meant to show that Iraq is about the size of your average suburban split level and even a child could have known what was going on there during the period 1991-2002. If they were making WMDs, we would have known. If they had made them, even the stupid Americans would have found them by now. There weren't any, they won't find any, and it's not because Saddam is resting in prison and a late model Russian Mig has been dug out of the sand that *Envoyé Spécial* will ever have to update the second film.

It is engraved on French retinas, and will be thrown in my face at the next friendly gathering. *Aha, tu as vu, Nidra, il n'y avait pas d'armes de destruction massive et ton gouvernement le savait! Il est formidable, ce Hans Blix. Et l'autre, Greg Thielman, quel sourire* !

Speaking of lies, I would like to figure out the physiology of this kind of bald-faced lying. Why is it that such shallow, manipulative, naïvely dishonest misnamed investigation seems to suck the oxygen out of the very air one breathes?

National Review Online[15]

TEAR ON THE DOTTED LINE

31 December 2003

"Monsieur this is not the true France," Daniel Ben Simon, *Haaretz,* December 26 2003, Tevet 1, 5764

Try to make sense of this puzzling mixture of true and false! It begins with some only too familiar sad tales, real life testimony from Jewish residents of Sarcelles exposed to every sort of harassment, assault, threat and insult from their Muslim neighbors. You wouldn't want to live one single day this way. You can't believe that Jews in a supposedly modern democratic country can be expected to put up with such mistreatment. And I know even worse stories coming from the same lawless territory. So I suppose the pâtissier, the Oriental pâtissier sighed and said to monsieur Ben Simon, "*Ici ce n'est pas la vraie France....*or maybe "*Monsieur, ici ce n'est pas vraiment la France,»* or "*Nous ne sommes pas vraiment en France ici, monsieur.* » Something of the sort, meaning this is not really France. However he put it, for anyone who has been to Sarcelles recently, the plaintive assessment is thoroughly convincing.

One would expect the article to continue in this vein. There are so many avenues to explore. Are these occupied territories an epiphenomenon or, heaven forbid, a vision of the real France of the near future? Are the persecuted Jews of Sarcelles dispensable... in the eyes of the real French, including the real French Jews? Or are they a warning of what awaits all of us?

Ben Simon does indeed ask, *What are France's Jews undergoing today?* And then, instead of searching for answers to this heartbreaking question that inhabits our days and nights, he throws us a whopper: *"in the past three years, which were studded with anti-Semitic attacks and incidents, not one Jew has been hospitalized, not one Jew has been injured or has required medical treatment of any kind against this background."*

What a slap in the face of the embattled banlieue Jews! And it happens to be totally false. Tear on the dotted line.

March 22 2003: Muslims participating in an anti-war demonstration attacked six members of Hashomer Hazair. All six required medical attention. One of the youths, Yoni M. was beaten over the head with iron bars and almost lost an eye. The attack was (partially) captured on video by Digipresse. Nicolas Sarkozy visited the HH locale one week after the incident and promised to bring the assailants to justice. Three months later the case was closed.

Ignoring the fully publicized peace march incident and dozens of others of equal violence, Ben Simon goes on to claim: "*The one serious incident was the puzzling stabbing attack on Rabbi Gabriel Farhi...*" Wrong again. The attack against Rabbi Farhi is one of the more *puzzling* incidents, because of allegations that the superficial abdominal wound was self-inflicted. And it is one of many such cases where incidents have been reported, denied, confirmed, discredited. Where do you go for the truth when the entire Jewish community is accused of self-inflicting antisemitism because of its support for Israel? How do you establish the truth when anyone who denounces an antisemitic act or crime is dismissed as an extremist, a fabulator, a holocaust profiteer? What is really happening to Jews in France?

Sébastien Selam (z"l) was not hospitalized.[16] No medical attention could have brought him back to life. His throat was slit. Twice. His face was gouged. I spare you the details.[17] He was murdered by a Muslim neighbor in his 10th arrondissement low-rent apartment building. Obviously the wounds were not self-inflicted. The murderer was whisked into a mental hospital and no one knows if he will ever be brought to trial. So is this an antisemitic crime, or just one more puzzling incident?

An eleven-year-old boy was systematically persecuted by two Muslim schoolmates from September to December of this year. Twice he required emergency-room treatment for his injuries. The affair was handled with the same mixture of secrecy and confusion that has prevailed over the past three years, but it happens that a journalist's daughter was in the same class as the persecuted Jewish boy. So the story came out. In *Le Monde* no less. This is not a Sarcelles anecdote, it isn't a case of friction between immigrant Jews and immigrant Arabs in the scary *banlieues*. It happened at the prestigious Lycée Montaigne in the 6th arrondissement of Paris. The bullies confessed, then retracted, then confessed but one of the boys, sincerely baffled, said he didn't understand what all the fuss was about; this kind of thing [beating up Jews] is common practice today.

A 31 year-old Jewish woman was assaulted, raped, and injured on the 30th of November near her home in the Bellefontaine neighborhood of

Toulouse. The assailant scribbled an anti-Semitic message on her chest with a ballpoint pen.[18]

How can a journalist write about what is happening to the Jews in France and scrupulously avoid reporting these incidents... and hundreds more?

Skittering away from *la banlieue*, Ben Simon briefly interviews a few prominent, well-integrated French Jews living in good neighborhoods who confirm the troubling rise of antisemitism. But he undercuts each example with a disclaimer and tops it off with an extravagant compliment for France. As we say in French, *je connais la musique*. France is not antisemitic, French Jews are elected to high office, President Chirac is not antisemitic, he officially confessed to France's Shoah guilt.

After a long detour in the *beaux quartiers*, Ben Simon takes us back to the horrible *banlieue* for another lurid example of persecution, reported by students in a Jewish lycée. You could cry! All of the students have been insulted, threatened with death and extermination, attacked, mocked, spat upon. They have to hide *kippot* and *Magen Davids* but they can't hide their Jewish souls. It's happening one half hour by commuter train from the center of Paris. No one can stop it. These kids are on their way out: they see no future for themselves in France. But Ben Simon, in magnificent intellectual tradition, far from the bruised bodies and hearts, wonders if we are dealing with "*Real or imagined anti-Semitism?*"

Another dotted line.

Philosopher Alain Finkielkraut, driven "*to the verge of hysteria... has been relentlessly spreading fear and anxiety...*" Well, my friends, if you want to see some real hysteria I recommend a walk on the wild side, *chez les jihadistes*. Take a look at the attack on the Hashomerniks in the abovementioned video or enjoy some authentic peace march scenes in Jacques Tarnero's film-essay *Décryptage*. Israeli flags covered with swastikas, Zionism = racism, Sharon = Hitler, and hordes of modestly hijabed Muslim women screaming unveiled virulent hatred.

Ben Simon has other fish to fry. And, for want of a better frying pan, he digs up a Raymond Aron review of a book by Bernard-Henri Levy... published 25 years ago. BHL, says the late Aron, "*With his hysteria is nourishing hysteria in segments of the Jewish community...*" This passage is so garbled I had to read it three times. How could the "*late Ray-*

mond Aron" review BHL's *Who Killed Daniel Pearl?* When I finally realized that the accusation of hysteria goes back a quarter of a century, I couldn't understand why Ben Simon would want to undermine his already shaky article by proving the contrary of what he is claiming to say. Given the thousands of nasty to serious incidents in Sarcelles alone, BHL is more of a visionary than a hysteric, Finkielkraut hits the nail on the head, and yours truly should get Ben Simon's job at *Haaretz*.

Is France an antisemitic country?

The question is futile. You can argue it up, down, and sideways. As this *Haaretz* article shows, you can give hair-raising examples of persecution of Jews, and then throw in a statement, an evaluation, a declaration based on unfounded generalities, and conclude that France is not an antisemitic country. Tear on the dotted line. Is French antisemitism really French? Because the hoodlums who attack Jews are Muslim. Yeah, but they are in most cases French Muslims. Citizens. With voting rights. And they can't be kicked out. You can quote discerning thinkers who express serious concern about the pervasive antisemitism in French society and then cancel them out with meaningless disclaimers. You can, based on nothing but vague supposition, entrenched ideology, or wishful thinking, claim that this brief upsurge of antisemitism is directly related to the Arab-Israeli conflict, and seems to be waning. So what if it flares up again tomorrow? As it did last month. And what if it is enflamed, next time, by some other conflict or some other aspect of the conflict?

This is why I opt for a practical, pragmatic, easily verifiable question: how much antisemitism is acceptable in France? Is it acceptable, when you belong to a French family that goes back hundreds of years, to know that Jewish teenagers in Sarcelles are insulted and attacked daily? Is it acceptable, when no one has put a hand to your child, to know that an 11 year-old boy is beaten up in a good school in the intellectual heart of Paris? Is it acceptable to be told that the Muslim murderer of a young Jewish DJ is mentally ill, and the antisemitic component of his act is calculated at 1/3rd of the total motivation? Have French Jews settled for a *seuil de tolerance*, a tolerable level of persecution beyond which they will... would... should react? Or is this tolerance measured on a sliding scale? Three years ago we were horrified to hear pro-Palestinian demonstrators shouting "Kill the Jews" in the streets of Paris. Today, when Jews are beaten, hounded, forced out of schools, neighborhoods and maybe the country, are we dumbstruck or, as Daniel Ben Simon suggests, hysterical, or manipulated by hysterical Israelis beating the bush for candidates for *aliya*?

Ben Simon winds up his article by accusing Jewish men of a longstanding disrespect for France's secular values, by flouting yarmulkes or Stars of David, and warns that this practice will soon be forbidden. Aside from the fact that no one ever claimed that ostensible or ostentatious or outward or obvious or highly visible signs of Judaism or Christianity have perturbed French tranquility, and knowing full well that these signs were dragged in by the hair to hide the real concern of French society—Islamic conquest—who ever said hijab and yarmulkes would be forbidden in public? Tear on the dotted line.

But, says Ben Simon, *Some Jews are already preparing themselves for the new reality.*" And suddenly, with no apologies, French reassertion of secular values against Islamic inroads is made to coincide with Jewish insecurity in Islamized France and the whole mess is dumped on the head of Chief Rabbi Joseph Chaim Sitruk who recently advised Jews to wear baseball caps over their *kippot*. So they won't be attacked. Tear on the dotted line. End of article. Now reduced to shreds.

Can we blame the kind reader who just wants to be helpful? Tries to put the article back together. And ends up applying the wisdom of the late Raymond Aron to the... uhhh... hysterical Rabbi Sitruk. Why should Jewish men stoop to hiding their Jewishness if they've already been attacked for three years without requiring even a snitch of medical attention? And why do *lycéens* in Sarcelles think they have no future in France when the worst that can happen is to suffer a self-inflicted wound like the publicity seeking Rabbi Gabriel Farhi? And, finally, monsieur, how could the true France be antisemitic if President Chirac says it isn't and he isn't. *M'enfin, c'est lui le président. Il aurait été le premier à le savoir. Si c'était vrai.*

Haaretz [19]

BETRAYED BY EUROPE
AN EXPATRIATE'S LAMENT
January 2004:

[The original text submitted to *Commentary Magazine*, "Meet me at Starbuck's," began with this account of my meeting with an unidentified journalist. The final version, edited in collaboration with Neal Kozodoy, begins on page 210.]

It's not so easy to know when you're deluding yourself and when you're finally seeing the light.

I have an appointment with a distinguished journalist who does not see eye to eye with me on a burning question but isn't afraid to talk about it face to face. Instead of the red carnation of olden days, he sent me the link to his picture on a website. I said I'd be wearing a purple hat... and kept my promise, though I had to take it off as I came out of the metro and headed into a blustery wind sweeping across a broad anonymous avenue somewhere out on the red line reaching into Maryland if I'm not mistaken. Now safely inside this small Starbuck's flooded with winter sunshine I put on my fedora and wait for the link to activate.

He walks in, I rise to meet him, he goes off to get our coffee and, height of *galanterie*, brings me my espresso in a real cup. I didn't even know Starbuck's had such things. Over the years I've imbibed quite a few espressos *de misère* swishing despondently in the lower depths of a paper cup that had sucked out all flavor and warmth but I never complained. In my adopted hometown of Paris I can't even swallow the coffee in any run of the mill café. It is, as we say, *infecte*. I order a coffee as a sort of shield against the glowering waiter, and let it get cold in its thick porcelain cup. I can drink a café at the Chaie de l'Abbaye in St. Germain des Près. And where else? Well, soon perhaps, at Starbuck's... in *le Marais, qui sait*?

Now I am deep in conversation with the journalist. Every word counts. I take no notes. This is not an interview. Page proofs of his coming article lie under his elbow on the small round table. We are making our way through the thicket of a thorny matter involving partial evidence and purportedly impartial judgment.

It's a pleasure to be able to speak freely, to disagree without antagonism and elicit the deep truths which, I am convinced, will ultimately lead this intelligent man to become a precious ally. Maybe he'll never change his mind on the specific question that first brought us together-- and still separates us—but he is too honest to deny that it raises the broader question of responsible news reporting in a 21st century democracy. *A suivre.*

My purple hat is set at a jaunty angle, the conversation is humming along, but I am having a hard time holding my own with the Starbuck chair. Too high, too deep, too hard, too slippery for petite madame Goldilocks. This structural engineering problem, amplified by the slippery effects of the silky lining of my elegant long skirt, results in a constant slide to the rear of the chair. I inch forward, trying to get a bit of traction but my feet barely touch the floor. The angle of inclination and degree of slipperiness preclude any status quo.

I know a lot about adjusting to foreign countries, feeling at home with strangers, acquiring exotic skills.... The question is, how do you adjust to your native land? What makes us feel at home? Why do we leave home? Where would I put myself, who would I be if I came back home?

I never thought of myself as an expatriate. I wasn't an American in Paris. And I certainly was not French. If anything I thought of myself as a free-floating European in a swishy ballet. I had returned to the Europe of my origins. Not Budapest, not Przemysl, those were places we don't go back to. But Europe, and all it can boast of. Beautiful cities that are really lived in, monuments at every street corner, savoir faire, craftsmanship, savoir vivre, boutiques, refinement, manners, health care and free education, history, French windows and parquet floors, and...

...the Shoah?

Another sort of high, hard, slippery, deep chair that is throwing me off balance. And no matter how I try to inch forward and engage in honest discussion there is no distinguished gentleman across the table for that conversation.

I came back to be European and, irony of ironies, Europe is showing me why my grandparents left. For a novelist and student of history, this is a fantastic experience. For the...

"Betrayed by Europe: An Expatriate's Lament"
An American in Paris is subjected to a lesson in European and Jewish history.
Washington, D.C., November 29, 2003
It is not so easy to know when you're deluding yourself and when you are finally seeing the light. When I look back at my reasons for leaving the United States for France in 1972, some seem to me as outmoded—

and, in retrospect, as endearing—as Beatles haircuts and Vietnam-war protests. Others stubbornly persist. In any event, my career as a serious American novelist having been short-circuited, I opted for the improbable exploit of becoming a writer in French and a professional translator, and I succeeded. I am long settled in Paris; the three youngsters I brought there, tucked under my free-flying wing, are mature adults with fast-growing children of their own. We have excelled in flexibility, risen to every challenge, transformed somewhat slapdash beginnings into a harmonious whole.

What happened? The sea change began on September 28, 2000, when the domestic repercussions of Arafat's prefabricated "al-Aqsa" *intifada* in Jerusalem struck me in a dizzying instant of recognition. I was hardly alone. Stunned and dazed, the formerly integrated, assimilated, liberated, progressive, and (in some cases) indifferent Jews of France found themselves—ourselves—thrust out of the body politic and herded into a virtual ghetto. In the years since then, things have only gotten worse, much worse.

Here I stand, endowed with an intimate knowledge of French language, thought, and reality—and on the threshold, perhaps, of France's, even Europe's, downfall. I know a lot about adjusting to foreign countries, feeling at home with strangers, acquiring exotic skills. I can eat with *ohashi* (don't ask me to call them chopsticks) like a native, I know how to take a shower with a pail of water in an African hut, I can dance... well, let me not string out my credentials. The question staring me in the face at the end of this three-week visit is, could I readjust to the United States, my native land? How could I get used to it, where would I put myself, who would I be if I came back home?

I never thought of myself as an expatriate; I'd let my American identity slip away while retaining the free-floating grace of being a foreigner. Instead, I'd been a "European," picking up after a brief interruption not exactly where my family had left off—not Budapest, not Przemysl, those were places we would not go back to—but Europe and all it could boast of. Beautiful cities that are really lived in, monuments at every street corner, savoir faire, craftsmanship, savoir vivre, boutiques, refinement, manners, health care, free education, history, French windows and parquet floors.

And . . . the Shoah? I came back to be European and, irony of ironies, Europe is showing me why my grandparents left. For a novelist and student of history, this is a fantastic experience. For a grandmother, it is agony. How can I explain to French grandchildren whose very existence is the consequence of my once flighty decision that I cannot entrust them to *their* native land? But how can I lead them to safety if I myself do not know how to go home?

I will have to change my way of looking at things. To some extent, I already *have* changed my way of looking at things. The post-Thanksgiving stampedes at the shopping mall? How I would have slathered them with leftist contempt decades ago. Today I see them as expressions of the common man's patriotism. No, the malls are not for me, I cannot live in a suburb; but it is incomparably better for people to shop their nation to prosperity than to be marching in the streets of Paris for jihad against the Jews or demonstrating for higher wages, shorter hours, and "justice" in Palestine.

The question is, how would I fit into the picture? Walking down a street in Brookline, Massachusetts, I can recognize myself, barely. But months of snow? I couldn't take it. Washington? Too square. New York? Perfect in theory, but in practice too frantic, and too expensive. Wouldn't it be great to reconnect with family, coast-to-coast cousins and nephews and nieces with their children, all so bright and energetic? Yes, but with grandchildren off to college so far away it might as well be Siberia or South Africa, I'd see them once a year if I was lucky.

Where, then?

En route to Paris, December 2, 2003

On my return flight—Air France, *bien entendu*—I pick up a copy of *Le Nouvel Observateur*. The images of President Bush's Thanksgiving trip to Iraq are still fresh in my mind. My heart went out to those men and women fighting to defend our lives, our freedom. Would French audiences ever see their shining faces, I wondered? Now, from the cover of the French weekly, a disheartened GI stares out at me, and I have my answer. "Iraq: Close-up of a Disaster," reads the headline. We see only the left half of the soldier's face, full front. His skin is reddened and smudged, sullen defeat veils his blue eyes, his mouth is pouting in reproach. Don't cry, poor boy, the *Nouvel Obs* is here to tell the world the true story of your debacle.

212

I keep in my archives a gem of an article from the same magazine, published shortly before the first Gulf war over a dozen years ago. It vividly describes—with photos, computer graphics, diagrams, interviews with retired generals—how the Americans, or rather the coalition in which the French were then nominally included, were heading for a fate worse than Vietnam. I'll never forget that article, or the dozens like it. But your average *Nouvel Obs* reader, chortling with delight over the current American "disaster" in Iraq, has no idea of his magazine's track record.

Last year, the journalist Sara Daniel (the daughter, as it happens, of editor-in-chief Jean Daniel) distinguished herself with an article in the *Nouvel Obs* on Arab honor killings in which she alleged that Israeli soldiers deliberately rape Palestinian girls knowing they will be killed (honorably) by their families. This caused an uproar, finally squelched by some wimpy verbiage about inadvertently dropped quotation marks and other such lies. Today, brave Sara is slogging around in Iraq. She spent a few days with the boys (and girls) of the 101st Airborne and, clever little French journalist that she is, found one willing to gripe into her tape recorder.

You know those amateur theatricals in which two people play ten roles? That's Sara's cut-rate journalism. A few quotes from the disgruntled soldier, a few lines about an ambush, a description of the dead and the mangled, and suddenly a whole company of miserable soldiers don't know what they are doing in Iraq and only want to go home. The hitch is, it's a company of one. Evidently the morale of the troops was *so* low that she could find only one soldier to whine for her.

Sara and the *Nouvel Obs* have access to all kinds of information. If you think al-Jazeera possesses the only doorstep at which mysterious videos are delivered to bring Americans the tidings of their imminent destruction, you might be surprised to learn that someone—who could it be, my goodness?—dropped a video at the feet of Mlle. Daniel. In this clip, courageous Iraqi freedom fighters are shooting a missile at a DHL cargo plane. Might this have something to do, perhaps, with some still photos published recently in *Paris-Match*? Same scene, but shot in two forms? I don't know (I've been back in the U.S. and couldn't follow all the threads), but I mean to ask around as soon as I return to Paris.

Already this much is clear. You've heard how terrorists invite al-Jazeera and other insiders to "come along and see us attack the Americans." Well, it seems that for this particular photo-op, *Paris-Match* was included. The way *Paris-Match* tells it, they received only the first half of the invitation, the "come along" part, when to their utter surprise, after three days of hanging out with the brave resistance—lo and behold!—a missile, a DHL plane, and pictures that no one ever expected to materialize.

As they say in French, *il ment comme il respire*, he lies as he breathes.

Paris, December 10, 2003

I used to run back to the U.S. for visits of ten days, just to see my family. Then I would return to my true love, Paris, and to my real life. That delicious sweet buttery butter, the perfect bread, our local open-air market. I loved the proportions: the distance on foot necessary to buy food for a day or two, eating all you could carry and nothing more, holding the whole country in the palm of your hand, all of it reachable by clean, modern, relatively inexpensive public transportation. I loved speaking French, couldn't wait to get back to it, loved my favorite boutiques, my fashionable clothes, my daily elegance.

There must be something adulterous about my relation to countries. I had a native land familiar as family, no language problems, my rightful place. I needed another country, a lover who would carry me off to adventure. I came back to my European origins, flourished in a European framework, delighted in making the exotic familiar. And now, my sincere affection betrayed, I am unforgiving.

Back in Paris, on a dreary winter morning, I'd ridden in from the airport with flood warnings cackling from the taxi radio. By the time I got home, torrential rains were inundating the south of France. For the next week, the evening news showed us floods, evacuations, raging rivers, stranded herds. Devastation. Six feet of water in the lowlands. Homes and businesses washed out for the fourth time in three years. Desolate homeowners peeling thick swatches of sodden plaster from recently refinished walls. Tears welling up as the camera panned to take in furniture, household appliances, books, clothes, mementos damaged beyond repair. The entire south of France was wading through rivers of despair. As if the whole country had dissolved in waves of tears. Or divine anger?

Sheep herders, wine growers, shopkeepers, small businessmen displayed their grief with dignity and restraint. On television, unsuspecting families who had bought fake-Provençal homes with red tile roofs and wisteria-garlanded patios were interviewed shaking their heads in dismay. Was it their fault that the regional authorities had issued building permits for flood lands? Now what? The parade of despair formed a panorama out of Balzac: villagers sporting cloth caps and authentic local accents, charming Mediterranean women glowing with healthy sensuality, typical rural backgrounds, landscapes, the people and the products I used to love.

Suddenly they disgust me. What is this simulacrum of a country inhabited by characters pretending to be actors out of a 1950's French comedy? Is it any wonder that they conduct their foreign relations like village bumpkins? But of course I'm faking, too, forcing myself not to like what I liked and to like what I still have misgivings about, breaking loose from my moorings and sending myself into orbit. Because I don't want to leave France and I can't stay.

Paris, January 14, 2004

I'm being treated to a poignant lesson in European and Jewish history. The 30's: why did they stay? Why didn't they run for their lives? Couldn't they see what was happening? I see before me a vivid demonstration of the deep roots we dig to make our lives bloom, the intricate biology of a human life, irrigated with the lifeblood of a community, inextricably connected to a society, born of life to give life to keep life alive. Leaving is not packing up and tipping your hat goodbye. It is tearing live flesh out of a living matrix.

I am, or was, the first American-born generation in a family that fled Europe before World War I: a lesson in the wisdom of leaving before it is too late. Now I am the first stage in the story of a three-generation "French" family. Why don't people just pick up and go while they still can? It's always the same. There is an ailing grandmother, a son in medical school, a daughter who just got married, a business too good to throw away and not good enough to sell. There are in-laws and obligations and unfinished business and . . . hope. Hope that it will all blow over. That people will come to their senses, reason win out, normal life resume. And so, blinded by hope, people minimize danger and cling to an imagined stability.

Jews are being persecuted every day in France. Some are insulted, pelted with stones, spat upon; some are beaten or threatened with knives or guns. Synagogues are torched, schools burned to the ground. A little over a month ago, at least one Jew was savagely murdered, his throat slit, his face gouged with a carving fork. Did it create an uproar? No. The incident was stifled, and by common consent—not just by the authorities, but by the Jews.

Some Jews are simply frightened; they are reluctant to take the subway, walk in certain neighborhoods, go out after dark. Others, clearly identifiable as Jews, are courageous and defiant. Many, perhaps the majority, show no outward signs of Jewishness and do not seek to know the truth about the rampant and increasingly violent anti-Semitism all around them. If you are Jewish but do not defend Israel or act too religious or look too different, you are not yet a target—so why insist on monitoring the danger when daily life is so delicious?

And the lies so tantalizing. A thick, hand-knit comforter of prevarication spreads itself over the French population. Every morning, instead of waking people up, the press tucks them in. France has become a nation of sleepwalkers. You sense it with particular sharpness after a visit to the U.S. How is anyone to face the truth about anything when the truth is hidden by 19th-century-style posturing, pretentious humanitarian hoodwinking, and low-down village tomfoolery?

France is in fact an adversary of the United States—as is its right, after all. But the French honestly believe their country is behaving like a reasonable ally, and there is no way to convince them of the contrary. They are hooked up to an intravenous flow of lies about the United States, fed propaganda disguised as information, molecules of fact dissolved in a carefully regulated solution to keep them on an even keel and save them from having to judge for themselves. No raw data allowed; one mustn't have people developing a taste for reality.

I don't see signs that any of this is about to change. Every measure taken in the right direction, or what might seem to be the right direction, hides a fatal flaw. After the floods, and with the exception of a brief parenthesis for a sourpuss acknowledgment of the arrest of Saddam Hussein, the subject of concern has become the *hijab*, the "Islamic veil." Enlightened by the findings of a national commission, the president spoke out grandiloquently in support of a law that would ban the wearing of "ostensible" signs of religious affiliation in schools and government offices. The time has come, said the president, to reaffirm the "values of the Republic" and to put an end to all these separate *communautarismes*, which he pronounced with a big zzzizzzy plural "s."

The law has not been drafted yet (it is scheduled for parliamentary debate in February), and even if it is passed, one wonders if it will ever be applied. But it is askew in its very conception. Unwilling or unable to name the problem for what it is—political Islam on the march—the government has turned headscarves into a religious issue and lined up its troops on the barricades of that peculiar French form of universalism known as *laïcité*. Since religion is the official culprit, the law will be evenhandedly aimed at the kippa as well, adding insult to injury for religious Jews just at a time when France's chief rabbi has advised them to hide their yarmulkes under baseball caps so they won't be beaten up by Islamists on the rampage.

So now, in the name of a doctrine originally promulgated to provide a bulwark against an overbearing Catholicism, the Jews are to be thrown in with those who really are hammering away at the secular values of the *République*. Jews lived quietly in France for centuries before the massive Muslim immigration started after World War II—but suddenly you cannot say anything bad about Muslims without saying something bad about Jews?

To be sure, the law is also going to mention that Catholics must not wear big crosses to school; but to my knowledge they have never intended to. Largely indifferent to the once-powerful Church that provoked the 1905 law mandating the separation of church and state, the vast majority of French Catholics swear by the principle of *laïcité* and don't even begin to suspect that they are being turned into *dhimmis* in their own country.

The handpicked leader of a recently created Muslim umbrella organization has called for reluctant compliance with the proposed law while already haggling for an Oriental compromise. But the major element in the organization, the radical UOIF, has mobilized against the law and against a Republic that would dare discriminate against Islam. You can't fool them by banning yarmulkes! And they intend to fight.

Will the pacifist and pacified French stand up and defend their nation? Or will we have to leave?

That is what it boils down to. Things have gone from shouting "death to the Jews" to firebombing schools and synagogues, to persecution, attacks, even murder. We have Muslim rage in schools, hospitals, and courtrooms. Police headquarters are attacked, hospital personnel beaten, judges threatened. The Republic is under siege, and what are the French doing about it? They are trashing America.

This, it seems, is their new Maginot line: the sneer of hatred. Hand in hand with the government and the intellectual classes, the French media are channeling the national dismay over lost grandeur into contempt for America. Watch these suave Europeans, snickering to themselves because American soldiers are getting killed in Iraq. Is that (they sneer) any way to risk your life? Go on a crusade to fight incurable disease, cross in front of a moving car, smoke a cigarette. But fight to defend your own country? It's indecent!

For me, the monuments are crumbling. The glistening golden dome of les Invalides. The châteaux and the triumphal arches, the obelisks, the buxom fountains, the wrought-iron balconies, the slightly tipsy 18th-century apartment buildings, the rivers winding through those darling towns and cities. How can so much beauty cover such deep cowardice? I lash myself to the mast and close my senses to the sirens, while my heart rings with pride for "the land of the free and the home of the brave."

We are not free in France. I know the difference. I come from a free country. A rough and ready, clumsy, slapped together, tacky country where people say wow and gosh and shop at Costco. A country so vast I haven't the faintest idea where I would put myself. A homeland I would have liked to keep at a distance, visit with pleasure, and leave with relief. A native land I walked out on with belated adolescent insouciance. A foreign land where I was born because Europe vomited up my grandparents as it is now coughing up me and mine.

If only the accusations bandied about so mindlessly by the French talking heads were true: American imperialism, Washington's insatiable drive for hegemony, the Yankee need to dominate the world, and all the rest, the whole stars-and-stripes version of the *Protocols of the Elders of Zion*. Just look at the American eagle spreading its wings, asserting its dominion: look at those sharp claws, that crafty eye, that hooked nose. If only it were true. Give me empire, my dear Yanks. Come over here and colonize this place so that I can put my suitcases back on top of the closet, keep my swishes and furbelows, my fanfreluches and baubles, my adopted family jewels and Continental airs, and live to a ripe old age here in the center of Paris, in the middle of nowhere.

Commentary March 2004[20]

Chapter 5/ Islamization

MUG SHOTS

21 January 2004

1: A pair of big beautiful round dark Indian eyes on the cover of *Le Monde 2*, the newspaper of record's jazzy new full-color weekend magazine. 2: the front end of an automobile exploded in Nantes, fully covered on prime time news with unanimous oohs and ahhs of reprobation. 3: the smashed up face of a 15 year-old Jewish boy attacked by a small gang of Muslims at a skating rink in Boulogne-Billancourt unbeknownst to the select readership of *Le Monde 2*, unsuspected to the popular TV audience, and underplayed by a good part of the Jewish media in France.

Close up: the babbling beauty on the cover of *Le Monde 2* is Arundhati Roy, "*la combattante*." And what a fighter she is! When she isn't busy being a French cover girl she's haranguing the crowd at the Social Forum in Bombay. I first discovered her in a text that went around the Net in the aftermath of 9/11. The towers were still smoking and Roy was ranting and raving. Her Bush-is-Bin Laden fantasies snaked and twined through thick paragraphs and abundant pages perfumed with Patchouli-flavored TNT. An imaginary chorus of longhaired barefoot latter day hippies materialized in the background, nodding and mumbling "yeah, that's right, ohhh." The victims of the horrendous Bhopal catastrophe were dug up to confront unforgivable America, precluding now and forever the slightest right to react against an attack aimed straight at our civilian heart. And all the rest was literature: Afghanistan would be reduced to rubble, to dust, to total oblivion and what would we gain by it? Everyone would hate us, deservedly so, and even more so. Anyway it was all our fault. We made Bin Laden, we cause poverty and misery, we selfishly enjoy the fruits of our labor.

Maybe I was too optimistic. I thought this kind of writing would end up in the attic under a heap of Afghan burkas. No, it mutates, recycles, and pops up at the *antimondialiste* Forum in the new version: Bush equals Saddam. And whatever was done to Saddam should be done to Bush. All of this is surely available online, if you want the details. Nothing in it could embarrass the editorial committee of *Le Monde 2,* it's all grist for the mill. And, give them credit: they put the saucer-eyed Indian on the cover instead of...

...Howard Dean.

Who blew up the automobile of Aïssa Dermouche, the newly appointed Muslim *préfet* or, as identified with his classic epithet, "*le premier préfet issu de l'immigration*"? Which certainly could not be true. There must be all kinds of *préfets* not to mention Interior Ministers whose parents were immigrants. But here we're talking about *the* immigration, that immigration, the only one that counts. If you live day in and day out with people who follow the rules of French logic you may be irritated by this kind of politics but certainly not surprised. Faced with the increasing lethal dangers of jihad in the *hexagone*, your government decides to act firmly and intelligently. A commission is named, hearings are held, recommendations are formulated, and the *président de la République* asks for a law prohibiting "ostensible" signs of religion in schools and public offices. The "Islamic veil," the kippa, and the big cross are precisely mentioned. No one is coming to school in saffron robes so Buddhism wasn't specifically included in the no-no's.

This has given rise to extensive debate in France and worldwide, showing that France has as many versions of "*laïcité*" as it has varieties of cheese. Nonetheless the exclusion of religious dress in the schools is based on the principle of *laïcité* which is the very foundation of *la République*. A *citoyen* or *citoyenne* is just that, a citizen with no adjectives, equal to any other citizen in the eyes of the French Republic. Now if you would like to know why, until very recently, let us say until 20 years ago, French parents had to choose their children's names from the saints on the calendar, then you haven't caught on to French logic and you are going to get into many arguments.

Girls should not come to school in *hijab* because it disturbs the universal harmony of *laïcité*. They should be good French citizens and accept the rules. Now how do you get that through to your public? Well, you send the popular Interior Minister, Nicholas Sarkozy, to Cairo's Al Azhar University where he pockets a decision from the great Sheikh Tantawi, more or less admitting that Muslims in France should obey French law. And what if he'd said the contrary? Or changes his mind? Whichever way the Sheikh turns, he can keep that feather in his turban: the French minister of his most *laïque République* comes to him for... advice? Permission?

We'll soon see. So you exclude hijab on the basis of solid secular principles, and that knocks out the kippa and the cross, which doesn't prevent French Muslims from accusing the government of discrimination and the jihad fringe from threatening sedition and worse. So how do you restore harmony? Try a slathering of mea culpa: We haven't been treating Muslim immigrants right (it's true), they aren't integrated (and hijab is going to help?), don't have jobs, don't live in everybody else's neighborhoods etcetera. And you name a *préfet issu de l'immigration*. The token Muslim just wants to be a normal French citizen. He doesn't hang out in the 'hood. He's director of a bright modern high performance business school. And, no surprise, he's Kabyle.

A few days after he's appointed somebody blows up his car. How dare they? The TV cameras focus on a car, its front end blackened and crumpled; pan to windows blown out all up and down the street, back to the place where the car was parked, scrutinizing for clues. The nation is up in arms. You don't do that to our *préfet issu de l'immigration*! No stone is left unturned. The investigation barrels forward and lo and behold the first suspect is the ex-boyfriend of the *préfet's* ex-wife. His second wife, actually; they divorced in 1994 and he's now on his third. A real Latin lover! But we're not finished with the ex's. A second suspect is brought in for questioning: the ex-boyfriend of the once and forever daughter of the *préfet* by his ex-wife. And a buddy of the ex-boyfriend. Then they are all released. And someone puts a bomb in front of the door of the beautiful modern business school brilliantly directed by Monsieur Dermouche. Pictures of his car with its front end exploded reappear on prime time news.

The fifteen year-old Jewish boy was skating at a rink in Boulogne-Billancourt just outside the city limits, a clean, well-kept neighborhood, not one of those outlaw *banlieues*. A bunch of Muslim kids ranging in age from 14 to 17 ganged up on him and beat him while snarling antisemitic insults. As usual they went for the head. And remember, they are wearing ice skates. It could have been worse but, according to news reports, skating rink personnel intervened. The assailants were arrested and arraigned in juvenile court. And the boy and his parents were received by Interior Minister Sarkozy. Patrick Gaubert, president of the LICRA (International League against racism and antisemitism), was there. He related the scene in a hushed voice on *Radio J* today. "The boy's face is smashed."

And the parents asked the Minister, "What are we supposed to do? Our children are beaten up. Are we supposed to protect them ourselves? What shall we do? Shall we stay? Shall we leave?"

Last Saturday thousands came out for a pro-hijab march in Paris organized by Mohamed Latrèche, leader of *le Parti des Musulmans de France* a virulent Islamist fringe group (religious political parties are against the law in secular France), with the backing of the UOIF, the Muslim Brotherhood organization that makes up the majority of the new government-created Muslim umbrella group. Latrèche made a moving speech in which he claimed that the Jews in France have everything, the Muslims have nothing. His sympathizers can't be fooled; they know the Jews are behind this anti-hijab law. The Jews control the press and the government, and they want to keep Muslim women from obeying Allah. The girls were out in force, most of them 3rd generation French, wearing *hijabs* made out of French flags and wrapped in all the principles of *la République*.

Latrèche's antisemitic acid bath was mentioned in passing in the French press. No indignation. The disgruntled lover who blew up the *préfet's* car will be discreetly imprisoned and the *préfet's* 1st, 2nd, and 3rd wives need fear no paparazzi. The 15 year-old Jewish boy whose face was smashed by Muslims wearing ice skates will remain unknown to the

French public, and president Chirac will continue to proclaim that France is not an antisemitic country. And where's the Arundhati Roy who'll morph him into Pinocchio? Not on the cover of *Le Monde*, that's for sure.

SLINGS & ARROWS
OF OUTRAGEOUS MISFORTUNE
21 February 2004

The controversy was set in motion when Armitage's comments were printed in Foothill's student paper on Jan. 28th. In an interview with the *Sentinel*, Armitage said of Israeli treatment of Palestinians, "And what they're doing with Palestinians every day? They're killing them. They're walling them in, they're essentially doing the same thing that was done to them ... It's exactly what Hitler did to the Jews."

Not only do we have to listen to this nonsense within the halls of academia, we are also expected to bite our tongues, bow to the idols of freedom of speech and not, definitely not, accuse the good Professor Armitage of antisemitism. Then again, if professors are to be held accountable for the clarity of their ideas and the quality of their thinking, antisemitism might in this case be a lesser crime. In this imperfect world, Professor Armitage can be as antisemitic as his heart desires without losing his tenure (I assume he has tenure), his salary, his perks. Can he also display crass ignorance of history and utter disregard for the meaning of words without incurring some kind of academic penalty?

It's exactly what Hitler did to the Jews.

Note the precision: *exactly*. He could have said "as bad as." He said *exactly*.

They're essentially doing the same thing that was done to them.

Again, note the use (in fact a misuse) of the emphatic qualification *essentially*.

What could be more inescapable than this condemnation of Israeli treatment of Palestinians?

But wait a minute. Is professor Armitage really talking about Israelis? What essentially did Hitler do to whom? He essentially conceived and implemented a clear-cut program to eliminate the Jews from the face of the earth. The fact that he was stopped short of victory takes nothing away from his program. However, the extermination project was aimed at Jews, not Israelis. And the people to whom it was applied could not apply it in turn to Palestinians or anyone else. They are dead. Essentially dead. And essentially Jews.

Does this explain why Armitage misuses the word *essentially*? The Israelis are not "essentially doing" they are essentially <u>Jewish</u>.

As for the *exactly*, if Hitler exactly killed Jews every day and walled them in, why in the world did it cause such an uproar in history? Saddam Hussein killed Iraqis every day, the taliban walled women in their homes, black Sudanese are being killed this very week in Darfur, prisoners are behind walls in every country in the world, justly or unjustly but exactly walled in. What was so bad about Hitler? Why can't Israelis do to Palestinians exactly what Hitler did to the Jews if what he did was kill them every day and wall them in? These things happen.

I would not deny that Israeli soldiers are killing some Palestinians some days. Would Professor Armitage deny that some Palestinians are killing some Israelis some days? What, then, is the essential quality of these killings? Do we need to know anything more about them? The whys and the wherefores? Apparently not. So the logical conclusion would be that Palestinians are doing to Israelis exactly what Hitler did to the Jews.

Aha, good professor, I hear you! I see you wagging your finger. No, no, no, the Palestinians are not fencing in the Israelis. You are right. You win. Winner takes all, rake it in, I won't even play my joker, not a word about the impenetrable invisible wall of Arab countries surrounding Israel. You win. *Exactly* means exactly and the Palestinians are not essentially fencing Israel in...

...because the Palestinian Authority and its conglomerate of armed militant activist groups have their own clearly announced project; they plan to kill so many Jews that the rest of them will flee Israel, and the last remnants can easily be reduced to exact essential dhimmitude.

This amply documented extermination project has more than one wing. The military wing went into action today, 22 February 2004, in a crowded Jerusalem bus, killing seven, maiming 62. Without the concerted action of the propaganda wing, this atrocity, one in a series of more than a hundred, would stand starkly, unmistakably for what it is: AN ATROCITY. The murder of innocent civilians, a crime against humanity.

Civilized people would not only condemn this atrocity, these atrocities, they would come forth and put an end to such barbaric actions. Which is why the propaganda wing took care, before kicking off the killing spree, to construct a narrative within which these atrocities would be presented as noble acts of resistance against intolerable oppression.

Essentially that narrative is constructed on the basis of a stinging accusation: they are doing to the Palestinians what Hitler did to them.

By what magic can Professor Armitage blithely incorporate the narrative and remain innocent of complicity with the project it promotes? Is he exactly antisemitic, essentially antisemitic, or inadvertently antisemitic? The question is academic.

SPME Faculty Forum[21]

DECONSTRUCTING CHOMSKY'S WAIL
29 February 2004

"A Wall as a Weapon," Noam Chomsky, *NYT* February 23, 2004

Chomsky's title speaks volumes: Israel builds a fence and in the words of the eloquent linguist it becomes a wall and a weapon. If Israel held out a flower it would be a dagger lily. And if Israel did and said nothing, it would be the silence that kills.

In a brief article that spits fire like a machine gun, Noam Chomsky throws the book at Israel. But he takes care to anchor his volley of accusations to a clever lie: "Few would question Israel's right to protect its citizens from terrorist attacks like the one in Jerusalem on Sunday..." No need to prove this wholesome reassuring thought? It happens to be utterly unsubstantiated and easily countered by hundreds of statements from identifiable sources including the very Palestinians who argued the case before the International Court at The Hague. The terrorist attacks are a strategic weapon (as lethal as a wall?) meant to achieve precise if unstated political, territorial, and religious ambitions. If Israel can protect itself from the attacks and, in addition, inflict political and territorial losses on the enemy that has been perpetrating them, then it would mean that humanocide bombings failed to achieve their strategic goals. When human affairs work in a normal way, losers lose.

Chomsky says that the problem with the wall is the frontier it traces. But then he claims that Israelis have been committing "politicide" against the Palestinians, that they have already turned the West Bank into an impossible hodge podge, that they have been killing Palestinians for 35 years of "brutal occupation," stealing their land and water, giving it to greedy colonists, leaving the Palestinians with not even a drop to drink, and all of this oppression, murder and privation is nothing less than an underhanded means of achieving Israel's final goal: expulsion.

Then how could an adjustment of the frontier traced by the fence undo the evil done by Israel? Last Friday, Palestinians who had gathered to worship on the Temple Mount (their Harum el Sharif) threw rocks at Jewish women praying below at the Kotel; in his spitfire op-ed, Noam Chomsky throws peace-plan rocks at Israel. It would take a whole issue of the *New York Times* to accommodate the reliable historical data that debunks all these allegations of perfect two-state propositions that were offered to an ungrateful Israel. But that is not the point and there is no reason to fall into the trap. The peace plan argument is no more valid than the land and water grab accusation.

No matter how many times we reply to those arguments they will be thrown back at us with renewed vigor. They must be attacked at the roots, shaken to their very premises. Chomsky's arguments, which we've heard hundreds of times, are tacked up against the pure white background of a falsified presumption that nations behave like angels. All nations, except Israel, play by the rules of chivalry, conduct foreign affairs like elegant ladies and gentlemen at a royal dinner party, behave like innocent children preparing their first communion. Because Israel is deprived of the holy whitewash, its normal behavior as a sovereign nation is painted in lurid colors and the Palestinians, consequently, are awarded the halo of the aggrieved party. This is their essential quality; nothing the Palestinians do can harm their status as the aggrieved party. If they lose it is not because they played badly, if they commit evil they must not be punished, if they lie their words become truth.

Against the pure white background of a world without conflict, without history, without causes and consequences, in the static space of this artificial configuration, a wall is a weapon and killing 900 civilians is asking for a drop of water and a crumb of bread.

The wall, according to Chomsky, is a weapon because it does not follow "the Green line established after the 1948-49 war." And if the combined Arab armies had achieved their goal and swept the Jews into the sea, the beach would now be the internationally recognized border? All the word games, op-eds, UN resolutions, Durban Conferences and travesties of international justice will not make that twisted logic come true. Let us hope that one day the Palestinians will find decent statesmen who will lead them into reality and out of the prison they have made for themselves.

SPME Faculty Forum[22]

HOLY SCOLDERS: EXPLANING KASHRUT TO A HAM HOCK

25 February 2004

Two days after the murderous attack against the Number 14 bus in Jerusalem and smack in the middle of the "off the wall" deliberations of the International Court at The Hague, France's public channel *France 2* broadcast one of those investigative panoramas of Israel that we watch with well-earned trepidation. It is all so familiar and still it hurts as the same nerve is hit and the same insidious message is transmitted to an all too credulous audience. The February 24th episode of *Un Œil sur la Planète* opened with France's favorite talking heads: Israel's soul-searching breast-baring holy scolders, always on call when it comes to scourging their country, their countrymen, their countrywomen. It's not as if their message brings any kind of new tidings. We've heard it all before. Avrum Burg can get space in *Le Monde* at the drop of an eyelid, the refuzniks are invited to speak to hot-headed Muslim kids in the *banlieues*, any Israeli who has a word to say against the government of Ariel Sharon, the doings of Tsahal, the g-d awful stubbornness of the "colonists," the dangers of theocracy, or the shabby treatment of Arab Israelis is welcomed by the French media.

There is nothing inherently evil in soul-searching, even in wartime; it may well be motivated by the highest Jewish values and the difficulties of respecting them in a beleaguered Jewish state. There is always room for honest debate about ethical values within a community which, at least theoretically, respects them. But why, if they are so intelligent and so ethical, do the holy scolders line up to confess our sins to a tacky French journalist *cum curé*?

Do they have any idea how ridiculous they look as they pour out the secrets of their true Zionist hearts to Thierry Thuiller who drools as he gathers the salt to rub into Israeli wounds? Egged on and flattered, monsieur the-conscience-of-Israel accuses the army of atrocities, the "colonists" of indecent settlement, the government of failure to comply with peace plans, the ultra-orthodox of oppression and draft dodging, and Israelis in general of deep-seated imperfections and indelible stains.

Who exactly are you talking to, *monsieur-la-conscience-de-ton-peuple*? Beyond the nervous little journalist hopping around like Jiminy Cricket, lies a French audience that is kept on intravenous anti-Zionism. Do they live by the higher values you profess? Do they ask their government to prove it heard the message of Sinai? Do they expect their compatriots to be kind to widows and orphans... if the cost of kindness comes out of their own pockets?

You are speaking to France, a wannabe world power jockeying for paternalistic leverage in the European Union and drugged on the fantasy of being the leader of the Arab world. You are tour guides for an Eye on the Planet that looks down its nose at *yeshiva bochers* rocking back and forth while their fathers and mothers are fruitful and multiplying; an eye that cuddles up to a poor Cohen who can't marry his divorced beloved because of the stupid rules of the nasty rabbis; an eye that scowls at the armored cars taking Jews in and out of their shamefully neat and pretty neighborhoods provocatively nestled in Palestinian lands. An eye that accidentally glimpses an exploded bus with scattered bodies seen from a distance and connected to no one and nothing. A bus that exploded like a can of Coca Cola on a hot day.

Israel is its own worst enemy. Because the real enemy is kept out of the picture. So Daniel Ben Simon can tut-tut about all the money spent on the military that could be better used elsewhere. He sounds so reasonable... and it's not just because he's wearing a turtleneck sweater. Compared to the modern offices of *Haaretz*, the Judean hills look as old as Methuselah and the wild men who live there—the one who shows the reporter a little archeological site attesting to ancient Jewish presence, the other who refers to the biblical promise—are made to look like prehistoric atavisms. Even the good looking young ladies and men dancing in a Tel Aviv nightclub on Friday night are turned into a reproach against the comical throwback dressed in black, blowing his horn to close a Jerusalem market before shabat.

All of this might seem like slim fare hardly worth fifteen minutes of indignation. But wait until you hear the punch line. The pearl in the oyster, the gold nugget buried in this take-a-look-at-this-and-that stroll: Israeli soldiers kill Palestinian kids for fun.

The sequence takes place near "the wall." Which is in reality a fence, seen from a distance in the background. In the foreground, a formidable Tsahal-watcher named Yvonne Mansbach explains to Thierry Thuiller that some Palestinian kids were horsing around near the barrier. The soldiers said "we're going to have a good time," ran over to the fence and, without even firing a warning shot, killed three Palestinian kids. This is supposed to be happening in real time. Yvonne Mansbach makes a phone call. She says she reported the incident to the army spokesman and he (I thought it was a she but maybe I'm wrong?) asked if the kids had done something to the fence and she replied what does that have to do with it, is kicking the fence punishable by death?

The army spokesman is deaf to ethical entreaty. The French journalist hears the testimony and draws the logical conclusion: Israelis know this kind of thing is happening, they approve, it doesn't even get a line in a newspaper.

This is the *France 2* that brought us the Mohamed Al-Dura "death" scene, the blood libel that kicked off these long years of murder and maiming of Israeli civilians. That day, September 30, 2000 at Netzarim junction, *France 2* stringer Tala Abu Rahmeh was in the right place at the right time. Thanks to his too good to be true scoop, the whole world was fed the Jews-are-child-killers story. The repercussions are global and enduring.

Riding on the credibility of the poster boy—a *France 2* / PA production—a jumpy little journalist can blithely claim that IDF soldiers just killed three Palestinian kids. He doesn't even have to ask his cameraman to zoom in on the scene or run over and film the bleeding corpses before they are rushed off for a Hamas funeral.

Muslims can beat up Jews in French streets and schools, burn synagogues and kosher butcher shops, without stinging the French conscience. They provoke a shrug of the shoulders, a solemn official declaration—France is not an anti-Semitic country—and a low mumble: what can you expect, when they kill Palestinian children for fun! Palestinians can kill and maim Israelis by the thousands, and a blasé French public yawns and mumbles: what can you expect, they build a wall and then use it as an excuse to kill Palestinian children for fun!

I have a suggestion: instead of explaining *kashrut* to a ham hock, the Israeli holy scolders should come over here and make a film about France, its ills and misdeeds, its failings and disappointments, its untroubled conscience that takes a handful of NGOS for G-d's gift to the world, its Salafist mosques and antisemitic comics, its pacifism funded by Saddam's oil money, its anti-Americanism fed by bitter jealousy, its Pravda press and defenseless borders...

But don't expect the special report to be aired on French television. Holy scolders are not kosher if they turn their scorn on France.

National Review Online[23]

2 JULY 2004

In mezza camina della vita, smarrito... my all-purpose citation. Half way down the road of life, lost... I set the Fourth of July as the cutoff date for these *Notes* and, in the most lifelike manner, precious time was devoured by other obligations, leaving me three thin days to tie up the loose ends and close the book, this book, for the next one is already germinating in my mind. Three days to give coherence to thoughts that have been taking shape for months. So what do I do? Tack on an extra session to make up for the time outs, the detours, the miscellaneous others, or respect my own rules and leave the scene the way we leave our lives, grabbing up a few essentials and rushing off in a dither. Our lives are unfinished. They do not end like a symphony with a resounding flourish. They are interrupted. Power outage. Blackout. No comment, because the Commentator in chief is no longer. Emmanuel Levinas is, to my terribly incomplete knowledge, the only philosopher to have accurately described death. A non sequitur. Life is the ongoing physically present existence of a unique individual and the self-commentary it inspires. We know that the material existence ends but prefer to ignore the fact that the commentary is not there to record the ultimate event.

And yet there is a conclusion of sorts in human affairs. When I set my cutoff date, I did not know that the 4-year stretch of jihad violence against Israel, sold under the misleading label of "intifada" would be an acknowledged flop... as I had predicted in November 2000. That an interim Iraqi government would assume sovereignty, that Saddam Hussein would be indicted by an Iraqi court. That the UOIF (French wing of the jihadist Muslim Brotherhood) would make public its intention to turn *la rentrée* into an onslaught of girls in hijab. That Jacques Chirac's popularity would be down to 34%. That Israeli scientists would discover an x-ray vision technique that can see through walls. That the Israeli economy would be recovering and the French economy going down the tubes.

I didn't know anything about Karen Armstrong, Eastern Christians, or replacement theology when I opened this notebook with a reaction to her op-ed about sharing Jerusalem. I didn't know, when I wrote the letter published in the *International Herald Tribune*, that Mohamed Al Dura was not killed in a crossfire, he was killed in a Pallywood fiction film. And so there is a wrapping up of sorts when *France 2*'s I-know-everything-about-Israel reporter Charles Enderlin, the same Enderlin who turned a 2-bit Palestinian propaganda film into a 21st century blood libel, makes his last stand on the security barrier. Enderlin is a phenomenon and a half. There are all kinds of ways to manipulate the facts. He does it with a hallmark voice and delivery system reeking with latter day saintliness. Where did the prophets go after the end of prophecy? They went to the Jerusalem desk of *France 2*. No matter what the subject, Enderlin's voice condemns Israel. If Israel handed out Ramadan baskets to every last Muslim in the disputed territories, Enderlin would report it as an affront, a crafty maneuver, a heavy-handed interference in the lives of noble Palestinians, a too little too late and too much too soon.

These days Enderlin's on the fence, exposing Israel's crimes. An Arab from East Jerusalem who is working on the security fence is captured live as he discovers that his home has been destroyed by Israeli government forces. Before our eyes he phones his boss and says he doesn't want to work for him anymore. Who could blame him? Why was his house demolished? We see him with a thick file of official papers. Repeated requests for authorization. Post-construction. The house was built without authorization. Is that any reason to destroy it? Can't I build a house in that lovely little square on boulevard Saint Germain, or why not in the middle of la Place des Vosges? Doesn't a man have an inalienable right to build a house wherever he wants, however he wants, and all the more so if he's an Arab living in East Jerusalem? Enderlin leaves no doubt. His voice is judge, jury, and jailor. Israel once again is thrown in jail. Clang!

End of reportage. A few days later it's a Palestinian crying because the Israeli fence is going to cut him off from his olive trees. Might as well cut off his head. In fact, beheading is more common these days than separating peasants from their olive groves, but you wouldn't know it because Charles Enderlin is there to replace an old guy named Solomon. The olive trees belong to the man who is crying. And if you're not impressed, listen to this: his olive trees are 200 years-old.

You might think that separating a man from his olive grove, even if he's owned it for 200 years, is not as serious as shooting a 12 year-old Palestinian boy in cold blood, but think again. The sins of Israel are all the same size, infinite, and punishable by the same sentence: extermination. It can be meted out anywhere. Against Israeli civilians, of course, but also against the tombs of Jewish soldiers killed defending France against the Nazis, against *yeshiva bochers* in the streets of Paris and its *banlieue*, against synagogues, Jewish day schools, torah scrolls, wherever.

I have sworn on my own head that I will not let this happen again. I have lain my hands in blessing on the heads of all our generations every day every hour to protect them from this scourge, I have blessed our generations, I've erected a security barrier around them without asking for permission from the worldly judges and holier than thou sinners. This must not happen again. There is no fatality in history, there is no minimum battle-ready battalion strength required to change the world. Anyone can do it.

The Israeli Supreme Court has ruled that one portion of the security fence must be taken down and relocated because it deprives certain Palestinians of their rights. The French press snickers and announces a slap in the face for Sharon. Lucky old Chirac, he doesn't have to worry about any bad news from the courts; they heard his case from inside a barrel of whitewash. But I have to worry about the security fence, erected when all else failed, the very image of all else failed, attacked from all sides, costly, dangerous for the workers and the soldiers who guard them, that security barrier, a thin line between life and death, a sigh of relief for every morning newscast that doesn't being with "twenty Israelis killed and 115 wounded when a kamikaze [sic] exploded on the number x bus in Jerusalem...," relief confirmed by statistics, a drop of 65%, or is it 75% or 85% in the number of attacks perpetrated. The victory that wasn't supposed to be possible. How many times have you heard it, Sharon promised security but he couldn't deliver, military strategy will never bring an end to terrorist attacks, nothing resists against a people who resists. Is that so? Yassine is gone, Rantissi is gone, the promised vengeance did not happen, the invincible desperados are made of flesh and blood, they disintegrate when impacted, their successors hide, slither, cower, and fumble.

And the self-appointed pro-Palestinians betray themselves at every link in the fence. A slap in the face for Sharon. They didn't say "a victory for Palestinian plaintiffs." No. Because they don't care one way or the other. And the nice Palestinian guy who is going to be able to go to his teaching job without making a long detour will become a patsy for the local jihad chief and the courts will be filled to overflowing with complaints aimed at tearing down the "wall of shame." This is the logic we are asked to swallow: women have to be barricaded behind *hijab* to protect them from their neighbors and brothers, Israel must stand naked and bare its breast to receive the death blow from its sworn enemies.

No, I don't trust the leftist judge Barak. I heard him speak in Paris this winter and my heart turned away from his lofty words. A fence runs through every encounter today, every conversation, every thought in our minds. We can't sit on the fence, we have to choose. If we refuse to choose, the choice is made automatically. The labels aren't clear. Maybe it's not a question of right or left anymore, but up or down. Up or down in a world that's spinning. Sometimes down looks like up. I mistrust this lofty ruling. Dread the consequences. It smacks of Judaism hung on the rope of its own best values. Yes, I understand the humanity of judging that an Arab should not be separated from the olive trees he has cherished for 200 years but shall a Jewish man be bereaved of his wife, a father of his son, a family of a whole branch because the owners of the olive trees are steeped in an altogether different brew? How can the material losses and inconveniences caused to individual Palestinians be balanced against the loss of Israeli lives? The terrorists do not come into Israel to uproot olive trees! How can Palestinian rights be protected on an individual basis when collectively they are at war with Israel? How can that war ever be ended unless it is finally called by its name?

Conversations today are thin lines that separate us from people who think they are sincere. Fences with no breaches. Openings that are closings. Cheap litanies picked up in the press and drawn at my feet like a line in the sand. Booooussssshhh (that's how they say "Bush" in French) is the opening shot, and all the rest follows, sadly predictable. This war in Iraq, it's a personal vendetta. There was no justification. Where are the WMDS, haha, there aren't any, and Saddam wasn't in on the planning for 9/11. All lies. Booooush is religious! That's like saying he's a lying, thieving, murderous devil. One person told me that he's a fundamentalist Catholic. How does she know? Because he went to visit the Pope. Another said he's a born-again Christian, and someone else informed me that he's a 7th day Adventist. The reason these people can give me the straight dope on the president of my country is that they get all their news in French. So obviously they know better than me. Okay, they admit, Saddam Hussein was undesirable (yes but he doesn't provoke their indignation, he isn't accused of being religious) but it was no reason to go to war and anyway as you can clearly see the Americans have lost.

It isn't an argument, not even a position, it's a fence. All requests for further details are considered to be a hostile intrusion. The fence is electrified. The conversation burns out. Every person who throws me this challenge is convinced that he or she is giving me the lowdown, the real story. Since I am regularly accused of being too well-informed, they apparently think that I know as well as they do but just won't face the truth. In April the "*résistants*" of Falluja allied with the formidable army of Moqtada Al Sadr, brought the Americans to their heels. Calling it another Vietnam was too kind. This was a new kind of debacle that only the Americans could deserve. That's it, the anchorwoman announced, in her soft sweet French voice, with her lovely French hairdo and finely designed French features, that's it, they've managed to incite the Sunni to unite with the Shia, and it's total disaster, *c'est le moins qu'on puisse dire*, to say the least. That was the cliché in April. And once the least has been said, there is nothing to add. The attacks are directed against Iraqis, the US hands over sovereignty as promised, Saddam Hussein is indicted by an Iraqi judge, so what? Sharon got his slap in the face, and so did Bush. The Supreme Court has ruled that the prisoners at Guantanamo can go to court and sue for their rights. In the eyes of the French public, their homeboy Gitmo inmates are the very image of the unfairly detained. *Ah bon*? Weren't they arrested in Afghanistan *nom d'un chien*!

What were they doing there? There's no sidewalk cafés in Afghanistan. So what would a Frenchman, even a *Beur*, be doing there?

Parallel fences will never meet. Iraq will never be a decent, law-abiding, democratic country. Israel should pull out of the "occupied territories" and let the Palestinians have their decent, law abiding, democratic state. The Americans should never have put their desert boots into the Iraqi trap: look at the violence. Yes, look at it, and you will observe that it is not coming from American troops. French media cluck over the lack of security, simple, plain, everyday security. Obviously the lack of security, like the lack of clean water and electricity, is the fault of the Americans. When the Americans are attacked, it is their fault. When Iraqis and foreign jihadis kill Iraqis, it is the fault of the Americans or more succinctly Boouuuusssshhh. It is their fault because they never should have opened the door, they shouldn't have stirred up the hornet's nest, they shouldn't have provoked legitimate anger against their illegal occupation, and they should have known that you can't force democracy down Middle Eastern throats. And that's why the Israelis are wrong, Israelis are guilty of the violence directed against them, Israelis are guilty of provoking the development of terrorist groups like Hamas and Islamic Jihad which, first of all, are creations of their own cynical policies, and second of all are not terrorists but militants, *résistants*, freedom fighters. The Americans should have stayed out of Iraq and the Iraqis would have deposed Saddam Hussein, effortlessly, the same way they tore down his posters from the walls, and the Israelis should get out of "Palestine" and let the Palestinians govern themselves as they clearly are able to do. And the Iraqis aren't.

There's no reality check to cast doubt on these arguments.

And no attempt to untangle the logic by which entire European populations are tormented day and night by the suffering of Palestinians mistreated by Israelis and the same sleepless humanists would have no problem enduring the sufferings of Iraqis mistreated by Saddam and his cronies.

3 JULY 2004

I know why Judaism provokes hostility. There are endless ways to express it, one does not exclude another. I offer two this morning: Judaism is questions put to people who cannot live without certainty. But Judaism is the certainty of an ethical imperative that people want to question by misbehavior, not because they are searching for greater truths but simply because it is too difficult to respect the Law. The anger, discomfort, and revolt provoked by Judaism is eternal. It does not spare Jews either, and cannot be solved by the advent of any reign, Jewish or otherwise, that would finally be able to answer all the questions posed by pesky Judaism. This is not a fatality it is the honor of Judaism. All kinds of intermediate forms of questioning have come and gone, all sorts of apparent subversion of deathly certainties have melted away, blended in, disappeared. If we want to call this enduring wall thrown up against and around Judaism antisemitism, then, yes, antisemitism too is eternal.

And that doesn't bother me in the least. The great danger lies in thinking it can be eradicated. This misleads us into sighing with relief every time it goes underground, misinterpreting it as it begins to surface, dilly dallying with it as it gathers storm force, succumbing when it bears down on us like a hundred billion dragons only to believe again, as our scattered remnants emerge from the maws of the beast, that this time they really really saw the damage antisemitism can cause and finally they understand, and they won't do it again. Yes they will. At least they will try. And it's up to us to make sure they can't do it again.

The security barrier is my metaphor of hope. The world was created by separating the light from the darkness. The road to freedom passed through the separated waters of the Red Sea. Lucidity is making distinctions. We have to erect a security barrier in our minds and keep deathly confusion off limits. The fatality is attached to antisemitism and NOT to the extermination of Jews. It seems innocent, harmless, even noble to confuse friends and enemies. No, it is deathly. Why did I know on 28 September 2000 that I had gone through a sea change, and there would be a major war? I knew it in a flash of light. And everything that has happened since that day has borne me out. My connection to France was severed. It will never be repaired. I was not rooted here, but I was linked.

At every stage of the current European war against the Jews, in which France stands first and foremost, denial paves the way for the next stage. In four short years the transformation is total. What was marginal has become mainstream, what was punctual has become essential, what was unthinkable has become ordinary and acceptable. The acts of lowdown thugs and the thoughts of lofty writers concord. Muslim killers, French writers, and Jewish victims cooperate to spread lies over the truth and express indignation whenever it slips out. 17 November 2003: Sebastien Selam (z"l) was murdered by a Muslim who killed a Jew exactly as prescribed in the Qur'an. 4 June 2004, Israel Ifrah was stabbed by a Muslim who shouted *Allahou Akbar* as he knifed a Jew according to the precepts of ritual murder. Ifrah survived because he got help before bleeding to death, but his lung is punctured, and his life is certainly spliced and bleeding. Selam's throat was slit in his building's underground garage, the murderer had time to kill him and then mutilate him with a carving fork. The crime was premeditated. The murderer had been antisemitically hassling the Selam family for several years. Since the Fall of 2000 in fact.

And yet when the *yeshiva bocher* was stabbed, Jewish media no less than the mainstream French media gasped in horror: now look what's happening, an antisemitic act has drawn blood! They had such great respect for omerta that they had sincerely forgotten the earlier bloodier fatal crime that is being hushed up. And the misinformation was picked up and spread worldwide.

It is so ridiculous I am ashamed to write it. Let's put it this way: the order came down from the top, I mean the Real Top *de la République*: the murder of the Jewish DJ was not an antisemitic crime. Nothing so gruesome happened on my watch, says the Top. And the effect is monarchical. It didn't happen. Ask your friends and neighbors, they never heard of it, or if they did, only vaguely, and if there has been no official reaction, there must be a reason. Ask Jewish community leaders and one will tell you that it's hard to prove, and another will say it's a terrible injustice (but that's just between him and me... in public he says nothing at all), and still another will explain that it's best not to mention things like this, it can do no good and may give ideas to those who would do as bad or worse. The same rules hold for jihad terrorist attacks in France. Everyone and his brother will explain that the French won't really wake up until there is a big bad terrorist attack on French soil. Well, there was one. The AZF factory, blown up on 21 September 2001. Selam's murderer is snug and out of harm in the nuthouse, and the AZF explosion is officially declared an accident though there has never been the slightest scientifically sound explanation of what exactly accidentally happened.

No, there won't be any reality check here, not on this go 'round. Reality is like Judaism in France today: it's all right if it knows its place.

On my lunch break I caught the last ten minutes of *Rumeurs du Monde*, a consensual Saturday afternoon urbane pep rally whose sole function is to show how Reasonable is the newspaper of record, *Le Monde*, and its director, Jean-Marie Colombani. At the end of today's program they were celebrating the coming election of John Kerry. It was all soft key, like coffee and pastries, but opinionated nonetheless. Kerry's chances are excellent, opined a French expert working out of Washington DC, because of all that's happening in Iraq, the tortures inflicted on prisoners (by Americans of course, the tortures inflicted by Saddam's boys never really made it into the headlines over here), the fact that they haven't found any WMDs And what would be Kerry's policy in the Middle East? Well it would resemble Clinton's. The fact is that Clinton admits, in his just-on-the-market book, to a certain bitterness about the failure at Camp David. It happens that Clinton holds Arafat responsible for said failure. But don't expect to hear that among the hustle bustle of *Le Monde*. So Kerry, if elected, well, when elected, might well choose Clinton as special envoy to solve the Middle East conflict. Absolutely entranced with his intelligence, the commentator went on to suggest that Bush might send Clinton on this high priority mission. But no one choked. Except me. And no one questioned the smooth suave logic of this high IQ fortune teller, predicting good chances for a Kerry win, which they all agreed would be a European victory, because he's with us and we're with him and Clinton was the kind of president we like to have in our White House, including Monica, in the hallowed French tradition. And I wasn't invited to say that Clinton's book was timed to pour mustard on Kerry's hot dog and leave a juicy vacancy for Hillary. Because Kerry, admit it my friends, cannot win. And a Bush victory now is a window of opportunity for Ms. Clinton in 2008 whereas if Kerry could win in 2004 he would be a serious opponent four years later. Why doesn't Kerry run for president of France? Anyway, I'm on record here saying that Bush will win. By more than a slim margin. And while I'm at it I'd like to add my highly personal explanation of why Kerry cannot under any circumstances be president of the United States or any other country developed, underdeveloped, or hopelessly primitive: his wife's hair is not done. That might seem silly, irrelevant, stupidly superficial but look around, you will never ever see a First Lady in any country of the world, whatever the political system, who does not have her hair properly done. Why is this so? Why must her hair be properly cut and set and brushed and styled and held in place? A woman can be Secretary of State in some countries with a disgraceful mop. We had a Justice Minister under Jospin who looked like her hair was cut by a juvenile delinquent with a dull razor. But a First Lady, be she a billionaire, cannot look like a floozy.

While I was writing the above, a communiqué from the CID dropped into my box, reporting the 6th anti-Jewish attack in or near Antwerp. And the Belgian government makes the usual promises. Did the good burgomasters intend, when they rubbed their hands and licked their chops at the thought of judging Sharon for crimes against humanity, that an army of thugs would start knifing Jews in the byways of Antwerp? Did the press imagine that a steady dose of anti-Israel poison could inflame some dull spirits and propel them against innocent Belgian Jews strolling down innocent Belgian streets? Do any of these good people want to know that there is no settlement on the horizon of the Arab-Israeli conflict so if that is the reason for the attacks then they will increase, spread, become more and more violent and utterly commonplace and acceptable?

What should we do? Wait in the wings and take comfort in knowing that the first choice victims are easily identifiable Jews? And as long as nothing happens to you or me, the situation is not serious? Life has a way of putting one foot in front of the other. Look at all the bona fide antisemitic acts committed in the past four years and we're still here, so why shouldn't we be here tomorrow and the day after. Just because the Europeans exterminated half their Jewish population why should that suggest they intend to exterminate the other half? Or half of the remaining half.

An article in *Maariv* arouses more indignation than all the synagogue burnings, swastika slatherings, Jew bashing and beating. When *Maariv* reports that the Jewish Agency is going to send its recruiters to France to encourage beleaguered Jews to make *aliyah*, adding the succulent detail that the project is code named "*Sarcelles d'abord*," meaning they are going to start with the Parisian *banlieue* where Jewish residents suffer the most, French Jewish media and community leaders finally let themselves go and blast out in no uncertain terms. Mind your own business, we'll make *aliyah* when we're good and ready, and no clumsy outspoken Israeli carpetbaggers are going to muscle in here and spoil our good relations with *la France*. These same people can swallow any kind of *goyishe mishegas*, and all the fancy high falutin' French official hogwash, but don't let those uppity Israelis get out of step. No *non-dits* for them.

What's touching is this family relation Jews have with Israel. That's how adolescents treat their families. I'll come to you if I need you but in the meantime keep your nose out of my business. But it's not so touching when you live in Paris and any chance promenade offers up a brief history of the extermination of the Jews. All the schools have memorial plaques now. Well and good. But these are the dead we cannot retrieve, the young lives nipped in the bud. What about today and tomorrow? This time we are not stateless, helpless, and unarmed. Then tell me, please, how can you convince so many people, including Jews, that what's wrong in the world today is that Israel is overarmed, overmilitarized, overreacting, overbearing, overreaching and the United States is a *hyperpuissant* disgrace? If an individual is standing in the street—in Antwerp or Sarcelles, for example—and he sees fifteen Euro-Muslim jihadis coming at him with knives and iron bars and qur'anic verses and, just before they can land the first blow, an overarmed Israeli soldier, just one, lassoes the whole lot of them and drops them in a desert prison, isn't that better than finding the Jewish man lying in the street bloody and unconscious, and the criminals scot-free?

There's a lot of easy talk about the lessons of history. The fact is people prefer not to learn. So they invent stupid little questions at the end of the chapter, and think that by answering them they can get a passing grade. Europeans do not feel guilty for persecuting and exterminating the Jews in the forties or at any other time. They may know that they should feel guilty. Some individuals certainly do understand the extent of the forfeit. But collectively Europeans are proving by their words and deeds today that they do not feel guilty and don't mind having another try at it just as long as the little superficial details are changed. I think that it's history itself that gives the lessons, and it takes time and intelligence to realize what has come over a nation that has committed, for example, a serious affront. Believing that the Europeans gave Israel to the Jews as a way of making up for the Shoah and, unfortunately, by oversight this little consolation prize turned into a new same-size injustice committed this time against the Palestinians, is a curious way of actually pursuing the enterprise of the Shoah. The restoration of Jewish sovereignty in Israel is the achievement of political Zionism and the logical development of religious Zionism and in both cases it is a Jewish achievement. With outside help, of course. Willing and unwitting, honest and calculating, partial and intermittent but absolutely necessary and duly recognized.

But look at the thin fenciness of all that's being said around us today. What if Israel was really given to the Jews as a consolation prize for the loss of one third of our population; was it a ten-minute respite or was it really meant to prevent further extermination? So forget it, and don't cry over our dead, and don't deplore our battered and beaten and blown up victims of insincere repentance. Could there be any sentiments more thin and transparent than these crocodile tears dried into curses against the Jews for doing the only thing that could ever liberate our persecutors from their own repetitive bouts of evildoing followed by insincere guilt, namely taking care of business. Defending ourselves.

It would seem to be obvious but it is one of the hardest arguments to put across. Another good reason for putting up a fence, for making a distinction between us and our enemies. So we can have a fair fight. That's what these "France is not an antisemitic country" declarations are all about. My reply is, don't apologize, put up your fists and fight. Because France has every right to be an antisemitic country, as much or as little as its little heart desires. But French domestic and international politics puts Jews in great danger, and that's easily verifiable, and that's what's at issue. The same for "France is a loyal ally of the United States but doesn't have to agree on this or that policy." No. France is not an ally. America is at war, America was attacked, America has the courage to face the enemy and fight, and France does everything a weak nation can do to make America loose. So okay, let's be faithful enemies.

There's something so ugly about smiling and grinning at someone as you trip him and make him fall on his face or to his death. And this ugliness seems to be seeping into the news in strange ways. Some phenomena are truly consequences of willful human policies. Others are simply emblematic. Such as the recent murders of children. It can happen anywhere. But when you see the images of country roads where young girls and boys disappear only to turn up days or months or years later naked and dead in streams, ponds, or buried in the grounds of the killer's castle, all that bucolic countryside that the news services have been peddling this year to show that France is the good guys and the Americans—"violence again today in Iraq," gloats the newscaster—are the bad guys, is suddenly yielding strange fruit. Yes, it can happen everywhere, but isn't there something terribly 21st century French about these men released from jail halfway through their sentences, men who have already raped a handful of youngsters, who are thrown back into their stalking grounds to rape and kill again. Isn't there something so human rightist, don't punish, understand, don't create data banks, it's an affront to civil rights. And then deplore the dead children on the evening news. And those rural landscapes meant to draw our attention away from the nasty quarrels of those bully Americans, these simple peasants in their rustic cottages, *la France profonde,* like we say the "Deep South".

What's this baseball team in Paris where all the players are Jewish boys? You can recognize them in a mini-second. Baseball caps that stand for yarmulkes and fool no one.

PIBULLS FOR PEACE
15 June 2004

You've heard of Moveon.org, you know about the dirty doings of the International Solidarity Movement, maybe you're in on the secrets of P10K, but do you know about the latest fashion in peacenicking—Pitbulls for Peace? The phenomenon is so new that I had to name it myself, and so secret that I couldn't cross check my information so, in the interests of accuracy, I will stick to what I saw with my own eyes on the boulevard Beaumarchais on Saturday 5 June 2004 at approximately 6 PM, namely: the barbarian hordes. Boulevard Beaumarchais marches from la Bastille to la République, carrying in its wake just about every protest movement France has produced. For some reason that a Parisian history buff would be glad to explain, the boulevard takes on two aliases—or maybe they are pen names—before it reaches its destination, which is la Place de la République. On second thought, maybe it's the boulevard du Temple that leaves la République, becomes the boulevard des Filles du Calvaire and finally, elegantly attired in high culture, dances into Place de la Bastille with all the pomp of a boulevard Beaumarchais.

Ugly posters were spread up and down the three-in-one boulevard in anticipation of the demonstration, denouncing "Bush, the world's worst terrorist" and putting in a word for "Justice in Palestine." Translated into demonstrationese this gives "Bush Sharon Assassin." A bit worn out, we've been hearing it for years, but the sudden appearance of Pitbulls for Peace just shows that we didn't know the half of it. The official version of this year's D-Day commemoration was *la patrie reconnaissante.* We saw hoary veterans parachuting onto green Normandy prairies, walking with teary eyes on the wet sands of Omaha Beach, welcomed royally in all-expense-paid luxurious hotel suites. There were a few shots of grateful local people, and a pinch of young enthusiasts whose admiration for the GIs and their British buddies is derived from the history books. Long blurry archive footage replayed the original operation, awakening chilling memories of young men mowed down as they jumped out of landing craft and landed chest-deep into their last ocean waves. But none of this served as a basis for any mass media reflection on—heaven forbid!—military courage. The American-British alliance that liberated France from its own Vichy government and the German occupation it had welcomed with open arms did not inspire any contemporary parallels. On the contrary! Everything was done to make sure that no stray citizen might imagine that the unilateralist American hyperpuissance and its British lapdogs currently Occupying Iraq could in any way be related to the 1944 liberators. The thinking media—newspapers, magazines, and radio—took care of spelling this out in intense sessions of ideological indoctrination. And of course they could always come up with a stiff-tongued American ready to gobble, in French on crutches, along the same lines: "That was then, this is now." Ah, if only the French could have their way, it wouldn't have been Boussssshh but *notre copain* John Kerry up there on the podium, speaking for the America we hold dear... at a safe distance.

But Booooouuushh was really and truly coming to France and the powers that be had to make the best of it, excuse me, the worst of it. Well, let me tell you, they were clever. The 60th anniversary of D-Day became a golden opportunity for reconciliation... with our American ally? Try again. With Chermany! Bush is out *les Boches* are in, the parallel is turned inside out and served up in *demi-teinte.* Spielberg showed you those white crosses and Magen Davids lined up as far as the eye could see? French TV brings you the solid granite German crosses that we may now freely decorate with flowers and tears. Nothing better than human interest stories to reconcile erstwhile warring peoples. Can you resist this lovely French lady who goes to visit her German half-sister? Are you not moved by the love story that brought her into this world, the Wehrmacht officer lodged in the hotel in her mother's village, love at first or second sight but love real love stronger than Big Berthas or cattle cars trundling Jews to the death camps, stronger than *résistants* tortured and killed by the Gestapo, all irrelevant details that have no role in this beautiful love story and even though the handsome officer went off to the Eastern front where, instead of dying a hero's death he survived, the cad, to return not to his French fiancée and her love-conceived daughter but straight home to Germany and the first *fraulein*. His French daughter arm in arm with her German sister cries sweet tears onto his grave and reserves her bitterness for the despicable villains who shaved her mother's head in a fury of revenge after the *libération*.

Libération indeed, you wonder who needed it when you hear the stories of survivors of the Allied bombings of Caen and neighboring towns. And the GIs with their chewing gum? Maybe you didn't know that they were raping French women in dark alleys and sordid hotel rooms. An unruly lot to say the least. Is it any wonder that today, 60 years after the famous landing, your average Frenchman feels closer to his German buddy than to some eagle-eyed sharp-clawed specimen of American imperialism? However, we were told, the world class terrorist Bush had no choice but to shake hands and make up with the Prince of Peace Chirac because the Americans need Europe (and what would Europe be without France) to pull them out of the quagmire in Iraq.

Just in case some two-bit barely harmful Al Qaeda activist might have wanted to get a shot at Bouuuussshhhh the French, *grand seigneur*, provided all the security a president could ask for. Another occasion to hear from disgruntled Parisians who couldn't get to their offices in the vicinity of the American embassy without passing through the gauntlet, showing their ID, getting frisked.

Finally, on D-Day minus 1, the Saturday before the Sunday commemoration, the big guns gathered at la Bastille to express their heartfelt opposition to war. *Non à la guerre* and don't ask which *guerre* because you might get a punch in the face or at least a snarl. Everyone knows which war they are against, it's the one that took place in Iraq a bit more than a year ago. You know, the war that left Baghdad in ruins, sent hundreds of thousands of haggard refugees on the roads, killed untold civilians and then some, and deprived the Iraqis of the 100% pure sovereignty that they have been struggling ever since to recover... with the help of the French press and French politician's speech writers.

By the time I got to the Bastille it looked like the march had already broken up. I saw fortyish and fiftyish plumpish ladies with short hair and *Non à la Guerre* stickers sipping cool drinks at the café. No tight ranks were visible on the boulevard. I heard a strange noise as if the earth underneath l'Opéra de la Bastille were having a heart attack, but I wasn't sure it had anything to do with being for or against the war. But I did see the up-front angels on TV that evening: Americans against Bush. Besançenot, the cutey pie mailman *Ligue Communiste Révolutionnaire* candidate, some Greens, some Union Leaders, some sexy young ladies.

Just when I was about to conclude that the demonstration had been a flop, I found myself nose to nose with a Falluja style jihadi cum sandwich man. A swarthy fellow with five o'clock shadow and a red and white keffieh wrapped around his head. He wasn't holding an RPG but he wanted you to think that he had just put it aside for a half hour to leave his hands free to distribute leaflets. His chest & back armor was made of colorful posters for the new Euro-Palestine party led by the not so funny comic Dieudonné who is making a big leap forward in his career by bashing Jews. Ever since this Rap Brown / Louis Farrakhan kind of a person started doing heavy antisemitism he has more gigs than ever. And now he's running for deputy to the European parliament on a ticket that warns that there'll be no peace for Europe without justice in Palestine.

The crowd thickened, spread across the boulevard and onto the sidewalk. A female voice like a machine gun hammered out the Euro-Palestine message from a mean sound truck. There were red and black anarchist flags (the Palestinian and Iraqi flags were already way up on the boulevard des Filles du Calvaire), some contingents from the Provinces, a few trade union hydrogen balloons and then suddenly the center-of-the-earth pounding swelled into deafening techno noise, and the barbarian hordes emerged. The Pitbulls for Peace were on the march! Sticking devilishly close to the ghoulish throbs of the sound trucks, pitbulls and Rottweilers flex their muscles, clench their teeth and narrow their steely eyes, looking for trouble. No, every scraggy grunge freak marching as to mayhem did not have a pitbull. But they all had beer bottles, and most of them were stoned on something, and many of them did have pitbulls, and they all had murder in their eyes. Girls with matted dreadlocks peeking out from dingy rags wrapped around their heads, wearing prison drab dresses over wide droopy pants, with tattoos here and cheap metal nose rings there, paired up with guys in the same scrungy style, came storming up the boulevard shouting guttural cries. Come to think of it, there's something punk hijab about this getup.

Their slogans were pure skuzz. *Nos désirs sont le désordre*. You bet! The Hausmanian windows shook as they went by, pouring out like lava from the volcano of their own desire for disorder. *Bush get out of here*. Yeah. Their centerpiece was a mockup Statue of Liberty, battered and beaten, supposedly because Booooouussshhh didn't treat her right. Yeah, sure. Three tender gendarmes in short sleeved blue shirts watched from the sidelines. What if these battalions of lumpenproletariat decided to charge? An orthodox Jew dressed in black rushed out of a building and swiftly led four young men to the corner, an eye on the hordes, an eye ahead to the intersection where they finally turned left into relative safety and my heart sunk. Germany in the 30s. Rumania. Warsaw, Prague... the hooligans, the hoodlums, the dregs and the toughs, cutting off rabbi's beards, making Jewish men scrub the sidewalk with toothbrushes, beating Jews to death. I could smell that not so distant past in the ugly anti-war crowd and read it in the light rapid step of the Orthodox Jews, slipping by like spirits, on their way to Sabbath evening services.

It seemed to go on forever, but finally the green garbage trucks trundled behind the last rows of heavy metal punk skinhead techno anarchist pitbulls-for-peace marchers. A rough estimate would put them at 1/3 of the total that marched that day to express their heartfelt pacifist indignation at the outrageous visit of President George W. Bush. Okay, let's say they were only 1/4th of the total. I've seen all kinds of peace marches in Paris this past year, one scarier than the next, but this is the first time I ever saw pitbulls marching for peace.

Apparently this passes for acceptable diversity in 21st century France. Because no one thought fit to mention it. It wasn't shown on the evening news. It wasn't noted in the newspaper of record. I keep asking people if they've heard about the Pitbulls for Peace, and so far no one knows they even exist. People who didn't see the march think it was all angels, cutey pies, plumpish matrons and Americans against Bush. Journalists who covered the march must have stayed up with the front ranks.

Leaving me all alone to meditate on the phenomenon.

PS: They came back during the night and slathered the shop shutters with slogans promising death and destruction to all and sundry and warning that Bassora chaos will come to Paris but in French it rhymes: *A Paris comme à Bassora, le chaos vaincra*.

Naïve optimists are hailing the "defeat" of the Euro-Palestine list, which scored only 1.83% in the European parliamentary elections. In Trappes, where a synagogue was burned to the ground in the winter of 2000, the list got 10%. And it was only presented in Ile de France... this time. Fifty thousand people, count them, fifty thousand French men and women cast their vote for Euro-Palestine. And you think the Pitbulls for Peace don't have a rosy future?

Chapter 6/ Gaza withdrawal

4 JULY 2004

Enemy, adversary, opponent there's no game unless the sides are clearly marked. And the rules clearly stated. Watching a game in this year's Euro 2004 championships I wondered what it would be like if the Reasonable Director of *Le Monde* were invited to give the blow by blow description of the games. For each match he would decide which team should win. His decision would be based solely on ideological considerations, totally unrelated to the qualities of strikers, defenders, coaches, captains, or strategies. And if the team he had chosen to lose should make a goal, he would simply deny it. And if his favorite team played badly, he would blame everything on their opponents. Ahhhh, look at that, Karim should have been able to score that ball if only the playing field were leveled and the resentment caused by centuries of colonization had been soothed, and then, look at the goalie of the enemy team, how can we accept his sacrosanct overprotection of his goal, doesn't everybody have a chance to win, what's this discrimination against Karim...

Asking for a fence—a clear separation between us and our adversary, not only in Israel but wherever the issues are raised, not only on the ground but in our hearts and minds—I am crying out for survival. We have the means today. We didn't have them in the past. But we will lose if we fall into the shared values trap. The world is not happy soup, it is conflict. The well-meaning bystanders who advise Israel to just do as it's told and stop making waves do not mean well for us. Can anyone deny that European Jews were softened for the slaughter by a whole string of legal dispositions? Why didn't they say no to the very first measure? Because they believed in law and order, they trusted their governments, they thought they were law abiding citizens of law abiding states and they didn't know what was in store for them. Today we know, so why do we submit, even if only in our minds? Today the scope of the war against the Jews is worldwide, the crippling dispositions come from all those nifty international organizations created to prevent replays of World War 2, Shoah included.

The International Court at the Hague is going to announce its security barrier decision this week. A general decision on all security barriers as befits an international court? Last spring an excellent tour of fences of the world was going around the Net. But this world's court is only going to judge one security barrier, guess which one? And if perchance the fence should be condemned, the UN Security Council may well follow through with a binding resolution. You would think the world would die of shame. I mean literally, the planet, you would think it would shrivel up and fall into the void. There's an image I have been trying to develop for months, a most graphic image of the world, our planet, like a Christmas tree ball but one made of lead, even heavier than lead, hanging on a tinny little hook marked "Palestinian suffering." And the hook is bending, bending, bending and breaking and the world is going to come crashing.

Can you imagine condemning Israel for putting up a fence to keep out inhuman beings trussed up in explosive belts diced with nails and bolts and all manner of poisons who have a pressing need to enter the land of Israel and transform its citizens, at random, into mangled flesh and piercing screams? These atrocities are not hidden behind the walls of death camps only to be discovered years later by a world that didn't know and couldn't have helped if they did and really is terribly sorry about it all old boy. These atrocities are visible to the naked eye. The intention of committing further mayhem is clearly stated. The means are concretely available. The effectiveness of the barrier is proven beyond a shred of doubt. And a court could actually condemn Israel for this fence?

Then why don't the thieves of Paris, for example, take us to court for barricading ourselves behind the heavy doors of our buildings firmly sealed by secret codes? Why should car owners be able to lock and unlock their car doors with little remote control gadgets instead of giving thieves a chance? Why should car doors be locked in the first place, and schools be allowed to keep out strangers? I don't need to carry this to further lengths to show how shamefully ridiculous such a decision would be. Could they possibly do it?

Yes.

And the joke is you can't get into the courthouse without going through all kinds of checkpoints!

What should we do if the decision goes against the fence? We should form Diaspora brigades, go to Israel with money and manpower, and finish the fence in one miraculous day.

I couldn't help replying to a message received this morning about another debate that is wracking the community: the Gaza pullout:

J., I have to make this hasty comment because I'm rushing to finish the book today. But I am wrestling with just the sort of issue raised here, so I can't keep from getting into the debate. It's heartbreaking, really. In all reasonable tranquility you have to agree with both sides of the question! We in the Diaspora can't tell Israelis what to do, where to put their necks on the chopping block, where to hunker down. Yes, but we are standing out here among the dogs and the wolves in sheep's clothing pushing Israel to cut off a finger so that later they can order Israel to cut off an arm and a leg. When you speak as an individual, you can just say what you think. I can say that it is a mistake to give an inch of territory to the Palestinians. On the contrary, Israel should have been taking territory away from them. As an outspoken individual I can say that Israel should have taken x amount of land for every terrorist attack. The Palestinians would not have a backyard to cry in by now. And the problem would be settled. You don't attack Israeli civilians. You don't commit crimes against humanity and get away with it. The consequences are immediate and painful and irreversible. And if the Palestinians had been forced to back off into the surrounding countries, and the terrorist attacks continued, you take land from them too. A piece of Syria, a piece of Lebanon, half of Iran, why not?

This is not a practical solution, it's a kind of fictional response. And yet... And yet, there will be no peace unless something like this is done some day.

In the meantime?

Obviously the Israelis will decide. But the Israelis include those who are against the Gaza pullout. Their arguments are no more indefensible than the arguments in favor. And there is one argument that to my mind is worth zero: we will pull out so that no more Israeli soldiers will get killed there (defending a handful of *meshuggas*...) and the world will see that we want a peaceful solution. The Lebanon retreat should have put that argument to rest forever and a day. As you so rightly comment, you cannot pretend that the jihadis across the way are going to interpret your moves according to noble principles and Talmudic wisdom. Your pullout is not their pullout.

They have shown that they are ready to sacrifice any number of lives for the sole purpose of getting the Jews off what they consider their land, and we know the extent of the territory they claim. Their logic is madness to us, but we have to realize that it is really their logic. And it overwhelms any rational, fair-minded individuals within their community who would like to make real peace and lead real lives.

As for the world recognizing Israel's good intentions, forget it! I mean forget it!!!!! Here in Europe the prevailing beliefs are only a stitch behind the jihadis. The latter believe that the Jews have to get off their *waqf* land because they defile it, the Europeans think the Jews have to get out of there because they are hurting the feelings of noble Palestinian savages and making trouble for peaceful Europeans who want to live in harmony with their own Muslim buddies.

So they will interpret the pullout as too little too late, and push for more, and keep pushing all the way down to the line, the '67 line, which is the '49 line, and any other line except for the original Jewish homeland endowment (when was it? 1917, or earlier) that included all of the present Jordan.

There is one illusion that I would not buy if you gave it to me: if and when Gaza becomes Terrorstan, and the terrorists strike the heart of Israel by all sorts of means and missiles, then Israel can strike back like any self respecting sovereign nation and the world will not lift a finger to condemn or restrain Israel. No. Talal Abu Rahmeh and his gang of fellow stringers will be there to film the damage and the UN will pull out the resolution they've already drafted for the occasion, and it will be a field day for Jew killers all over the world.

I guess I'll have to put all of the above in my book.

Hurry up please it's time. I feel pressed and pushed. Writing is the creation of an endless space of reflection. It's a journey into the unknown. However haltingly I may begin, I quickly reach a breakfree point. I soar. These past few days I am writing laboriously, heavily, my words drawn down from the heights by sadness. Leaving a manuscript is like leaving a home. I want to say this one is finished, I need to feel free to rest my mind and gather new energy for the next adventure. I need to be sure that writing this *Notebook* doesn't become a habit, a routine way of thinking and expressing myself. I can't get caught in the rut of reacting, always reacting to the same affronts. I don't want to rehash.

I gave up reading the French media. Dropped the *International Herald Tribune* too. I can't be picking lice out of their heads every day. I drew a line, put up a fence. These people are on the other side. Their arguments have no value...for ME. That's the point, that's the separation we seem to have so much trouble making. Someone sends me a sort of sloppy hand-written extreme lefty cutesy op-ed from the let it all hang out *Charlie Hebdo*. Look at this. The scribbler describes a TV debate, vomits on Maître William Goldnadel who dared to say he supports the policies of Sharon's government and adds, would you believe it, "Pierre Rehov was even worse." Pierre Rehov is the filmmaker who went behind the lines and brought back scenes of Palestinian newsmen in collusion with Palestinian doctors to cook scenes about Israeli atrocities (you've heard about the massacre of Jenin? Well these are its real authors). And our Charlie boy goes on to sing the praises of France's latest political innovation, the Euro-Palestine party. The party was a prominent element in the anti-Bush march (see "Pitbulls for Peace"). Their prime candidate, Dieudonné, is currently scowling nazistically from the oh so typically Parisian kiosques, dressed in a Wehrmacht uniform, advertising his show "*Mes Excuses*," held over for another triumphal series of performances. Ever since Dieudonné came out as a gutter antisemite his popularity has multiplied a hundredfold. Earlier posters for this *Mes Excuses* in which I would guess he excuses himself for everything he said about the Jews because it wasn't nearly nasty enough, showed Dieudonné black and mean. But now he's closer to the bone. His face is faded to nearly white on the new poster, he's proudly wearing the Nazi uniform, and he's scowling like a death camp director sicking (?) his dogs on a skin and bones Jew. Dieudonné's apology for previous defamation is clearly "kiss my ass!" And he can afford it. Because the courts not only judged him innocent of reprehensible hate speech, the judges explained the thinking that led to this decision, confirmed on appeal, and it is chilling!

But the point is, their arguments are absolutely valid...for THEM. We aren't in the same world, we aren't going to the same destination, there is no debate. Sometimes I think that the fence is going to cut into the earth and leave us on separate continents... from the point of view of history, at least, I'm sure it will. I'm not going to enter into the details, I won't grant them two and argue for three and quibble over five. If I hadn't set today as my cutoff date I could write pages and pages about recent court decisions in France but I will have to content myself with a brief outline: the thugs who attack Jews and get caught are released, the Jews who bring their assailants into court are disgraced and punished, verbal attacks against Jews are considered valid and their authors washed, dried, ironed and sent out fresh as a rose to begin again. I think that sums it up.

These people mean what they say, judge as they see fit, are fully aware of the consequences of their judgments, which they serenely accept. What are you going to discuss with them? How can you care what they think? What makes you think there is anything we could do to find grace in their eyes? They are going to go all the way to the outer limits of their present state of mind. There is nothing to stop them.

Did you know that real *résistants à la mode de l'Islam* do not cover their faces? Did you know that they operate proudly *à visage découvert*. Which proves that the so-called Muslim terrorists you see on those websites —and, by the way, how is it the Americans let those sites operate, isn't it somehow to their advantage—anyway these scenes with the masked hooded men who garble words and then behead someone who is dressed, take note, in something similar to if not exactly an orange prison jumpsuit such as can be seen at Guantanamo (or Alcatraz I suppose, but the voice speaking here doesn't know that) are not at all what you have been led to believe. The killers are Mossad agents or Israelis. That's why they hide their faces. The beheadings are a clever technique to make Muslims look bad. There are Mossad agents all up and down Iraq. They are tracking 7,000 Iraqi scientists, wiping them out one after the other, one was killed just recently, all the others are afraid. The American Generalesse who ran the prison at Abu Ghraib where the Americans tortured Iraqi prisoners, shame on them, well she just admitted that there were Mossad agents all up and down the prison, and Mossad advisers telling the soldiers how to torture... Muslims, of course. Did you know that people from the Zionist entity are buying up land in Iraq hand over foot, especially in the Jewish quarter of Baghdad? And the first gesture of this Iraqi puppet government was to vote indemnities for Iraqi Jews. It's clearly intended to destroy the country. Native Iraqis are poor and starving, and this will finish them off. Indemnities to Iraqi Jews, how about that! There is not a single Iraqi who likes the Americans. They all hate the Americans. The Americans commit atrocities every night. Our witness personally saw them firing from an Apache helicopter at some Iraqi police who were arresting prisoners. The prisoners escaped. Why would they do that? Simple: they want the prisoners to escape. Do you know that former Iraqi military men who fought under Saddam are unemployed today? Did you know that if your cell phone rings when you pass in front of an American soldier he shoots you? The Shia and the Kurds want Saddam killed, they don't even want a trial. But everyone else is shocked by the way he is being mistreated. Humiliated. Why didn't they show the whole speech on television, why did they cut out part of what he said? He said this trial is a farce, its only purpose is to serve Bush's re-election campaign (are you guessing who provided all of this precious information, did you already guess Michael Moore?) But how about the *résistance*, is it true that it's Al Qaeda, or is it foreigners from different Arab countries come to help the Iraqis resist against the cruel American occupation? Well, says the invited guest, some Iraqis don't believe Al Zarqawi really exists. You know, a few weeks ago they said they had killed him, then they say he's in the North, then the South... they don't believe there is any such person. Yes, some of the *résistants* are foreign fighters. They only attack the Americans. Sometimes Iraqis get killed [sure, like when they bomb a mosque, it was meant to kill American soldiers but it happened that they hadn't come to prayer that day].

This is what I heard today on *Radio Méditerranée*. Tawfik Mathlouti, the Mecca Cola man who isn't afraid to advocate the dismantling of the Zionist entity and the dezionisation of France, opens the two hour call-in hate feast with an unambiguous warning: you know the rules, no defamation, no incitement to racial hatred, no foul language. And then he opens the cages and lets the wild beasts into the ring. One after the other his callers vomit, spew, and sputter murderous hatred of Zionists and Americans. Smoke comes out of the radio as they fire verbal barrages against us. Nothing else interests them, nothing can stop them, if the program went on for 20 hours instead of 2, they would fire away for 20 hours. The fact that there are not a hundred murders every Sunday afternoon is proof that even inflamed fanatics take time before acting out. It's only been four years. Give them time.

They follow the rules. They call Jews "Zionists." And inciting hatred against Americans is apparently permitted, because Americans are not a race. Jews, by the way, are not a nation; Rad Med reminds us of this basic tenet at least once a session. Judaism is a religion, period! (And we are to understand that Judaism is an Ashkenaz religion that originated somewhere in Poland, though there were Jews in Arab lands, and they were treated better than your mother treats you, but wherever they are they are a religion and should all go home.)

However, the source of the precious inside information on Iraq resumed above is not a wild-eyed *Beur* calling in before taking his butcher knife and stalking a *yeshiva bocher* in the streets of Paris. It's not even Tawfik Mathlouti. It's his guest. A journalist, a real life- size French Arab-speaking journalist who has a paying job on French radio stations, namely Radio Monte Carlo, and government-owned Radio France Internationale, Arab language section.

Don't even bother to be shocked. Because he is on the same side of the fence as his distinguished colleagues in the French press. Maybe they don't have the Mediterranean guts to come out and say these things, and maybe they don't have the opportunity to slink around Sadr city and get the inside dope, but the news they bring to willing French ears is just a polished up toned down version of the eyewitness testimony of Tawfir

Amjahid. By the way, he recommends a great site for further information: www.almoheet.com or, if I am mistaken, www.usalmoheet.com.

5:50 PM SUNDAY JULY 4TH

No grilled hot dogs here. It's raining and chilly.

So what do I do? Turn off the switch and say that's it, *Notes from a Simple Citizen* ends here, unfinished...

And interminable...

Or do I throw in a few extra days to make up for the endless interruptions?

Date?

Separation fence... once again Jews are rebuked for showing what others want to hide. The fence as separation. Creation begins with the separation of light and darkness. Today, in the name of humanism, separation is abhorred: man / woman; good / evil; permitted / forbidden; life /death; truth / lie mustn't be distinguished one from another. The security barrier erected to separate Israel from death-dealing terrorists is splattered with sloppy metaphors. Fence = ghetto, they are creating a ghetto, a ghetto to enclose the poor innocent Palestinians, a ghetto to confine themselves in the good old persecution tradition. And public opinion, led by the publicly opinionated chatterers, giggles and says, "How ironic." But the fence says just the opposite. It says no one ever again can huddle us into a ghetto, antechamber to extermination. We are the ones who put up the fence, and it comes with instructions for openings and ultimate dismantling. "To dismantle this fence, abandon all hope of exterminating us, abandon all preparations for murdering us. Look to yourselves, create a civil society. Look at this fence and recognize that it is the concrete representation of the metaphor of creation: separate light from darkness in your souls, learn the difference between good and evil, stop pretending that death is life and murder is liberation. You are up against the wall built out of the chains you forged for yourselves."

Date?

I saw it. And the appropriate description slipped into my mind like a contact lens slipping into its familiar eye-slot. I saw it, a flat gray snaking ribbon almost indistinguishable against the background of the hills of Judea, and its real designation spoke to me in a small revelation: fortified city. It's not an apartheid fence, not a wall of shame, not the walls of a shameful ghetto, it's a fortified city. Israel is a fortified city. That's what you do when the barbarians approach and encroach

MARCH - AUGUST 2005

18 March 2005

Am I a tired old war horse ready to be put out to pasture... or, worse, melted down to glue? Where is my perspicacious eye today when alarm bells ring out from my inbox even while I slept, turning the office corner of our bedroom, where I work with relentless devotion, into a war zone. Just a few hours ago I was informed by a cherished comrade in arms that Bashir Al Assad is on the lam. Coup d'état in Syria, and I'm informed before Fox News finds out but it's not cause for celebration—the cross-eyed ophthalmologist has been overturned by the worst faction in his rotten kingdom. Maybe the boy was slinking out of Lebanon the better to control it with a long arm. I was informed, earlier this morning, that he— or the Syrians, maybe the mutineers already getting the upper hand—is sending lean & mean Palestinians into Lebanon to stir up trouble and transform the Cedar revolution into a devastating forest fire. Sunlight pours into my eyes as I write these words in a shimmying TGV headed south, taking me on a brief furlough, a moment of respite. In ten days I'll be off to the United States again, my third trip since the first week in November, another 5-week stint of intense activity, talks, meetings, con-tacts, strategy sessions. My life is transformed. The combat against jihad has brought me an incredible level of activity and satisfaction. These few hours in the train are my window of opportunity, my chance, my only chance to sign off and leave this notebook forever open-ended, not with a conclusion, not with a solution, but with a simple wave of the hand. Arbi-trary.

My informants say that the coup d'état in Syrian confirms their worst fears. Bush has blown it. Pretending to be a don't tread on me world class sheriff, he comes up dupe, putty in the jihadi hands that are now digging their claws into the soft white flesh of the Middle East. Syria is rid of the stupid kid who never even tried on his father's boot, Iraq is in the democratically elected grip of the Shia Islamists, Syria and Iraq form a *ménage à trois* with nuclear Iran, Lebanon delivered over to Hizbullah is poised to aim its exterminating warheads at Israel, Israel is slitting its wrists with Sharon's jiveass Gaza disengagement *mishegas*, and Putin's Russia, back in the saddle, is pumping second-hand nuclear weapons and fuel into the jihad maw. They won't even need help from North Korea. And probably don't want those Chink infidels mixing into the apocalypse project. As for the Europeans, France first and foremost, they'll be in charge of the curtain raising dilly-dallying. A bit of belly dancing to distract the media, a bit of intellectual floozy woozy to befuddle the left, and behind the scenes the same treasonous sellout to the nearest bidder. As usual.

I didn't have time to read my messages carefully this morning. I was struggling to finish an article for *Makor Rishon*. How many messages do I receive every day? Fifty? A hundred? Manna from heaven. Static too. Stressful incitement to read, reflect, respond. Magnificent connection to world upon world, invigorating circulation of life-giving information. And a trap. A labyrinth where multitudes enter and the lucky few emerge, invigorated and armed for action. It's like sperm. You sit there at your keyboard like an ovule inviting fertilization and awash in waves of spermatozoid aspirations. Which one will click and multiply? Most will go down the drain. Does it mean they are all unworthy?

Alain Finkielkraut chose the monastery. No e-mail, no computer, no cell phone. It's not a solution it's an artificial serenity and I'm sure he has all kinds of assistants, *shabes goyim* who handle the profane objects and deliver their wisdom beautifully printed on white paper, purified of electronic sin. OK, that's cheating. But AF has so much soul, so much mind, so much elasticity and rigor, that I forgive him everything.

I almost got invited to speak with him at a conference at Bar Ilan University but the organizers told E. N. who was promoting me that they were looking for big names that would attract sponsors. Now E. N. says the conference might be canceled for lack of funding. I'm not suggesting that if they had only invited me...

It's okay. I'll find my way back to Israel soon. I'm earning shekels writing for *Makor Rishon*. Somewhere in my heart I never dried my legs after paddling for a few sweet minutes in the waters of the Mediterranean just before sunset, before the ocean closed for shabat. No time to linger and enjoy on that trip, in that delicious September of *mission inaccomplie*, of wasted opportunity, of tearing myself away from the beach, from the little terrace of my beautiful room at the Cinema Hotel, denying myself the sun roof, not a minute of extra leisure to fully enjoy the Israeli breakfast, rushing out to the studio, shut in behind dark shades, working by fits and starts and to so little avail.. But nothing is wasted on me. I found a way, later, to make the desert of that project bloom. It's a good story. I might come back to it. Or I might not.

The question is—do I really not think that Bush and Sharon have created a royal mess, or am I too tired, after five years of war on all fronts, to even imagine the possibility, let alone admit it. The ink hasn't dried on my brilliant defense of their policies, strategies, tactics, and intermediate results, and now I'm being asked to fold my texts into dunce caps for the two leaders who have done the most to fight against jihad since it reared its raging head in our times.

How can I refuse to send them to the back of the class, beginning with Arik, who is pulling up stakes in Gaza, blind to the dire predictions of all my trusty Zionist friends?

The same talking mouths of French radio who were squawking about Israeli atrocities in the fall of 2000 are now cooing up a storm about Mahmud Abbas, the real peacemaker who is turning Hamas into plowshares and Islamic Jihad into boy scouts, enlisting terrorists into his 100% legitimate army-police force, releasing prisoners and putting "collaborators" to death, in short, showing himself to be deserving of a state. Give him a state, quick! You know a *hudna* can't last longer than a soap bubble.

And the same smart alecks who have been saying that Bush's democracy-in-the-Middle East snake oil is downright foolish—that's not the way it's done, and who says they want it, and even if they did want it they surely couldn't do it—are telling us to give the Pals a state. What for? To balance out Israeli democracy and live happier ever after? That or the opposite, it doesn't matter. Give-the-Pals-a-state urgency is chronic and incurable.

But the same people who have been guffawing since G. W. B. decided to reply to 9/11 like a man are not the same people who are organizing rallies to support the residents of Gush Katif. The latter are my friends.

And I don't know what to think.

22 March 2005
(TGV en route to Paris)

So, haverim, where did your Syrian coup d'état disappear to? Not a word in the press! They could hide it for a day or two but not for four. False alarm? And the precocious springtime is gone too. And my cell phone... but that's another story. Or maybe not. I hope I left it behind. I don't think I lost it between the house and the train station. I'll know for sure an hour from now when I get home, because precisely what is missing is that lovely compact instrument of communication by which you find out if you left your address book on the dining room table or let them know that you will be late. Or on time. The only comforting thought is that it's on its last legs. I have to replace it anyway. And what's the point of mentioning it except to say that I never ever left my phone behind when traveling, and if I did this time it is a measure of my distress. That lovely city is a wreck. The garbage collectors were on strike. Street cleaners too, it's the same company. Dog shit everywhere. On the sidewalks, on the streets, smashed by feet, smashed by cars, soaked in rain, dried in sun; flattened, spread, slogged, slimed, clumped in every conceivable shape and consistency. Broken glass glinting in every nook and cranny of the paving stones. Graffiti on all the facades. Broken down shops, sleazy shops, boarded up shops. The Bronx? No, that last ditch steely-eyed killer glinting lower depths hard edge Bronx poverty doesn't exist there... or not yet, or further down the road in neighborhoods we don't see. But down at the heels dilapidated has now leaked into every inch of that sweet city of the Midi. And shreds of decency are right there in the midst of it, no barriers, no fine membrane of separation, no up and down, no them and us, just one big dirty soup. Shady characters stand on the street corners, dealing in lowdown merchandise; shabby old men with empty eyes come and go in threadbare nightmares, and the local people are sinking with the ship.

It happened slowly.

The conversation hits a bump. Such good friends, decades of fidelity, the ones we can disagree with and see again ad again. But the bump takes me by surprise: G. says that France is the leader of Europe. How can he even dream of believing such a fantasy? France is the leader of no one and nothing. France is a dying organism offered to every sort of carrion eater. All vital systems are shutting down. Europe has been invaded, gave up without a fight. Europe is defeated worse than ever before and doesn't even have a mind to observe its own demise. The little puffs of lost majesty that survive here and there are so ridiculously foppish. How can we take anything seriously?

Dominique de Villepin with his diplomat's hairdo shows his toothy smile on prime time news. What is he really? The big bad wolf! Shaking hands with the hypocritical imam of the Paris mosque, embracing the diabolical imam of the Muslim Brotherhood, and what's the good news? The Foundation of Islam, latest trick in the book of sellouts. Money is already pouring in to build mosques. Haven't you noticed the dearth of mosques? And after the signing ceremonies and the handshakes, Oriental pastries are served by a woman in a bright colored headscarf. Sweet pastries and the Islam of France and vote yes for the European constitution because if in fact it might be dragging in a few stray cat problems, not to worry, it will all be smoothed over in two years or five.

Journalists went to a technical lycée at Montreuil and interviewed a few *casseurs*. Their faces are snuffed out to protect the guilty. Why did they attack their natural allies in the March 8th demonstration? The smasher speaks in rap. Pours out his gripes. They have everything, you can tell by their "*look*," they're on their way, we're stuck in a rut, they have this kind of *baskets*, we have that kind, so we beat them up, and we'll keep it up.

No one serves sweets after the rap.

16 July 2005

If the law of gravity applied only to apples it would have been replaced long ago by one that works for all objects. What of the explanations for the miseries that befall us? OK, they are only explanations. But people manipulate them as if they were laws.

My favorite: Bush and his band of neocons are half mad half Jewish = plotting to rule the world for their own narrow ends. Even if they can be [almost] forgiven for getting rid of Saddam Hussein, their cockamamie idea of imposing democracy on the Middle East is unacceptable and impossible. There we come to a fork in the road: it's impossible because the Middle East can't be democratic until the Israel-Palestine conflict is resolved to Palestinian-Arab–Muslim satisfaction or it's impossible because democracy is not their thing. In fact there are several forks; it's also impossible because Islam is incompatible with democracy. And because democracy can't be imposed.

But there won't be peace in the Middle East until there is a Palestinian State complete with running water and other amenities. That is, an undemocratic, let's say a tyrannical Islamic dictatorship similar to Iran and determined to exterminate the Jewish State.

So, the US and its allies should get their dirty hands off the Middle East, pack up, and pull out.

EXCEPT in Israel.

Because the Palestinians won't have a state unless the Americans create it out of whole cloth.

Conclusion: it is wrong to spend American money and lives to help the Iraqis build a budding democracy. And it's right to deliver a dictatorial Palestinian State with forceps.

After which the American role would be to step back and give modest nominal support to the usual Middle East = the status quo ante, which, if you listen to the same critics, is the reason why all the trouble began. They love to say that the US backed Saddam, the Taliban, and still today is buddy buddy with the royal family of Saud. Then, confusing democracy with elections, they accuse the Americans of cheating because they don't want newly liberated states to elect Islamic theocratic dictators into office. Guilty of backing Usama (which they didn't) and guilty of not liking Moqtada al Sadr, but guilty of not knowing how to get rid of him.

As for the mathematics—1,700 military deaths in Iraq is proof of US defeat; 1,500 civilian deaths in Israel is proof of Israeli wrongheaded stubbornness; and 1% of Muslim fanatics willing to die to kill us is proof that there's nothing to get excited about. But, killing 50 to 70 people at random in London is a demonstration of the extraordinary capacity of Islamic militants to bring a country to heel. Hundreds of their fellow jihadis arrested or killed in Iraq doesn't enter into the pacifist equation because they are not reported [in France].

Has anyone noticed the Sabra-Shatila effect in Iraq? Iraqbodycount and others of the same ilk are tallying up the victims of car bombings and putting the total in a column marked "Iraqi civilian dead since March 2003" meaning, killed by the Americans.

27 July 2005

The unsurpassed genius of Shakespear is the simultaneous portrayal of inner and outer drama. Conflict in the human soul is externalized, played out in intricate relations between lifelike characters. But this is far from primitive artificial allegory. The external drama is no less true; it has its own dynamics, exists in its own right. No, the genius of Shakespear is far more intricate than what I just described. It is the above, multiplied to infinity. The play within the play of reality. Psychology that dictates history that informs psychology that drives history that draws its source in psychology that twists and turns under the influence of history...

Israeli soldiers are training in the Negev. It's not exactly Hollywood, but the usual urban warfare sets are in place. Arab village. Jewish settlement. How do you enter a Jewish home without traumatizing the children, how do you drag Jews out of their home without tripping and falling into any previous historical experience not to be mentioned here? Apparently there is some kind of cage that can be used as a temporary prison. How does an IDF soldier extirpate a Jewish family from its home, presumably with his right hand, while warding off a Hamas horde with the left hand? And whose fault is it? The settlers who don't want to leave? The government that has dreamed up this nightmare evacuation? Or the great white hope, Mahmoud Abbas, who has made it perfectly clear that he has no intention of extirpating Hamas from the ongoing drama. Though he will go through the motions whenever necessary. Put yourself in his position. Can he triumph over Hamas in Gaza? Not on your life. More likely on your death. His only hope is to ride on their coattails (or more precisely bullet clips), share their triumph in kicking the Jews out of Gaza, share their power in Gaza and deal with them over the next territory they intend to occupy, namely Judea & Samaria. What can he gain from trying to win out over Hamas, and losing? Hamas will celebrate a double victory: over Israel, over the PA. His only hope is to give the appearance of reining them in, while in reality clasping their blood-soaked hands.

The struggle in the Jewish soul is played out in the Jewish State. Our strength is our weakness. Other people lash out in rage, destroy indiscriminately, submit and revolt with equal futility. We turn against ourselves the aggression that should be aimed at those who attack us. And yet we survive and they go down the tubes. Jews scuffling with Jews while Qassams rain down their destruction. Jews turned against Jews, while Palestinians—Hamas, al Aqsa Brigades, Islamic Jihad, and PA mixed together—kill Jews. A young woman sitting on the porch with her fiancé is smashed out of existence. The porch isn't in the "occupied territories," it's in Israel proper. Whose Israel? The rocket launchers see no Israel, hear no Israel, accept no Israel. All withdrawal is partial in their book, until there is no more Israel to withdraw from, no more Jews to withdraw.

For years the ticket of respectability has been "I don't agree with the politics of Ariel Sharon." Jews who want to be considered normal, reasonable, and reliable opened their conversations with this *laissez passer* and went on to plead for some kind of respite from *shahid*-imposed atrocities. Antisemitism turned their ticket in the other direction: why should I be accused of antisemitism just because I don't agree with the politics of Ariel Sharon? Today, Ariel Sharon is on a state visit in France and I don't hear anyone saying "You can say what you want, but you have to give credit to Ariel Sharon..." Oh, they do give credit. But they don't tear up their old tickets.

I am certain that Jacques Chirac will blow it. Sorry to be so crude. I know that he will not be able to contain his smoldering Muslim-induced hatred for Israel. He'll be obsequious, hypocritical, pretentious as usual, but the anger against the very existence of the State of Israel will seep into his voice, glaze his eyes, and turn his clownish gestures into repressed slaps in Sharon's face. Why did he invite the Israeli prime minister to Paris? To give him one brownie point for the Gaza withdrawal? *Même pas!* To put him on notice: if the withdrawal does not satisfy the full range of Palestinian demands, including free access by land and sea and from the air, not only to Egypt and beyond, but to the "West Bank" and to Israel itself... woe on you! Ambitious France wants to play lead violin in the Quartet. Macho paternalistic France thinks he can put the screws on Condi Rice and get her to put the screws on Arik. Concessions, and more concessions, and still more concessions. And nothing will ever be enough to satisfy His Majesty Jacques, more royalist than the king, more uncompromising than the jihadis of Hamas, Hizbullah & cie.

Will our local jihadis organize mass demonstrations against the visit of the "butcher of Sabra and Shatila"? Not likely. First of all, their rank and file is on vacation in the old country (that they pretend is utterly foreign to them when they get into big criminal trouble and are threatened with deportation). And even more first of all, because we are in a new post 7/7 era. Europe has been jolted out of its slumber. Three British men carrying bombs in knapsacks blew themselves up in the bowels of the Tube, and the fourth did his deed in the upstairs of a typical red London bus. Take a closer look at the blokes. Didn't you see them leading the march against Bush's imperialist war in Iraq? Aren't they just the type that explained to willing British intellectuals that this was a war against Muslims? Oh, maybe those four operatives were instructed to lay low, to not arouse the slightest suspicion. But their political wing was surely at work, pumping the anti-Zionist / anti-American / antisemitic poison into the mainstream. Europeans are potheads. They can't turn against their dealers.

A week later, a second team fanned out in the same formation, three in the tube, one on a bus. I immediately understood their logic. After the first attack, you get the true Brit strutting. No one can stop us, we are going on with our lives, I take the tube, it can happen anywhere (and it did, on a Turkish beach and then at Sharm el Sheikh) we stood through the blitz, we'll stand through this. So, one week later, boom, you hit them again. One-two knockout punch. The same thing will happen at Sharm El Sheik unless the Egyptian police can prevent it. The undaunted couple interviewed by French television, sunbathing on the beach, fully intending to pursue their vacation like the brave tourists they are... Al Qaeda intends to shred them in its next operation, ASAP. Three thousand out of the six thousand sunbathers left the day after the attack. Two thousand out of the three thousand survivors will leave after the next one.

So why did public opinion and French media dilly dally over the most unlikely explanations for the second, fortunately failed, London attack? They imagined things that simply don't exist, a sort of very low-power explosion that would just rip apart the knapsack without causing any collateral damage. A copycat team thrown together hastily and wastily. Anything but the obvious: a second attack exactly like the first. Except that, according to the rare down to earth well-informed scientifically reliable specialists, the batch of explosives mixed for the two attacks had deteriorated. Now it is apparent that the 7/7 jihadis worked together with the 14/7 team. They underwent a joint training session, whitewater rafting in Wales a short while before going into action. Was this meant to firm them up? Or was it a way of discussing final arrangements, out of reach of MI5? I opt for the latter explanation.

I'm not setting up shop with a crystal ball. I'm testing my sense of reality. From the very first entry in July 2000 to the last word, which I will heroically try to write before the scheduled evacuation of the Gaza settlements on the 17th of August 2005, I have been trying to analyze the situation with sufficient acuity to yield accurate predictions on the next step. When I began, I was on the sidelines. And in France, writing in French. My text was a plea to French media. Don't set Jews up for the slaughter. One more time. Wake up! Look at what you're doing. And besides, I warned them, this time the catastrophe will not consume us before spreading to your neighborhood. We don't do victim anymore. We know how to step aside and let the flames go directly to your address. Wouldn't it be wiser to stop right now? If you can't understand the Middle East conflict, just shut up. But don't vomit up lies from morning to night. You'll choke on your own upchuckings.

Just five years later the balance has tipped. I write articles in English that are published in prestigious magazines, in print and online. My potential audience is enormous. Theirs is small and rapidly shrinking. Instead of pleading with them, I expose them to an international audience. I influence public opinion in countries that have real power. They talk to themselves. Their predictions turn out to be as ridiculous as their analyses. And mine? Let the reader judge.

What will happen after withdrawal? But, first of all, will withdrawal really occur? Yes, I think so.

But first, a brief report on some inside information that sheds light and perhaps even more so darkness on all that is said in this notebook. The scene takes place in the garden of a home not far from Mont Valérien where the Nazis executed up to a thousand résistants. A birthday party. Over a glass of champagne, one of the guests lines up four prominent women and sweetly shoots them down with a volley of gossip. It goes more or less like this: Do you know why (the online news magazine) *x-x* shut down? The X.X.X. withdrew its financial backing, furious because S. wanted 100,000 euros to do a report they requested on the undergoing negotiations between Hamas and the European Union. They pulled the plug on her! Well, what really happened is that the couple S-L exploded. L. started writing strongly anti-Chirac editorials, S. was still writing pro-Chirac but it wasn't enough to calm the pro-Chirac French financiers, they backed out. S. was having an affair with C.C. ... cheating on L. and, what's more, with C., who was going with X.C. Shortly afterward, C. was appointed Minister (of X).

In the space of one glass of champagne we go from a supposedly scrupulous unbiased source of information on the Middle East to the cabinet of Dominique de Villepin, with a leapfrog over the head of the news director of state-owned *France 2* who has been handling the spin on the Al Dura affair. At other dinner tables in other gardens in Paris and in the provinces and even in the far flung vacation spots where this cardboard elite is drinking, partying, and switching partners, similar tidbits are served with the champagne. No, France is not a banana republic, it is a royal farce.

A friend drives me into the city after the party. She drops me off in the middle of the scrunge at Place Clichy where I take a cab the rest of the way, going past the Opéra in all its splendor, down quiet summer streets between rows of Hausmanian architecture, balconies, mansard roofs, giant *porte cochères* where carriages no longer drive into paved courtyards, I see Paris as the best preserved ruins in the world. The architectural glories stand firm, the aristocracy that created them, that ruled from them, is gone forever. The plebes have moved into the palaces, the masses stumble in constant confusion, the barbarians have seeped in through the cracks, the servant girls are frolicking with the master or the mistress or each other, according to their tastes, butcher's apprentices jump out of state limousines and into gold embossed offices, and the journalists dutifully cover for them. Talk to any journalist off record, he'll describe the mess. Not only the mess, but the pettiness of it all. But you mustn't quote him, mustn't say anything that could identify her. Why? So they can keep their jobs.

Has it occurred to any of them that if one or two or six or eight started to tell the truth, they could all tell the truth? No, it does not occur to them.

They all know that *France 2*, in collusion with a Palestinian cameraman working for Al Aqsa brigades or Islamic Jihad or both or all of the local jihadis, fabricated a news report about Mohamed Al Dura, the Palestinian boy "killed by Israeli soldiers." This kicked off the intifada, primed the *shahid* pump that poured death and destruction on Israelis for four years, now reduced to a trickle by Israeli action, but ready to go full force again. And rapidly spreading in Europe. By now, all French journalists know that the Al Dura news report was a crude fabrication. They know that *France 2* Jerusalem correspondent Charles Enderlin knows that it is a fabrication. I think he knew from the very beginning. They think that if they come out and say it, they will lose their jobs. They don't understand that by their silence they have lost their jobs. They are not journalists, they are courtesans.

Ariel Sharon is visiting Paris. What a joke! Chirac's clothespin smile is going to convince Israeli public opinion that Gaza withdrawal is a summer valentine that will cure decades of heartbreak? And our rolly polly Arik's outstretched let bygones be bygones hand is going to jack up Jacquot a few points on the popularity scale? As for the anti-Sharon demonstrators, the hundreds of thousands of pro-Palestinians have melted down to 300 lost souls holding a candlelight vigil outside the Madeleine, not even mentioned on the radio. That whole circus has packed up and moved out of town. Or underground. The real jihadis are preparing their bombs. The fellow travelers are left to fall by the wayside.

29 July 2005

Ariel Sharon will be taking off from Orly in a short while. He will land in reality. The three days he spent in Paris were surreal. As if they took place in a time warp, or in an isolation capsule. Setting aside the apparent realpolitik reasons for this fake handshake, except to remark that, as usual, France had more to gain than Israel, I want to know what really happened. Judging by French TV and radio—nothing. Commentary was reduced to the strict minimum, and even less. Following well-worn principles of French media, the line was decided, and mindlessly repeated. The chosen theme was *aliyah*. Last year, said every journalist including some on Jewish stations, Sharon caused an uproar by telling French Jews to flee French antisemitism and settle in Israel. This year he congratulates the French government for its fight against antisemitism, and advises French Jews to come and settle in Israel but doesn't tell them to flee antisemitism. And that's it, for your general public that looks no further, and may not even be watching because, as French TV informs them for half of every newscast, they are on vacation. That's the sum and substance of the new tone of diplomatic relations between France and Israel. *France 1, 2,* and *3* aired chilly interviews. I suppose they took place at the newly reopened Israeli embassy (the fire last time!), in a wood-paneled library. Sharon stiffly seated at an antique desk, the Israeli flag at his left. The journalist stiffly seated in an armchair at a safe distance from Sharon, as if he had SARS. The brief interview was static and inconsequential. As was appropriate, given that neither journalist nor audience was in any way prepared for any major change in policy.

This visit, at the end of July, when every second shop is closed for *congés annuels*, was treated by the Israeli press, according to reports on Jewish radios here, as a fantastic breakthrough, a heartwarming improvement in hitherto stormy relations, the dawn of a new era, and maybe, just maybe, a return to the pre-1967 glory days. My French bullshit minesweeper is working full time. Did the Israelis send only Francophone journalists to cover the event? That, and left wing peace-now philo-Europeans? I'll have to check it out with my *haver* Amnon Lord of *Makor Rishon*. He won't be bluffed!

The image came to me this morning as I listened to a 45-minute interview with Sharon (Elkabbach on *Europe 1*) and then to a long program of analysis, with many invited guests, on Jewish radio: it's the battered wife syndrome. The brute beats up his wife year in and year out, and suddenly realizes that the neighbors are starting to look askance at him, that his boss is having second thoughts, in short, that his reputation is in danger. And the battered wife conveniently decides to make amends for one of the thousands of crimes of which she is accused as the blows fall on her hide. Suddenly the wife-beater tells her to get dressed up and invites the most nondescript couple in the neighborhood for dinner. He praises his wife, she praises him, they don't exactly kiss, that would be too much, the dinner is awful, the neighbors go home, the whole incident is forgotten until one day the wife-beater goes to jail or the wife goes to the cemetery.

I'm realistic. I can take a heavy dose of realpolitik. If it's good for Israel, fine. If it's also good for France, even better. I have no objection to this fifth class state visit. What matters is how it is interpreted by sane healthy individuals, especially when their interpretations influence public opinion.

Chirac giving Sharon a gold star for demonstrating, by the Gaza pullout, that contrary to all that was said and thought, Israel is willing to make a teensy weensy step toward peace, *NON*! Who is France to judge? France has been playing footsie with every Middle East dictator and jihad chief for the past thirty years. France was chummy with Saddam Hussein when he was sending $25,000 to shahids' families for distinguished service in the cause of killing Israeli civilians. I do not need to dress a résumé of French faux pas on this route—because I have been chronicling them day by day since the summer of 2000.

Sharon's visit is a non sequitur. It is not surrounded by any rethinking of French foreign policy in the Middle East, it is not buttressed by any revised analyses in the press or in the minds and mouths of government officials. It is not connected to what came before and so it will have no connection with future policy or actions. It's like a mediocre film tossed onto the screens in the doldrum month of August, just to fill a bit of space and time.

Sharon wants the French to influence their Francophone Arab friends? What influence does France have in the Arab world? What Arab world, in fact? Syria? Only if France backs Bashir's intransigence and duplicity. Lebanon? Only if France backs the democratic movements against Syria and the Hizbullah. The Hizbullah? Only if France betrays Lebanon, Israel, the US and so-called moderate Muslims the world over. The Maghreb? Only if France continues to pursue its Eurabian policy, which includes hoping for the destruction of Israel without actually attacking. Iran? Only if France helps Iran hide its nuclear weapons development and avoid the consequences of its dire projects. Egypt, Iraq, Jordan? They know that France is blustering and powerless.

And what does France want from Israel? A seat at the card table. The sexiest game in town. The Arab-Israeli conflict. Will Arik let France have a say in any future peace processes? *NON*!

Which doesn't mean that no good will come of this paltry exhibition of mutual insincerity. The press will not be able to go back to its joyous game of pouring acid on Israel. They had already lost interest some time back. It won't be revived. The jihad attacks in London have even silenced the news from Iraq. Any car bombs these days? We hardly know. The bombs that burst into the press this week are the stock found in a car in Luton, left behind by the 7/7 bombers. For their comrades in arms? Or did they think they were coming back for a refill? Either way, it shows how little they understand about the countries they are trying to destroy.

It's quite human to put together familiar stories in which to insert extraordinary incidents. I suppose I do it too. But you have to be ready to change your story when the facts hit the sidewalk. This is where the French media, among others, fail completely. That's why the news is so old and tasteless here. Maybe *Fox* overdoes the hype. Breaking news every ten minutes. The same tidbits of breaking news all day long. But here the news never breaks. *Interdit*. It has to be passed through a series of filters, then washed, starched, and ironed. Except for the great big catastrophes that hit all the screens at one and the same time (and for which, I suppose, the agencies can offer images at reduced prices because of economies of scale) the news is a day or two old. And repeated at noon and prime time and again the next day. When it's too mediocre to bear, I zap. And usually come upon the same subject on the other station. State-owned or privately owned, French TV is all coming from the same source, controlled by the same political power, tailored along the same lines.

When the facts disturb the scenario, the scenario wins. No matter how many or how weighty, the facts are systematically discarded and the scenario is pushed ahead miserably. You might ask what does it matter. I reply that you can't have democracy without a free press.

British police shot a man to death in the Tube last week. Early reports claimed he had run out of one of the houses under surveillance, and refused to heed warnings to stop and hold up his hands. Then it turned out that he had nothing to do with the jihad attacks. And he wasn't a Paki or any such thing, but a totally absolutely completely wholly innocent Brazilian. You can believe that the French media slurped over that story. I heard it fifty times. It's called a "*bavure*" in French, meaning a blot, like an ink blot on a pupil's penmanship exercise. Something that seeps out, spills over, oozes. And did they ooze!

Does that mean that I was overjoyed to know that a Brazilian was shot in the head when in fact he didn't have a bomb around his waist? How many Israeli border guards, checkpoint soldiers, and utterly vulnerable shopping center guards have died because they kept a *shahid* at bay, blew up with him or her instead of letting them get into the shopping center or restaurant? So, *nu*, Jews don't shoot people in the head without asking for their permission first. Or maybe they do, sometimes. For the same good reason.

My scenario had multiple pathways. Why did the man run as if guilty? Is it because the police were in plain clothes, and he thought they were criminals? Was he carrying a few grains of hashish? Maybe he'd planned to take the train without a ticket? News reports over here kept hammering away at the absolute. He was a mechanic, he had lived in London for several years, he had a visa.

Only it turns out that his visa had been extended with a fake immigration stamp, and even the extension had expired two years ago. If he'd stopped and put his hands in the air, he might be back in Minas Gerais today, alive, not in a coffin.

I'm ready to be wrong about the newfound French-Israeli friendship. I'm all ears to discover the real reasons behind this maneuver. Is it possible that Jacques Chirac woke up one day and realized that they can hit Baghdad, they can hit London, and they can hit Paris? Not the way they hit in 1995, that was sardine *shahids*. Not the way they hit the AZF fertilizer factory in Toulouse. That could be kept hidden, in a country where the press is led around by a ring in the nose. But hit like London. And the secret services that are working secretly (M.L. always tells me how efficient they are, and how they hate the government that tries to keep them from being efficient) will have to come out and admit that they are in the *banlieues* and in the *provinces* and in the *arrondissements* of Paris and maybe in your building! Honeycombed throughout your society of pacifists, ecologists, antiglobalization angels, and masses on the dole. Despite all the blarmy retailed in his very own media, does Chirac suddenly realize that unless the Americans win in Iraq and wherever else they choose to deploy we are lost here? Or is he simply tailoring himself a new shirt in preparation for campaigning against Sarkozy for the presidential nomination of his party?

The best news I heard today is that the Israelis are going to build a three layer fence on the border with Gaza. To tell the truth, this and some of the things said by Sharon in the interviews he gave in Paris, have convinced me that he knows what he is doing in pulling out of Gaza. Strangely enough it corresponds to my own off the wall plan: take a chunk of territory away from them every time they commit a *shahid* attack. Suddenly I've changed my perspective. Pulling out of Gaza seems to translate into giving land for terrorism. Ah, but no. Pulling out of Gaza and building three rows of fence, with all kinds of robotics to patrol the border, IS a way of taking territory away from the Palestinians as punishment for their jihad terrorism. The land taken away from them is Israel proper. They won't be able to sneak in. And when they try to shoot over the fence, the counterpunch WILL be terrible. The problem with this idea is that there is already a fence around Gaza and it has been keeping terrorists out.

30 July 2005

And I am on the fence. On the question of withdrawal, I'm on the fence. Yes, I admit, I'm convinced by Sharon's reasoning. It's a strategic move that will make Israel stronger and more resistant. It is not the beginning of a tumble of concessions, under international pressure, stupidly rewarding terrorism and delivering Israel up to its enemies. I think it is a military decision. Shoring up the line of defense. Ready for the next onslaught.

I think Sharon knows what he is talking about when he says that in the Middle East there's a lot of talk, a lot of promises, a lot of signatures on agreements, and they are meaningless: what counts is action. He knows Abbas is playing a double game, and he is confident that he can beat him at it. Hamas can bluster and boast, claiming to have kicked the Israelis out of Gaza. The few decent citizens—or maybe they are potentially many, I have no way of knowing—left in that enclave that nobody wants have already had a taste of what is coming. Something worse than taliban Afghanistan. It's happening already, but the media aren't allowed to film it. Courageous journalists like Khaled Abu Toameh report it. French media don't care to cover it, even indirectly. So you get the usual biased image of Gaza. Those terrrrible *colons* (as I observed long ago, this word goes beyond the hateful identification with old-fashioned colonizers, it is a 100% equivalent of *youpin* meaning "kike") on the rampage to prevent the return of Palestinian lands. The settler's movement and its tens of thousands of active allies have not done one hundredth of the damage done by a single winegrower's demonstration in the south of France, or a rowdy bunch of *banlieusards* on the 14th of July. Two hundred, or was it four hundred, cars burned on French independence day. Sovereignist Philippe de Villiers, interviewed by the twinkling star of French newscasteresses, Claire Chazal, mentioned the fact as a disgrace to *la République*. Claire pouted and scolded him with her velvet voice: really, monsieur de Villiers, it's a tradition, there's always a bit of rowdiness on the 14th of July.

I guess so. It goes back to decapitating the king.

Stories on the ground are heartbreaking and heartwarming. Soldiers pray and cry with the marchers they are ordered to contain at all costs. A small minority of crazies torment them with stupid Shoah analogies, but the overwhelming majority is like me, on the fence. Even as they bravely express their opposition to withdrawal, they know that they will respect their government. They know the soldiers are doing the right thing, obeying orders, no matter how badly it hurts. I remember Dany Seaman telling me that it is important to state Israel's right to remain in the disputed territories, even if withdrawal is a necessary strategic decision. That is what the demonstrators are doing: staking claim, even though they know they will pull up stakes and leave. They express Israel's right to Gaza with their heads and feet, not by writing intellectual op-eds. They are Israel's expression of the right to remain.

Can the Left make the same claim to integrity? I don't think so. Where are the Shalom Aschavniks today, when soldiers are torn asunder? Last year, or was it two years ago, they were drooling over the refuseniks who publicly proclaimed their refusal to serve in the territories. They brought them to France and sent them on the speaking circuit like dancing bears. Do they have a word for the brave soldiers in the other camp who do not refuse to obey today, though their convictions are at least as strong as those of the refuseniks they spawned and fawned over?

Voices on the Left, the Israeli Left, the French-Jewish Left, have no shame in trotting out their threadbare Oslo illusions. These people are always on the fast track to peace. They absolved Arafat of 99% of his responsibilities, they shower Abbas with 99% of unearned praise, they kiss the 1949 armistice line as if it were *tsitsis*—and disguise it in a 1967 label—they read the road map in Arabic, they make the most preposterous proposals in the most reasonable voices; terribly mistrusting of anything vaguely resembling religion, they take themselves for G-d.

And from their high heavens they zing down thunderbolts of judgment. Those settlers, *ces colons*, with their knitted *kippot*, biblical beards, and damnation rabbis, are a mortal threat to Israeli democracy, to the very existence of the State of Israel. They must be suppressed at all costs. The damage they have already done is incalculable. To the point of making us—the ones who know the right path and read by divinely rational light—wonder if there's something inherently wrong with the very notion of a Jewish State. Fortunately we have allies in Europe, in the US, and in the Arab world, ready to declare peace, if only these wild hordes can be contained.

And the Left is not subverting Eretz Israel? Shimon Peres, spoon fed by European interests? It's all so elegant on their side. All bowing and scraping and... what's the equivalent of crocodile tears when applied to cooing? Hyena cooing is too strong. Leave it at that. Just think, if Israel had done like other moderate sized powers, and seized as much land as it could grab in each defensive war—and don't forget, those were not quibble wars, they were extermination wars against Israel—Israel could give back a chunk of Jordan, a chunk of Syria, a chunk of Lebanon, a chunk of Egypt, and keep Gaza and all of Judea and Samaria, and earn the eternal admiration of the international community. If it were really about land. I said at the beginning, in the year 2000, the territories are a red herring. Compared to what I know today, I was like a newborn child. With the innate knowledge of a newborn child. Today I can repeat this statement with conviction upheld by wisdom and nourished by a treasure of reliable information: the territories are a red herring.

What use is intelligence without critical thinking? It's like a fast sleek car with no steering wheel. Just point it in some direction, and it goes straight ahead until it crashes into a wall. That is the condition of the French population today. One of the four bombers who were to serve as weapons of mass destruction in the London transit system on the 21st of July was arrested in Rome yesterday. On his way to Rome, he passed through Paris. I scoured through the French press. No one mentions that the *shahid*-dud passed through Paris. Isn't that an interesting detail, given that we are on *"vigipirate rouge,"* the next to the highest level of alert, and we are being congratulated by various well-informed sources for being particularly vigilant, particularly effective, particularly better than the Brits when it comes to shielding the population against terrorists. Hmmm. So this most wanted man slipped into and out of Paris without being observed. *Très intéressant, non? Non.* Censored out. It can't be possible that no journalist wanted to mention it. They can't. They don't have to be told in so many words, they get the idea. Our message to the world today is that we are not only the great lovers and maximum perfume creators, we are also tops in anti-terrorism. The fact that this man whose picture was broadcast every way imaginable slipped in and out of Paris is not acceptable. It disturbs the idea we want to get across. An English journalist writes an article in praise of the French way of handling Islamist extremist. The pivot of his argument is the truly excellent surveillance of radical mosques, with ejectable seats for bad imams who preach hatred. *Supair*, as they say. If only I could remember the names of the books published years ago exposing those same mosques that have been spilling out hatred for years. They were being watched and listened to. French undercover agents know all about them. And the French government let them operate unhindered, just as the British let theirs preach indoors and outdoors, in the mosques and in Hyde Park Square and in their dedicated newspapers and in the mainstream press and through the mouths of useful idiots. The murderer of Sébastien Selam (z"l) went to one of those mosques, the one on rue Tanger I believe. The mosque continued on its merry way, the murderer is cooling his heels in a comfortable psychiatric ward and will most likely be released without ever being tried. The other two London dud bombers were arrested yesterday in a spectacular operation fully covered by the British media and available to any journalist who wanted it. The operation was filmed for heaven's sake! Scant, sparse echoes reached the French media yesterday. We'll see what happens today.

The news is being leaked slowly through an eye-dropper. Some sources are getting the name straight: the bomber arrested in Rome is not a Somali named Osman Husain, he's an Eritrean named Isaac Hamdi. He took the Eurostar from Waterloo Station on the 26th of July, and from Paris continued on, probably by train, to Milan and Rome, making dozens of calls on his cell phone all along the way. He claims that the 21st of July bombs were not really meant to explode, they were just to scare people. Combing through different sources of information, I discovered—once again—how ideology forms cataracts that cloud the vision. While French media just barely begin to mention that the flunked out bomber passed through Paris (think of it, he got off the train in our very own *gare du Nord* and from there, probably in the *métro*, to *gare de Lyon* where he took the train to Italy) as if it were no more interesting than Great Lakes WIS as a jihadi destination, *FoxNews* has the most comprehensive information I could find. *La Repubblica* tells less than *Corriere della Sera*, the *New York Times* is almost as hazy as *Le Monde*. Aren't they interested in the news? I think I'll ring up the SNCF on Monday and ask which train Hamdi took and how he got through passport control.

Two months after French voters said *NON* to the proposed European constitution, Eurabia seems to be hitting bumps. Europe without borders, post-nationalist ultrapacifist Europe is donning flak jackets and setting up checkpoints. They'll soon wish they could build a wall!

I love the pace of this modern world where my passion for history hooks up with my sense of adventure and things discerned in the thick of the fog come out into full light in the space of months or years. It is not simply a technological change, it is the possibility of an ethical leap. Because the consequences of miscalculations are so rapid that they cannot be disguised. The invasion of Europe under cover of multicultural claptrap is already revealed for what it is. The figures were there, the statistics, the sharp observations of a courageous few, but the masses were fed a completely fake story of traditions of immigration. And whoever said otherwise was immediately boxed "extreme right." No society can absorb so many foreigners in so short a time, especially when they are undereducated, untrained, unskilled and, as if that were not enough, hostile to the host country. But now it's no longer a question of words. The seeds have sprouted and blossomed and given bitter fruit. Reality will get the upper hand.

The masses of illegal immigrants will be swept out, the good along with the bad. Hamdi's brother had a call center near Roma Termini station. He fabricated false identity documents, among other activities. Counterfeit document rings have been uncovered in France, but how many are still going strong? Sarkozy has already announced that he has the means to revoke citizenship of people convicted of preaching or promoting terrorism. Muslims born in Europe will be sent back to their parent's and grandparent's native lands. Between injustice and jihad, Europe will choose injustice.

And it will be better for all concerned. Don't think I don't care what happens to France, to Europe, to Muslims the world over. My anger may be stunning but there is no hatred in my heart. Not even indifference. And I know that my self interest is best served when others prosper. I am not French, I will never be French but I take no pleasure in watching this old country dig its own grave. This jihad immigration should be pushed back and the reflux transformed into reality pressure on Muslim countries. It will drown their tyrannical dreams.

Musharaf just decreed that foreign students will no longer be allowed to study in Pakistani madrassas. Isn't that a beauty? I hope he'll send home the ones who are already there. Brothers of French jihadis who ended up in Guantanamo are always explaining that the innocent young man just went to Pakistan to study classical Arab. Will the French police be waiting to catch them as they come bouncing back? Or will they let them dance through, like Hamdi alias Husain?

I love this information age. CAIR does a public relations stunt, issues a phony fatwa against terrorism, and before they can leave the press conference a dozen online magazines and blogs have presented all the evidence necessary to show that the fatwa is a fake, and the fatwa makers are terrorists themselves.

31 July 2005

The beauty of a chronicle is that it captures events as they occur, embedded in the totality of what is going on, the essential, the incidental, the filler, the body and soul of life. A chronicle captures what history will strain to retrieve. No other genre, except for fiction, can ever convey history in its lifelike vitality. I am a novelist, I will always be a novelist even if, as is likely, I never write another novel. My eyes are trained by novel writing, and what I see is material for fiction. Editors are reluctant to accept such an approach. If you live beyond my intimate circle and you are reading these lines, it means I made it over the endless hurdles. Talk about a security barrier, an apartheid wall... I could write a book about it!

I am perfectly capable of writing a journalistic article, a theoretical essay, a well-documented research paper. But here, in this intimate place where my mind speaks for itself, I can give the best of myself.

This is why I cannot always explain, journalistically or historiographically, the myriad details drawn from reality busying itself all around me as I write from France in English for readers who may know very little about daily life in France at the dawn of the 21st century. When I was a student, readers were expected to go on a search for background information in order to understand the words of writers worth the effort. Perhaps this does not go with the modern way of life that I praised just a few paragraphs ago.

France 3 is the regional channel of the State-owned French TV network. *France 2* is the national station. And there's not much else to speak of. The third partner, *TF 1*, was theoretically privatized a long way back. You wouldn't know it. They get their images from the same pool, and by some miracle come up with the same bouquet of subjects for almost every newscast. One half hour at 1 PM, one half hour at 8 PM, approximately 20 minutes of the most frivolous, vacuous, inconsequential babble about nothing, and 10 minutes of something resembling news.

Last night, *France 3* covered a momentous incident in l'Hérault, a department in the south of France, le Midi, whose main urban center is Montpellier. A local man who had shot at three *Maghrébins* [interruption...several hours later:]

How can I resist gathering news as it comes, like the blithely free spirit that I am, wandering down the byways of current events, where every hour yields arms full of wildflowers? While researching precise details on the above incident, I came upon an article in the left wing daily *Libération*: "Anti-terrorist commando terrorizes a family." The article recounts, with obvious indignation, how an innocent Moroccan father, Mohamed A., and his French son, Ahmed A., were mistreated by the French police. The facts and the commentary are inextricably joined. Let's try to separate them. Commentary: the police were excessively brutal, violent, disrespectful, vulgar, and threatening. The man and his son are totally innocent. The famous anti-terrorism judge who ordered the arrests was contemptuous of their rights, only saw them for five minutes. And of course, being totally innocent, they were released. An exemplary tale. This is the way French society is going to go. Overreacting to the so-called terrorist threat, taking vile pleasure in harassing Muslims.

And, one might add, if one swallowed the commentary, wasting tax-payer's money, aiming at soft targets instead of going after the real terrorists. (Readers of *Libération* might fill in the names Bush, Sharon on that one...)

The facts: Mohamed A.'s cousin has a son named Mohamed Belhadj. Seven major suspects in the Madrid bombings (11 March 2005) were holed up in an apartment belonging to him in Leganes, Spain. When the police came to arrest them, they blew themselves up. No remains of Belhadj were found. According to the family of Mohamed A., his brother, who lives in Spain, was questioned after the bombings, cleared of all suspicion, and released. One must suppose that Mohamed claimed, in an earlier investigation, to have had no contact with his cousin's son. Now the police show him the video of a wedding in Morocco in August 2000. And there's the young Belhadj. Mohamed A. says it's the one and only time he ever saw the boy. And why did the French son Ahmed go to Spain with his brother Ismael in March of 2005? To deliver a Mercedes 109, replies the totally innocent young Ahmed. But the French police rough him up, slap him, tell him he's going to go to jail, that he'll be sodomized there by fellow inmates (it isn't mentioned when the French media slurp over the Abu Ghraib scandal, but this is par for the course in French prisons). Ahmed breaks under pressure. Admits that his father spoke to Belhadj on the phone, let him stay at their home. This fact is followed by words that we are obviously supposed to attribute to Ahmed: "It was the pressure." Followed by: "Then he retracts." Retracts where? In front of the journalist? In front of the police? the judge? Alone later with his father?

On this same 31st of July, the *Sunday Telegraph* published an interview with France's terrorizing-terror judge Bruguière. With typical cockadoodle-do bravado the Judge explains that the Brits better take off their kid gloves if they want to fight effectively against terrorism. He praises the French way, based on repression, preemption, and blatant disregard for the niceties. This is how France has managed to keep a smoke-free zone in the middle of a hellzapoppin' world. There's just one little problem, according to the judge: even though France doesn't have troops in Iraq, it seems that this badge is wearing thin. Trouble may be brewing. One can assume that greater repression will be called for.

Put two and two together: the judge's word can be trusted. Witness the case of Mohamed and Ahmed A. How's that for repression? You won't catch them puttering around with terrorist cousins in the future!

Meanwhile, back at the train station, the most wanted terrorist Ousman Husain was able to take the train from London to Paris to Rome.

And Gaston Malafosse, 61 years old, was buried in the village of Bessan, population 4,000. *France 3* filmed the demonstration the day after his funeral. 1,500 typical French men and women marching silently down narrow lanes lined with linden trees in a typical Midi landscape, red tile roofs, a central square, a fountain, a café-restaurant. Local government officials came from miles around, mayors marched with their tricolor scarves across the chest. They carried a banner marked "*Plus jamais ça.*" The slogan dates to the period when the crimes of Vichy during the Shoah were, tardily, revealed. It's become an all-purpose expression, more likely used to accuse the Israelis of Nazi crimes against Palestinians than to remind French people that they are, once more, setting up the Jews for slaughter.

But in this case, *plus jamais ça* means never again shall an honest burgher be pushed beyond exasperation by the violence of "the young." The young in question are usually Muslim or Black. In this case they were Maghrebis. And Gaston Malafosse felt, it is reported, that they were harassing him. He shot into the group. Wounded three, one of them seriously. And hung himself two days later in his jail cell.

5 August 2005

I went away for three days of peace and quiet. But did not totally lose contact with the outside world. I was at a very worldly beach resort, with comfort and luxury and CNN. The first time the name passed on the ticker, all I saw was "Steven Vincent." Ah, I said, I know him. Maybe they are going to show a report he did in Iraq. Ten minutes later the ticker came around again, and this time I saw the whole sentence: *Reporteurs sans Frontières* expresses outrage at the murder of freelance journalist Steven Vincent. Unreal. I know him, but we didn't meet. He knew me through my writings, and through a mutual friend. We tried to communicate by e-mail but his provider was one of those snooty services that block certain correspondents. We had to pass through relays, but finally we set up an appointment in New York. Shortly before he was to leave for Iraq. But I had to leave NY suddenly for private reasons. Finally Steve and I arranged a meeting by telephone. We spoke for an hour or more. I remember asking him if he had any information on Florence Aubenas. Who? "Aubenas, the French journalist who has been a hostage in Iraq since January 5th. The whole story is so fishy." He told me that he didn't even want to think about kidnapping. And now he's dead. Captured, probably by Shia renegades who have infiltrated the police force, and shot dead two hours later.

7 August 2005

Early on a Saturday morning in August, I tune in to *France Culture* to join me for breakfast. I'm probably listening to a rebroadcast. There is no news, there are no features, there is no reflection in France from the 13th of July to the end of August. It is the time of *vacances*, of emptiness. The program is about diminishing fuel supplies, the tone is exactly the same as the religious programs dutifully broadcast on one or another state-owned radio station, the ideology is flat-earth: supplies will run out, the only solution is to diminish demand. The ecological ayatollahs cast damnation on our sinful consumption. Mechanized farm machines, lustful food imports, unholy travel, and all the way to the daily bath, each sin is calculated in tons of fuel. Passion knows no bounds. The unbridled castigators unwittingly carry us, by a process of hapless subtraction, to the dregs of the unwashed masses of olden times, and beyond to the very images of destitution flashed on our television screens from Niger. The famine in Niger is a smokescreen to hide massacres in Darfur and jihad on our doorstep. Horrible images of starving children tug at the heart-strings. Interspersed with shots of peasants hoeing desperately arid earth. Drought, crickets, and the indifference of rich nations has led to this: an infant the size of a cricket, heaving for one last breath. It is men-tioned in passing that the birthrate is 8 children per childbearing wom-an. And in fact, the mothers are not skin and bones, they are normally nourished, and probably bringing the eighth offspring to human rights organizations for emergency lifesaving. The lifesavers arrived by plane, just like the bananas decried by the specialists in ecological Puritanism, who went so far as to castigate people who want bananas in the winter, as if Europeans could have homegrown bananas in the summer.

End-of-the-earth thinkers don't travel to the end points of their logic. Maybe they want to preserve intellectual fuel as well? They stop in the romantic zone, with images of a rose cheeked neopeasantry plowing the fields with hefty horses, dressing in homespun cloth, riding to market in open carriages, frugally saving shoestrings, whittling authentic toys for authentic children during the long evenings of authentic winter.

The same romanticism prevails in the conception of foreign relations. The Palestinians are romantic revolutionary heroes, the Israelis are voracious cruel colonizers. Jews are profligate spenders of rare and precious commodities, Palestinians are authentic tent dwellers in flowing robes that live by candlelight. Even the rockets they shoot at Israelis, destroying property and lives, are "*artisanaux*" or hand-crafted. Surely justice is on their side.

Like so many others, I climbed out of my foxhole in the fall of 2000, dazed and shaken but determined to fight. I transformed my existence, my private and professional relations, discovered vast new sources of information and a world of new friends and devoted readers. I moved from the sidelines toward the center. And today I face a new border dispute. Withdrawal. My cherished friends and colleagues are mobilized against withdrawal, my inbox bursts with resounding speeches, relentless demonstrations, admonitions, accusations, calls to action, alarm bells, heartfelt appeals, horror stories, imprisoned adolescents, cages for recalcitrant settlers, and the thuds and thumps of heroic scuffles, all in the sweltering heat of Eretz Yisroel. My heart is torn and twisted. I can no more heap curses on Arik Sharon today than I could condemn Bush-Sharon-assassins four years ago. I can no more applaud withdrawal from Gaza than I could have condemned armed intervention in Jenin. I truly don't know what is right, strategically. I do believe that the decision is totally and uniquely strategic. It has nothing to do with making peace with Palestinians. This is not a time for making peace. I don't think the Sharon administration can clearly enunciate its strategy any more than the Bush administration could baldly state the real reasons for taking military action against Saddam's Iraq.

Trying to see my way clear, I have to continue to spin out these don'ts. I don't think that the Israelis, individually or collectively, are duped into believing that they are exchanging a territory for peace, not even for a bit of peace. I don't think that asking the families to leave their harbors of peace, their idyllic neighborhoods, their orchids blooming in the midst of filth and depravity is in any way comparable to the cruel uprooting of Jews from their homes and countries that has marked our history since the beginning.

It is all shot through with paradox. To a Diaspora Jew who doesn't know how to hold a gun let alone shoot it, the sight of Israeli soldiers dragging away Israeli demonstrators is a battle of Titans. All of these people know how to fight, they have been defending themselves against a ruthless enemy, they are born tough. Tough and clever. Think of it! Jews infiltrating the Gush Katif, under the nose of Jewish soldiers trained to defend those very settlements against Palestinian infiltrators.

I don't think this is the war of the Jews that will destroy Israel. I don't think Israelis will shed Israeli blood. One crazed kid did a Baruch Gold-stein. Shot four Arab Israelis, wounded a dozen in a bus. Young men from the village smashed him to death with bottles and stones. The po-lice had already arrived at the scene but they couldn't do anything to stop the instant primitive revenge. Couldn't even get to the wounded. Maybe they could have saved some lives? In England, a young black man was killed with an axe blow to the head, in revenge for the subway bomb-ings. Arab Israelis in a bus, a black youth walking in his own neighbor-hood, no, we don't do that, we don't kill people that way, we don't even think of them that way, we don't hate them indiscriminately. I can write about Muslims and Islam in the harshest terms, I can never justify mur-derous hatred against them. Today, I can say that I want massive emi-gration of Muslims out of Europe, voluntary and involuntary, the good with the bad. For the sake of everyone. But I can't condone animosity against them.

Let me not dissolve in my *bons sentiments*. Why can't I participate, emotionally or intellectually, in the current outrage against withdrawal from Gaza? Am I wrong in my own terms? Have I lost my capacity to react? Or am I expressing what so many others dimly feel? Let me state it simply: I do not agree on the principle of a Palestinian State. I do not think that Israel has any obligation to give any territory to any Palestini-an authority. And I imagine that the withdrawal from Gaza and its ulti-mate aftermath will lead to widespread acknowledgment of these two essential principles. If the withdrawal takes place under fire, which is the most likely scenario, the expected conclusion will be more rapid. If the

PA is able to get its military wing—Hamas, Islamic Jihad and all the rest—to hold its fire until the day after the withdrawal is completed, it will take a bit longer. But not much.

The paradox is that Israeli residents of Gaza could set a retroactive example for Palestinians by bravely accepting to leave their beloved homes, greenhouses, schools, synagogues, and land. They could leave with broken sobbing hearts and brave feet. Turning, as they go, to say: *Here you are. We gave up what is precious to us, so that you can feel at home here. Now give up your dreams of return, so that we can feel at home in Israel.* It won't happen that way.

Palestinians who would like to live in peace, side by side with a Jewish State, won't even have the chance to live in peace within their own *Judenrein* Gaza. They are already caught in the claws of jihadis and crushed in the maws of warring schools of corruption. Their children are killed by Qassams that fall short, stabbed to death in family quarrels, indoctrinated to blow themselves up as *shahids*. The nihilism that cannot vent itself against Israelis turns against its fellow citizens. Decent Palestinians don't have any hopes for a decent life in Gaza. It will become one vast launching pad for attacks on Israel. Whether the international community approves or not, Israel will have to retaliate. No more pinpoint operations. Ah, but there I go, all the way to the limits of my logic, and believe me, I have no stomach for what will happen to the man in the streets of Khan Younes, el Bureij and the former Netzarim. I don't want it to happen. How are we going to avoid it?

Ariel Sharon explains that the next step after withdrawal is to return to the Road Map. His opponents, my dearest friends, say that the next step will be withdrawal from parts of Judea and Samaria... international pressure for further concessions... a renewed campaign of massive attacks against Israeli civilians... international pressure to prevent Israel from taking decisive action against its enemy... the destruction of the state of Israel.

And some people think we cannot win the war "against terrorism." The same people thought Israel could not, by military means alone, bring an end to what they call suicide bombings and what the Palestinians call martyrdom operations. On the same page with the report on the abduction and killing of Steven Vincent, the *International Herald Tribune* reported on improved car bomb techniques in Iraq. If I had time to read the blogs and other reliable sources, I would know pretty well what is going on in Iraq, good and bad. As it is, I have to make educated guesses. We are not losing. It is not a worse Vietnam. As one might notice, critics of the war keep comparing it to Vietnam. But the United States has fought many wars. Vietnam was the exception, not the rule.

The French word is "*décalage*," meaning gap or lag. Jet lag is "*décalage horaire.*" There is a huge *décalage* between the common ordinary perception of Iraq and what is actually happening. For the French, the *décalage* is so great, we are not even speaking of the same time and place. Nothing is happening in Iraq but car bombs and other jihad attacks. The killers are called "*résistants*" or at best insurgents, and the people they murder with their horrendous methods are just as quickly chalked up as American-caused casualties. Perhaps Americans have a slightly broader picture. Being against Bush and against the war in Iraq is a badge of honor in our Western societies. The arguments I hear—that I provoke—are always package deals, and inevitably include expressions of aversion for George W. Bush. I don't think these arguments can be based on personal conviction, because all sorts of very different people give me the exact same reasoning. And I'm not talking to whacko pacifists or vicious pro-Palestinians. These are intelligent, reasonable people who behave righteously and responsibly in their personal lives. I think they would be surprised if they could see the sources of their arguments. If they looked at the vile propaganda spread in the Arab-Muslim world, if they visited the Islamist websites, if they learned about the intermediate propaganda spun out by jihad fellow travelers, and if they more carefully analyzed what they read in *Le Monde*, the *NY Times* and other such elegant sources, they might see that they are swallowing jihad propaganda reprocessed for their refined taste.

You can like or dislike Gorge W. Bush, agree or disagree with him on questions of religion or abortion, consider him stupid or bright, sincere or phony but can you deny that he rose to the occasion of 9/11 and led his country into courageous, defensive warfare? The domestic social changes occurring under his influence are nothing compared to the upheavals of the sixties; their negative effects will be negligible and easily balanced out by future administrations. Why would people hate Bush and forgive Clinton for slothfully exposing us to a stunning military attack on our own soil?

I don't pretend to be a military strategist; I rely on intermediary analysts whose arguments are convincing. My well-meaning friends and relatives tell me that we should have attacked Iran or North Korea, not Iraq. That we should have stayed in Afghanistan and not gotten distracted in Iraq. That we should have fought terrorism, not Saddam Hussein who had nothing to do with 9/11 and had no WMDs. It is like saying we should bring the 9/11 *shahid* pilots into court and try them for reckless airplane driving. No political party or potential presidential candidate has elaborated an aggressive strategy for fighting the jihadis. And no one can take us back to the 20th century. Where do we go from here? Well, in the first place, we go from here, not from some theoretical starting point in the past, illuminated by hindsight and bathed in divine omniscience.

And here we are with a war on our hands, at a period in history when thinking people think you can make a war go away by reconfigurating it in the press. We are attacked by powers that want to destroy us, and it becomes an unjust war led by that idiot Texan Bush. Instead of hating the war that is being waged against us, people hate Bush. Because he recognizes it, and wants to fight it.

The *décalage* between the Steven Vincent I knew and the announcement of his death in the press is so great, I can't close the gap. Here's the first message I received from him:

"Dear Ms. Poller:

"X X was kind enough to provide your e-mail to me. I am a fan of your writing in the New York Sun and was very pleased to find out that X (whom I met only two weeks ago) knew you. I would like to meet you—I understand you will be in New York at the end of this month. Perhaps we can meet? I would love to hear your take on the situation in Europe.

"And while I'm at it, do you have any connections in Iraq? I plan to return to the country this spring—specifically to Baghdad—and could use any and all contacts. Just thought I'd ask.

"In any case, I hope you can spare some time to meet me when you come to New York. Meanwhile, I will continue to look for your by-line.

"Best,

"Steven Vincent"

He was an art critic, transformed by 9/11. We talked about the sharky smarky art world. Between that first message and our final conversation, he had changed his plans and decided to go to Basra. Not because it was less dangerous, but because it had become impossible to move around in Baghdad. He didn't want to spend his time in a hotel room, or at the bar drinking with other foreign correspondents. Did he say that last line or do I imagine it? If his provider hadn't indulged in some stupid kind of profiling, we would have exchanged many written messages that I could retrieve today. We spoke about Europe. He had remained somewhat skeptical after Bat Ye'or's presentation at a Washington bookstore. But I know her work, I had already read *Eurabia*, I was able to tell him that it was based on scrupulous documentation, and borne out by the facts on the ground. I think he said that he would have to make a trip to Europe sometime this year. He was visiting with his parents when he called me, or just before, or just after. A leave-taking visit of an attentive son. He was modest. He'd already published one book about Iraq, *The Red Zone*, and yet he asked me if I had any contacts. I almost bought his book at the airport on my way back to Paris in May, but I decided to read Sharansky's *Case for Democracy* first.

It seems that he had tried to blend in. Grew a beard, dressed like a Shia. Fatal error? He could no more pass for a Shia than Johnny Weissmuller for Tarzan. The *décalage* is too great. If, as it seems, he was murdered by Moqtada al Sadr's boys, it shows that you can't make soft ultimatums with warlord ayatollahs. You have to be ruthless with them. All the showdowns with Al Sadr ended in backdowns. But what can you do? How do you deal with a society in which tyranny is soaked into the very bone? That's why a guy like Steve Vincent couldn't blend in, despite his flowing robes and Shia beads and Ali someone or other t-shirt. You have to have pools of tyranny in the depths of your eyes, your muscles have to flex with tyranny at every move, your saliva has to be bitter and your sweat acrid. It doesn't matter if you are dealing it out or taking it, tyranny is the very sound of your voice, the very air you inhale and exhale. So what do we do with these people? How can you save the freedom-lovers among them? And protect yourself from the others?

[interlude] "Le kiosque arabe" (*Radio France Internationale*) is my top unfavorite radio program. Broadcast from Beirut on Saturday afternoon, it brings together two Arab specialists who comment on the week's events in the Middle East. Sometimes it's two journalists, sometimes one journalist and one professor. They are usually Lebanese, or Syrian, if not Palestinian. Once they had an Israeli. I can listen with my eyes closed, I could play the role of the invited guests or the French Arabophile moderator, just give me the subject and in two seconds I'll turn it against Israel and the United States. The only subjects worthy of attention are those that can be used to the disadvantage of Israel and the United States. Well, today's program should reassure my anti-withdrawal friends. Everyone agrees, on the Arab kiosque, that Ariel Sharon has a trick up his sleeve. He is unilaterally withdrawing from Gaza so as to avoid getting on track with the Road Map. And you don't have to be told that the Road Map, being an internationally concocted document, is decidedly to his disadvantage. So the foxy old general sidesteps the roadmap, pulls out of Gaza, and pursues the colonization of the West Bank. Unless the international community bears down on him and forces Israel to get on the Road Map, there is a good chance that we are heading for another confrontation.

Doesn't this square with what we are saying? The Pals intend to complain to International Mama that the withdrawal from Gaza is incomplete, insufficient, unsatisfying, inconsistent with their express demands, in short, a provocation no less than the previous Ariel Sharon show, namely the visit to *l'esplanade des mosquées* on 28 September 2000. Just as they prepared for their jihad-intifada during the Camp David talks, they are revving up for a new round of the same while we at home are wringing our hands and rending our clothes over the withdrawal from Gaza.

8 August 2005

On my way to the market this morning I discovered, just around the corner, on a little side street, the remains of a burnt motor scooter. A motor cycle parked a few feet away was melted down, obviously by contact with heat or flame. As I stood staring at the wreckage, its reality superimposed on images of car bombs in Iraq and fire trucks swallowed up by forest fires, a neighbor passed. He looked at me looking at the carcass and said, "It burned."

And that's the French mind in a nutshell. Of all the comments one might make, none could be more inconsequential and, with respect to me and my curiosity, insulting. It burned, *monsieur*, yes, I may be a foreigner but I'm not an idiot. I can see that it burned. And that gives rise to all kinds of thoughts in my active mind. Here I discover a tiny corner of Baghdad on my own street. If it had been parked a few meters further into our street I might have been awakened by the light of the flames. I'm still surprised that I didn't hear anything. None of the guttural sounds of late night street fighting that so often tear me from sleep. On this quiet street in this lovely *quartier*, late night revelers explode in last ditch frustrations, seething quarrels, triangles, warring factions. They scream bloody murder but so far we haven't discovered any bodies strewn on the battlefield.

For my neighbor, it's clear: it burned. And he goes home and I go to the market, shaking my head in dismay. It seems to me that French TV news is perfectly tailored to his mind. I did a quick press review at the international news stand at the market. The British papers reveal that the London *shahids* received money from Saudi Arabia. The *Corriere della Sera* showed a picture of a passenger from the Tunisian airlines crash. A young woman, undoubtedly pretty, with dark hair and a lovely figure. She had lost her dress in the crash, her innate body dressed in fresh white underwear floated head down in the green waters off the coast of Palermo. The flight was on its way from Bari to Djerba. The plane was built in France in 1992. A spokesman for the airline reports that it was regularly serviced. It just happens that the motors lost power after the takeoff, the pilot tried to get to Palermo for an emergency landing, he didn't make it, the plane landed with such a thud that it broke up into three pieces, the passengers in one section survived, the others are dead. Information has leaked out about the Air France jet that overran the runway at the Toronto airport and landed nose first in the ravine. Two of the evacuation toboggans failed to function. One or more of the emergency exits wouldn't open. Nevertheless, says the journalist, the plane was evacuated in two minutes. I've heard that at least a dozen times. How can three hundred passengers get out of a plane in two minutes?

Disappointing news for the French media: Discovery looks like it's going to make it back to earth safe and sound. They were banking on a catastrophe. Never mind, other juicy subjects are available: the 60th anniversary of the nuclear bombing of Hiroshima. Hiroshima, world capital of pacifism. All nuclear powers should give up their weapons, enjoins the mayor of Hiroshima. Young and old engage in heart rending ceremonies, but there is only one message for French viewers: the Americans did the dirty deed. WW 2 disappears, the Japanese never fought, allied soldiers didn't die. Atrocities? Never heard of them! *Radio France Internationale* announces a special program today: the Americans dropped the atomic bomb on Hiroshima even though the Japanese were ready to surrender.

Doesn't it remind you of Saddam Hussein? He too was ready to do anything the international community could ask of him. But those Americans don't listen to reason. And French radio and TV couldn't care less if the Saudis financed jihad attacks in nearby London. They have scores to settle with the pilot of the Enola Gray. And then they are off to the festival of Bayonne. Traffic jams on the vacation routes are another big subject. The news coverage of traffic jams rivals with news reports on the beach, which rival with ten minute broadcasts on seasonal jobs at French resorts. So what else is new?

If you don't live in France or don't watch the domestic channels, you would never in your wildest dreams imagine the way the news is covered here.

I started catching up with the news from Basra by the late Steve Vincent. How did I manage to miss all of his articles? Sites that I often visit were off my route this summer. I kept thinking that someone would forward one of his articles to me, or a day of his blog, and I'd follow from there. It was because of our phone conversation, so intense, so real, that I expected some kind of direct channel to fall into place, and when it didn't, I wasn't sure where to look. Now I discover him everywhere: in a *FrontPage* symposium that ends abruptly with news of his death. In a series of articles on *National Review Online*. In the *NY Times*. I would have caught his last article in the *International Herald Tribune* if it had fallen on one of the days when J. returned from covering an event; he buys the IHT when he's traveling, or gets it for free in the plane.

But it didn't happen, and now his words from Basra come alive at the same time as I haggle with my mind to accept his death. I see why he liked my writing. He and I have the same literary approach to the subject. Writers of fiction aim at capturing life with utter precision in time and place. A character isn't a tiny dot embedded in a block of statistics, a sociological sample, a theory: a character is one person, that we try to create in lifelike uniqueness. What happens in a novel really happens. I am not denying the truths that can be told in other forms, but I have special affection for this embodied reality of fiction. Steve Vincent's characters are alive. Will live forever. And Steve is dead.

The *décalage* is too great. Between the art critic who saw the world end on 9/11 and the reborn journalist who went snooping around Baghdad in 2003 and then Basra in 2005, the distance is too great. I imagine him walking with large strides on long thin legs. Too thin, ascetically thin. Between the aesthete turned journalist, engaging in respectful truth-seeking conversations with specific individuals, and the *untermensch* grabbed off the street by empty-headed thugs and murdered in cold blood, the distance is too great. They didn't have to kill him! His revelations did not endanger them. They have decades of corrupt power-grabbing stretched out before them. Neither the central government nor the so-called occupying powers will ever get to the stage of cleaning out the dusty corners where they operate, feeding on the offal generated by Saddam Hussein.

When we were students, my fiancé roomed with an Afghan whiz kid whose mathematical genius took him out of his benighted Pashtun village in the Khyber Pass to high school in Kabul and from there to the University of Wisconsin. He used to tell us stories of his homeland. Any foreigner who set foot in those regions was automatically labeled a spy. Punishable by death. On the other hand, if the government dared to jail a criminal from their village, the villagers formed a posse, shot up the jail, and released him. The men spent all their time cleaning their guns and shooting them.

I imagine that Steven Vincent was killed in that kind of a tribal gesture. Someone's honor was offended. Someone's territory was defiled. Someone's power was just ever so slightly endangered by the shining light of an honest man's truthful writing, and the punishment was death. Nothing to discuss.

While the enlightened world is shivering in its boots as Iran develops nuclear weapons, France is scolding the US for dropping the bomb on Japan. And French experts are speculating on the distant possibility that Iran might just make some steps in the direction of acquiring nuclear weapons, though most likely they are just blustering. Of course they need nuclear fuel for civilian uses, because someday their oil supplies will run out. You understand, my friend? Stupid Westerners are spending like there was no tomorrow, but those Iranians are so postmodern, so far seeing, that they are developing nuclear energy for the far distant future when their very own oil supplies will dwindle to a trickle. I bet they signed the Kyoto protocol too! Why are they blustering? Because they feel so threatened there in the Middle East, surrounded by nuclear India, nuclear Pakistan, nuclear Israel, and nuclear US-occupied Iraq. You'd feel threatened too. The perfectly neutral perfectly objective journalistic voice wonders: why can all those countries have nuclear weapons and Iran can't?

Indeed. Why not? In a world without borders, without order, without values, without reality, there's no reason why Iran can't have the capacity to wipe the world off the map, there's no reason why Muslims can't immigrate into Europe by the millions in a few short decades, there's no reason why disgruntled young men and women can't blow people to smithereens by the dozens in Israel or anyone else their disgruntled hearts desire. There is no reason in that never never land slapdashed out of confusion, aimlessly roaming through unmarked space.

To make sense out of this world, one word will suffice: war.

We are at war. A different kind of war. What might be called an a-military war. I regularly stumble into conversations that begin with the other person serving me a tray of hors d'oeuvres prepared precisely by our mortal enemy but processed by an elegant staff of purveyors. They come in different assortments. One tray offers: Israel should retreat to the 1967 borders, stop colonizing, give the Palestinians their rights including the right of return and half of Jerusalem or three quarters if that's what they ask for. Another includes: there were no WMDs in Iraq, if they had to invade it should have been Iran, the US can't ignore international law. I am impolite, I won't gobble down the snacks, so I get scolded. And the most common punch line is, "We can't win against terrorism."

Why in the world would anyone in a modern, industrialized, civilized, high tech society think that we can't win against terrorism? There are myriad intermediary explanations that you can develop on your own. I think the essential reason is that these people are fed jihad propaganda from morning to night. Jihadis are incompetent bullies. They pull off gory operations against soft targets, and make people think it is the beginning of an endless onslaught that will leave no corner of the earth unbloodied. They can strike anywhere, I am told, and we are over-extended in Iraq.

8 August 2005

The idea that we cannot vanquish terrorism comes from the same origin as terrorism itself: jihadi bluster. A retrograde mentality with no coherent sense of time, exacerbated by the flames of ideological passions that consume the mind of the perpetrators who delude themselves into thinking they are destroying the enemy. Jihad operations (I won't speak of terrorism anymore unless directly or indirectly quoting) are, in reality, punk fireworks. Cowards and bullies can wreak havoc but they never win. Al Qaeda will be known as the sheikhs of miscalculation. The 9/11 attacks were to bring America to heel; they provoked brilliant military retaliation. Even Saudi Arabia responds with a lopsided crackdown of sorts when attacked by its native sons. Only the macho Spaniards did as they were told. But it won't last. Zapatero got elected, fine, but now he has to remain in power, and he can't do it while dhimmying with the devil. Four explosions in London mass transit and Al Qaeda is hollering from the top of Al Jazeera's minarets: we spread fire in the heart of London. What they did is destroy one super safe haven. The irony is that if Europeans would wake up and see clearly, if the Left would stop dabbling in suicidal alliances with evil, if international opinion would get it straight, if the media in free countries would simply report modestly and accurately on highly complex situations, the jihadis would be sent back to their caverns... and the moderate Muslims everyone loves to imagine just might begin to emerge and throw off their shackles.

This a-military war imposed on us by frustrated bullies is wrapped up in narratives that should be deflated as cleverly as their phony apocalyptic flame-throwing operations. And they could be much more easily deflated if they were not processed and packaged by a series of intermediaries before being delivered to the very citizens who should reject them with as much disgust as they express for lesser evils like GMOs and junk food. Deporting imams is fine, and better late than never. But someone has to expose the witless journalists, analysts, and politicians who are retailing jihad propaganda. Here's an example from the *International*

Herald Tribune, an op-ed by Abdul Cader Asmal, published on 4 August 2005, under the title "Binladenism / Terrorism is not Islamic." The author begins by making a clear distinction between the admittedly Muslim terrorists and Muslims in general. He explains "While the recent terror acts have been committed by Muslims there is nothing 'Islamic' about them. They are totally antithetical to the fundamental principles of Islam..." Then, in typical fashion, he veers from this brief introduction to deliver a long indictment against all and sundry who point the finger at Muslims and ultimately demonize the religion by labeling the terror "Islamist" and spewing hatred of Islam with "malevolent glee." The author proposes the term "binladenism" to more accurately describe the terrorism he decries, for which he finds no excuse, no justification... despite the legitimate concerns he apparently shares with the binladenists, to the point of warning that "Until the issues are addressed, the war on terror will smolder on." He argues for "unwavering, unconditional" opposition to binladenism, as exemplified by the fatwa issued by the Fiqh Council of North America, "a small first step." And closes with a quotation from the Qu'ran—a solemn injunction to Muslims to stand for justice—and a note of hope for the future.

Why would anyone object to this heartfelt message? Simply because it is not true? Let's see. Take out the word terrorism, and replace it with jihad. Why? Because that's what binladenism is. Bin Laden, his henchmen, his disciples, his fans, his pawns, all the way down to your local *shahid*, all quote from the Qu'ran, all claim to be pursuing the sacred obligation to wage jihad against the infidels. They aren't inventing apocryphal verses, they are just quoting a few lines, a few pages further than the sincerely moderate Abdul Cader Asmal. Is jihad some kind of mysterious, abstruse, complicated intellectual concept disputed by scholars over the centuries? No. It is so simple it hurts. Where can you find it, besides in Qu'ranic verses? In history. It has been practiced according to the same rules all through the history of Islam.

Recently, conversing with a very intelligent person whose subtle mind is a constant delight to me, I came up with a sort of statistic that needs to be verified but couldn't be far from the truth. My debating partner, the kind you love to agree or disagree with, had read an article that downplays the religious aspect of Al Qaeda, preferring to highlight the modern, political influences, including Soviet communism. I came back with some of the things I know about the importance of the religious motivation. And suddenly, without aforethought, I said: "the only times the Muslims stopped practicing jihad was when they were colonized by the West."

Making war by peace talk has been practiced for decades against Israel. Now it has spread to the whole democratic world. People's heads are stuffed with sugarplum peace, starry visions of peace twinkle in front of their eyes, they wear more peace badges than a five star general, they decorate themselves for virtue, bravery, foreign policy acumen, military strategy, humanism, humanitarianism... And how do they win so many medals? By saying "I am against the war in Iraq." Robin Cook died the other day after a hike in the Scottish hills. He was described as the former British foreign minister who resigned (actually as Commons leader) in 2003 because he was opposed to the war in Iraq. The good die young. Cook was only 59.

It is like a Greek epithet, "against-the-war-in-Iraq." It has no relation to reality. What war are they against? The snaky underhanded jihad war being waged day and night against Iraqis? So let them go to Syria and wear their "against the war medals," let them go to Iran and tell the "spiritual leaders" to stop fomenting war against Iraqi civilians, let them stand up in a Shia mosque and denounce the war against Sunnis, and vice versa. Are they against the 3-week brilliant military campaign that brought down Saddam Hussein? Not really, but they are for the people who are against it. Are they against American fumbling in the aftermath of that war? Yes or no, it doesn't matter, because they are not for helping in any of the practical ways in which allies help. No, they are just parading around with their badges, and convincing masses of people to nod their heads in agreement. You can't discuss the issues with these distracted disciples, because they are not really interested in going into the details, not really interested in foreign affairs or military strategy or the history of jihad.

We can't blame them even if it is their fault. We have to think up new arguments, approaches, tactics to enlist them in the army of their own defense. But it can't be done unless we block the flow of propaganda. It sometimes seems like a hopeless task, but our jihadi allies step in and hand us treasure troves of information and corrosive material that destroy their own vile projects. One little 4-point bombing in London, and a second beautifully botched attempt has done as much to upset the long march of Eurabia as the collected works of our most brilliant minds. Which doesn't mean that their research and writing was insignificant. My educated guess is that the very authorities who are suddenly discovering Al Qaeda termites from the basement to the rafters in Europe knew all along that the charges made against them by the likes of Bat Ye'or and Robert Spencer were true. They pretended to think it was ultra-right ultra-Zionist Islamophobe ranting, but they knew it was an accurate description of their outmoded secret diplomacy. France in the forefront, with its *"politique arabe"* that even the Arabs don't trust.

9 August 2005

Swifter than the speed of light! Yesterday I read an exposé on Omar Bakri and his Neanderthal followers. A *London Times* reporter, Muslim of course, who infiltrated the group for several months, reports on their sayings and doings. It's like an x-ray, no, what am I saying, that's old-fashioned, it's like an ultrasound image in the belly of the beast. Look no further for the causes of jihad warfare, it is all there. In the same way that you can see thousands of Muslims bowing in simultaneous prayer, you can be sure that thousands of groups, just like Bakri's, are growling in the bowels of Europe, ready to lunge. They go for the carotid artery, slit the *kuffar* lifeline, they explode with anger, spit nails and rat poison to the furthest limits of their destructive perimeter. This has been going on for decades, and European intelligence services know it, and European leaders have not only allowed it, they have encouraged it, in their proud tradition of violent revolution and their cowardly politics of Eurabia. When the bombs went off in Casablanca, aimed at Jewish points of interest but killing mainly "innocent" Moroccans, the Spanish did not expel or imprison their fair share of conspirators. Who, less than a year later, aimed their jihad fire at Madrid commuter trains. And still the British allowed their lot of high power explosive Muslims to rant and rave in mosques, street corners, and stately homes. With relays in the *Guardian*, the *Observer* and the *Financial Times*. I clipped a book review entitled "The terrorist weapon of choice" (*FT* 2-3 July) by Louise Richardson, executive dean of the Radcliffe Institute for Advanced Study, Harvard University. The review is illustrated with a 4-column photo of jihadis in baklavas, carrying kalashnikovs. The front and center fellow stares us straight in the eye. The general tone of the review is fuzzy apologetics. Here are a few choice quotes:

It opens with: "There are many reasons for the current fascination with suicide terrorism. It is disconcerting to encounter a person who is willing to sacrifice his or her life in furtherance of a cause." Commenting on a collection of essays, *Making Sense of Suicide Missions*, Professor Richardson relates, "...several of the authors attack the myth that suicide terrorism is a religious phenomenon.... The more philosophical carefully parse the statements of Osama bin Laden and the perpetrators of September 11 and find them too wholly secular. As Holmes argues, they hit the twin towers not as icons of blasphemy but of arrogant power. Al Qaeda is not fighting the west until it says 'there is no God but Allah,' but until it gets out of the Middle East. He makes a compelling case that it was not religion, not Islam, but the pooled insurgencies of the Arab Middle East and a specific narrative of blame that made the US the target of al-Qaeda." And she concludes with this pithy thought: "In the end, one begins to wonder if suicide missions, or martyrdom operations, are indeed a unique phenomenon. Military historians long ago persuaded us that what drove young men over the trenches, and out of the foxholes, was loyalty to their small band of brothers. In all our societies, we reserve the highest honors for those who have given their lives for their country. Having read these studies one is left wondering whether suicide bombers are so different." I spare you the quote from Horace that winds up this homily to Hamas and its band of brothers.

May I wonder, in turn, why Louise Richardson is being richly rewarded by Harvard University for wondering if there is any difference between a *shahid* who blows himself up in a pizzeria and a soldier who lands at Normandy on D-Day? If there were any justice on this earth, Harvard would immediately send me the equivalent of one month's wages paid to Professor Richardson. And the *Financial Times* would publish my review of her review... which came out 5 days before the martyrdom operation in the London tube and bus.

Well, my friends, Omar Bakri skipped town! He went to Lebanon to visit his ailing mother but, according to his wife, he may decide to extend his stay, because of the hostile climate in Great Britain. Didn't I say so? The guys are bullies and cowards. He hightails it out of London before the police can arrest him and send him to jail for aggravated incitement, and the pitbulls he trained are left with no guide and master.

France 2 just loves those scenes of Israeli soldiers training to drag "colonists" out of their homes in Gaza and dump them in cages. The IDF keeps trying to find ways to get the media to simply tell what is going on instead of crucifying Israel on everyone's TV antenna, but no matter what Israel does it turns against us. The Palestinians are killing each other in Gaza. A rocket meant for Sderot fell short, killing a 10 year-old Palestinian boy and seriously wounding his siblings. Mayors, governors, police chiefs and judges resign after their homes are attacked and sacked by Hamas or Al Aqsa brigades or the local al-Qaeda cell. Fiancés are dragged from their cars and executed on the spot for unseemly behavior. And these are just a few vague details out of the mass of information available from reliable sources. While the IDF invites the media into training camps where soldiers play recalcitrant settlers and other soldiers drag them kicking and screaming across the ground, the PA has forbidden cameramen to take pictures of internecine mayhem in Gaza. Charles Enderlin, who kicked off the jihad-intifada with his al-Dura superproduction, is still there with his velvet voice in an iron glove, reporting on the latest ramifications of his one-man foreign policy.

Peter Jennings died of cancer at 67. Wim Duisenberg had a heart attack and died in his swimming pool near Orange in the south of France. His wife Greta, famous for flying the Palestinian flag from her balcony at a time when Israelis were being killed by the dozens, discovered the lifeless body of her husband, former director of the European bank, floating in the pool.

What if I am wrong? What if the worst case scenario is the accurate reading of our situation today? George W. Bush, Israel's best friend, Condoleeza Rice, Bush's best Secretary of State, and Brother Ward, the General appointed to keep an eye on the situation on the ground are all ganging up on Israel now. The Palestinians attack, and our American friends counterattack... with words of caution to our one and only reliable ally in the Middle East. Hold your fire. Don't over-react. Bolster Abbas. Don't aggravate the situation. Let's just get this retreat behind us and move on to the next stage. And what if the next stage is: you've got to start pulling out of the West Bank so Hamas will not get the upper hand in Gaza? Make hay while the sun shines, withdraw while the rockets fly, take my word for it, signed, your pal from Texas.

Meanwhile, one US congregation after another is voting Israel divestment resolutions. They've been worked over by Palestinian Christians who promise to liberate them from their connection to Judaism without telling them that they will be disconnected from the Bible and the Holy Land and won't even be able to turn the other cheek when triumphant Islam comes to behead what's left of them. I observed the sharp rise in antisemitism concomitant with the increase in murderous attacks against Israelis. Now we see a sharp rise in Israel boycott movements parallel to the withdrawal from Gaza. It is all so predictable, so monotonous, so easy to see through and so difficult to combat. It's like an invisible stain. You rub and rub and rub, but how can you get rid of it when people can't see it?

But it's there.

Discovery should land in California in about two hours. French media have been hoping, yes, that's the correct word, hoping it would blow up on re-entry, just like Challenger. They have shown so many images of the tragic fate of Challenger that you can forget that we're now on Discovery, the damage was repaired, all systems go. Yes, but, the newscaster smiles, looks you in the eyes, and declares: "it might not work." The re-entry temperatures are something terrible. The slightest defect, the tiniest tear, who knows if they really repaired it...

Forest fires are raging in the south of France. Flames shoot into the sky, threatening Manosque, Aix-en-Provence, Hyères. Exhausted firefighters lug hoses through the underbrush. Thousands and thousands of acres burn. Camp sites and homes are reduced to cinders. And the Canadairs are grounded since the first days of August when one plane split and crashed in Corsica, killing the two pilots. Investigators have not been able to identify the cause of the accident. Why is it taking so long? Maybe they are all on vacation. Don't expect the press to inform you. They are too busy imagining Discovery transformed into a ball of flame.

Safe landing for Discovery. I watched it on French TV, zapping from *France 2* to *TF 1*, both equally neurotic. Columbia, Columbia, Columbia (not Challenger as I mistakenly wrote above) here is where Columbia disintegrated, are crew members thinking of Columbia, do you remember the accident of Columbia, can anyone forget death in Columbia. And how was the re-entry covered in the US? I don't know. They wouldn't tell us. So I imagine "oh say can you see by the dawn's early light," but it wasn't dawn yet in California, I can imagine American confidence, energy, optimism, and even though the sun is finally shining in a blue sky on the first summer day in weeks, I want to go home.

Victory is not only predicted, it is pre-celebrated for one French athlete after another at the World Track & Field Championships in Helsinki. Defeat is feared, anticipated, half-way predicted, half-way solicited, as if some fantastic French gods were stationed in the mid ground between the real divinity and the center of Paris, ready to do the media's bidding. It is so neurotic! Do you think I hate the French? How could I? I live here. How can I not wish a rapid recovery for the people around me? Why don't people and societies want to get well?

I'm going to think about that in the nearest park.

[later] The pilot of the spacecraft was a woman for heaven's sake!!! Couldn't they have said one word about that? No. Maybe there will be a small bouquet for her on tonight's news. The jihadi sheik I referred to above is named Omar Bakri Mohammed. When I do articles for publication online or on paper, I fact check before transmission, but here in this chronicle where I speak to you *en tête à tête* I let the corrections show. I don't do this for stylistic effect. But you understand, I don't have to explain.

Daniel Pipes, Frank Gaffney, Meyrav Wurmser and a handful of other visitors to my inbox these past few days have convinced me in my opposition to the Gaza pullout. But I keep saying we have to plan our next step, because it's obvious we can't stop it. And I keep saying we have to know what time it is, from minute to minute we have to be sure to know what time it is. Things are moving fast, we can't lose crucial battles, our survival is at stake. What if I'm wrong, what if I don't realize that it is already zero hour? The worst case scenario could be upon us. The pinpoint attacks here and there might be the first inklings of what is in store. Israel could be in existential danger. If the American government has lost its guts, lost its clarity, who is going to protect us? The Europeans are making noises now, but nothing proves they won't fold under a few more jihadi blows. They could back down at any moment, decide that the deportations were arousing anger in the Muslim communities.

My sunny temperament always shows me a way out of trouble, a glimmer of hope, a reason to trust in humanity and the future. I reassure my friends: don't worry, they'll realize we're at war, they'll fight back, we'll win. Don't be afraid.

What if I'm wrong?

Scenes from British streets flash on the news. It's like Tashbi said: you'd think you're in Beirut or Cairo. That didn't exist when I lived in London forty-five years ago. So...it means that these old men in native dress had not yet arrived.

10 August 2005

I woke this morning with visions of Gaza settlements, IDF outposts, armed convoys, islands of order and prosperity in a sea of violent confusion. And before my eyes were completely open, I accepted the fact that they cannot stay. It is not a stable ongoing situation. And yet their departure will not solve anything, won't have any positive results for anyone. The world's media would have us think that these settlements are an insult to Palestinian pride and misery, that their beauty and comfort is stolen from innocent Palestinian victims, that they are the sole and unique example of such a clash of civilizations in the heart of occupied Gaza (which the ignorant are led to believe was taken from the Palestinians). This is because it is forbidden to photograph the sumptuous villas of the PA nomenklatura. Those mansions are really stolen from the downtrodden local population!

Judaïques FM's Israeli correspondent reported today from the Gush Katif. I do not claim that individual reality is more real than collective or historical reality: both are necessary. But if these political decisions didn't pass through the lives and bodies of individuals, they would be no more important than comic books. If only the Gaza pullout were nothing more than a subject for conversation in Parisian cafés. I listened to two interviews, and my mind started racing ahead to an idyllic epic conclusion to this heartrending dilemma. The key concepts of the soon to be vacated residents are faith in G-d, trust in *haverim*. A miracle will occur, we won't have to leave. But if we have to leave, that does not prove that G-d is not with us. Or that it is not his will that we leave. The soldiers and policemen will not harm us, they are our brothers, our sons and husbands and fathers. We will not lift a hand against them. The journalist remarks that nothing is packed, no one is getting ready to move. And yet, he coaxes, realistically you know that August 17th is the final date for expulsion. Yes, she knows. She already received the letter. In Neve Deka-lim, the leader of the French residents of Gush Katif is interviewed among the hustle and bustle of a normal day's activity. No moving vans, no packing boxes. He too is realistic. He admits that many families have filed their relocation claims. When the time comes, he says, we will leave with our heads high.

And the image bursts into my heart. It is corny, I know. It won't hap-pen that way, at least not exactly. But it captures something of the truth of my people and perhaps expresses nothing more than my love of Juda-ism and my pride in being Jewish. They are so tough, so stubborn, so honest and trusting, so fervent, so close to the heavens and so down to earth, and so rooted in reality. Let this withdrawal—because I don't think anyone or anything can stop it—take place with the most astonishing dignity. May the pain, sorrow, and evil of precedent movements—exodus from Egypt, expulsion from Spain, deportation to the death camps—be refined and transformed into a gesture of Jewish strength. Yes, there is a way to express the sublime contradiction of reality. The Palestinians will celebrate with malignant joy, convincing themselves that they chased the Jews out of Gaza like they will chase us out of Israel and off the face of the earth? So? Who can stop them?

The whole world and his brother will be there to film the event. Freely, as usual, on the Israeli side, under censorship in the Palestinian camp. Could we show them something they've never seen before? The Jewish residents of Gaza standing tall and proud, walking freely out of Gaza and into their future, side by side with the soldiers and policemen sent to force them out, singing Hatikvah together, crying together, pray-ing and dancing together.

Being very practical, I have to find a solution for their belongings, which they will leave behind because this is their way of saying it is their land, their home, even if they must go away. So I am thinking that the members of Sharon's cabinet could go in and fetch their belongings. Since they trust Abbas to keep his dogs at bay, there's nothing to fear. And it would be their way of showing that they understand the sorrow they have been forced to impose on their fellow man and woman. The soldiers and policemen can help with the move, since they won't have to drag the settlers kicking and screaming from their homes. They too have nothing to fear from the Palestinians who will wait patiently on the outskirts.

So you see, my big budget film is not that much less convincing than the real plans of a real government.

We can't ask for any gratitude, recognition, or recompense from the Palestinian side. The withdrawal is unilateral because there is no one to negotiate with. But we can ask for something from our own, from those who live in what they think is really Israel…

Suddenly the precedent comes to mind: the way the secular communist Jews mistreated their religious brethren in the *shtetlhk* of Central Europe when the Russians invaded.

The other day I bumped into Y. She was with an Israeli friend who lives in Paris. A Tel Aviv type, with a little gold earring. Handsome and virile. Y. is the one who sent me one of those peace petitions that were going around after 9/11. Initiated in Sweden, it had been signed by dozens of Israelis before she sent it to me. She's Polish-Israeli-American-Parisian and I am sure a fervent advocate of withdrawal. I asked if she's leaving soon on vacation. She is. To Israel? Not now, it's unbearably hot.

I was in Israel last year in August. It was so bearably, so wonderfully hot. Except for some evenings in Jerusalem when I was actually chilly. It was a strange visit, I was intensely there, but at the same time kept away from so much that I wanted to experience, and still it was a wonderful way to begin to make a bit of a home for myself in Israel. I went back again in September, still working on the same project, still cooped up in a recording studio, hardly any time to taste my surroundings. I never wanted to go to Israel as a tourist. Now there is a part of my life there, just waiting to take root and blossom. The project I was working on never came to fulfillment. At least not in the form in which it was conceived. I had made endless concessions in order to collaborate with a friend I cherished and admired, but it was no use, we couldn't combine forces, we were like reverse charge magnets, pushing each other away, despite our warm friendship and sincere appreciation for each other. I don't want to describe our differences, because I will be on my side, and my intention is not to prove I was right. He wanted to be the great conceiver, he needed an implementer. I can't work in the service of someone else's imagination. At someone else's pace. I conceive and implement, I have to work with neat precision at every stage, I always finish what I started, I always respect the deadlines I set for myself, I always accomplish what I set out to do.

Suddenly I found myself in someone else's mess. Twenty-five versions of the scenario were floating around. Modified by hand on paper, modified in Word in red, blue and italics. Modified in the video work in progress but not on paper. The project advanced two steps, floundered, started over, covering the same ground, floundering, backstepping. And consuming huge amounts of time and energy. Then suddenly it would lunge out in a new direction, a parallel project, just as ill-conceived as the primary one, but dependent on it, and calling on other collaborators, making commitments that could never be fulfilled. I was so embarrassed by the sloppy work, but at the same time I was weaving strong friendships that would endure. On the first trip, I worked with a laptop that belongs to the recording studio. I would safeguard my work at the end of the day. But the next morning, it had disappeared. Along with all the applications. I had to call for help from the IT man who would come with his USB memory stick and transfer my files to I's desktop, and again in the morning, I'd have to get someone to transfer them back. In the meantime, the studio would be busy with bigger clients, the technician would run off and leave me in the lurch, and there I was in that air conditioned room with the black shades drawn, while outside it was unbearably hot, just the way I love it. But I couldn't run off to the beach and come back, I had to wait, and fiddle around with the scenario, desperately searching for what was missing, the coherence, rhythm, focus. On the second trip I brought a little laptop that D. fixed up for me. But when I downloaded the files from the studio's desktop, all the texts in my computer were writing right to left. I struggled for hours, for days trying to get it back into left to right. I'd finally get it, and then suddenly it would switch again.

And the beach was calling and I couldn't answer. I had to rush off to the studio early in the morning. And plunge once more into an infernal chopped up working day. It was no one's fault. Everybody worked like that at the studio. They laughed when I described it as the essence of Israel: *balagan* combined with New York Jewish pace. The technician had three cell phones. When he left the room, he left them all on the table. Suddenly they'd start vibrating, ringing, shaking the whole room. I couldn't answer. I can hardly speak any Hebrew. My own language, and I can't speak it!

I was trying to polish something that fell apart whenever you touched it. And time was running out. We worked in front of a battery of screens, with all kinds of functions I couldn't even fathom let alone use. We went over and over the same sequence of images, half asleep with boredom, and he would tell me that he'd gone to bed at 2 AM, because he had to finish this project, and at 3 AM for that project, and he sent his wife to Ashkelon for shabat but he would join her the next day, he was exhausted, she was fed up with his working all the time. They were young.

One day, I asked the technician to show me what was in the data base. He opened the files one after the other. A wealth of images we had not exploited. Finally the project took shape in my mind. He translated the Hebrew. TV interviews, documentaries. I had it! A carefully constructed video argument, a sequence of images that proved our point, realities that spoke for themselves. I replaced the heavy discourse of the earlier versions with these new elements. But cautiously. My collaborator was back in the States but I could feel him looking over my shoulder. And I wanted to be fair to him too. So I conserved elements that seriously bothered me, heavy elements that dragged down the whole document. And so much material that he had borrowed from others. Not to mention the inextricable problems that arose with investigators who had, willingly or unwillingly, provided the material in the data base. Under false pretenses, they said.

A few days before I left Israel, the whole thing exploded. My collaborator, who considered himself producer, director and all the rest, wanted an implementer who would make his video work, without changing anything. He was furious with me because I innovated. For me it was only normal, for him it was high treason.

And we were such good friends, we had such a fantastic intellectual complicity. I've tried to keep the friendship alive. He has too. But it's touch and go. It took me months to get my professional life back on track. And that absolutely worthy, not to say urgent, project was lying undigested in my mind. How could I abandon it?

A lovely summer evening. When I closed the shutters at midnight the sky was clear dark blue, and the street was empty. Paris is a ghost town in August. I didn't even go out for a stroll this evening, I spent the whole evening re-organizing my files on the Al Dura affair. Glancing at papers here and there as I went, asking myself for the thousandth time if I could be wrong. What if it's not a fake? Could I have been misled by the investigators? Shahaf, Juffa, Huber? But Rosenzweig is an old grisly retired *Monde* reporter, and he believes it's a fake. I don't think I'm mistaken. But I ask myself every day. Just to make sure.

The reports from Gush Katif were rebroadcast this evening. I caught one that I had missed this morning. A disagreement between the Diaspora Jewish journalist in Paris and his colleague in Gaza. You interviewed someone who said, "it's a paradise here... except for the Arabs." We can't accept that, it's racist. The reporter in Gaza was taken aback. The Qassams are flying, a 10 year-old boy was shot in the head the other day, Hamas is breathing down their necks, today Gaza tomorrow Jerusalem, and they're not allowed to say "except for the Arabs"? How about if he had said "except for the Palestinian militants"? That would have been acceptable?

Décalage.

11 August 2005

I just realized: the deadline for that little translation I accepted to do for a Belgian film producer is... August 17th. The same day as the deadline for Jews in Gaza. 180,000 prayed at the kotel yesterday, imploring the heavens to save them from... from what, in fact? From the terrible decree of public opinion, relayed by a government under fire. Under fire from its closest ally. My very own US of A. How did we get into this mess? The decline of democracy is demagogy, the reign of public opinion, like the long locks of a dead princess waving in the waters, moving to the dictates of courtesan journalists who have usurped the role of poets and thinkers. I did not think that G W Bush would go that way. What went wrong?

It may be that there are limits to the reach of any leader of a free country. The downside of democracy. A dictator pursues his personal vision, unhindered, to the utmost possibilities of catastrophe. President Bush, his Secretary of State, his administration can only go so far beyond existing notions about the Middle East, Islam, jihad... The hard knocks of reality will do the rest.

Let the Palestinians dance for joy. Will they hang their heads in shame when Muslims are pushed to the exits in Europe, and the scaffoldings of the beautiful Eurabia project are gradually dismantled? Europeans should take notice. Why do the beautiful Jewish homes in Gaza have to be destroyed? So that they will not be desecrated. If Gaza is not Israeli it is no more Palestinian than Egyptian. And Paris is France only as long as the French can hang onto it. It is not racist to observe that some populations come with their own laws, laws that are incompatible with those of the host country, and the resulting conflict cannot be solved by blissful ignorance.

Journalism is a fascinating failure. Though some journalists do actually ferret out the facts and report them with admirable skill, most journalists simply adopt a reporting style that gives the illusion of being more factual, more informative, more reliable than other sources. One of the techniques they use is to latch onto a model and follow it like a pilot bird. The informally designated leaders, the newspapers of record—the *NY Times* in the US, *Le Monde* in France—specialize in a tone of reasonableness that can be used for any and all subjects, to report any mixture of truth, fantasy, propaganda, wishful thinking, rumor, investigation, supposition; what matters is not the weight of the facts but the style of discourse. Reporting on the death of Steven Vincent, the *London Times* favored the sexual over the political angle. What got Steven in trouble was the way he hung around with his interpreter Nour. Tongues were wagging. And in those parts, when tongues wag, swords swing and bullets zing. The *Telegraph* went even further, to my surprise. According to their reporter Steven intended to marry Nour so that she could emigrate to the United States. His wife Lisa Ramici who, for the *Times*, is quoted as saying repeatedly that she thinks the relationship was platonic, is portrayed by the *Telegraph* as actively cooperating with this plan. Did she agree to divorce so he could marry Nour? For immigration reasons alone? And afterwards? Was he going to divorce Nour and remarry Lisa? Nothing revealed in Steven's carefully documented articles would seem, for these journalists, to explain the murderous reaction of his killers. What death squad in a white Toyota? Wasn't it just the collective Shia indignation that pumped bullets into a man who dared to disrespect the strict honor code of proud Muslims? Remarking that Nour is said to have survived the attack whereas it is usually the woman who is killed, the journalist doesn't even bother to speculate on the fact that when the man is an infidel he does not benefit from the benevolence of Allah's servants.

Global communication, internet, instant connection notwithstanding, the authors of these gossipy speculations are apparently unaware of the mysterious adventure of Florence and Hussein. The French journalist was allegedly held captive for five months in extremely close quarters with her faithful Iraqi guide. They too had palled around town in most unvirtuous proximity. Their French support team did not hesitate to place them side by side in giant portraits, apparently fearing no dire consequences from the obvious romantic overtones that continued after the couple's liberation and Hussein's arrival in Paris. Did he plan to divorce his wife and marry Florence? If so, he would not fear for his life in France. But the whole hostage story is off the table now. All the better to avoid pesky questions about the glaring inconsistencies.

A new era has opened with the July bombings in London. The spotlight has done a 180-degree shift. Not long ago it was glowing on France's turbaned and three-piece-suited Muslims dashing off to Baghdad—to Jordan, actually, but it's all one *umma*—to save French hostages, while on the home front beautiful young ladies in *hijab* served Oriental pastries to the anguished families surrounded by opportunistic politicians. Now France deserves a distinguished medal for distinguished repression of antisemitism and radical Islamist terrorism.

Imagine someone who attended one of my lectures last year in the United States, now reading about this French distinction in the *New York Times*. And not only there. In the *Boston Globe* too, and the *Washington Post*, the *LA Times*, *Newsweek*, and seeing it repeated on countless reliable unbiased websites and online magazines. If they say so it must be true. Some people will remember listening to me in the JCC in Oakland, the synagogue in Fairfield, the university lecture hall in Charlotte, and thinking I must be exaggerating. If things were that bad in France, the *NY Times* would already have reported it.

Let us not forget that France is the country that spends the most time and money fighting against dog shit on the streets of its towns and cities. The result is there for all to see. And step in.

But did you know that one half of the prison sentences handed down in France are never executed? Meaning that criminals are sentenced to prison, but no one comes to get them and take them to jail, and they just disappear into the population. Criminals sentenced to life in prison are often released after serving something like ten years. This includes murderers, even child molesting murderers. When they go back to their tried and trued murderous molesting ways, there is a public whimper: why were they allowed to roam freely again? The official reply is a statistic: recidivism is very low, around 2%. First of all I don't believe it and second it's no comfort to the bereaved parents of the recidivistally murdered child. People who lose their licenses for reckless driving have found the perfect solution: they drive without a license. Leading some very clever thinkers to think that taking away licenses is not a good thing. No-smoking laws already exist in France. But you can't see them through the smoke that fills the air of cafés and restaurants.

From September 2000 to the end of 2001, there was no public recognition of antisemitic acts. Since that date there has been a sort of recognition, including statistical measurement, law enactment, and official pronouncements. However, one of the most effective measures employed to reduce antisemitism in France is the two-channel classification system: words and deeds draped in the colors of Nazi type 1940s anti-Semitism are given the appropriate label; attacks on Jews by Muslims and jihad fellow travelers are classified as "inter-communitarian strife" when they are not dismissed as understandable expressions of *résistance* on the part of oppressed peoples and simili-Palestinians of our *banlieues*... and universities. Because it would be a mistake to think that these expressions of *résistance* are limited to the thuggish classes. They reach into the highest intellectual spheres, the banner flies from the smokestacks of respected semi-governmental think tanks, and sympathies for this movement drive French foreign policy.

While France gets medals for vigilance, the parents of the young Jewish woman who was beaten within an inch of her life in *banlieue* X do not want any exposure; they are afraid the murderers will come to finish the job if the story is brought to light. I can't give a single detail that would identify her. The bereaved family of Sébastien Selam has yet to find a crumb of solace from the French courts. Twenty-one months after the crime, the murderer is still in a psychiatric hospital, the magistrate has not even opened the investigation, the case will never be tried. The three young men, aged 15 to 19, who threw bottles of acid into the courtyard of a Jewish school, where children were playing at recess, were released after a preliminary hearing. Given the pace of French courts, their trial could be expected to take place three years from now. Or maybe five. The black comic Dieudonné, who rose from marginal success to national fame when he turned to serious antisemitism, is collecting royalties from the DVD of his Jew-hating show, featured in the highly popular FNAC stores and who knows where else. And the DVD of the Franco-Lebanese-Syrian co-production, *La Porte du Soleil*, which portrays Israelis in 1948 as Nazis subjecting Palestinians to Shoah style atrocities, is distributed by the high class artsy European TV channel, *ARTE*.

As for imams, if anyone has been deporting them, it's news to us. Jihad preachers, Al Qaeda sleeper cells, accomplices to bomb squads operating in Turkey, Spain...

August 12 2005

...Casablanca, support groups for the shoe bomber, financiers for the Madrid bombers, jihad recruitment cells in the 19th arrondissement of Paris, training camps in the Bois de Boulogne or maybe it was the Forêt de Fontainbleau, just ask, we've got it. The complete jihad kit: intellectuals, chemists, converts, thugs, foot soldiers, bogus charities, jihad political parties, web sites, radio stations, gang rape for women running loose without *hijab*, and an abundance of conciliatory intermediaries who produce the smoke screen and the apologetics and the cockeyed interpretations behind which all of this danger grows, develops, digs deep roots, spreads. And we have the reputation for being tough on terrorism? Who did the PR on that one?

Yesterday's issue of the *Daily Alert* included an article on Steven Vincent from the *Scotsman*. It goes even further than the previous articles, actually gives a figure, $2,500, for the dowry Steven paid to Nour's parents. I went back to my inside informers. What's this all about? Wasn't he married to Lisa? Are these rumors coming from the very police department he accused of running a Moqtada Al Sadr-faithful death squad? In the *Scotsman* version, Steven and Nour were abducted from their hotel. Will the Irish come along and have them torn from their bed of iniquity? Stateside, the political motivation holds good. He wrote accusing articles, they bumped him off. I tried to research the story. Google poured out hundreds of blogs. Nothing but reactions to the basic report. I came upon the *NY Times* article, with the photo in color. And saw how much was lost in the black and white copy posted on *FrontPage*. I was wrong about the thin legs. No, he was much more physically present than I had thought. Dark and handsome. I see how he could try to pass for a Middle Easterner. But I stand by what I said about the eyes.

Whenever a man and woman work closely together there are sensual innuendoes. In the old days, when only men were free to dilly dally, the innuendoes were often verified. Men slept with nurses, secretaries, students. Sexual attraction is a wonderful lubricant for the necessary thorniness of human concourse; I find it easier to navigate than female-female jealousy. Of course repressive societies can't let men and women get near each other unless they are married, that is, unless the man has control over the woman. What the men do in secret is another story, an ugly exaggeration of sexual freedom combined with sexual bondage.

If I were in New York I would go to see Steven's wife. She would tell me the truth. Someone should do it. If an Iraqi police officer in Basra lies to me, either because he himself is in on the plot, or just because he wants to save his own skin, I'm neither surprised nor betrayed. But I don't expect my friends and colleagues to lie to me. Human motivations are so complicated, the public and private are tangled together. It is so hard to get to the truth of things.

Yesterday, or was it the day before, I heard shouts and screams in the street. I looked out the window, in the direction of the boulevard, and saw a young man and woman turn into my street. She was screaming hysterically. Screaming at him, screaming for help. *Au secours, au secours.* She fell to the ground, shouting, writhing, accusing him. She crawled over to a parked car and fell back against it, still screaming, shouting, hollering. He had walked ahead. He went back, crouched near her, spoke quietly. She screamed, "Don't touch me!" I wondered if I should do something. He seemed to be calm, but she was pushing, pushing, pushing. He might lose his temper and strangle her. Or stab her.

Hearing no more screams I assumed that they had moved on. I went back to work. Then I heard the sizzle of talkie walkies. Looked out again. There were two police cars and five or six policemen and women. The young man was to their left. The young woman, wearing an orange hooded sweatshirt (nothing to do with the Gaza pullout, I'm certain) despite the heat, walked off to the right and down a small side street. It looked like she made a little shrug as she passed the small island of police. Quite a comedown from the hysterical screaming twenty minutes earlier. The young man, dressed in black jeans and t-shirt, continued down my street in the direction he was going when the incident broke out. Apparently the screams had alerted a woman whose apartment directly overlooked the scene. I suppose she called the police. Now she spoke to them for a few minutes. Then went back into her building. The police left. Case closed.

Things are not what they seem.

Yesterday I went to visit an old friend I had not seen for years. He lives in a quiet section of the 17th arrondissement. I took the métro. The train was new. Compared to the NY subway it's imperial luxury. But there was a crazy guy standing not far from where I was seated, talking to himself, a low mumble of threats and imprecations. The métro stations smell bad. As I came out at Pereire, I passed a guy going down the stairs with a pitbull. He's going to take the metro with an attack dog. No muzzle of course. When I got into the train going home, I sat down on a *strapontin* at the end of the car, and quickly realized that the guy sitting next to me was stinking drunk. The smell of alcohol was overpowering. I decided to get off at gare St. Lazare and take the bus.

In the bus, I met a neighbor who knew Chantal Piekolek, a woman who was murdered the same day as Sébastien Selam. She was stabbed more than twenty times. As usual, information was sparse and incoherent. They said she was recently widowed, her deceased husband was Jewish but she wasn't, the motive was robbery. But friends of the Selam family told me that she was Jewish. And then I found out about this neighbor, who knew her. They both had stands at some kind of market... selling leather goods, I believe. At the end of the day they would have coffee together before going home. She was divorced. Used her maiden name, Piekolek. When her father died, she took over his shoe store. In the 17th. That's where she was murdered. How much cash can there be in the register of a little neighborhood shoe store?

The guy who killed her was a multi-recidivist. He was caught because he tried to kill another woman after Chantal. He was hitchhiking, she picked him up. In broad daylight. He was about to slit her throat but she called for help. *Au secours, au secours.* Somehow she escaped. I saw a picture of him. You'd have to be looking at the world through extremely rose colored glasses to give that guy a ride!

The first time I asked the neighbor about the case, he told me the murderer died of cancer in prison, without coming to trial. Yesterday he said he thinks the prison guards did away with him. He was always threatening to kill them when he got out. They had good reason to believe he would be released.

The next time a French person throws statistics on the US prison population in my face, I'll have something to throw back. OK, it's not exactly PA style revolving doors. But there is something slightly lax about not implementing half the prison sentences, and letting murderers out of jail after seven years, *n'est-ce pas*?

This summer there has been a spate of prisoner escapes from mental hospitals. Convicted murderers are sent to ordinary mental hospitals. They don't have prison hospitals or special sections for criminals. No protection for staff and the other patients. The convicted murderer walks into the hospital and becomes a suffering human being, worthy of respect and freedom.

Repression is a bad word in French society, at least since I've been living here, which is post-1968. You know the master thinkers, Foucault and the like. Everything from Saddam Hussein's people-shredding system to ten year-old juvenile delinquents and including dogs that shit on the sidewalks, everything is to be handled with kid gloves. No repression will be tolerated. In fact, it's almost the only thing that isn't tolerated.

Which makes it all the more surprising to discover, in international media, that the French are doing a much better job at controlling the rowdier aspects of Islam, because they don't hesitate to use repressive methods. While the Brits are wringing their hands and fretting about habeas corpus, the antiquated French legal system can practically chop off their heads without a trial. The super duper anti-terrorist judge, Jean-Louis Bruguière, has a free hand. He kept a few dozen Muslims in prison for three years before they were tried and released for lack of proof of terrorist activity. But in the meantime, a strong message was sent to all concerned. People can be arrested and held for days or weeks, without seeing a lawyer or contacting family.

There may be some truth to it all. Contemporary French secret diplomacy operates on an antique *côté rue côté cour* system: all courtly bows and lace handkerchiefs on the street side, dismal dungeons and targeted killings on the courtyard side. It couldn't function without the cover offered by a dutiful press. Journalists disguised in the trappings of freedom function like courtesans. It is so ingrained that they can describe it shamelessly and feel no guilt about the consequences.

They don't feel free, so they don't feel pinched. They can tell you privately that they know the Al Dura news report is a fake. But they won't come out and say it publicly, they won't write it in an article, they won't quote someone who says it. Why? Because it's not true that it's false? No. Because they don't want to lose their jobs.

Does this explain why they can portray jihad murderers as freedom fighters? Because they don't know what freedom is? And they don't have any sense of responsibility. Look at the vertiginous decline of France over the past five years. Of course you can go back further and find the roots and sources and origins; you can go back as far as your education will carry you. But in this chronicle that began in the summer of 2000, I have recorded a headlong fall, a momentous slice of contemporary history that began with trumpeting triumph and fatal illusions. That is why I insist on capturing events as they happen, instead of gathering my notes and re-organizing reality into a coherent whole in which the beginning knows its conclusion.

The population of this country was led down the garden path and straight into a cesspool, and it could not have been done without the media. Puffed up pride was fueled with misguided notions of the outside world. The French were led to believe that their country was the leader of a great power that would challenge and defeat the American *hyperpuissance*. France was on its high horses, thundering over the paving stones of Europe, galloping across Muslim desert sands, courageously opposing the forces of evil, that is, the capitalist warriors, raising high the standard of peace and international law. A whole nation, nominally sophisticated, was precipitated into the ruinous fantasies of a mediocre president and his cohorts. And, believe me, they believed.

[interlude] *France 2* news, 1 PM. Flick of the eye coverage of the mass anti-withdrawal meeting at Rabin Square last night. Attendance is estimated at 100,000 (a few minutes later, on *TF1*, the figure is 200,000). Followed by a long, extensive, drawn out, heavy-handed report from Netzarim, signed Talal Abu Rahmeh and, for some reason, four or five other journalists and/or cameramen. The subject is a Franco-Palestinian biologist who had returned to his native land and built a comfortable three story home cheek by jowl with the "colony" of Netzarim. I stare at the images, trying to recognize the layout. I don't think I'm seeing the famous junction, but I can't be sure. Vague towers rise in the distance, but our attention is focused on the foreground. The good doctor (in the sense of PhD I suppose, not M. D.) tells us that it will be the happiest day of his life when the Israelis leave. These past years you couldn't step outside, or even onto your terrace, without getting shot. Every foray was a mortal danger. Now that they are leaving, he's going to fix up his house. There are at least three hundred bullet holes inside the house. Israeli soldiers occupied the house at least three times. All the other houses in the vicinity were destroyed. We see ruins here and there in a desolate landscape, nothing but sand and scrub, nothing like the green lawns of the Jewish neighborhoods in Gaza. Of course this barren soil on the Palestinian side of the line is the fault of the Israelis. You can't expect a man to tend his garden when he risks his life from sniper fire. Now the biologist caresses the misshapen leaf of an abandoned plant. He's going to fix up his house and garden. A new era is dawning. The sea is visible in the near distance. He put all his savings into the construction of this house. Did he ever live there? There is not a stick of furniture, nothing but bare walls and bullet holes. At least the house is still standing, he consoles himself. Maybe it's because of the French flag he put on the roof from the first day.

This is Talal, the father of the al-Dura story. Way back when—on September 30, 2000—the jihad-intifada was in its infancy, Talal composed the touching story of a 12 year-old Palestinian boy whose father couldn't protect him from Israeli gunfire. The same Israelis who pockmarked the home of the Franco-Palestinian biologist with hundreds of bullet holes shot at the al-Duras for 45 minutes on that fateful day. Now we are led to believe that if only Jamal al-Dura had thought of waving a French flag, they might have been spared... the embarrassment of participating in this shameful hoax. Could someone in his right mind please tell me why heartless cruel bloodthirsty Israeli soldiers would be daunted by the red white and blue French flag? Why would decent, self-defending, ethical, law abiding Israeli soldiers destroy all the houses save one, the one that is flying a French flag?

Five years later, Talal proves that he is not only a bad liar, he's a lousy storyteller.

But it's good enough for *France 2*. I zap to *TF1* and catch the report they chose to couple with the scene at Rabin Square. The elegant home of a doctor Schemla (or Chemla) and his wife in the Gaza Strip. They will stay up to the last minute, in case anyone needs medical care. His wife has prepared the relocation request that she has to file before the end of August; after that date there will be a 30% reduction in indemnities. There are no signs of packing. The interior is luxurious, refined, tasteful. It could be an elegant Parisian apartment. We go to another home. Here the father is packing up, with the help of friends. He doesn't want his wife and children to be exposed to the trauma of evacuation, forced or voluntary. In the final scene, a bearded man enters a beautifully furnished room carrying the back end of a Qassam. He says that Gaza, or did he say the Gush Katif, used to be known for its lettuce, now it's known for its Qassams. And he tells how many thousands of rockets have been shot at the Jewish neighborhoods of Gaza.

Can anyone blame me for being fascinated by every detail of all this? *France 2* has to eliminate 100,000 demonstrators from Rabin Square, half the estimated crowd, in order to lend credibility to its version of the wanton destruction of Palestinian homes near "Netzarim." Where's the logic? What can be gained by dividing the figure in two? What does it prove?

And what of the two missing persons? The unmentioned mythical mystical al-Duras? In all the pith and pathos of the evacuation coverage, not a word to commemorate their "ordeal" at Netzarim Junction when "all hell broke loose" at 3 PM on the 30th of September 2000.

Seven thousand Palestinian policemen are surrounding the Jewish neighborhoods, ostensibly to prevent Hamas forces from approaching to take credit for chasing the Jews out of Gaza, moving into the homes before they can be demolished and, why not, taking pot shots at the fleeing occupiers. Will they be able to hold their line? And if they don't, I'd like to see them dislodge the jihadis the way Israel dislodged its own protestors.

Lebanese authorities released Bakri.

[interlude]

A communiqué from the Israeli embassy in Paris chills my blood—it obsequiously explains disengagement as a Road Map move in the interest of peace for Israelis and Palestinians. The two worst arguments for withdrawal are that it doesn't make sense to have 8,000 Jews in the midst of 1.4 million Palestinians (some are still using the 3.8 million figure but I think my friend Roberta Seid and her team have sufficiently debunked it), and that it will favor peace. If 8,000 Jews can't live in Gaza, how can 6 million Jews live in Israel, surrounded by how many billions of Arabs and Muslims? As for peace and the Road Map, sure, try setting out on the highway without a car, following a road map designed by a comic book artist for a new version of Treasure Island. If that's the map, right, the Gaza pullout is exactly where it should be.

I can understand that the Americans would put pressure on Israel to ease up the steam they are getting from Islam in all its forms. After all, we know that the US is not a puppet in Sharon's hands. It's a country of its own, that follows its own mistaken notion of its own national interest, like all other countries. Like you and me, if we were countries or presidents of same. I can understand that the Israeli government and its assorted embassies (was that communiqué a French exception or a form letter sent all over the world?) might have to talk this kind of nonsense on the international scene. I can understand that the plan looked like a good idea in its early stages, and now that the Palestinians are reacting as could be expected but as the plan did not exactly foresee, it isn't looking so good but a government is not like a freelance writer who looks you in the eye and says oops, I made a mistake. I can understand that the pullout is a bad idea, and doing nothing was worse, and anything else anyone could have done would not have been any better. I can understand that some people, many people in Israel think that it's like going to the dentist. Do it and get it over with and you'll be glad you did. And I can understand that 100,000 people praying at the kotel and 200,000 singing and dancing in Rabin Square can believe that they will make a miracle happen.

I can understand all of this. I too want a miracle. Not a corny cardboard miracle but the kind that is performed by human beings, informed with divine light. If writing is prayer, this is my prayer for the miracle. Let the world see us as the miracle we are. Miracle of dignity, survival, decency, love for our fellow man. Miracle of energy, imagination, invention, flexibility, elasticity. Miracle of hope.

This is not the expulsion from Spain, this is not the deportation from despicable European countries, this is, yes, this is Jews asking Jews to leave their homes, begging them, imploring them, forcing them to leave their homes. For the sake of the entire nation. Even if the decision is wrong. There are ways to correct the error. Believe me, there will be ways to correct this mistake. But we have to stay together.

I saw images of Islamic Jihad marching in Gaza. Small boys in uniform riding with armed men. Riding through the ruins of the city these people made for themselves. And Mahmoud Abbas— I think he was speaking to this IJ crowd—promising "today Gaza, tomorrow Jerusalem."

No. Not Jerusalem.

Again, and once more, and with wicked curiosity, French television shows Israeli soldiers and policemen playing out the violence of the evacuation. I pray it won't happen that way. I pray for an earth-shaking surprise. Men, women, and children walking out of Gaza intact. Please, *haverim*, do it that way. Walk out of there of your own free will. How many hundreds, thousands of journalists are there for the countdown? They want to see scuffles, worse than the training sessions. They want to see Jews shed Jewish blood. Not all of them, of course. But this depraved conscience that has been hovering over Israel since September 2000... Think of it, they call Tony Blair the lapdog of Bush because he had the courage to send troops to Iraq. But they are not ashamed of being the lapdog of Arafat, of bin Laden, and al Zaqarwi, and your local backpacking jihad bomber?

There has to be a judgment on the withdrawal from Gaza. I seem to be seeking it stupidly in the media, like trying to get water from a stone. Why? Simply because that is the source, for the masses of people all over the world, of knowing what is happening there where they cannot be. And they do make judgments. That lead us to disaster.

There has to be a higher judgment on this gesture, this turnover, that is neither desperate nor suicidal nor calculated. It is totally unjust. No, I can't even say that Israel is giving Gaza to the Palestinians. Whatever Islamic Jihad, Hamas, and the others will try to make it seem, Israel isn't giving them Gaza, Israel is turning its back on them. And that is what they deserve. Despite the fact that decent people will suffer along with the criminals responsible for their hopeless situation, Israel is turning its back on them. They will wither like plants without the sun.

Or they will deal with the evil in their hearts.

Either way, this separation can be justice.

And the judgment must be final: the path taken by the Jews out of Gaza will become a rampart for Jerusalem.

August 13, 2005

Talal is back with a vengeance. What's going on there? Another one of his home-cooked news reports on *France 2* this evening. The Israel-Palestine segment begins on a warning note: Jerusalem is swarming with policemen, Israeli authorities are afraid that extremist Jews will try to get to *l'esplanade des mosquées*, Islam's third holiest site, and provoke the Muslims and prevent the Gaza pullout. We're back in September of 2000. Ariel Sharon visited Temple Mount, the most sacred site of Judaism and, in the intifada narrative, this desecration of Islam's third holiest place caused an easily understandable outbreak of violence that escalated into years of martyrdom operations by the Palestinians and use of excessive force by the Israelis. Why is state-owned French television fanning the flames of violence on the eve of the Gaza separation? No extremists in sight. That segment is over in a few seconds. It is followed by a long drawn out visit to a Syrian family whose home is a stone's throw from the colony of Kfar Darom. The family has remained in the home these past years despite the fact that Israeli soldiers are living there. The family is confined to the ground floor. They are not allowed to go upstairs. Like the Franco-Palestinian biologist on yesterday's news, this family scurries inside. It's too dangerous out there. You can get hit by a stray bullet for no reason. Farida, the *RFI* correspondent in Gaza, tells the same story on the radio today. The Palestinians are so happy that the Israelis are leaving, now they can go outdoors without getting hit by stray bullets. The Syrian man of the house shows the cameraman the room where the Israeli soldiers sleep. It looks like a typical Arab bedroom. It's on the ground floor. Our host explains how they point guns at him from all directions (at bedtime?) and he and his family are confined to certain rooms, they can't even go to the bathroom. Now he shows us the room where the soldiers tried to kill him. The master bedroom. An imposing wooden headboard. And right behind it, a broken window covered with a rag. Here it is. A mortar shell came right through the window. Wounded in the head, Mister K. survived by a miracle. Now we see him with the whole family. His son was shot in the back by Israeli soldiers. He too survived by miracle. Neither father nor son show any signs of permanent damage from these serious wounds. They seem to be in perfect health. Like the wife and the daughter. All in good health, well dressed, well fed, living in a comfortably furnished well-equipped home.

We are shown the wall that surrounds the colony. And told that the family is not allowed to approach it. One might wonder why they would want to approach it. But one must wonder nothing, one must take everything as given. An Israeli tank passes by the kitchen window. "We had to hide to take this picture." Why? Don't ask. These people live in a gilded prison, and the only reason they are still there is that Mister K. absolutely refuses to abandon his home.

His children made a beautiful work of art out of spent shells. It spells peace. In bullets. How much more peaceful can you get? The last shot shows the whole lovely family united under a rainbow colored *PACE* flag.

Five years after the al-Dura story, Israeli soldiers are still trigger happy monsters taking potshots at Palestinians who are only asking for peace, *pace, paix*.

Shabat leads directly into Tish Be'av this evening. And in Paris it's the August 15th weekend. Withdrawal will begin in earnest tomorrow evening and Monday. *TF1* does not visit any bizarre Palestinian homes this week. They show Jews moving out of Gaza. And give them a chance to express themselves. It's all very calm, and true to life.

This "homes of Palestinians who have suffered" series smacks of manipulation. Israeli soldiers living in a home with a Syrian family? For how long? Under what conditions? For what reason? It doesn't make sense.

August 15 2005

Whether the report comes from an Israeli correspondent on a Jewish station or a Muslim correspondent on a French station, the master word is the same: violence. Will these Jews be violent? Beyond the simple, I might say the stupid sensationalism of the media, there is a deeper reason: the fear of the power of Judaism. What energy is captured in those cells? What danger lurks in that religious fervor? And, again, the *décalage*. Every close up takes us face to face with gentle people whose open faces shine with inner light. I don't deny that there may be pockets of seething revolt waiting to pounce. But the main thrust of these people, their families, their gestures, their homes, their gardens is gentle and productive. Even in Israel, so many people talk about them as if they were monsters. The settlers. Religious fanatics. Dragging us into confrontation, making our lives dangerous. I don't want my sons going into the territories to protect a handful of nutcases. They never should have been allowed to live there in the first place.

Suddenly they stand before us. Their homes are so beautiful. How did they build those neighborhoods on the fringes of Gaza? The accepted wisdom, seen from France but not only from here, is that if they are living in luxurious comfort they stole it from their Palestinian neighbors who live in squalor. The truth is that the Palestinian leaders stole from their people, and the palaces they built with some of that money are standing in Gaza today. No one is allowed to photograph them. I know, I've said this before, but I am saying it again.

I listen attentively to the interviews. And what I hear echoes my innermost thoughts this week. Neither violence nor Gandhi style nonviolence. Something different. An Israeli correspondent interviews a soon to be evacuee, presses for answers: but what will you do when they do come, you do have a sense of reality—he speaks kindly—and you know that sometime within the next few days, the soldiers will come... The answer is calm, determined, and subtle. Yes, they do have a sense of reality. No, they do not want to clash with the soldiers. And who looks the best in the rare images I have seen? The soldiers on military bases practicing strong arm techniques, or the residents of a settlement preparing shabat with friends and neighbors, in large, beautiful, clean, clear, kitchens? They do not want to turn against their fellow man. And woman. And they will not leave of their own free will. Many have already packed up and left, some burned their homes and greenhouses so that the Palestinians couldn't desecrate them or profit from them. And some will wait until the last minute, and walk away with their heads high.

Their material existence must enunciate the principle. Packing up, preparing, protecting their belongings would mean acquiescing in the decision. They refuse the decision, but will accept the law of the land. At the last minute.

Another interview, with a Frenchman from Judea Samaria whose son lives in Kfar Darom. He and his son make it clear that according to their way of life, you cannot at the same time defend your values and calculate how you will compromise if all fails. Their force of conviction depends on unflinching fidelity to a vision and its concrete implementation. But, near the end of the interview, the father explains that the majority of Israelis are against the pullout. And he gets lost in a sort of casuistry that could suit an American Leftist—in fact, I heard Amy Goodman argue that way, explaining that even though Bush won the election, it wasn't really the will of the people, and even if the polls show x% of support for the war, that isn't really what the people think. Are the heavy handed tactics Sharon is using to bring off this withdrawal truly a betrayal of democracy? Or a sign of its eternal imperfection?

There are other cases, far less emotionally charged, cases where life and death are not in the balance, where there is no lethal enemy at the gates, but a part of the population is opposed to a government decision, and resists by all means possible. The expansion of Narita airport, for example. The battle went on for decades. With quite a bit of violence on both sides. When a democratically elected government makes a decision that is unpopular with a certain segment of the population, and the opponents mobilize large numbers, should that overcome the government decision? Two hundred thousand people praying at the *kotel* is tremendous, but it is a tiny minority of the Israeli population. Here in France the unions mobilize half a million for a demonstration against a government project that would help the economy but deprive them of some of their privileges. The government gives in. The economy slumps further. Unemployment increases. The unions are strengthened. The social fabric is weakened.

I don't want to hear about the war of the Jews, civil war between Jews, cleavage between religious and secular Jews. Yes, the conflict exists. It's not a war. It exists inside of us too. If I think of Judaism as a concentrate that rose to the surface of existing societies in the time of its origins, and separated from their barbaric practices, the constant tug to go back to the original medium is almost chemical. Giving up the framework of *kashrut* and observance of holy days feels like liberation. The doors to the world open wide. Choices multiply. Within and without. Personal budding and blooming brings to fruition another person, other people that had remained buried like barren seed. You change the way you dress, the way you walk, the very shape of your body. Taste forbidden pleasures. Take risks. Mix unashamedly with foreign bodies. That new life seems more true than the past hampered by observant separation.

And then one day you realize that you have lost something precious and irrecoverable. All the exotic pleasures have faded and become ordinary. There is nothing more exotic, more enticing, more deeply intellectual, highly spiritual, profoundly sensual, utterly desirable than the Jewish life.

Fast track Israel with a little gold earring in its pierced earlobe is making a pact with the devil, coddling jihadi terrorists, swallowing the junk food of international promises, and allowing armed Palestinians to surround Jewish settlements in Gaza, under the pretext that they will prevent Palestinians from making an ugly spectacle of themselves on the evening of the 17th of August. I predict that nothing will prevent this spectacle. And perhaps the photographers posted there to capture Jew on Jew violence will turn their cameras on the evil faces of Palestinian hatred.

If I am wrong, if the Palestinians keep their rage in check, accept law and order in the shape of their own military forces, and if the policemen themselves do not turn their weapons on the departing Jews and shoot them in the back, could it be a sign of a small change for the better? But who can even imagine it?

16 August 2005

A *France 3* soundman was kidnapped in Gaza Sunday evening. Hasn't been heard from since. He's a Franco-Algerian. The two Franco-French journalists who were with him when he was abducted tried to intervene. To no avail. There have been several abductions this month. They usually end after a few hours. Not this time. The UN has pulled its personnel out of Gaza. Other NGOs too. But French media never seem to have any leftover "violence" to apply to the situation there. Violence is the violence expected to occur when the ultra-extremist ultra-religious ultra-rightist colonists are forced to leave Gaza against their will. The violence that will occur has been predicted so often, the few scuffles that really occurred have been shown over and over so that distracted public opinion will apply the violence label where it belongs, on the Jews, no matter what actually happens.

Jewish radio has been running interviews with Gaza residents. Heartbreaking. In their tearful voices I hear echoes of centuries of displacement and persecution. The same story repeated endlessly for thousands of years. Wherever Jews are allowed to settle, they labor and improve, they fruitfully multiply, they create wealth and beauty. Then it is plucked like ripe fruit, by the rightful owners of the land, and the Jews are thrown out with only the clothes on their backs.

Does this mean that a Jewish state is now persecuting Jews? I don't think so. Listening to the residents express their bottomless sorrow, their love for these so-called colonies that are nothing but lovely Jewish neighborhoods surrounded by fences and guards because the Palestinians want to destroy them, listening to the sound of men, women, and children torn from their homes, torn limb from limb, I remember images of the armored busses that transport them to and from Israel proper, or to and from other neighborhoods in the same area. That was the way they lived. And they love their neighborhood to death.

On the midday news *France 2* promised a report by Talal Abu Rahmeh about the abduction of the *France 3* journalist. The newscaster did his intro, looked down at his screen, mumbled something about coming back to the subject later, and went through the rest of the newscast to the very end without another word about the abducted journalist. No surprise. Between the PA censorship, Talal's "militant" obligations, and the prickly Quai d'Orsay, it must be rather difficult to report on such a sensitive subject. I heard some comments on the radio this morning... perhaps it was a *France 3* colleague of the abducted soundman... I caught it in the middle, but the gist of it was that they don't quite know what to think, this isn't Iraq, there have been no demands, political or financial, it will take time to puzzle it out. One might wonder if this is the thanks France gets for adoring Arafat and painting Palestinian atrocities in the glorious colors of *la résistance*. I remember Malbrunot telling me that the Palestinians don't take hostages.

Nissim Zvili, the Israeli ambassador to France, was a guest on today's *France 2* newscast. The young, half way competent, good-looking, suntanned newscaster treated the ambassador with whippersnapper insolence. Zvili made some points, but I was so disappointed to hear him repeat the words "colonists" and "ultra-extremists." It was a mistake on our part to not combat the vocabulary right from the beginning. It's still not too late. An overview of Gaza was presented in the course of the same program. Conspicuously absent: all mention of the jihad-intifada that had turned Gaza into a battlefield. And of course no explanation of how Israel happened to be "occupying" it, no reminder that Gaza would be under PA control if the offer made at Camp David in the summer of 2000 had been accepted, no mention that Gaza had been administered by the PA after the Oslo agreement. All of these irrelevant details are swept aside. What counts is that 8,000 Jewish colonists occupy 25% of the land; 1.3 million Palestinians live in squalor in the rest, most of them in refugee camps. Not even a veiled hint of the existence of sumptuous villas rising above the Palestinian squalor.

The smart aleck journalist challenged the ambassador to deny that Sharon was pulling off a dirty trick—getting rid of Gaza the better to hold onto the colonies in the West Bank.

Further evidence of the really fantastic PR results of the pullout as provided this morning on *RFI*'s talk show. Juan Gomez is on vacation. The African journalist who replaced him was surprisingly candid and fair-minded. One caller ranted and raved about how Israel was pulling out of Gaza but would Israel develop Gaza after the pullout as it should, make it viable, give it water, electricity, jobs, roads, ports, schools, hospitals... The host suggested that perhaps it would be up to the people of Gaza to develop the territory.

The worst is a left wing Israeli who calls in to scold the extremist colonists who have been making so much trouble for Israel ever since 1967. Her voice exudes confidence that she is among friends, among the good people of all races, creeds, and cultures who know how to pinpoint the faults of the bad people. Like the French Jews in the 30s who joined in the chorus of contempt for Eastern European Jews. They thought they were creating an island of safety for themselves. Instead, they were destroying the little bit of ground still left to stand on. She doesn't know that she is no less a colonist than the residents of the Gush Katif whose tears now leave her cold.

The investigation into the London bombings progresses. The latest leaks undo previous leaks. Now they are saying that there is no discernible connection with Al Qaeda, no links between the A team that succeeded on July 7th and the B team that flopped on the 21st.

August 17 2005

It looks like my prayers are being answered. Too soon to be sure but it seems that I have correctly read the Jewish soul. The Jewish residents of Gaza want to state—with their hearts minds and bodies and with their treasured household goods—their right to live in Gaza and enjoy the fruits of their labor. They want to leave with their heads high, singing, praying, dancing, crying but not defeated. They do not want to make a tear in the fabric of Israel by opposing the soldiers and policemen who have been sent to evacuate them. They do not want to force those soldiers and policemen, their brothers, to treat them with cruel brutality. When the Portuguese revolted against Salazar, they put carnations in the barrels of the rifles pointed at them, they brought the army over to the side of the people. But Tsahal is a people's army.

The families will leave. The young activists (isn't that cute, these kids are given the same label as the Hamas goons and their ilk who are preparing at this very moment to conquer the evacuated settlements and turn them into a terrorist bastion) who infiltrated will fight, but they won't be a match for the army, even though they are the very stuff the army is made of.

All day yesterday I was subject to the ugly vocabulary of the French media. I know those releases are concocted by *Agence France Presse* in Cyprus. I am familiar with their pornographic approach to language when Jews or Americans are involved. But it's still painful to listen to them drool at the prospect of Israeli soldiers forcibly removing colonists from their homes.

Mohamed Ouathi has been in the hands of his abductors since Sunday evening. The incident is downplayed in the press. I suppose the French don't want to up the ante. They have to pretend that it's not all that important to get the guy back, the way you do when you bargain in the *souk*. Besides, it would be embarrassing to admit that those darling Palestinian *résistants* could mistreat a French journalist.

Why do I resist the drastic interpretations of my American comrades? Am I tired of the struggle? I don't think so. Maybe it's because I don't want to give up the struggle or the hope. I know that the Bush administration is making crucial errors in Iraq. But they are still on the right track. Yes? More or less? Or are they retreating, leaving the job one tenth done, leaving the Iraqis to their own mess? I think that Sharon is making a strategic move that will leave Israel in a position to act more decisively against the jihad networks in Gaza. But maybe I'm wrong? Maybe he is strengthening them and leaving them a free hand, an open border—like the Saddamites have in Iraq—through which to bring in reinforcements from Lebanon, fan out into Judea Samaria, create the same kind of troubles there as they've been fomenting in Gaza since 1993.

The jihad-intifada story is ending as it began. With stories of Israeli soldiers shooting at innocent Palestinians for the fun of it. The area around the settlements is described as a shooting gallery. The Palestinian violence that initiated this state of war in the year 2000 has vanished without a trace. Vanished from the French media... If I were following the story in the US there would at least be a variety of viewpoints.

As I understand Judaism, religious people like those who are now being forced to abandon their homes, their land, and their livelihood, must in the final hour obey the law of the land. Even if it is unjust. This is the true separation of religion and state. Even in a Jewish State. Without the protection of the state, our religion is in danger, exposed to the same forces that have been constantly trying to make us disappear. Without religion, our state is weakened. By showing themselves to be noble, these religious Jews can strengthen Israel. I have never accepted the comparison between our extremists and their extremists. This pullout is a demonstration of the difference.

Reports are coming in that Hamas is taking up positions around the evacuated neighborhoods, ready to move in and take over before the PA can lift a finger. Meaning that if the PA is serious about establishing law and order in its own camp, the jihadis could be caught in a pincer movement between PA and IDF forces. They wouldn't stand a chance! But the PA won't dare to move against them, because it can't protect its rear guard. It's the PA that will be caught in the pinch, and the ordinary citizens of Gaza will be put through the meat grinder.

I can't follow events closely today, I have to do a translation.

Which is more realistic? To trust in G-d, in a Jewish way, which is a way of trusting in life, of making life bloom, of making heaven wherever one sets one's feet. Or to trust in a hypothetical solution based on the belief that if Israel retreats to the 1949 borders, gives the Palestinians half of Jerusalem and a right of return that they only want for the form but won't exercise, the conflict will end?

August 18 2005

This French propaganda media loves to cry with the bereaved. Except when the bereaved are Israeli Jews. That's another story. One hundred fifty two Martiniquais killed in a particularly dreadful plane crash in Venezuela monopolizes newscasts for two days. Empathy oozes from the screen. This is a small island, everyone knows everyone, it's all one family, unbearable sorrow, overwhelming moral support. Reporters are in Saint-Esprit, François, and other communities that are particularly hard hit. A Martiniquais family on the outskirts of Paris, also touched by the tragic crash, and a couple miraculously spared—they decided at the last minute not to go on the week-long holiday to Panama because their son was ill. Given the age of the couple, they couldn't be less than 50, one must suppose that their son is not a toddler. But his illness saved their lives. French authorities are at work, consoling the sorrowful, ferrying them to the morgue, more exactly *la chapelle ardente* set up in a town near the crash site, expediting forensic teams that will help identify the bodies. No detail is left untouched. The anchor in the Parisian studios has tears in her eyes. We see a priest from Martinique leading a service in a chapel in Cologne where Catholic Youth are gathered for their annual jamboree. He reads the names of the victims. Breaks down. Can't go on. One family, his own friends, relatives, parishioners are on the list.

And of course we are told that there was nothing wrong with the airplane, it had been checked very recently, it's very difficult to explain how both engines could fail almost simultaneously. A Colombian charter plane. The co-pilot was 21 years old. His accumulated flight hours placed him in the category of debutant. What went wrong? Technically the plane was fine. As a matter of fact, since the crash at Sharm el Sheikh (a year and a half ago if my memory is correct) new regulations have... well, they have not exactly been applied, let alone implemented... they have been more or less outlined and should eventually be applied sometime before 2008. Except for one requirement, which is already implemented: travelers who book charter flights with agencies must be informed of the name of the company with which they will be flying. A quick check reveals that the requirement is blissfully ignored.

And so we come to understand the purpose of this niagra of emotion pouring from the television screen: to cover the fact that French travel agents are still booking flights with unreliable companies. Every crash bounces back with the same promise. The flight recorders will be analyzed to ascertain the reasons for the crash. And then you never hear another word about it. Unless a class action suit pops briefly into the news. Then you find out that the victims' families have never been informed. And the years go by. The Egyptian company was above suspicion, the Tunisian plane that crashed off the coast of Palermo was operated by a reliable company, the Cypriote charter that crashed on its way from Cyprus to Athens was not a fly by night operation. In fact, the Cypriote plane had already been hit with depressurization incidents, and the company was well aware that the fatal flight was subject to the same problem. Now we discover that the Colombian charter company was notorious. In both cases the pilots refuse to fly.

They talk about ultraliberalism—meaning modern capitalism—and the miseries of globalization and deregulation, and people die by the planeloads.

No tears left for the Jews of Gaza. Enderlin is the master of ceremonies, granted full indulgence to project his skewed view of Israel, protected on his Palestinian flank by a total blackout of unflattering images or even a sentence or two of balanced reporting. Mohamed Ouathi was kidnapped by armed Palestinians on Sunday. Today is Friday. Talal's promised reportage never appeared. Has he been trumped by a new generation of more "militant" propagandists flourishing on the powder keg of jihad-intifada? Shams Oudeh, the Reuters cameraman whose raw footage has been so useful to us in figuring out what went on at Netzarim Junction on September 30, 2000, was stabbed the other day by a Palestinian. His wounds are not life threatening, but it may be an indication that we were right in guessing that he deliberately, honestly recorded the manipulations taking place that day in the Palestinian camp. A *comité de soutien* has been created for the latest French hostage, but his portrait hasn't gone up on the façade of City Hall yet, and we don't know, from French radio and TV, if he has a distraught wife or mother waiting for the slightest shred of news.

I had to find out from Khaled Abu Toameh of the *Jerusalem Post* that Chirac personally sent a message to Abbas, threatening to withhold all further payments to the PA if Ouathi is not released, safe and sound.

A bit embarrassing, isn't it? And what if it turns out that he's being held by a Palestinian branch of Al Qaeda? And what if the French hostage file has been transferred from Iraq to Gaza, with notations on how much ransom to expect, and how to negotiate. Will Didier Julia mobilize his network?

The transfer of Jewish populations from Gaza is taking place almost according to my most fervent hopes. More tears than scuffles, more psalms that insults, more brotherly hugs than punches. It doesn't matter if we don't get credit in the salons of international opinion, we know in our hearts that this is the right way to do. Our future will be brighter.

On one condition: that the Israeli government stands firm, respects its word, refrains from additional unilateral withdrawals unless and until the PA reins in its jihadi killers.

A Jew in Judea Samaria killed four Palestinian workers yesterday, wounded two others. The news was reported on Jewish radio with misplaced integrity: the murderer is labeled a terrorist, an extremist, and his act is called "*un attentat*," a terrorist attack. I can imagine the reasoning: when a Palestinian blows himself up in a public place, maiming or killing dozens of Jews, we want the media to call him a terrorist. They don't. They call him a militant. And make excuses for him. We don't want to do that. Result? A murderer is called a terrorist, his isolated crime is now associated with a military strategy of planned atrocity with genocidal ambitions, and the next Palestinian who murders Israelis will still be a militant for the outside world.

Three hundred fifty low level bombs exploded almost simultaneously in Bangladesh yesterday. The aim of the operation is to institute Shari' a. What shall we call that? A missionary operation?

E-MAIL TO J.

J., I don't agree with you on this. The truth is that the Palestinians have held their fire during the evacuation. By focusing on a few isolated incidents, you are missing the really important point: Abbas does control these jihadi groups. When he wants them to strike, they strike. When he wants them to be still, they don't move. The infighting in Gaza is far more important to observe. Since the foreign media can't do any free honest reporting from the Palestinian side, they show all the sturm und drang in the Jewish neighborhoods. I suppose you get a more honest mix between the confrontations and the shared prayers and tears. Our reporting here is coming from the same Enderlin who brought us the Al Dura fiction. And his sidekick Talal is just the other side of the line, doing his thing.

Today, *France 2* invited PA spokeswoman Leila Shahid to explain the ins and outs of the liberation of Gaza. Talal's report had shown Palestinians who want to reclaim their land that was requisitioned during the intifada (they always make it sound as if the Israelis started it) to create a no man's land between the Palestinian villages and the Jewish neighborhoods that they call colonies.

Later, they asked Leila if the farmers were going to get their land back. She said, "Yes, if they have proper deeds... which would be true of 3% of the land now occupied by Israelis. 97% of that land is dominial." She didn't use the term "dominial," she said it was public lands.

So there you go about Israelis stealing land from Mohamed and Bashir and Hassan. Just more Palestinian fairy tales.

An *RFI* journalist was interviewing Palestinians in a Gaza teahouse or some such place. And they were telling how Gaza was a paradise before the Israelis occupied it. With date palms, pomegranates, almond trees and so on and so forth. I'd love to see a picture of Gaza when it belonged to the Egyptians. I know that it was a hellhole in '67, and the Egyptians refused to take it back. Another tea drinker explained that the Palestinians got along fine with the Israelis until Abu Amar came back. Why did that create trouble? Because he started attacking them? No, of course not. It was because he said he would take back the Palestinian land. So the Israelis got nervous, and relations deteriorated.

N'importe quoi!

Now I have to finish a translation, but I'll listen to your side of the argument.

It's really crying times.

[extended interlude]

25 - 27 JANUARY 2006

25 January 2006

There is the educated guess before the reality and the appraisal after the reality... and then there is the Middle East soup in which the whole alphabet floats indiscriminately and no one is ever held accountable. The Gaza withdrawal was not exactly what the doctor ordered, no, it fell far short of the irredentist claims made against the Jews in that part of the world over the past 100 years, but it was declared in all the usual places that this was a step in the right direction. Removing a Jewish thorn from the tender Palestinian foot would certainly be beneficial. It raised high hopes. Everyone was setting the table for imminent negotiations. Ah that wonderful peace process, what a delightful banquet in store. The Palestinians stormed in and desecrated the synagogues. Hmm, yes, the synagogues, well, what did you expect, synagogues are a terrible provocation for Palestinians, put yourselves in their place. And they sacked the greenhouses. Well of course it would have been better to leave them intact and use them productively but... but by then the press had covered its eyes and here in France there were no more news reports from Gaza. Qassams rained down on Israel. Not on the wicked "*colons*," but on Israelis in Israel "proper." Most of the time they fall short, or off the mark, or do slight damage, or only kill one person and commotion dozens and destroy a few houses. Armed factions fight each other in the streets of Gaza. Kids get killed in the crossfire. PA officials are attacked. Their houses are gutted. Some flee. The only news to filter from Gaza to France was the triumphant announcement that the Palestinians were harvesting their first crops. And the sacked greenhouses? What sacked greenhouses. You don't need greenhouses to grow a press release. You didn't need gunfire to kill Mohamed al-Dura, why would you need green, red, and orange peppers to make a harvest?

And what about those landed proprietors waiting feverishly in the lens of Talal's camera last August, ready to move back into their liberated land, and take care of their olive groves? Did they get pistol whipped by Hamasniks or did they go back to their apartments in Ramallah once they had played the two-bit role in the *France 2* advertorials? They served their purpose: to show that Israel had caused untold, now fully told, Palestinian suffering and whenever Jews leave, things get better. No need to show the happy ending.

Where are the commentators who painted the rosy picture of post-Jewish Gaza? I'll tell you where they are, they are now covering the elections, and in the space of 24 hours they have transformed Hamas from a terrorist organization dedicated to the extermination of the Jewish State of Israel into a political party poised to win close to a majority of seats in the Palestinian legislature. Hamas leaders shout from the rooftops their intention to pursue armed struggle. They respond directly to timid declarations from European officials warning that it will be a tiny bit difficult to continue to deal with the Palestinian government in the event of a massive influx of Hamas members but then after all if they are in the legislature that will make them automatically legislators and legislators are not terrorists so of course the question of armed struggle will be left at the door. No, declares Hamas, we will not give up armed struggle and we will be in the legislature.

But their voices are whitewashed, their arms are dumped in the soup, *before* and *after* go round in circles as the soup is stirred, and tomorrow's news will wipe out today's predictions.

So let me say here and now that the PA will try to rig the election results while at the same time trying to tighten its bonds with Hamas. But the PA will not be able to keep up its distribution of goodies, because Hamas will take the lion's share. So Fatah gangs will shoot up administrative buildings, while trying to get into Hamas coffers. And Europe will look the other way and suddenly bow down to democracy in the Middle East. Hamas will get the same beauty treatment as the ex-rebels in Côte d'Ivoire. Even the Americans will bend. Iran, having bought another precious span of time by offering to let the Russians enrich the uranium on its territory on condition that the case not be referred to the UN Security Council, will pour money into Hamas Palestine. Shari'a will be imposed. Decent Palestinians will leave, Christian Palestinians will flee, terrorist attacks on Israel from Palestinian territories will intensify, and public opinion will forget that Hamas was going to go straight. All eyes will turn to the "West Bank." Unless Israel withdraws, Hamas will not be able to govern properly. Put yourself in their boots.

I wouldn't be surprised if Mahmoud Abbas were assassinated. Or flew the coop.

26 January 2006

France 2 of al-Dura fame was clearly rooting for a Hamas victory. And they got it! Last night the news was all doe-eyes for Hamas. We watched a woman in hijab...voting. She wore a white headscarf that almost covered her eyes, a veil that almost reached up to the bottom edge of the headscarf, leaving a tiny slit through which she might navigate, but only with a male escort.... She proudly voted Hamas. To end Fatah corruption and bring virtue or more precisely Shari'a to Palestine. No footnote to mention that the EU bears a fair share of responsibility for the Fatah corruption. French Eurodeputy François Zimmeray lost his mandate, punished for trying to impose accountability on the PA, beneficiary of extraordinary EU largesse. The EU, Chris Patten *en tête*, paved the way for this Hamas victory, and if *France 2* is any indication, so much the better. Another voter stepped up to the plate, described as a modern, liberated Palestinian. Not for long. She too was fed up with Fatah corruption, and had come to vote Hamas. "If they give me what I want, I'm ready to give up the superficial, my makeup, my jeans..." Of course. And the other superficial, my right to choose my husband, own property, raise my children... and all those other frivolities that disappear under Shari'a, like the face under the veil? And who says that *hijab* won't be replaced by the *burka*, or the *abaya* in the coming months?

Hamas candidates, from the top down, proclaim their intention to relentlessly pursue armed struggle, all the way to the liberation of Palestine. And French journalists, for some strange reason, now admit that this means the total elimination of the Jewish State. And yet they and the experts they love to invite agree that once Hamas is in the government they will tone down the rhetoric. Isn't it obvious? Look at Ahmadinejad. A model of moderation. They prefer to look the other way. At Erdogan. Poor fellow, he has to send his daughters to school in the US because they aren't allowed to wear *hijab* in their own country. Now he can send them to Gaza to study.

Eyes that do not focus see everything in a vague haze. This is the image of world affairs peddled to public opinion. Mixing up past present and future instead of clearly separating time into the segments that exist in reality, twisting clearcut statements and fitting them into baseless generalizations, opinion-makers lead people into a state of hopeless confusion.

But that still doesn't explain why *France 2* comes out unashamedly for Hamas. And our comic book Minister of Foreign Affairs, Douste-Blazy, mumbles a mealy-mouthed declaration implying that France has no inhibitions about chatting with Hamas. And *vive les élections*!

Prime Minister Dominique de Villepin subscribes to the parenthesis concept of the Jewish State: Jewish sovereignty in Israel is a parenthesis in modern history. And the sooner the brackets are closed, the better. President Chirac is known to say that he cares sincerely about "his" Jews here in France, but doesn't give a fig for Israel. And Charles Enderlin, chief of the *France 2* Jerusalem desk, working hand in hand with his trusty sidekick Talal Abu Rahmeh, seems determined to accomplish what all the fiercely united Arab armies never managed to do: defeat Tsahal.

OK, I can't help it, I have to shoot one little spitball at my former editor, *Metula News Agency*. Last night, they published an excited release from Palestinian correspondent Sami El Soudi joyfully announcing the victory of Fatah. According to El Soudi, Fatah would be able to make a coalition with several small parties, obviating any pressure to appoint Hamas ministers. This morning, Palestinian PM Ahmed Qorei resigned, and invited Hamas to form a government.

So, move over Sami, and let me repeat my prediction: *ça va barder*. Fatah gunmen will not take this sitting down. Many shootouts are to be expected, and many Palestinian youngsters will be killed in the crossfire, real deaths, real crossfires. I do not take any delight in the prospect. But I have to tell the truth as I see it.

Breaking news: Sami El Soudi admits his error. And offers his resignation from *Metula News Agency*. I take back the spitball. Never should have sent it.

Mahmoud Abbas has resigned too.

27 January 2006
Commemoration of the liberation of Auschwitz

No, Abbas didn't resign. Not yet.

A novelist strives to give the illusion of time apace, time in motion, time inextricably united with characters and events. Non-fiction writers make time stand still. For five years I have been writing about reality with the tools of fiction. Palestinians voting freely in democratic elections have chosen to be represented by a jihad faction consecrated to the extermination of Jews and, in the immediate, promising to establish shari'a. Until the exact moment when the votes were counted, well-meaning commentators and election observers took pleasure in describing the elections as free, democratic, legitimate, correctly and calmly conducted. *France 2* propaganda network showed jihadis coming up to the polling station, handing over their weapons, going in to vote. One of them couldn't suppress the trademark snicker of fake news. Now, the votes have been counted. Look back at these five years. Who described Palestinian society accurately? Me? Or the *New York Times*, *Le Monde*, Javier Solana, and your favorite academic? Suppositions about Palestinian normalcy, willingness to compromise, reasonable aspirations, hunger for freedom have gone up in smoke. Hamasniks tore the Palestinian flag from the Parliament building and replaced it with the green banner of Hamas. Now what?

Now, now is now, now is not we should have, they should have, it would have been better if. Now is what do you do with an outlaw population living within a hair's breadth of a lone tiny democracy bravely navigating on a sea of hostile Muslim nations. What do you do with the Palestinians? We don't exterminate people. We don't pick them up by the skin of their necks and throw them out. We have been negotiating with them... under pressure from our allies and motivated equally by our own highest values, but it is time to admit that the Palestinians we were negotiating with are the same people who just knowingly chose to be governed by Hamas. As for those—I don't need to name them—who will argue that Israel created Hamas by not giving the Palestinians what they wanted, the answer is so what? We could no more give them what they wanted when they were governed by Arafat and called it a peace process than we can give it to them today when they are governed by Hamas and call it jihad.

The "I told you so" game is perilous here. The I told you we should have negotiated with the PLO are trumped by the I told you we couldn't negotiate with the PLO because they never kept their word who now trump the I told you we should give back the "colonies" and half of Jerusalem, because the Palestinians have freely, democratically, unambiguously announced their goal: destruction of the Jewish State and, ultimately, extermination of the Jews.

As we say in French, *ouf*! Now we can deal with the problem. Despite massive heroic efforts to reconfigurate it, to make it into a small problem that any decent government would have solved in short order, the problem has stubbornly defined itself. What do you do with a mortal enemy standing at your front door?

Today we hold our aching hearts and commemorate the Shoah [actually, no, it's the "liberation" of Auschwitz that is commemorated today]. Blacks and Muslims in France are competing for a place in the ovens. It seems strange, doesn't it? Why would they want to be deprived of their civil rights, rendered helpless by a relentless series of legal measures that would leave them defenseless, rounded up in an endless series of legal operations, transferred to the intermediate hellholes of domestic concentration camps, separated from parents and children, starved, humiliated, delivered into a living hell, starved, tortured, beaten, frozen, reduced to numbers, reduced to skin and bones, reduced to ashes. Why would they aspire to such atrocious suffering? Today they covet the starring role of victim. They want to be cast as victims of the worst crime ever perpetrated against humanity. When the atrocities were underway, they did not come forward and ask to be included. They want the gravy without the ashes. What they mistake to be the gravy.

Victim is not a cushy job. Jews have better ways to use their energy than jockeying for a place in the victimary limelight. Just the opposite, we want to stop being victims of everybody's inferiority complex! How about that? Political Zionism, fulfilled in the creation of the State of Israel, is precisely the refusal of the Jewish people to be stateless, defenseless victims. And our enemies manage to twist that around and claim that we were given "their" state as a sop, to pay us off for the losses of the Shoah. The truth is, the more the world claims to remember the Shoah, the more it is used against us, in a diabolical enterprise that aims at a new improved extermination of Jews. And no matter how much recognition is granted to the suffering of peoples enslaved and colonized by Europeans, the aggrieved parties still pout and fume, stamp their feet, break their toys, and holler that it's not enough.

Judaism recognizes the suffering of others. But this recognition is inscribed in a comprehensive ethical system. That's what the others should compete to embrace. Not the taste for victimhood they mistakenly ascribe to us. They should overcome their vengeful hatred against the descendants of those they accuse of victimizing them, and construct decency in its place. Then they could stop being jealous of us.

And of course the whole "how terribly we suffered" shtick is disqualified, because it draws a veil over the jihad conquest. In fact, it comes in handy just when a new breed of scholars is shedding light on the true face of Islam. A new, and let's hope it's the last, round of jihad conquest looms on the horizon, poised to advance in the night of "how terribly we suffered." It worked for the Palestinians, didn't it? Convincing the whole world that their suffering, at the hands of the wicked Israelis, was the mother of all causes, they quietly enrolled in the Al Aqsa jihad. Day breaks, and we discover the Arab legions mounted on thoroughbred missiles, poised to strike. Hamas, Hizbullah, Iran... and the Saudi princes bringing up the rear, up to their necks in oil revenues and steeped in the very origins of the Arab conquest.

Instead of cousins and uncles, Jews have memories of the Shoah. Each of us carries an extended exterminated family. Trapped by their naïve faith in humanity, in nationality, in what is healthy and reasonable, pushed gradually but inexorably through a series of ever-narrowing passages, hoping against hope, enduring beyond endurance, snuffed out like candle stubs, they left us a heritage of abbreviated life stories. An image invades my mind and heart. The sewers of Lvov. The narrow slimy ridge. Inching along. Above, machine guns, blowtorches, man-eating dogs. Below, rat-infested poisonous waters, death by drowning. They inched along. One step, hope, another step, hope, another step, hope. How could a human being muster, in that last murderous second, enough hope to take one more step?

The bomb blast sometimes destroys all vital organs. The person looks normal on the outside, but on the inside it has turned to something like applesauce. Other times it leaves nuts and bolts in the brain. They enter through the eyes. Sometimes the organs escape unhurt, but the envelope is crumpled beyond recognition, like a piece of paper to be tossed into a wastebasket. Members are blown off at the root. Children, grandmothers, fiancés on the eve of their wedding, brilliant students, charitable doctors, lovely young ladies whose laughter hangs in the acrid air. Families picking up the pieces and bravely getting on with their lives.

You can't get away with committing atrocities against Jews. That was the lesson of the Shoah, and it hasn't been learned. It looks like you can get away with it. But the price is utterly terrible. Today, the price is Iran with nuclear weapons. And all the trimmings.

We've come a long way from the days of naïve insolence when we asked why our families let themselves be led to slaughter. But we haven't come far enough. Our lives look so stable. We fret about small inconveniences. But I fear we are in the same situation as our *shtetl* generation. Waiting for the exterminators to arrive. And this time it is worldwide. If they should have run for their lives, where can we go?

We hear voices from some quarters warning that we must not snub a Hamas government because that would mean we don't respect the outcome of free and fair elections. It shows how far we have drifted from anything resembling lucidity. No state is obliged to have relations with any other state. That is a way of respecting the people's choice! In the very same breath we are told that if Hamas won, it is Israel's fault for not giving the Palestinians what they wanted when Abbas and, before him, Arafat was in power. By the first logic, Israel should have declared its intention to wipe the Palestinians off the map, and the world's busybodies would have forced the Palestinians to maintain normal relations with Israel.

[interlude]

Pierre Shapira, Socialist Eurodeputy and official observer of the recent Palestinian elections, interviewed by Shlomo Malka on *Radio Communauté Juive*, expounds in his eminently reasonable voice typical leftist nonsense about world affairs. He doesn't think the Palestinians really voted in favor of the extermination of Israel, they were just frustrated over Fatah corruption and Israeli checkpoints. I'm probably combining the declarations of Shapira with similar nonsense mouthed by Maurice LeRoy, whose official titles I didn't catch. One or the other or both opined that the international community definitely should not cut ties, refuse to talk, cut off funds, refuse to negotiate with Hamas now that the faction has become the government. And the bla bla bla about the wonders of power and responsibility when applied to extremists. A Muslim professor at Berkeley explains, in an *LA Times* op-ed, how Israel paved the way for Hamas. Checkpoints again. The real responsibility of a real entity is lost in the shuffle: the European Union that refused to make accountability a prerequisite for funding. And, I might add, the Quartet that refused to enforce the first provision of the Road Map: disarmament of all factions, unification into one official armed force under direct PA control. And, finally, and why not, the Israeli government for pulling Jews out of Gaza and thus handing Hamas a great big fat juicy victory to exploit to the hilt in the just-finished election campaign. We kicked them out of Gaza we'll chase them out of the rest of Palestine. Fatah promised it, we delivered. Does it cross the mind of the eminently reasonable Eurodeputy that Palestinians voted to reward Hamas for its triumph in Gaza? Maybe voters thought the Hamas extremists would win, but moderately. If so, too bad. Let the men start growing their beards and the women ironing their *hijab* and the Christians packing their bags.

Clashes between partisans of Fatah and Hamas began today. Three wounded.

I just decided that I will close this notebook today. I am not—or no longer—observant, and I wish I could do it before shabat, but I won't make that deadline. I'll finish before midnight. Today is the right day to taper off into thoughtful silence. First, for personal reasons, in honor of my father Lou Poller (z"l) who would have been 97 today, in homage to my father whose Zionism I rejected from the arrogant heights of my passionate Third Worldism, my father, born in Przemsyl, near Lvov, brought to the United States at the age of two, my father who joined the Marines in 1941 at the age of 34, to fight the Nazis, to try to save his people caught in the European trap his parents had escaped, my father, who raised millions for Israel, my father who spoke Hebrew and quoted from the Bible, a poor immigrant kid educated at the yeshiva and then thrown into the world to earn his living, an American success story, a self-made man who became wealthy, sent me to the university to learn how to reason against him, my father who gave me a priceless education in Jewish ethics, American capitalism, stubborn determination, innate elegance, beauty, talent, joie de vivre and *naïve maladresse*.

Ariel Sharon lies in a coma at Hadassah hospital. The blood of life courses through veins as fragile as lady's sheer stockings. A man like Sharon who held the destiny of his country, of his people, in the palm of his heart, and any old man anywhere in the world, equally fragile. Determinists of different stripes will read their own reasons into this arbitrary stroke of bad luck. Israelis do not go in for theatrical mourning. No women in black weeping and wailing for the little father. Three generations of wartime, the nation's survival guaranteed by a citizen's army, young kids braving death, has forged a society that cannot indulge in languorous sorrow. The tears flow, uninhibited. Then they are dried with the back of the hand, and the tearful pick up their rifles and go back to active duty.

Sharon isn't forgotten. What matters about Ariel Sharon is what he did when he had all his faculties. The glorious deeds and the mistakes. Today, flicked aside like a piece of dust, he can't be enlisted in any cause. And no one can refuse to report for duty on the grounds that Sharon is indispensable. I hate to hear Rabin dragged into arguments like a ventriloquist's dummy ...if he had lived, if he hadn't been killed, if he were here now.

It's called a lifetime. It endures the time of a life. And it ends in slow long-drawn agony or in the snap of unseen fingers. The certainty of death drives our courage. My father taught me to strive without limits to reach my goals, to never ever give up.

When you think courageously it is like a lifeline. Every word of this text is connected organically. That's what gives a novel the heartbeat of life. I will have to strive against editorial pressure in order to bring these words to you still alive with the pulse of my singularity. Editors will want me to remove this passage, that e-mail, some previously published articles. They will want me to explain things that have been left in the wings. They will say certain passages are too long, readers will lose interest, and others are not clear, readers won't understand. They will object to the mixture of styles and circumstances.

And I'll fight to defend Jerusalem.

What? To defend Jerusalem?

When you write courageously, in the truth of the instant, the text weaves itself intricately, creating myriad connections that self-conscious editing could never achieve. The commentators who have been serving as purveyors of jihad conquest, transforming the shockingly crude raw material into easily digested processed high class news, are left today with nothing but loose ends. Each day's twisted description of reality unraveled before dawn the next day. A new version had to be concocted, but it would end the day in shreds. When you have the courage to think for yourself, you see the present instant clearly and that sheds light on the past and the future. These *Notes* took me from French back to English—I have translated the entries from July 2000 to September 2001, originally written in French—took me from France back to the United States and from there to Jerusalem. Striving to understand what was happening as the world I live in crawled to the brink of disaster, I produced light and found my pathway. I changed my life. From an unknown novelist who couldn't break through I became a novelist-journalist published widely, read by tens of thousands. Because I recognized on the very day that Arik Sharon stood our ground on the Temple Mount that Europe had lost its moorings, I drew strength from deeper sources.

Remember sleazy Arafat signing peace treaties, slobbering for peace negotiations, and promising that millions of Palestinian children would die for Jerusalem? Meaning—would murder for Jerusalem. Jewish children did not seek martyrdom. Death was brutally thrust on them. Their unspent lives are our heritage. They will form the invincible ramparts of Jerusalem.

Peace is not absolutely necessary. Human beings can live with war, they can live through war, and they can die in war but life goes on. If there is ever to be peace in the Middle East, it can only radiate from the Holy of Holies. There can be no peace in the Middle East or in the world until the plan to exterminate the Jews is defeated, totally defeated. Muslims have lost all claims to Jerusalem because their claim is based on an evil ambition to replace the Jews. Third holiest site of Islam, *tu parles*! They need three holiest sites and we can't have even one? No, my friend, their need to replace us is what keeps them from finding the center of themselves. There will be no peace as long as that hollowness rages in the pit of Islam's stomach.

Iranian President Ahmadinejad has already done the math. Didn't someone say he looks like the Arab grocer who runs the corner store that stays open to all hours and sells overpriced bruised fruits and vegetables? He licked the tip of his pencil and figured it all out. He can wipe out six million Jews in one fell swoop. And so what if he loses 12 million Arabs? There are more where those came from. He still comes out ahead.

Aha? I thought they just absolutely had to have Al Quds? After Israel is nuked, it won't be worth a wooden euro. And forget about the golden dome. Jerusalem without the Jews is nothing but a piece of mediocre real estate. Islam wants Jewish Jerusalem to be magically, simultaneously Yerushalayim and Al Quds, Islam wants to be Judaism, to exterminate the Jews by becoming the Jews, becoming Jews who are Muslims but still keep the treasure of being Jews. Islam smolders with rage and keeps tearing its heart out, Islam is exploding in a gigantic death cult, a mushroom cloud released by the impossible equation of fusion fission.

Isn't it a crying shame? All those well-meaning people, and even if they're not sincerely well-meaning they dress up as well-meaning, and they put on their best suit & tie voice, those voices of reason, and they hitch up their skirt or their trousers and raise their shoulders and look down at me and say, "you have to share Jerusalem. It's the only decent thing to do." Every single day for five years has brought proof of exactly the opposite, but their days are numbered and mine flow in a steady stream.

I am responsible for Jerusalem. Here in this book, everything depends on me. There will be no more mass extermination of Jews. Those who are plotting the extermination, marching with their multicolored banners, are heading for exquisite defeat.

Can you imagine, can you just imagine what would be happening now if Jerusalem had been divided, and the Hamas government had sovereignty on the Temple Mount? Did the brilliant peacemakers who thought that one up include in their contingency toolbox the January 2006 victory of Hamas in the Palestinian elections? Of course not!

Well, even so, Hamastan is too close for comfort.

[interlude]

France 2 makes a specialty of *décalage* between image and commentary. For "*le petit Mohamed*" it was a dramatic commentary propping up the most nondescript uneventful image. Tonight, scenes of heavy fighting in the territories somehow slipped through the censors. Other sources are already reporting 13 people injured—*France 2* prefers the original count of 3—in scuffles between partisans of Fatah and Hamas. A Hamas leader interviewed after Friday prayers on Temple Mount—as I said, too close for comfort—gleefully announced that the first thing they are going to do is set up courts to judge the previous administration for squandering the people's riches. *Ouh la la*, watch the villas empty before the Virtue squads come calling. A Christian Arab in a bar says, "If they impose shari'a, I'll leave."

Somewhere in a corner of my mind I see an exodus of freethinking Palestinians. Something worse than checkpoints is on its way.

[*It is Saturday 28 January but I want to keep the 27th as the end date. Poetic license.*]

Leaving this book is something like leaving home for one of my frequent trips to the United States. I make up lists of what I have to do before I leave, what I have to do when I get back, what I need to take with me, what I need to buy before I go, and at the same time everyday life goes on, fills the days completely, unforeseen important events occur, filling the days to overflowing, and underneath it all I'm wondering what the weather will be in Boston, Washington DC, Irvine CA as, most often, I not only change latitudes but arrive in periods of transition, from winter to spring, from autumn to winter.

Pages and pages of notes I jotted down at times when I couldn't develop the ideas in writing will be left by the wayside. I won't even look at them. Even more important, from the point of view of readers, hundreds of pages of articles I've published in the past two years remain outside the limits of this book. They will be collected in a separate work if I can make it happen.

As it stands, the Chronicle did end more than a year ago. Or, more exactly, it metamorphosed into something closer to journalism. Events covered in those articles are not even mentioned here. But it would be a mistake to standardize this adventure by extracting the articles published between 2000 and 2003 and, eventually, regrouping them with those published in the past two years.

These *Notes* not only recount what has been happening in the world, but what has happened to me by writing about it in this particular way. If historical novels fictionalize the past by inserting characters made of whole cloth, this chronicle functions like a novel in which I, a real person, am the protagonist. It follows me as my fortunes change. And it matters, not because I matter, but because it gives credibility to my vision of the near future. In the same way that I carried myself out of the pocket where I was unwittingly hidden, a small voice reaching up to the Great Commentators of my Adopted Country, pleading with them not to construct the ideological scaffolding for the extermination of my people, and rose to a position of strength, where my voice carries far beyond theirs and exposes their mediocre parochialism, our voices can reach the front lines and determine the outcome of the battle.

Your corner ecologist thinks the same thing. He's within his rights. The question is: who sees clearly? The effort to see clearly is what gives us power to influence the outcome.

Something eventful occurs, Hamas wins the Palestinian elections, you read all the commentaries you can get your hands on and 95% of them spin around the same assumptions and usually arrive at the same conclusions. Elections. Result. Taking office. Well, I don't think it's going to happen that way. Commentators are quick to dump on Bush and his cronies, it's the world's favorite sport, and they are having a field day with these elections. Oh ho ho and ha ha ha, you wanted democracy in the Middle East, now look what you got. Professional pro-Palestinians are having such a good time pooh poohing democracy that they forget that the Solution was Two States living Side by Side in Peace and Security. They forget that both States would necessarily have elections, choose governments, express the collective will.

Jimmy Carter has no shame. He declares that the US government can no longer fund the Palestine Authority, now that it's in the hands of terrorists... so, what we should do is give the money to the UN and let them finance the PA. Shows respect for the UN, doesn't it? What with the oil for food scam and all, they won't mind dealing with terrorists. A majority of the countries in the UN are half-way terrorist themselves.

What will the members of the defeated Fatah do now? Stop for a minute, before Hamas imposes shari'a and sends ambassadors here and there, and think about the Fatah payroll. All those people who are going to lose their jobs. All of them fully armed. What are they going to do? Collect unemployment benefits? Join the unwashed masses in the "refugee camps?" Apply for jobs in high-tech enterprises in Ramallah? What in the world are they going to do with themselves in Palestinian territories administered by Islamist fanatics, ostracized by the world and its brother? Do you think a man can reconvert from PA policeman to garage mechanic—if he's lucky—and, in addition, accept the rigors of shari'a? For every Fatah gunmen ready to turn his coat there is already a Hamas gunslinger already standing at the head of the line.

I don't think the Fatah personnel will take a bow and walk off stage any more than Saddam's forces stepped aside and accepted the liberation of Iraq. Between Hamas that doesn't know how to even pretend to run a government and Fatah that has no intention of being pushed out, the elections won't carry much weight.

The crossfire invented to patch up the lie of Israeli gunfire deliberately aimed at 12 year-old Mohamed al-Dura will be more than real in the coming weeks. Ordinary citizens will lose their lives as if they were afterthoughts. No pro-Palestinian movements will mobilize in Europe. European Muslims will be out on a limb.

Palestinian populations in Gaza and Judea-Samaria grew, if they did not flourish, under the rule of wicked Israelis... and cried "genocide" and wailed "apartheid" and hollered "open prison." Today it may all come true. As Hamas and Fatah fight it out over their heads and with utter disregard for their welfare.

It is hard to imagine an outcome. If the population gets into the fray, that will make just one more warring faction. What peace process could ever separate them? Could the "decent people who just want to get on with their lives," the ones that Israel should have made peace with, ever make themselves heard? Saudi and Iranian money may be forthcoming but even they won't pour endless funds into a smoldering ruin. It is not easy to plan jihad attacks against Israel when you have to protect your back, your house, your post office, your armory, your next meal.

The UN wouldn't be able to impose law and order. No Arab country would send troops. Don't tell me the world is going to expect Israel to do it, when we're not busy taking out Iran's nuclear sites. Poetic justice would be to see the Palestinian-held territories returned to the condition of Israel in the centuries of Ottoman rule. Underpopulated. Desolation.

[interlude]

In that case the picture would be complete. On each side of the line we would see the land of Israel, on one side as it was when inhabited by Jews, on the other when inhabited by their enemies. And it would be clear: Jerusalem belongs to the Jews. If you take Jerusalem away from the Jews, it will still belong to us, it won't exist physically anymore, only its meaning would exist, in our hearts.

That is the key to peace in the Middle East: Recognize that Jerusalem belongs to the Jews. From that point onward, all the pieces of the puzzle would start to fall into their rightful place.

When I said that in July of 2000—Jerusalem belongs to the Jews—no one knew what would transpire in the space of five years. Other hypotheses were retained. Bringing us to the brink of disaster, worldwide disaster. Even China is in danger. The destructive force that is thundering and churning with raging white heat has been feeding on this covetous lust for Jerusalem. Do you understand? It's a lust that can never be satisfied. It would destroy life on this earth if... it will destroy... if we don't....

I always tell the truth. M. arranged for me to meet with Denis Jeambar. I explained to M. that I just want to talk to him, a woman to man talk, not an interview, not a challenge, not a scolding "how could you keep silent, you know the al-Dura reportage is a fake." I just wanted to talk to him, I wanted to understand how he reasoned. A colleague of Jeambar phoned to arrange the appointment. Everything was going smoothly. Then he asked me why I wanted to see him. I was taken aback. I thought he knew. I told the truth. Did his colleague tell the truth? Did he say, "Ah! In that case, forget about it. He doesn't want anything more to do with that affair"? No. He said the secretary would call me. And no one has called.

I could have spoken to Jeambar in perfect confidentiality. I would never have mentioned a word he said, wouldn't even tell people I had spoken to him, certainly would not have written an article about it, not even hinted at it, no "anonymous source" business for me.

These people think the al-Dura affair will disappear, because they don't talk about it. And now the French media think that the Hamasity of Palestinians will go away because they won't comment on it, they won't give the concrete facts about the violent Hamas-Fatah clashes. A thousand angry men storm the legislature, *RFI* reports a hundred. Several people were killed, hundreds injured, the French media report 3 wounded. They didn't hesitate to report on the massacre of Jenin, the refugee camp reduced to rubble. Later, when it turned out to be false, the media explained that you have to understand, they work under pressure, deadlines, news is precisely that—news—and it has to come in and go out as fast as it's happening. Later they back up and rectify.

They're not ashamed. How can they not be ashamed? What does it feel like, to lie all the time and be proud of your métier? It becomes second nature. You decide what you want to believe, what you want your audience to believe, and you snip, and tuck, and trim, and inflate, and powder and paint and touch up and tone down every last concrete detail until they fit the picture you decided to paint. You can multiply the number of Israeli tanks and shrink the number of Fatah gunmen, kill people in front of the camera, hide bodies where no one can find them...

But the problem is that today's facts come to fruition, generating new facts, new facts to be manipulated, and all those banged and twisted facts pile up like wrecked cars in a dump. And five years later you have the Palestinians freely voting for a Hamas government. How can you not be ashamed to discover that everything you have been saying about this explosive situation for five years was wrong?

They aren't ashamed. They keep skiing down the same slope. Wagging a phony finger and putting Hamas on notice. Hey you guys, you have to say you renounce terrorism and recognize Israel's right to exist. Otherwise, we won't be able to give you any money, and that creates a terrible problem for us.

Lucky for me, Hamasniks are pure in heart. Arafat made those promises, the money flowed into his pockets. Abbas picked up where he left off. But Hamas leader Khaled Maashal, still hanging out in Damascus, says what thousands of commentators seem to have overlooked: we won't be an armed faction anymore, we will have our army, like any other sovereign nation.

[now it's the 29th and I have ten minutes to write this morning]

The Arab League won't have it! Yemen and a handful of other enlightened states of the same type have already announced a boycott of Danish products. The League demands an apology from the Danish government. The scandal has been brewing for months, ever since a Danish magazine published caricatures of the prophet Mahomet. If I would even attempt to compose a brief synopsis of the ghoulish cartoons published in Arab-Muslim countries depicting Jews, Israelis, President Bush, PM Sharon it would require a whole chapter and still it wouldn't suffice. A Danish magazine publishes some pale, thin, barely perceptible drawings of the prophet and the highest Muslim authorities convene, convoke, threaten, and mean what they say. Denmark is the quintessence of European style tolerance. A tiny nation that behaved with honor when great European powers like France rushed into Nazi arms and filled them with tens of thousands of Jews to exterminate. But Denmark, like all European countries, has awakened to find itself pinched in the Eurabian trap.

Harboring an embryo foreign power, its share of the millions of immigrants purportedly seeking refuge, now setting up camp for the final reckoning. The Arab League wasn't importing Danish bacon, the boycott won't necessarily have any economic impact, the point is that Denmark is notified of its dhimmi status, and the penalty for non-compliance will be a pincer movement between the domestic and the foreign branches of the umma.

[interlude, and change of schedule. I forego all or part of the program on Levinas that I wanted to attend. I must go to the limits of my thought...today.]

I went to the outdoor market this morning. One hour outdoors, the temperature is above zero Celsius, the sun is shining, the wind is not strong, I was warmly dressed from hat to boots, only my gloves are a bit flimsy, they look like warm gloves but they're cheap synthetic, and my fingers were stinging by the time I started home, I couldn't wait to get inside my warm apartment. I am well fed and healthy. I live in comfort. How did anyone survive the camps? So few survived, I know, but how did anyone survive? Yesterday the roof of a building in southern Poland collapsed under the weight of the snow, killing 60—or a hundred and sixty, they are still combing through the ruins—people who had come to see an exhibition on homing pigeons. Yes, I thought of my relatives, the lost branch of my family. Did they pass through that town on their way to the death camps, did they huddle in that snow on that January 27th when the first camps were discovered by the Russian troops?

And whenever I'm cold, I wonder how could they possibly survive?

And how can we, in all our lush comfort, in all our royal privileges, with all our ways and means, how can we fail to redeem them now?

Saudi Arabia must allow infidels to visit Mecca and freely practice their religion. Foreign women visiting the country should be free to dress in miniskirts, bikinis, topless and even bottomless bathing suits, and all funding to jihad-preaching *madrassas* should be immediately curtailed. No one is yet naïve enough to offer such conditions to Saudi Arabia. Besides, Saudi Arabia doesn't have to meet any conditions. The long arm of its trillions of dollars can reach into our homes, our universities, our think tanks, and now they are even wrapping the World Economic Forum at Davos around their plump fingers. But at least everyone knows not to make such ridiculous demands on the beturbaned princes. Nissim Zvilli, interviewed on a Jewish radio station this morning, mixes a large dose of lucidity with a smidgeon of goo. He too thinks that Hamas should renounce terrorism and recognize the State of Israel; he thinks the exquisite Mahmoud Abbas will exert a beneficial effect as president in tandem with the recently elected Hamas government. And, if Hamas should dare to embark on a new round of terrorist attacks, the Quartet should definitely refuse further funding. In all fairness, the former Israeli ambassador to France, also spoke much common sense. Still, I can't countenance this widespread habit of oozing. Every time a truth needs to be told, part of it is allowed to ooze and fall through the cracks.

What will happen if Hamas continues to perpetrate terrorist attacks?

Why would they have to perpetrate terrorist attacks? They are the government. The Palestinians have raised an outright jihad movement to the level of legitimate government. They were asked what they wanted, and this is their reply. Now what?

Am I deluding myself? Am I recycling the normal reaction of panic that I should fully express, transforming it into a glorious expression of hope? I thought for a while that the United States would be, once again, our refuge. I drew closer, made new ties, tried to convince myself. (As I write these words, the birds have begun to chirp. It is such a long time since I heard them chirping, I almost forgot it could happen. The weather is going to improve.) Drawing closer, I saw more clearly. Muslims in America and Muslim money pumped into America are exerting the same influence as Muslim masses in Europe. I thought that American Jews would not stand for nonsense, I thought French Jews were cowed. And I waited. Wondering if this waiting was an ominous repetition of the attitude of European Jews on the eve of extermination. Only this time, I am in Europe, not in the United States choking back tears for my family in Poland or Hungary.

My thought constantly collides with the "ineluctable reality of the visible." This concrete illusion of peaceful everyday life that makes my warnings sound like anguished exaggerations.

Am I now deluding myself, in thinking I have found the x factor that reconciles my dire warnings with my involuntary hope? The barbarian hordes are massed on all of our frontiers, poised to pounce. The enemy is at our gates and in our streets. At every giant step closer to disaster, the same stunned surprise rises up like the smoke of thousands of little campfires. Ahmadinejad clearly announces his intention to destroy Israel with nuclear weapons. Gasp! Hamas wins the Palestinian elections. Gasp!

Am I deluding myself in thinking that the truth is dawning? And we will finally grasp it and accept the war that has been thrust on us and fight it intelligently? I thought I was going to reach the last page of this book in a state of equilibrium. I would confirm all the dire warnings contained in these pages. And I would reassure—first myself, then you— that they will be heard in time.

Times have changed. People in our democratic developed nations have tremendous assets and extraordinary freedom compared to citizens in the 30s. The jihadis are not tactical geniuses. They are too excited by their own passions. They make mistakes. They score constantly against their own team. Hmph! That's only a half truth. Saudi millionaires are as smooth as double rich milkshakes. Muslim Brotherhood in Europe dresses in suits and ties and gets access to every conduit worth exploiting. We are in for an avalanche of *faits accomplis*.

It's unfair to mention only one book when I have read hundreds of valuable works these past five years and learned so much from them but it happens that my current reading is taking me into the lower circles of hell across the centuries of jihad conquest: *The Legacy of Jihad*, by Andrew Bostom.[24] An immense graveyard as far as the eye can see. Mountains of skulls, rivers of blood, slaves by the tens of thousands, desolate landscapes, abandoned homes, torched fields, deathly silence, distant moans and somewhere in a far corner a sultan, a pasha, a sheik rapes young boys and comely maidens. The current exhibition at *l'Institut du Monde Arabe* in Paris is The Golden Age of Arab Sciences. Arab Sciences, got it? Is physics a Jewish science? Maybe it's German? Not even European. It's just science. But the Arabs have their own sciences, plural in the original, and a golden age that, if the truth were to be told, coincides with certain phases of the jihad conquest. While the comely maidens were raped and converted or converted and raped, the brilliant scholars were converted, co-opted, and transformed by that special Muslim alchemy into Arab scientists producing Arab sciences. Watch your step. If the umma loses patience with us, they may take back their sciences. Our ships will sink, the stars will fall from the heavens, our computers will blunk and go blank, and the warriors will scoop us up by the tens of thousands as they did once before.

355

The numbers of the slaughtered and the enslaved are staggering. *Legacy* is a collection of original sources, a taster so to speak. A few chapters of the conquest of India, a few on Byzantium, the Near East the Far East, it all blends together in one staggering monotonous repetition. The marauders rode out of Arabia and conquered the world. Okay, half the world. But when you've conquered half, you have powerful influence over the rest and, it would seem, you rise up and above and totally out of reach of any possible judgment of history. European colonization was so crude by comparison! The Arabs were so ruthless that they obliterated the otherness of their victims. Entire populations were dipped in Islam's acid bath, reshaped to fit a single unique model, and left to multiply to infinity. Why are there billions of Muslims in the world today? L. said to me, "Islam must have appealed to the hearts and minds of people... the conquest yes, but that wouldn't explain..." Hearts and minds to be sure. They bled the hearts and cut off the heads of those who refused to convert. And they took slaves. Tens of thousands, hundreds of thousands, perhaps millions of slaves. The accounts are so similar, they run together and blend over centuries and vast stretches of land, and seem to converge in present day scenes of multitudes prostrate in prayer, compact masses surging in pilgrimage, at football games, or in flag burning demonstrations, but always massed and mindless. European colonizers set up administrations, pushed people around, leeched out wealth, indulged in base impulses, disgraced themselves...

...I can't go on. I listened to ten minutes of news and I feel like I got punched in the gut. Seven thousand Israeli policemen are training to evacuate twenty-three families from an illegal outpost in Judea-Samaria. Whaaaat? *Haverim*, stop, will you please stop toeing the line and get ready for...

You're like a bride battered within an inch of her life by a brutal husband, who picks up the pieces of herself, limps into the kitchen, and tries to prepare dinner. Don't evacuate any more Jews. Don't give back any more territory. Throw away the Road Map. Don't you see? The famous apartheid wall that was treated like evil personified is fast turning into a Maginot line. All day long I'm hearing about terrorist attacks, Hamas has to renounce terrorist attacks and promise to recognize Israel. Don't you remember? Their champions explained that they used young men and women with explosives belts because they don't have F-16s. Now they will have airplanes. They won't beg Israel to open the airport. They won't ask for permission to cross from Gaza to Judea-Samaria. And that's what the Palestinians wanted, that's why they voted for them.

The new German chancellor Angela Merkel has an appointment with Mahmoud Abbas in Ramallah tomorrow. Diplomacy as usual. Will she have the stomach for what she is going to see? Will she tell the truth? Will Abbas be able to make a clearing through which she will pass, will he be able to keep from breaking down and sobbing in her arms?

I can't go on, but I can't sign off without completing the image. If you don't learn anything else this year, study the jihad conquest. Hundreds of thousands of slaves carried away from devastated villages, towns, and cities. Uprooted and scattered. Some were sold in distant slave markets, some were settled in previously devastated conquered lands. Talk about roughing up other people's cultures! Some were perverted into soldiers and enlisted in further conquests. They lived in misery, half-starved peasants like worker ants. Some were groomed and pampered for courts and harems. And some were allowed to pursue their magnificent arts and crafts and studies to weave golden ages and Islamic arts and sciences. Caged birds, they sang, and died out.

Is that memory totally abolished? Do the descendants of those defeated nations have any idea where they came from and how they got where they are? Think of it. Islam was a handful of Arab tribes. Now it has billions of adepts who are taught that their solemn obligation is to practice jihad, to kill or convert infidels, but preferably to kill them. But they themselves are the descendants of the victims of jihad! As if you could turn a cooked goose into a hunter.

Talk about occupied territories, let's talk! Twenty-two countries, x-million square kilometers, benighted populations still wandering in a daze centuries after they were smitten by the conquering horde. And who do they come up against? Jews. World champions in memory longevity. This is a fight that no one wants to miss. Even though the victory of Israel is a foregone conclusion. Even though the misguided audience keeps rooting for the wrong side. Even though the victory of the Arabs in Jerusalem would be an unmitigated catastrophe for the entire world. Even though the victory of the Jews will open the lock and release the invisible chains that have held those billions of Muslims in captivity for centuries.

Is that the origin Islam is furiously determined to hide? The rich and varied origins, the different religions and customs, the languages, the names of people and places, the stories and the histories of those conquered millions? By pretending that their right of return is to Jerusalem, by binding their energies and human potential and lashing their hopes to Jerusalem, by confining them to hopeless frustration, defining one single goal for billions of Muslims and terrorizing millions of bystanders into sharing that death-dealing desire, Islam is desperately trying to hide its crimes.

Just think of it: all these confused masses crying for jihad... they are the descendants of the victims of jihad. And the more they focus on the destruction of Israel, the more they themselves are enslaved. Iran. And now the Palestinians. Many of them transplanted from the Balkans, by the way. About to disappear into the depths of shari'a. Unless they are saved from shari'a by civil war. (I almost added "or bombed out of existence by Israel," but then I wanted to take back the thought. Israelis don't do that. But Israel doesn't commit suicide either.)

It is a mistake to think that what they need, what they always needed, was a state, two states, the whole state with Jerusalem as its capital. It would be preposterous to think that if in fact they had accepted a state, that famous living side by side in peace State that everyone talks about and no one has ever seen, they would not have voted Hamas today. If they had accepted the Camp David offer in the summer of 2000, maybe they would have voted Hamas in the fall of 2001. And don't forget, the Hamasniks tore down the Palestinian flag and hoisted the jihad green flag on the roof of their Parliament.

The more they vow to destroy Israel, the more they destroy themselves. This is the defeat/victory we have to offer them. And the tragedy is that the world keeps interfering, to delay the reckoning. In a mixture of good intentions and bad intentions, working with the erosive force of public opinion, a little trickle that can cleave mountains, in collusion with all that is worse for everyone, an international determination steps in every time the evil intention of taking Jerusalem and exterminating the Jews is defeated.

And this *masse informe* made up of descendants of slaves and the vanquished has come in droves to Europe, not to find their freedom but to take one last stab at conquest, and this shapeless mass is now giving us lessons in diversity!

The sheer numbers are constantly thrown in our faces. You can't insult a billion and a half people. You can't fail to take their exquisite susceptibility into consideration as you pour your coffee in the morning, set your alarm clock in the evening. Don't make them angry, whatever you do. Say "excuse me" even if you didn't do anything. You don't want to go to war with a billion and a half Muslims do you? Besides, most of them are moderate.

How do we know?

It's logical. They can't all be fanatics on the rampage.

Why? Is there a law against it? A law of nature, an international law?

I did not know that jihad had undone so many.

There were nations, peoples, governments, cultures all over the world in those times. And lost among the nations, a fierce warrior tribe. And in the heart of that tribe, a warlord. Who heard voices. A warlord who heard voices who cobbled together a bit of your holy book and a bit of my sacred writings and rode out to conquer the world. Warlords come and go. Hearing voices is not unheard of. Fire and sword, rape and plunder, terror and intimidation are familiar tactics.

But this warlord begat many warlords who raced from place to place slaying millions, enslaving millions, defeating legions, demolishing fortresses, pillaging, plundering for years, for decades, for centuries. Imposing one religion, one law, one language, one culture, in one long horrifying fait accompli.

They wiped out the story. And left the victims to populate the earth.

How did they do it?

How can it be undone?

Notes

1. Heine, Henreich, *Jewish Stories and Hebrew Melodies*, Markus Weiner Publishing, Inc, NY. 1987: 22-23, translated by C. G. Leland

2. Bellow, Saul, *To Jerusalem and Back*, Penguin Books, 1985, (Viking 1976): 135-6

3. Luke, *The Holy Bible*, King James version Electronic Text Center, University of Virginia Library

4. Metula News Agency http://www.menapress.com/article.php?sid=317

5. Metula News Agency 26 and 29 August 2002 (info# 022608/2 EV

6. http://spme.net/cgi-bin/facultyforum.cgi?ID=580

7. http://spme.net/cgi-bin/facultyforum.cgi?ID=1623

8 http://digipressetmp4.teaser.fr/jt2ie.htm

9. http://www.paixjusteauproche-orient.asso.fr/

10. http://spme.net/cgi-bin/facultyforum.cgi?ID=1640

11.//spme.net/cgi-bin/facultyforum.cgi?ID=1663

12. *Un jeu d'enfants palestiniens, quelque part entre la culture et la culture de la haine* [Palestinian child play, somewhere between culture and the culture of hatred] (info # 010606/3

13. *Observatoire du monde juif*, N° 6/7, June 2003

14. http://www.guysen.com/es/articles.php?sid=1537

15. http://www.nationalreview.com/articles/209035/seeing-believing/nidra-poller

16. Poller, Nidra, interview with mother of Sébastien Selam, http://archive.frontpagemag.com/readArticle.aspx?ARTID=13810

17. Lappen, Alyssa, "Ritual anti-Semitic murders in Paris" www.frontpagemag.com; Interview with Selam family and neighbors www.rosenpresstv.com/djlamc/index.html

18. www.guysen.com/mailinfo.php , based on an article published in La Dépêche du Midi, 2 December 2003

19. Abridged version published in *Haaretz*. No reference available.

20. https://www.commentarymagazine.com/articles/betrayed-by-europe-an-expatriates-lament/

21. //spme.net/cgi-bin/articles.cgi?ID=221

22. http://spme.net/cgi-bin/articles.cgi?ID=222

23. http://www.nationalreview.com/articles/209793/holy-scolders/nidra-poller

24. Bostom, Andrew G., M.D. *The Legacy of Jihad*, Prometheus Books, New York N.Y

By the same author

L'Harmattan
Karimi Hotel & autres nouvelles d'Africa 2011

authorship intl
Karimi Hotel & Other African Equations 2012
Al Dura: Long Range Ballistic Myth 2014
The Black Flag of Jihad Stalks la République 2015

ILLUSTRATED BOOKS
Je t'en prie Gregory images/Devis Grebu. Seuil 1993
as-tu connu machu-picchu? images/Jacques Soisson. Messidor/la Farandole 1984
A table! les histoires sont servies. images/Selçuk Demirel. Messidor/la Farandole 1982 diplôme Loisirs Jeunes
Cheval d'York. images/ Cogollo. éd. Ouskokata. Paris 1981 1st prize Mecanorma/Marker d'Argent. *Horse de Verve* (English)
D'oeuf d'habitude déjeuner etc. images/ Gentiane Gaussot. éd Cimarron Paris 1980 prize for best illustration, New Delhi. *Eggs as usual breakfast etc.* (English)

TRANSLATIONS

French to English
Levinas, Emmanuel, *Humanism of the Other,* U. of Illinois Press 2003
Levinas, Emmanuel, *Unforeseen History,* U. of Illinois Press 2004
Chertok, Léon. *Memoirs of a Heretic*
Morin, Edgar. *Les sept Savoirs.* UNESCO 1999
Dictionnaire européen des lumières. Dictionnaire de théologie (group
transl.) Fitzroy-Dearborn.
Jeanneret, Michel *Perpetuum Mobile,* Johns Hopkins University Press,
2000
Kourouma, Ahmadou, *Monnew,* Mercury House, San Francisco 1992
Roberts, Jean-Marc, *Hand me down children,* ⟨ *Les enfants de fortune*
Seuil ⟩
Maximin, Daniel, *Lone Sun.* U. Press of Virginia 1990

English to French
Potok, Chaim, *La Harpe de Davita* with Philippe Paddeu. Buchet Chas-
tel. Paris 1986
Potok, Chaim *Livre des Lumières* with Yvette Métral. Buchet-Chastel.
Paris 1985
Michael McClure *Ciels de Jaguar* with G. Louisy. Christian Bourgois
Paris 1978 .

Italian to English
Natalia Ginzburg "Mio Marito," "The Mother," & "Elegy & Lament for
England". *Mediterranean Review* 1971 & 1972

www.ingramcontent.com/pod-product-compliance
Lightning Source LLC
Chambersburg PA
CBHW031423270326
41930CB00007B/550